STUDIES IN WELSH HISTORY

Editors

RALPH A. GRIFFITHS   KENNETH O. MORGAN
GLANMOR WILLIAMS

———————

3

CARDIFF AND THE MARQUESSES OF BUTE

John Crichton Stuart, second marquess of Bute, 1793–1848;
posthumous portrait by A. R. Venables, 1852

CARDIFF AND THE
MARQUESSES OF BUTE

by

JOHN DAVIES

*Published on behalf of the
History and Law Committee
of the Board of Celtic Studies*

CARDIFF
UNIVERSITY OF WALES PRESS
1981

© University of Wales Press, 1981

British Library Cataloguing in Publication Data

Davies, John
  Cardiff and the marquesses of Bute — (Studies in
  Welsh history; 3 ISSN 0141–030X).
  1. Bute family
  2. Cardiff, Wales — Genealogy
  I. Title   II. Series
  929'.2'0941   CS439.B/
  ISBN 0–7083–0761–2

*Printed in Wales by Qualitex Printing Limited
Cardiff*

IN HONOUR OF MY FOREFATHERS,
WILLIAM DAVIES

AND

WILLIAM POTTER,
Rhondda colliers, creators of Cardiff

EDITORS' FOREWORD

Since the Second World War, Welsh history has attracted considerable scholarly attention and enjoyed a vigorous popularity. Not only have the approaches, both traditional and new, to the study of history in general been successfully applied to Wales's past, but the number of scholars engaged in this enterprise has multiplied during these years. These advances have been especially marked in the University of Wales.

In order to make more widely available the conclusions of recent research, much of it of limited accessibility in postgraduate dissertations and theses, the History and Law Committee of the Board of Celtic Studies has inaugurated this new series of monographs, *Studies in Welsh History*. It is anticipated that many of the volumes will have originated in research conducted in the University of Wales or under the auspices of the Board of Celtic Studies. But the series will not exclude significant contributions made by researchers in other Universities and elsewhere. Its primary aim is to serve historical scholarship and to encourage the study of Welsh history.

PREFACE

A quarter of the population of Wales lives within the boundaries of what were the lordships of the Bute estate.[1] The Cardiff Castle estate, held by the Stuarts of Bute from 1766 to 1947, was at the centre of the changes, social, economic and political, which transformed south Wales between the eighteenth and the twentieth centuries and which caused such a high proportion of the population of Wales to dwell in the towns and mining valleys of east Glamorgan. To that transformation, the marquesses of Bute made a crucial contribution. They were the constructors and owners of Cardiff's Bute Docks, recognised in the late nineteenth century as the world's greatest coal port; they were the landlords of the Dowlais Ironworks, hailed in the 1840s as the world's greatest ironworks; they were the initiators of the exploitation of the steam coal of the Rhondda, acknowledged as the most celebrated of coal valleys. Especially remarkable was the role of the second marquess, owner of the estate from 1814 to 1848, who, largely resident at Mountstuart and Dumfries House in Scotland, conducted an industrial revolution in south Wales through correspondence. In addition, he created in Glamorgan a system of paternalistic power which had a significant influence upon the social and political life of the county during the most fateful period of its history.

The contribution of landed proprietors to economic development and the relationship between established aristocratic families and new middle class industrialists and entrepreneurs are issues of importance in the history of modern Britain. Some landed families felt that the advance of industry constituted a threat to the social and political hegemony of their class and to such families 'the dread of the loss of feudal domination [seemed] too strong even for the influence of Mammon'.[2] The majority however were eager to profit from the rents, royalties, dues and capital gains generated by the development of

[1] See map below, p. 32.
[2] Robert Wilson, *History of Hawick* (2nd ed., 1841), p. 295, quoted in T. C. Smout, 'Scottish landowners and economic growth, 1650–1850', *Scottish Journal of Political Economy*, 1 (1964), 233.

transport undertakings and by the industrialization and
urbanization of their estates and, in receiving such profits,
were largely content to be rentiers rather than entrepreneurs.
Some aristocratic families went further and were concerned
actively to initiate economic development rather than passively
to benefit from it.[3] Among these the marquesses of Bute stand
pre-eminent. Under the second and third marquesses the
agricultural receipts of the Glamorgan estate paled into
insignificance alongside the profits from minerals and urban
and dock development. As the largest landowners within the
south Wales coalfield the Butes were able, to a high degree,
to establish the pattern and the pace of mineral exploitation.
Upon Cardiff, 'Lord Bute's own town', the family left an
indelible impression. Their activity there places them in the
front rank of British city makers, for of the British cities in
whose development a single landowning family played a
preponderant role, Cardiff is undoubtedly the largest. Although
the second marquess of Bute's relations with the new industrialists of Glamorgan were often tense, Professor Smout's
description of Scottish landowners as striving 'side by side with
the middle classes to develop a new kind of dynamic economy,
as they believed this to be to their mutual advantage', is
particularly applicable to him; equally apposite, in view of the
later history of the family, is Smout's concluding comment:
'and when they had succeeded, it became a Frankenstein to
rend off their limbs of privilege and leadership'.[4]

The materials available for the study of the Bute family and
its estates are at the same time profuse and deficient. There is
no single estate archive; the collection at Aberystwyth contains
records of fundamental value but many papers relating to the
estate are deposited at Cardiff, Edinburgh and elsewhere.
Materials documenting the Glamorgan estate under the second
marquess are abundant, the correspondence between the
marquess and his agents being particularly illuminating.
During the minority of the third marquess, the presence of a
resident trustee in Glamorgan reduced the need for extensive
correspondence as did the marquess's reluctance, on reaching

---

[3] See, for example, F. M. L. Thompson, *English Landed Society in the nineteenth
century* (1963), pp. 256–68.
[4] T. C. Smout, *op. cit.*, p. 234.

manhood, to be as closely involved as had his father in detailed estate administration. In consequence, while all aspects of estate activity in the period 1814 to 1848 can be closely chronicled, some aspects of the history of the estate thereafter, particularly agricultural policy and general estate administration, cannot. Yet, the fact that the material available for the first half of the nineteenth century is so detailed more than compensates for the relative paucity of evidence relating to the second half of the century: the decisive period in the history of the estate was the second quarter of the century and much of what occurred subsequently is consequent upon the well-documented decisions made by the second marquess during those decades. Furthermore, other aspects of the activity of the estate under the second marquess's successors, for example, the movement of rent, the leasing of building land and minerals, the developments at the Bute Docks and Bute policy towards railways, may be studied in detail through the rich and varied materials available at Aberystwyth, Cardiff and London.

In pursuing Bute documents in libraries and record offices in Wales, Scotland and England, I have had much cause to be grateful to librarians and archivists. It is a pleasure to acknowledge my indebtedness to the National Library of Wales, in particular to the staff of the Departments of Manuscripts and Maps and Prints, whose courtesy and assistance are always unfailing. I wish to thank Mr. T. J. Hopkins, late of Cardiff Central Library, and, among others, the staffs of the Glamorgan Record Office, Cardiff, Coal House, Llanishen, Register House, Edinburgh, and the British Transport Historical Record Office, London. I am indebted to the library staff at University College, Swansea, and at the University College of Wales, Aberystwyth, for many kindnesses and I also wish to thank both colleges for providing me with grants to assist my research. The maps in this volume were drawn by Mr. Don Williams of the Department of Geography, Aberystwyth, and the frontispiece is published by kind permission of the National Portrait Gallery of Scotland. I am grateful to Miss Tegwen Michael, Miss Siân Jones and Miss Linda Griffiths for typing the manuscript. At every stage of publication the assistance of Miss Lowri Morgan of the University of Wales Press has been invaluable.

I wish to thank Professor Glanmor Williams, Professor I. G. Jones, Dr. K. O. Morgan and Dr. Ralph Griffiths for reading the text and for their constructive suggestions. All errors that remain are mine. Above all, I wish to thank my wife, Janet Mackenzie Davies, although mere thanks seem preposterously inadequate.

John Davies,
Neuadd Pantycelyn,
Aberystwyth

Department of Welsh History,
University College of Wales,
Aberystwyth
June 1980

CONTENTS

LIST OF MAPS AND ILLUSTRATIONS

ABBREVIATIONS

B.D.C.	Bute Docks Company
B.T.H.R.O.	British Transport Historical Record Office
C.	*Cambrian*
C.C.L.	Cardiff Central Library
C.C.L., B.	Cardiff Central Library, Bute collection
C.R.C.	Cardiff Railway Company
C.T.	*Cardiff Times*
G.R.O.	Glamorgan Record Office
H.B.MSS.	Hamilton Bruce Manuscripts
L.	Letterbook
M.G.	*Merthyr Guardian*
N.L.Scot.	National Library of Scotland
N.L.W.	National Library of Wales
N.L.W., B.	National Library of Wales, Bute collection
P.P.	Parliamentary Papers
Scot. P.R.O.	Scottish Public Record Office
S.W.D.N.	*South Wales Daily News*
W.M.	*Western Mail*

I

THE BUTE FAMILY

THE FIRST MARQUESS OF BUTE, 1744-1814

'Your friend [Lord Mountstuart]', wrote Sir John Pringle to
Boswell in 1767, 'is a married man and I am persuaded, happy
in that state, although the match was made upon prudential
considerations only.'[1] The 'prudential consideration' was the
landed property of the Windsor family and this was the
marriage which brought the Stuarts of Bute into the front rank
of Welsh landowners. The bride, Charlotte Windsor, was the
daughter and co-heiress of Lord Windsor, whose family held
estates in Glamorgan as descendants of William Herbert to
whom, in the sixteenth century, the crown had made extensive
grants of landed property. Herbert was the son of William
Herbert of Ewyas, the illegitimate son of the first Herbert earl
of Pembroke. The vast possessions of the first earl went,
through the marriage of his grand-daughter, to the Somerset
family and were the foundation of the territorial power of the
dukes of Beaufort in Wales. Through the patronage of his
kinsman, Charles Somerset, first earl of Worcester, William
Herbert came to prominence at court, serving as an executor
of the will of Henry VIII and as a member of Edward VI's
Privy Council. In 1547, in fulfilment of his father's intention,
Edward VI granted Herbert estates in south Wales, including
the lordships of Miskin, Glynrhondda and Llantrisant, 'parcel
of the land of Jasper late duke of Bedford' (d. 1495). Two
years later, in recognition of his assistance in the suppression
of the rebellion in the west of England, Herbert received
further grants of land in Glamorgan, together with lordships
and manors in Monmouthshire, Breconshire, Wiltshire and
elsewhere, while in 1551 he was raised to the peerage as Baron
Herbert of Cardiff and earl of Pembroke.[2]

[1] F. Brady and F. A. Pottle (eds.), *Boswell in search of a wife* (1957), p. 50. The
marriage took place on 12 November 1766.
[2] *Dictionary of Welsh Biography* (1959), pp. 350–52; *Calendar of Patent Rolls,
1547–48* (1924), pp. 193–94; J. H. Matthews (ed.), *Cardiff Records: material for the
history of the County Borough* (1898–1911), I, 463–72; N.L.W., B., 141, 2.

THE BUTE FAMILY

THE BUTE FAMILY, A GENEALOGICAL TABLE

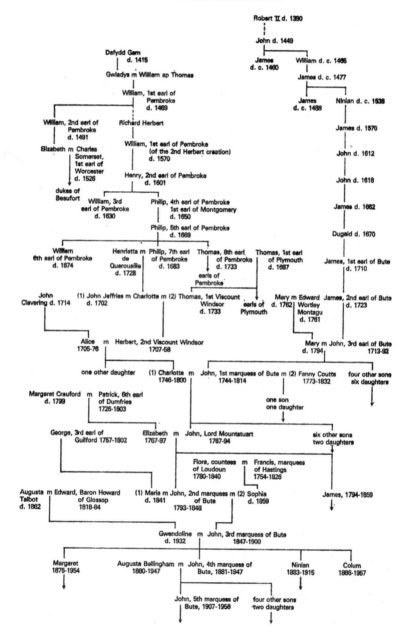

In the late-sixteenth century, the Welsh estates of the Herberts, together with their extensive property in Wiltshire around the dissolved abbey of Wilton, gave them a prominent position in the English aristocracy. In 1559, with an annual income of between £4,000 and £5,000, the earl of Pembroke was fourth in the table of wealth of the English peers. He was by far the most powerful magnate in Glamorgan, holding thirty-six manors and controlling five boroughs in the county. With a firm territorial base in Glamorgan and almost equal strength in Monmouthshire, the Herbert family dominated the political life of south-east Wales up to the Civil War. Nevertheless, in the mid-seventeenth century, during the lifetime of the fourth earl, it became clear that Wilton with its extensive lands in the rich Wiltshire countryside was the effective centre of Pembroke wealth and influence. During the Civil War, the power of the Herberts, supporters of Parliament, proved no match in south-east Wales for that of their kinsmen, the Catholic and arch-royalist Somerset family of Raglan castle. Under the fifth earl, the links with Wales weakened further. Members of the Herbert family continued to represent Welsh constituencies and offices in Wales were still granted to them, but after the Restoration the energies of the family were concentrated in Wiltshire and the fifth earl began disposing of his Welsh lands.[3]

In 1683 Philip, the seventh earl, died leaving a daughter, Charlotte. Philip had barred the entail of the Glamorgan estate on marriage but the Wiltshire estates had been settled in tail male. Therefore the title and the Wilton lands went to the seventh earl's brother, while the Welsh estates went to his daughter Charlotte. Thomas, the eighth earl, sought to dispute the division of the family property and the matter was brought before Lord Chancellor Jeffreys who decided in favour of Charlotte, soon to become his daughter-in-law. Jeffreys's decision was upheld by the House of Lords and the litigation ended with a private Act of Parliament in 1696. Charlotte, who married John Jeffreys in 1688, was left a widow in 1702. In 1704 she took as her second husband Thomas Windsor, son

---

[3] G. E. Jones, *The gentry and the Elizabethan state* (1977), *passim*; P. Williams, *The Council in the Marches of Wales under Elizabeth I* (1958), *passim*; L. Stone, *The crisis of the aristocracy* (1965), pp. 207, 760.

of the first earl of Plymouth. Windsor, who had distinguished himself in William III's wars in Ireland and Flanders, had in 1699 been granted the title of Lord Windsor in the peerage of Ireland and in 1711 he was raised to the British peerage as Lord Mountjoy.[4]

The first Lord Windsor died in 1738, his title passing to his son Herbert who, a year previously, had married Alice, daughter and co-heiress of Sir James Clavering of Axwell Park, county Durham. The Claverings, a vigorous and quarrelsome clan, were prominent in the coal trade of north-eastern England. Although the baronetcy and most of the Clavering property passed to a junior branch of the family, Alice brought her husband land, collieries and money reported to be worth £60,000.[5] Herbert, Lord Windsor, died in 1758 without leaving male heirs; his peerage died with him and his will directed that his estates, after his wife's lifetime, should be divided between his daughters, Charlotte and Alice. The bequest was subject to the curious condition that marriage to a Scotsman or an Irishman would bar either daughter from inheriting, a condition clearly defied by Charlotte when in 1766 she married Lord Mountstuart. The restriction in the will was circumvented by Lady Windsor, who obliged her younger daughter Alice to affirm that she would 'not claim any advantage from any breach in Lord Windsor's will'. In 1768 Alice married Lord Beauchamp, son and heir of the earl of Hertford. Lady Windsor, to make doubly sure of her eldest daughter's inheritance, purchased Alice's right to a moiety of the Glamorgan estate and bequeathed it to Charlotte. The precaution proved to be unnecessary for Lady Beauchamp died childless, leaving her sister Charlotte sole heir to the Windsor inheritance.[6]

Lord Mountstuart, Charlotte Windsor's husband, was the son of John, third earl of Bute, George III's prime minister.

[4] G. W. Keeton, *Lord Chancellor Jeffreys and the Stuart cause* (1965), pp. 351, 383, 470–71; *Complete Peerage*, XII, ii (1959), 804–6; J. H. Matthews, op. cit., II, 63; T. Lever, *The Herberts of Wilton* (1967), pp. 140–45.
[5] Lord Windsor's marriage settlement, cited in Lord Mountstuart's settlement (N.L.W., B., 137); E. Hughes, *North Country life in the eighteenth century, the north east, 1700–1750* (1952), *passim*; *Gentleman's Magazine*, VII (1737), 252.
[6] Ibid., XXVIII (1758), 46; Lord Windsor's will (N.L.W., B., 137, 1); deed relating to Lord Beauchamp (ibid., 137, 3); case for the Glamorgan Great Sessions, 1807 (ibid., 31).

Although the family was not ennobled until 1703 when Sir James Stuart was elevated to the Scottish peerage as earl of Bute, Viscount Kingarth and Baron Mountstuart and Inchmarnock, the Stuarts of Bute were of royal lineage, being descendants of Sir John Stuart, illegitimate son of Robert II of Scotland (d. 1390).[7] Robert II had granted his son the hereditary office of sheriff of Buteshire and had given him extensive lands on the Isle of Bute, the core of an estate which grew until it embraced almost the whole of the island. Yet, despite their paramount position on their island and the third earl's vigorous attempts to improve his lands, the Stuarts of Bute were not a wealthy family. In the late-eighteenth century their Scottish properties yielded no more than £1,500 a year and in 1746 the third earl's father-in-law was informed that 'they intend laying down their coach [as] their Scottish estates bring in very little'.[8]

Although the third earl of Bute was lampooned as a savage Highlander, the Stuarts of Bute were not remote Highland chieftains immured in their island fastnesses. The first earl was one of the commissioners appointed by Queen Anne to discuss the union of Scotland and England; the second earl was a Scottish representative peer from 1715 to 1722, a position also held by his son, the third earl, from 1737 to 1741 and from 1761 to 1780. It was as a member of the House of Lords that the third earl became first minister of the crown under George III.[9] One of the by-products of royal favour was the grant of a British peerage to the family in 1761, when the countess of Bute became Baroness Mountstuart of Wortley with remainder to her male issue.[10] The title was a recognition of the wealth which the countess had inherited in 1761 under the will of her father, Edward Wortley Montagu, consisting of

[7] *Complete Peerage*, II (1912), 440–46; J. A. Lovat-Fraser, *John Stuart, earl of Bute* (1919), p. 80.

[8] Ibid., pp. 4, 5, 39, 45; J. Wilson, *Tourists' guide to Rothesay and the Isle of Bute* (1862), p. 50; G. Chalmers, *Caledonia, or a historical and topographical account of north Britain* (1894), VII, 36–37; Mrs. Stuart Wortley (ed.), *A prime minister to his son* (1925), p. 10.

[9] *Complete Peerage*, II (1912), 440–46; J. A. Lovat-Fraser, op. cit.; J. E. McKelway, *George III and Lord Bute* (1973); H. van Thal, *The prime ministers*, I (1974), 105–13.

[10] Until 1782 this was the only method available to the crown of granting British titles to Scottish peers. A. S. Turberville, *The House of Lords in the age of reform* (1958), pp. 103–4.

property in Yorkshire and Cornwall variously valued at between £500,000 and £1,340,000.[11]

The use of the Wortley fortune, which the third earl enjoyed from 1761 until his death in 1792, enabled him to indulge his expensive tastes and belies the rumour that his expenditure was financed by his alleged mistress, the princess of Wales. Such expenditure was manifested above all in his passion for buying and building houses. In 1763 he purchased the mansion and 4,468-acre estate of Luton Hoo in Bedfordshire for £111,000; he employed 'Capability' Brown to landscape the 1,200-acre park and the Adam brothers, whose genius he was among the first to appreciate, to remodel and redecorate the house. Luton Hoo and the books and pictures it contained delighted so fastidious a tourist as Dr. Johnson, who obtained a ticket to visit it in 1781.[12] The third earl also commissioned the Adam brothers to build him a town residence in Berkeley Square and in addition he owned a villa at Brompton and a house in South Audley Street. His favourite home, however, was Highcliffe, a mansion which, at huge expense, he had built on the Hampshire cliffs near Christchurch. Following the eclipse of his political career, he retired to Highcliffe where he devoted himself to antiquarian and botanical studies and to his collection of books and paintings.[13]

On the death of the third earl of Bute in 1792, the title passed to his eldest son, Lord Mountstuart, husband of Charlotte Windsor. With the title, the fourth earl entered upon the life-tenancy of the family estates in Scotland and Bedfordshire, in accordance with the provisions of his marriage settlement. Lady Windsor having died in 1776, he was also in possession, *iure uxoris*, of the Windsor estate in Glamorgan and the Clavering property in county Durham. The wills of his parents brought him little in the way of additional wealth. Highcliffe and almost all the personal estate of his father went

[11] R. Halsband, *The life of Mary Wortley Montagu* (1956), pp. 275–76; W. S. Lewis and R. S. Brown (eds.), *The letters of Horace Walpole*, IX (1941), 338; J. A. Lovat-Fraser, op. cit., p. 15; *Gentleman's Magazine*, LXIV (1794), 1061.
[12] Ibid., XXXIII (1763), 515, LXXXVII, ii (1817), 5–8; *The Victoria History of the county of Bedford* (1908), II, 353; Mrs. Stuart Wortley, op. cit., p. 45; A. Cobbe, *The history of Luton church* (1899), p. 627; J. Boswell, *Life of Johnson* (Hill-Powell ed., 1934), IV, 127.
[13] Mrs. Stuart Wortley, *Highcliffe and the Stuarts* (1927), p. 7; J. Grieg (ed.), *The Farrington diary* (1923–28), IV, 210, VII, 23.

to his brother Sir Charles Stuart, while he was made responsible for a mortgage of £43,500 raised upon the Luton estate
to provide portions for his brothers and sisters. Under his
mother's will, the fourth earl received a legacy of £4,000, but
most of Lady Bute's considerable personal property was
bequeathed to her son William and her daughter Louisa. The
vast Wortley possessions went to his brother James and
provided the territorial justification for the bestowal of the
title of Lord Wharncliffe upon that branch of the Stuart
family. These provisions the fourth earl deeply resented; the
alienation of the Wortley lands he contested in the House of
Lords but the matter was settled in favour of his brother by a
private Act of Parliament in 1803. He sought to divest himself
of part of his responsibility for the Luton mortgage but in this
attempt also he failed and for the rest of his life he considered
himself a wronged man, cheated of his expectations.[14]

'Strange to say', noted the biographer of Thomas Coutts,
'save for certain references in Boswell's *Johnson*, the first
Marquess of Bute is almost unknown to history. His obituary
notice in the *Gentleman's Magazine* is brief and meagre and the
Annual Register, save for a mention of his death at Geneva, is
silent altogether.'[15] There are, however, other sources which
shed light upon the man who married the heiress of the
Windsor–Pembroke estates in Glamorgan. After being educated
at Winchester and Oxford, Lord Mountstuart went on the
Grand Tour in the course of which he attracted the attention
of James Boswell. '[Lord Mountstuart] is handsome, has
elegant manners and a tempestuously noble soul', wrote Boswell
to Rousseau in 1765. 'He has never applied himself earnestly
to anything . . . His money is for him in civilised society, what
physical strength is to a savage.' The young aristocrat's guardian
urged Boswell to join them on their tour believing, wrongly,
that Boswell's company 'would prevent [Mountstuart] from
being tempted by bad company to renew his dissipations'.[16]

[14] Wills of Lord and Lady Bute, marriage settlement of Lord Mountstuart,
case as to the will of Lord Bute (N.L.W., B., 137, 1); 42 George III, *cap*. 67;
Mrs. Stuart Wortley, *Highcliffe*, p. 17; A. Aspinall, *The later correspondence of
George III* (1963), II, 51–52.
[15] E. H. Coleridge, *The life of Thomas Coutts, banker* (1919), II, 117–19.
[16] F. Brady and F. A. Pottle (eds.), *Boswell on the Grand Tour, Italy, Corsica and
France* (1955), pp. xviii, 9, 10, 92, 93, 108 and 130; J. Boswell, *The tour in the
Hebrides* (Hill-Powell, ed., 1934), V, 58.

On returning from Italy in 1765, Mountstuart was launched upon London society. 'The new importation of the year', noted Lady Sarah Bunbury, ' . . . is [Lord Mountstuart who] is tall, well-made and very handsome; . . . he is very conceited and seems to me to be very proud and vain, but yet is very well bred and does vastly well as a *beau*.'[17] Mountstuart's ambitions were political but his father, whose influence over royal patronage was waning rapidly by 1766, was able to do little more than bring his son into the Commons as one of the members for Bossiney, an adjunct of the Wortley estate and one of the rottenest boroughs in the kingdom. Mountstuart, however, preferred the Lords, believing that his 'mode of speaking was better suited for that House'.[18] His ambition was realised in 1776 when he was granted the title of Baron Cardiff. He did not win prominence in politics. With his father's enemies in the ascendant, he was under pressure to do nothing which might be construed as approval of them, his wife hoping that 'the thinking part of mankind will always do him justice for sacrificing his own will to his parents'.[19]

In 1779 extravagance had driven Mountstuart to seek diplomatic office and in that year he was appointed envoy at Turin, a post worth £3,600 a year. The appointment was a great relief to his wife. 'He must go somewhere to save', she wrote, ' . . . He cannot remain content without having everything that other people have . . . A few years abroad will repay our debts . . . If we had an embassy we might very nearly live on our pay.'[20] Lady Mountstuart's wish was granted in March 1783 when her husband was appointed ambassador at Madrid, an office which carried a salary of £6,000. Although he remained ambassador until November of that year he did not visit Spain, for he considered that the embassy at Paris was

[17] The countess of Ilchester and Lord Slaverdale, *The life and letters of Lady Sarah Lennox, 1745–1826* (1901), I, 180.

[18] C. Ryskamp and F. A. Pottle (eds.), *Boswell, the ominous years, 1774–76* (1963), pp. 107–8; L. Namier and J. Brooke, *The House of Commons, 1757–1790* (1964), I, 223–25; III, 502–3.

[19] E. H. Coleridge, op. cit., p. 50; A. Aspinall, op. cit., II, 3–5; W. S. Lewis and A. D. Wallace (eds.), *The letters of Horace Walpole*, XXXIII (1966), 25; Mrs. Stuart Wortley, *A prime minister to his son*, p. 203.

[20] E. H. Coleridge, op. cit., I, 50; *Bulletin of the John Rylands Library*, XXXIII (1950–51), 252.

the only one worthy of his rank and ability.[21] After his father's death in 1792, the realisation that his fortune would be less than he had anticipated, caused him to consider embassies less exalted than Paris.[22] When Madrid was again offered to him in 1794 he accepted and left for Spain in 1795, hardly a propitious time for the arrival of a British ambassador there. During the fourth earl's term of office, the Spanish government, whose attack upon France had ended in disaster, signed a peace with France which was virtually an alliance. There is nothing to suggest that the earl distinguished himself in the office, which he resigned in 1796. When he was pressing for the title of marquess in 1795, the duke of Portland wrote to him: 'The king adverted . . . to the peace made by Spain and wished it to be submitted once more, fairly and candidly to your own consideration, whether this was exactly the moment in which you yourself would choose to accept any mark of distinction, or would advise him to bestow one upon an Ambassador under the same circumstances as yourself'. Although Portland hastened to deny that he considered the earl to be incompetent, he argued that the grant of the title of marquess might 'be construed as a sort of salve or skreen for supposed negligence or inability'.[23]

Despite his public career, the fourth earl was granted a marquessate. On 21 March 1796 he became Viscount Mountjoy, earl of Windsor and marquess of the county of Bute. The king had earlier been anxious to raise the third earl, as his chief minister, to the British peerage but the statute prohibiting the grant of a British title to a Scottish peer was not repealed until 1782. The fourth earl had angled for a marquessate before accepting the Madrid embassy and had apparently been promised one. By 1795 he was tired of the delay and in September of that year Portland informed Pitt that the earl of Bute would not wait 'for the completion of a wish, which I have reason to believe, he has for some years not only entertained but cherished'. When the title was

---

[21] A. Aspinall (ed.), *The correspondence of George, prince of Wales, 1770–1812* (1965), III, 162; Mrs. Stuart Wortley, *A prime minister to his son*, p. 210.
[22] A. Aspinall, *Later correspondence*, II, 3–4; Bute to Portland, 19 January 1793 and 14 December 1794 (University of Nottingham Library, Portland Papers, Pwf. 619 and 8629).
[23] Ibid.; Portland to Bute, 25 September 1795 (ibid., Pwf. 8630).

granted to him, the marquess considered that it was no more than his right and, in thanking the king, remarked that 'at least it secures the name and dignity of my family from being totally obliterated'.[24]

In January 1800 Charlotte, marchioness of Bute, died at the age of fifty-four. She was buried in London, but on 5 September 1800 her body was reinterred at the vault constructed for the Bute family in the parish church of Roath near Cardiff. Twelve days after his wife's reinterment, the widowed marquess married Fanny, daughter of the wealthy banker, Thomas Coutts. The Bute family's connection with Coutts and his bank was long-standing; both families were members of the Scottish community in London and the third earl had been arbitrator in the dissolution of the partnership of the brothers James and Thomas Coutts in 1774. The marriage was not of Coutts' own contriving. 'The match has been her own choice . . . entirely', he wrote, 'and she believes it will secure her happiness. If so, I ought to be content, though I confess that his age (56) appears to me a great objection . . . but he has remarkable good health and looks younger than any of his brothers.'[25] The marquess's second marriage put an end to his financial troubles. It was believed that Coutts gave Fanny £100,000 on the morning of her wedding and in his will he left £20,000 to each of his three daughters, directing his wife, who inherited the residue of his vast fortune, to 'reward them further according to their deserts'. In her will, Mrs. Coutts, by then duchess of St. Albans, stated that she had given her stepdaughter, Lady Burdett, a total of £118,602; Lady Bute pre-deceased the duchess but it is likely that she also benefited from her stepmother's generosity.[26]

After their marriage, the marquess and his wife wandered from rented house to rented house in England and on the continent.[27] In November 1814, almost forgotten by his

[24] Ibid.; A. Aspinall, *Later correspondence*, II, 464.

[25] E. H. Coleridge, op. cit., p. 119; R. Richardson, *Coutts and Co., bankers, Edinburgh and London* (1901), p. 18; G. Galbraith, *The journal of the Rev. William Bagshaw Stevens* (1965), p. xxiv. In 1814, when he was eighty, Coutts married Harriet Mellon, aged thirty-eight (C. E. Pearce, *The jolly duchess*, 1915).

[26] J. Grieg, op. cit., III, 181; E. Healey, *Lady unknown, the life of Angela Burdett-Coutts* (1978); E. H. Coleridge, op. cit., II, 369.

[27] Ibid., II, 193; C. 28 January, 10 February 1804, 8 November 1805, 16 May 1806; the duchess of Cleveland, *The life and letters of Lady Hester Stanhope* (1914), p. 94.

fellow-countrymen, he died at Geneva at the age of seventy. A month later his body was buried alongside that of Charlotte, his first wife, in the family vault at Roath. Eighteen years later they were joined by Fanny, his second wife. The first marquess lived an unfulfilled life; he had talent, charm, beauty and, in the last years of his life, great wealth. He failed to find satisfaction in any of these. In one sphere alone did he add significantly to the heritage of the Bute family. As a connoisseur of books and paintings he greatly augmented the collection which his father had built up at Luton. In 1817, when a list of the paintings was published, it contained a Raphael, a Rembrandt, a Velasquez, two Titians, two Cuyps, four paintings by Rubens, five by Reynolds and a large number of works by less distinguished artists. As a collector of manuscripts, the marquess bought much of the correspondence of his grandmother, Lady Mary Wortley Montagu, and all that was available relating to the political career of his father. In addition, he purchased James Grainger's papers, the foundation of Grainger's history of England, and by 1812 most of the Strawberry Hill manuscripts of Horace Walpole had found their way to Luton.[28]

The first marquess of Bute had seven sons and two daughters by his first wife, and a son and a daughter by his second. Family feeling was strong in him. Writing to his eldest son in 1793, he declared: 'The whole bent of my life has been an endeavour to aggrandize my family and, more particularly, the male branch.'[29] He made strenuous efforts to assist his younger children but it was upon his eldest son that he concentrated his greatest attention. John Stuart, born in 1767, showed all the signs of becoming a second edition of his father. After being educated at Eton and Cambridge, he was sent on the Grand Tour, a journey which, the scanty evidence available suggests, was as entertaining as his father's. On returning from his tour in 1789, he was declared to be 'a brilliant character and to the brightest parts and soundest

[28] W. S. Lewis and A. D. Wallace (eds.), *The letters of Horace Walpole*, I (1937), 313, 335, 354; II, 12, 27, 307, XV, 161, *Gentleman's Magazine*, LXXXII, i (1812), 146, LXXXVII, ii (1817), 5–8; R. Halsband, op. cit., pp. 289–90.
[29] Bute to Mountstuart, 28 August 1793 (Sandon Hall Archives, XX); A. Aspinall, *Later correspondence*, II, 3.

principles adds all the lustre of external accomplishment'.[30] In 1790 his father brought him into parliament as member for the Glamorgan boroughs, an act which marked the reimposition, after long neglect, of control by the lord of Cardiff Castle over the boroughs of Glamorgan. In October 1792, the young Lord Mountstuart married Elizabeth, heiress and only surviving daughter of Patrick Crichton, sixth earl of Dumfries. This marriage brought to the Bute family the Crichton estates which were larger and potentially more productive than those on the Isle of Bute. The Crichtons, like the Fitzalans, ancestors of the Stuarts, were an Anglo-Norman family which had been encouraged to settle in Scotland by David I. By 1240 they were landowners at Sanquhar in Dumfries-shire and by gift, purchase and marriage they gradually amassed estates in south-west Scotland which by the late-nineteenth century extended over 63,890 acres of Ayrshire and Galloway. The Ayrshire estate, the centre of which was the family mansion of Dumfries House at Old Cumnock, was particularly valuable for it included extensive farm land, property in the Ayrshire coalfield, urban land at Kilmarnock and Troon, and influence in the politics of the county. The marriage also brought to the already much-titled Bute family the additional dignities of earl of Dumfries, Viscount Ayr, Baron Cumnock and Baron Crichton of Sanquhar in the peerage of Scotland and a baronetcy in the peerage of Nova Scotia.[31] A rich match for his eldest son had long been the ambition of the first marquess of Bute. 'I am averse to all clauses', he wrote in 1787, 'which subject the possessor to the necessity of bearing alone the name or arms of Stuart. Why should a foolish, absurd vanity prove the means of defeating an alliance which might considerably increase the wealth and influence of . . . our descendants?'[32] The alliance between the Stuarts and the Crichtons was the

[30] Mrs. G. H. Bell (ed.), *The Namwood papers of the ladies of Llangollen and Caroline Hamilton* (1930), p. 183.
[31] P. H. M'Kerlie, *History of the lands and their owners in Galloway* (1906), I, 343–51; J. Bateman, *The great landowners of Great Britain and Ireland* (1883), p. 69; *Complete Peerage*, IV (1916), 499–501.
[32] Mountstuart to his son, 16 November 1787 (Sandon Hall Archives, XX); A. Aspinall, *Later correspondence*, II, 51–52. The seventh Lord Crichton was created earl of Dumfries in 1633 with remainder to his heirs male bearing the name and arms of Crichton.

occasion of long negotiations, culminating in a case brought before the Lord Chancellor in August 1793.[33] In February 1794, before a decision had been reached, Lord Mountstuart died following a fall from his horse. At his death at the age of twenty-five, he left a son, John, later the second marquess of Bute, born on 10 August 1793, and a pregnant wife who was to give birth to a second son, James Patrick Herbert, on 25 August 1794.

THE SECOND MARQUESS OF BUTE, 1794–1848

John, the elder son of the Stuart–Crichton marriage, is the central figure of the Bute estate in the nineteenth century and it is his activities which give the family's history its special significance. Yet, when he died in 1848, the *Times* hardly mentioned the fact and the *Annual Register* gave no more than a line or two to the event. The mass of published diaries and memoirs which cover his lifetime ignore him almost completely. But although he did not cut a figure in London society, his death plunged whole communities into grief. In Cardiff and Glamorgan his memory was cherished and when the newspapers of south Wales reported the death of his son, the third marquess, a far better known figure in London society, they gave as their headline: 'Death of the Son of the Creator of Cardiff'. The second marquess's life and character were strikingly different from those of his predecessor and successor. The first marquess was brilliant and amusing but feckless, profligate and irresponsible, a typical eighteenth century man-about-town. The third marquess was a religious zealot, talking endlessly of altars and liturgies, a student of clair-voyance with a wealth of esoteric knowledge; he was a remarkable product of the romantic Catholic revival. The second marquess was also a product of his age, a mixture of evangelical earnestness, aristocratic arrogance and the confident ruthlessness of an early nineteenth century industrialist. Dour, remote and overbearing on first acquaintance, he was a man with a deep sense of responsibility, considerable imagination and an enormous capacity for hard work.

[33] Sandon Hall Archives, XX and XXI.

Left fatherless at the age of one, he spent his infancy in the care of his mother and her parents at Dumfries House. Following the death of his mother in 1797 and of his grandmother, Lady Dumfries, in 1799, the young heir, then known by the title of earl of Windsor, came into the sole charge of his paternal grandfather, the marquess of Bute, spending his boyhood in Bute houses in London, Luton and on the continent. He proved an able child. 'He is so ambitious of acquiring knowledge', wrote Lord Dumfries in 1800, ' . . . that I fondly form the highest expectations of the happy result of such dispositions.'[34] Lord Dumfries died in 1803, his grandson inheriting his titles and his estates. In 1809 the young earl of Dumfries went to Christ's College, Cambridge, where he was strongly influenced by his tutor Dr. Kaye, later the eminent bishop of Lincoln. Between 1809 and 1814 he travelled extensively on the continent; during a cruise in the Mediterranean in 1809 he won the friendship of the duke of Orléans, later King Louis Philippe. He spent the winter of 1812 at Stockholm, where he became acquainted with Mme. de Staël and in the following year he visited Moscow, St. Petersburg and Vienna. In the summer of 1814 he visited Napoleon at Elba; in September he went to stay with his grandfather at Geneva and was with him when the old man died two months later.[35] Two letters survive from this period in his life. Written in Russia, they show that even before coming of age, he was fascinated by land improvement and economic development, a fascination which was to remain with him for the rest of his life.[36]

In 1814 the second marquess of Bute came into his inheritance. He was by then afflicted with a severe eye disease which was to be a permanent burden. He could read and write only with difficulty and had to be led when walking or riding. His malady caused him to be highly accident-prone. In 1845 he fell from his horse, splinters from his spectacles piercing his

---

[34] Dumfries to Bute, 18 August 1800 (ibid., XX).
[35] *A sketch of the life of John, second marquess of Bute, reprinted principally from the Cardiff and Merthyr Guardian* (1848); H. Cobbe, op. cit., p. 242; Orleans to Bute, 29 June 1813 (Sandon Hall Archives, XXI); J. G. Alger, *Napoleon's British visitors and captives* (1904), p. 242.
[36] Dumfries to Lady Bute, 13 June 1813, and to Bute, 29 June 1813 (Sandon Hall Archives, XX).

eyes; thereafter his writing deteriorated from the semi-legible to the wholly illegible.[37] Artificial light aggravated his affliction; evening parties were a torment to him, and in consequence he shunned London social life. Hardly had he attained his majority when the threat of blindness forced him to abandon all thought of active participation in estate management, and he spent the years from 1814 to 1820 largely in retirement on the Isle of Bute.[38]

In 1818, during his period of convalescence, the marquess married Lady Maria North, daughter of the third earl of Guilford, the marriage representing an alliance between the descendants of two of George III's prime ministers. The young couple were connected, for the marquess's stepgrandmother was the sister of Lady Maria's stepmother. Since the early-eighteenth century the head of the Bute family had in each generation married an heiress. The second marquess was no exception; of his wife's uncles, the fourth earl had died childless in 1816 and the fifth was unmarried and living as a recluse on the Isle of Corfu.[39] Lady Bute and her two sisters were therefore the co-heiresses of the North estates. She brought her husband over £40,000 in cash and on the death of the fifth earl in 1827 she became entitled to a third of the extensive lands of her family, the total value of which was estimated to be £345,474. Under the North Estates Act of 1831, Lady Bute received the 2,945-acre Kirtling estate in Cambridgeshire and the 350-acre Harlow estate in Essex.[40] Kirtling Tower and the North mansion at Wroxton Abbey, which was at the marquess's disposal until the marriage of his sister-in-law, Lady Susan, in 1835, were additional homes for the Bute family and further focal points of the marquess's endless travels.

Although Lady Maria brought her husband wealth and land, she failed to provide him with an heir; a chronic invalid, her recurring illnesses disrupted the Bute household until her death in 1841 at the age of forty-eight. Under the marriage settlement, the marquess had use of the income of his wife's share of the North estates until his death, when the property

---

[37] Compare his letters of 1845 with those of 1846 (G.R.O., D/DA 29 and 30).
[38] C.C.L., B., IX, 17; J. Wilson, op. cit., pp. 70–71.
[39] J. G. Alger, op. cit., p. 42; *Complete Peerage*, VI (1926), 210–18.
[40] The marriage settlement of Lord Bute and Lady Maria North (N.L.W., B., 137, 2); 3–4 George IV, *cap*. 32.

passed to Lady Susan, his wife's only surviving sister. In
memory of Lady Bute, a woman of great charm and kindness,
the marquess built a row of almshouses at Kirtling, whose poor
inhabitants 'looked upon the tomb of their former benefactress
as the shrine of a patron saint'.[41]

Four years after Lady Maria's death, Bute married again;
his second wife was Sophia, daughter of the first marquess of
Hastings and his wife Flora, countess of Loudoun. The Bute
and Loudoun families were distantly connected and their
estates in Ayrshire were contiguous. Lady Sophia was not an
heiress; she did, however, bring her husband estate responsibilities, for her brother, the second marquess of Hastings, died
in 1844 leaving a young heir, and Bute was obliged to
supervise the administration of his nephew's Loudoun and
Rowallan estates.[42] Lady Sophia had literary interests; in 1841
she published an edition of the poems of her ill-fated sister,
Lady Flora Hastings, and during her widowhood she edited
the journals which her father had written while governor-
general of India.[43] She was a less attractive personality than
Lady Maria. Bute's kinsman, John Stuart Wortley, found her
unsympathetic, his brother Lord James Stuart disliked her
intensely and her correspondence suggests that she was
querulous and obsessive by nature.[44] She did, however, fulfil
her husband's great ambition; twenty-nine months after her
marriage and six months before the marquess's death, she gave
birth to a son, thus ensuring that the returns upon the
investment which Bute had made in estate development would
be enjoyed by an heir of his body.[45] Left a widow at the age
of thirty-nine, Lady Sophia spent a wandering widowhood
and followed her lord to the grave in 1859.[46]

[41] De Grave to Richards, 29 September 1841 (G.R.O., D/DA 25).
[42] H. Blyth, *The pocket Venus* (1966), pp. 16–22; letters on the Hastings estates
(G.R.O., D/DA 30–31; N.L.W., B., 70, L. 1847–48).
[43] Lady Sophia Hastings (ed.), *The poems of Lady Flora Hastings* (1841); Lady
Bute (ed.), *The private journals of the marquess of Hastings* (2 vols., 1858).
[44] Lord Wortley and C. Grosvenor, *The first Lady Wharncliffe and her family,
1779–1856* (1927), II, 84; C.C.L., B., IX, 27, 21; Scot. P.R.O., H.B. MSS.,
196–198; G.R.O., D/DA, 32–33.
[45] Lady Bute had previously given birth to a stillborn child which was buried
in the gardens of Mountstuart (Lady Bute to Bruce, 10 May 1853: Scot. P.R.O.,
H.B., MSS. 198).
[46] But not to the same grave. The second marquess was buried alongside his
first wife at Kirtling. Sophia was buried at Mountstuart.

After 1820 the second marquess of Bute devoted his entire life to estate administration and improvement. Like a medieval monarch perambulating his kingdom, he spent his time travelling from Mountstuart on the Isle of Bute to Dumfries House in Ayrshire, to the Gibbs Royal Hotel at Edinburgh, to Newcastle-upon-Tyne, to Kirtling Tower, Wroxton Abbey and Luton Hoo, to his London houses at Camden Hill and 80 Piccadilly and to Cardiff Castle. His favourite home was Mountstuart and it was only with reluctance that he left Scotland at all. His perambulations required considerable forethought; when planning a journey from Dumfries House to Cardiff in 1846, he informed his agent, 'We propose to sleep at Kendal next Tuesday and at Wroxton on Thursday. Order four horses for my carriage at Chepstow and at Newport. Air the castle'.[47]

As estate manager, the second marquess was tireless. He wrote at least half a dozen lengthy business letters a day and kept copies of every one of them in letter-books.[48] His punctuality was legendary and his letters show that he had a firm grasp of affairs and a prodigious memory. 'The simplest expression or promise given by the late Marquess of Bute', noted the *Buteman*, 'was valued as much by the Bute tenantry . . . as a sixteen-page lease, well knowing that his retentive memory would not fail, even in the slightest detail.'[49] He expected the same punctiliousness and devotion to duty in his agents as he showed himself. This led him to attack every one of his employees in turn, and his letters often give the impression of an impatient and irritable man.

Although the second marquess did not care for London and its society, he did consider that he should take seriously his membership of the House of Lords. The *Cambrian* in its obituary of him did him less than justice in stating: 'The noble Marquess was a tolerably regular attendant in the House of Lords whenever business of importance was brought forward, although he but seldom troubled the house with any remarks'.[50]

[47] Bute to Richards, 26 March 1846 (G.R.O., D/DA, 30).
[48] Most of the letter-books for the period 1820–48 are in N.L.W., B., 70 and C.C.L. MSS. 4.173 and 4.860. There are original letters relating to the estate in G.R.O. (D/DA, 1–54), C.C.L. (B., VI, 33; VII, 44; IX, 27; XI, 55; XIV, 5; and XX), N.L.W. (B., 137 and 141) and Scot. P.R.O. (H.B. MSS., 196–98).
[49] *The Buteman*, 17 September 1859.
[50] *C.*, 24 March 1848.

An examination of Hansard shows that Bute did, in fact, address the House on fifty-seven separate occasions.[51] His position in politics he defined as agreement with his friend, the duke of Wellington, and avoidance of the excesses of the ultra-Tories. 'He persevered', stated the *Cambrian*, 'with a staunch consistency in supporting a Conservative policy, of which his interpretation was not so strict as to disqualify him ... from taking a useful part in public affairs.'[52]

The Bute family has won a reputation for being reactionary and obscurantist,[53] but the second marquess at least proved himself to be a judicious member of the legislature. An early champion of Catholic emancipation, he made a lengthy speech in its favour in 1828 and presented petitions on the subject from Cardiff and county Wexford. He was active in the agitation against slavery and in gathering information on the consequences of its abolition.[54] In the late-1830s he made annual speeches in the House on the necessity for abolishing religious oaths by municipal officers and in 1841 moved the second reading of the bill to relieve the disabilities of the Jews. He was a vigorous critic of the injustices of the new Poor Law, a consistent adversary of the truck system and an opponent of the Game Laws which he declared to be 'unjust and oppressive'.[55] Like his mentor, the duke of Wellington, Bute resisted parliamentary reform, but again like Wellington, and his own kinsmen the Lords Harrowby and Wharncliffe, he was not a last-ditch opponent. Nevertheless, he disliked reform sufficiently to quarrel with his brother over the matter, a quarrel which shook Bute political influence in Glamorgan.[56] On the issue of the repeal of the Corn Laws, he aligned himself with Peel and Wellington. His speech on the matter was a reflection of the

---

[51] He spoke on 'liberal' causes twelve times, church matters ten times, Scottish affairs five times, parliamentary reform four times, agriculture four times, taxes on beer twice, free trade, abolition of coal duties, the London and Westminster Bank, the Great Sessions and Ireland once apiece and fifteen times on miscellaneous matters.

[52] *C.*, 24 March 1848; Bute to Tavistock, 29 July 1830 (N.L.W., B., 70, L.2).

[53] E.g., I. B. Thomas, *Top sawyer, a biography of David Davies of Llandinam* (1938), p. 272.

[54] *Parliamentary debates*, second series, 7, p. 1122; 20, pp. 373, 803; 19, p. 1223; Bute to Wellington, 1 August 1846 (N.L.W., B., 70, L. 1845–46).

[55] *Parliamentary debates*, second series, 16, p. 1289; third series, 44, pp. 317–18; 58, pp. 1048–49, 1449, 1457.

[56] See below, pp. 122–25.

degree to which he himself was becoming more of an industrialist than an agriculturist, for by 1846 his profits from urban rents, mineral royalties and dock dues far exceeded those from agriculture. 'When he began public life', Hansard reported him as saying, 'he approved of protection, but having been directly or indirectly engaged in matters . . . connected with the commerce of the county, his opinion had undergone considerable change. He now thought that protection, as far as commerce was concerned, so far from being a benefit, was a positive injury.'[57]

Toryism to Bute meant essentially the defence of the established church, English and Scottish. 'It has long been the object of the Republican party in this country', he wrote in 1846, 'to identify the Tories or Conservatives with Corn Laws; but the Conservatives will stand upon their own true ground in defending the principle of the established church.'[58] He did not consider that emancipating Catholics endangered the establishment, but he was 'unable to trust himself to speak on the subject of those who sought to destroy the union of Great Britain and Ireland', for the weakening of the union would, he believed, threaten the position of the Church of Ireland. The claims of the Jews to full civil liberties were in his opinion stronger than those of the Nonconformists because the Jews had not attacked the principle of establishment.[59] His concern for that principle was political rather than theological; he was as vigorous a champion of the Presbyterian establishment of Scotland as he was of the Episcopalian establishment in England and Wales.

Outside the chamber of the House of Lords and outside the confines of his own estate, the second marquess played a minor but useful role. He was a member of the pilotage commission of 1835 and in 1841 joined the Select Committee on Copyhold Tenures. An advocate of emigration as an answer to rural over-population, he became in 1842 a vice-president of the British American Association for Emigration.[60] He continually

[57] *Parliamentary debates*, third series, 87, pp. 469–70.
[58] Bute to Nicholl, 9 February 1846 (N.L.W., B., 70, L. 1845–46).
[59] *Parliamentary debates*, third series, 1, pp. 16–17; 58, pp. 1048–49.
[60] Bute to Richards, 1 May 1835 and 2 February 1841 (G.R.O., D/DA 20 and 25); letters of December 1842, May 1843 and March 1844 in N.L.W., B., 70, L. 1840–44.

refused to involve himself in railway companies but was a leading figure in the London and Westminster Bank in its early, difficult days; chairman of its committee in 1833, he spoke in the bank's support in the House of Lords.[61] The crown of his public career came in the mid-1840s when, from 1842 to 1846, as Her Majesty's High Commissioner to the General Assembly of the Church of Scotland, he was a participant in the Disruption, the greatest crisis in the history of the Scottish church. He restored to the office some of its former dignity and splendour, clearly enjoying the ceremonial of residing at Holyrood House. He resigned in 1846 following misgivings over the queen's oath to the Church of Scotland.[62]

Bute was on friendly terms with the royal family, although his second marriage did identify him after 1846 with those who condemned Queen Victoria's treatment of Lady Flora Hastings. William IV took a sympathetic interest in him, the duke of York gave away Lady Maria North at her marriage, the duke of Gloucester made a three-day visit to Cardiff Castle in 1826 and the queen honoured him with a knighthood of the Thistle in 1843.[63] Lady Bute's poor health and Bute's bad eyesight, however, largely excluded them from the social round. Indeed, few of the traditional pastimes of the aristocracy appealed to the second marquess. He did not gamble, breed racehorses, flirt, hunt or shoot; unlike the rest of his line, he found no delight in collecting books and pictures and begrudged money spent on the upkeep of his residences. He was ill at ease in any large gathering and his political enemies considered him haughty and remote. Although he received warm praise for his conduct at the General Assembly of the Church of Scotland, it appears that he was an execrable public speaker. When he opened the Cardiff Eisteddfod of 1834, Lady Charlotte Guest noted that 'His speech was miserable, and made me tremble lest I should be betrayed into a smile . . . it was at length to my great relief, and I should think to

[61] Richards to Bute, 20 April 1833 (C.C.L., MS. 4.173); Roy to Bute, 5 March 1846 (N.L.W., B., 70, L. Roy, 1844–46).
[62] Letters in ibid., L. 1845–46 and N.L. Scot. MSS. 3444–45 contain material on the Disruption.
[63] Bute to Mrs. Abbott, 19 July 1841 (N.L.W., B., 70, L. 1840–44); E. H. Coleridge, op. cit., II, 157, 182; C.C.L., MS. 2.716, 12–14 August 1826.

his, concluded'.[64] There was a strong streak of vanity in the second marquess; when he received a congratulatory doggerel in 1846, he ordered another copy and gave the author two guineas. He was anxious that Glamorgan should recognise its debt to him and solicited gratitude. 'I sent you six impressions of my portrait', he informed his dockmaster in 1840, 'but it is twelve years old. I am free to say, *between you and me*, that I wish the county of Glamorgan would call for another by way of some set off to me for my trouble at the dock.' After his death, the county raised a subscription to erect a statue of him; much to the inconvenience of the traffic, the statue, which was unveiled in 1853, was placed in front of Cardiff town hall in the middle of the narrow High Street. A year earlier, a portrait depicting him holding the plans of his dock had been unveiled in the castle drawing room.[65]

The second marquess died at Cardiff on 18 March 1848 at the age of fifty-five. 'He was just at the height of his glory', wrote Lady Charlotte Guest. 'He had brought his long wished for little heir to Cardiff for the first time, he had received deputations of congratulations from the authorities on the event, . . . he was in highest apparent health and spirits, visiting day by day his docks and the institutions of the second Liverpool.'[66] His body was taken from Cardiff to Kirtling to be buried alongside his first wife. He would have been delighted to know that his funeral with its thirty-one carriages, its mutes and its muffled rolls of drums, drew larger crowds than did the funerals of George IV and William IV.[67]

THE THIRD MARQUESS OF BUTE, 1847-1900

On the death of the second marquess, his titles, his property and his debts went in their entirety to his son, John Crichton-Stuart, third marquess of Bute, an infant of six months. The third marquess was one of the most remarkable figures of the

[64] Lord Bessborough, *Lady Charlotte Guest; extracts from her journal, 1833–52* (1950), p. 33; N.L.W., Calendar of the diary of L. W. Dillwyn, 23 May 1818.
[65] Bute to Smyth, 26 December 1840 (N.L.W., B., 70, L. 7); memorandum, April 1846 (C.C.L., B., IX, 36); information from the National Portrait Gallery of Scotland. See Frontispiece.
[66] Lord Bessborough, op. cit., p. 206.
[67] *C.*, 7 April 1848.

nineteenth century British peerage. His immense wealth, his eccentricities, his conversion to Catholicism and his fame as the hero of the most successful of Disraeli's novels made him the object of much gossip and speculation. His early life, however, was not particularly auspicious. Two months after his father's death, he was constituted a ward in chancery, his mother being nominated guardian. A sickly child, he spent his infancy with his mother and a bevy of other women at Cardiff, Mountstuart and elsewhere.[68] His mother died in 1859, her will recommending that her relation, Lady Elizabeth Moore, and her late husband's relation, General Charles Stuart, should be joint guardians of her son. The guardians quarrelled over the education of the young marquess who, disliking General Stuart, connived when thirteen at Lady Elizabeth's scheme of smuggling him into Scotland. Litigation followed and a long dispute took place over the nationality of the marquess, for the courts of Scotland would not give up a domiciled Scot to a guardian appointed by an English court. The case, which became of significance in Scottish law, was taken to the House of Lords, which appointed General Stuart sole guardian.[69]

Stuart arranged for the young marquess to live in the household of the earl of Galloway at Galloway House. In 1860 he was sent to May Place, an aristocratic preparatory school at Malvern, and two years later entered Harrow where he stayed until 1865. His stay at Harrow seems to have been a happy one; although he was to become a fervent Roman Catholic, he sent his three sons to Harrow rather than to a Catholic public school. He entered Christ Church, Oxford, in 1865 where, despite his wealth and his high rank, he made little impression, a contemporary commenting that 'he was a retiring man and did not mix much with other undergraduates'.[70] At Oxford he was exposed to the full blast of the theological controversies of the 1860s. The second marquess

[68] D. H. Blair, *John Patrick, third marquess of Bute, K.T., 1847–1900, a memoir* (1901), p. 5; *Times*, 23 July 1860; Scot. P.R.O., H.B. MSS., 196–98; C.C.L., B., IX, 27, 21.

[69] N. Macpherson, *The appelate jurisdiction of the House of Lords in Scotch cases, illustrated by the litigation relating to the custody of the marquess of Bute* (1861); *Times*, 18 May 1861.

[70] Lord Braye, *The fullness of my days* (1927), p. 71.

had been an Anglican in Wales and England and a Presbyterian in Scotland, although he preferred Anglicanism, keeping
an Anglican chaplain and marrying his second wife in Scotland
according to Anglican rites. Despite his support for emancipation, the second marquess loathed Catholicism as a religion;
Guy Fawkes' night was celebrated with great fervour at
Mountstuart. Lady Sophia, as befitted the great-grand-
daughter of Selina, countess of Huntingdon, was a zealous
Protestant; she financed bands of colporteurs to distribute
bibles among the Glamorgan Irish and was in great perturbation in 1853 when her sister received an offer of marriage
from a papist. The Galloway household was dourly Presbyterian and the young marquess considered himself one of the
few Scottish aristocrats who was faithful to the national
church.[71]

Since his boyhood, however, the third marquess's fascination
with medieval Scottish history, with tales of saints and
monasteries and the fate of Mary, Queen of Scots, was drawing
him towards Catholicism. At Oxford he was befriended by
C. S. Murray, a Catholic Scot for whom Pugin had designed
a chapel, and by Murray's chaplain, Monsignor T. W. Capel
who, in descriptions of the marquess's conversion, is cast in the
role of *éminence grise*. The marquess was received into the
Roman Catholic church on 8 December 1868, three months
after his twenty-first birthday, a timing dictated by his advisers
who were anxious that his conversion, which they did all in
their power to prevent, should not weaken Bute influence in the
1868 election or poison the demonstrations of loyalty to the
Bute family at the coming-of-age celebrations. When news of
the conversion was made public, it caused a profound shock.
The Rothesay *Buteman* talked of the 'perversion to Rome' as
a public calamity and stated that the islanders were turning
their portraits of the marquess to the wall and even taking
vengeful pot-shots at them.[72] The news caused consternation
at Cardiff, although it was warmly welcomed by the growing

---

[71] Lady Bute to Richards, 1 March 1853 (C.C.L., B., IX, 27, 21); N.L. Scot.,
MS. 3447; D. H. Blair, op. cit., p. 4.
[72] Ibid., pp. 46–47, 61–65; *The Buteman*, 9, 16 and 23 January 1869; J. Jones,
River out of Eden (1951), chapter IV.

Catholic community there. 'We have here', wrote the marquess in 1869, 'between 9,000 and 10,000 Catholics who are, of course, delighted by what has happened . . . large mobs of people assembled to see me go to mass.'[73]

With his conversion, the marquess's life became dominated by Catholicism. 'It was like reading *Lothair* in the original', wrote Augustus Hare after meeting him in 1874, 'and most interesting at first, but became somewhat monotonous as he talks incessantly . . . of altars, ritual and liturgical differences; he often loses himself, and certainly quite lost me, in sentences about 'the unity of the Kosmos'.'[74] The marquess indulged in frequent fasts and spent large sums of money on allegorical jewellery and religious objects; he presented the Pope with a cross which was carried at the head of the Vatican Council's opening procession; when his wife gave birth to their eldest son he gave her a crown bearing in rubies the inscription 'a virtuous woman is a crown to her husband' in Hebrew characters, and he purchased a ring bearing a diamond in a crescent which he intended to give to his wife if Constantinople were taken from the Turks.[75] He was undoubtedly an attractive personality. Hare considered that 'he has great sweetness and gentleness of manner and a good looking, refined face'. 'It is pleasant', wrote Lady Knightley, who dined with him in 1873, 'to feel one is with people who are deeply religious and really do *care* for God.'[76]

Although diffident in public, the third marquess won for himself a leading position in the British Catholic community. He was prominent among the lay Catholics at the Vatican Council and led the Scottish delegation to Pope Leo XIII's ordination jubilee celebrations in 1888. He entertained Cardinal Manning at Cardiff Castle and in 1879 used all his energies to persuade Newman to accept the red hat. There was a strong streak of obstinacy in him; on Scottish educational matters he had very fixed views and entered into a long dispute on the

---

[73] D. H. Blair, op. cit., p. 78; J. V. Hickey, *Urban Catholics* (1967), pp. 56–96.
[74] J. C. A. Hare, *The story of my life* (1900), V, 169–71.
[75] D. H. Blair, op. cit., pp. 86–87; J. C. A. Hare, *The story of two noble lives* (1893), III, 365; codicil to the will of the third marquess of Bute, 1882 (N.L.W., B., 137, 5).
[76] J. Cartwright (ed.), *The journals of Lady Knightley of Fawsley* (1915), p. 246.

subject with members of the Scottish Catholic hierarchy.[77]
His Catholicism coloured all his attitudes and, as the *Western
Mail* said in its obituary of him, 'It would have been difficult
to imagine the Marquess of Bute as a Protestant'.[78] He linked
the name of Bute with Catholicism to such a degree that by
the 1890s it was being assumed that the family had always
been Catholic.[79] His interest in theology and liturgy led him
to show a warm and scholarly sympathy for the Greek and
Armenian churches. Like his father he was a strong supporter
of the Jews; he gave generous leases for the building of
synagogues in Cardiff and advocated the establishment of
a Scottish college for Jews at St. Andrews.[80]

It was widely assumed that on becoming a Catholic, the
third marquess, to be consistent, should also have become a
Liberal. When the news of his conversion became public, the
Leader declared, 'The Marquess of Bute is only half converted
after all, for he still announces himself a Conservative . . . We
do not see how he can easily help becoming an advocate of
the policy that would concede the fulness of religious liberty
to the Marquess's co-religionists in Ireland . . . many Roman
Catholics will feel suspicious of that conviction which, whilst
adopting a faith, still sanctions its persecution.'[81] There was
nothing progressive about the third marquess, however. On
coming of age he had announced himself to be a Conservative
and an old-fashioned Tory and, following his conversion, his
lawyer at Cardiff announced that 'the marquess of Bute is as
firm a constitutionalist as ever, and it would be no fault of his
if his social and political relations with Cardiff undergo any
change'.[82] Although he contributed substantial sums to
Conservative party funds, the marquess had no interest in

[77] M. F. Roskell, *Memoirs of Francis Kerrill Amherst, D.D., Lord Bishop of
Northampton* (1903), p. 178; A. Westcott, *Life and letters of Brooke Foss Westcott, D.D.,
D.C.L., sometime bishop of Durham* (1903), II, 43; D. H. Blair, op. cit., p. 158;
C., 9 September 1881; W. Ward, *The life of Cardinal Newman* (1912), II, 579. The
third marquess's contribution to Scottish Catholicism is discussed in chapters by
O. Dudley-Edwards, R. Macdonald and D. McRoberts in D. McRoberts (ed.),
Modern Scottish Catholicism (1979).
[78] *W.M.*, 10 October 1900.
[79] E.g. *Estates Gazette*, 4 October 1890.
[80] D. H. Blair, op. cit., *passim*; *Jewish Chronicle*, 12 October 1900; M. T. Shaw,
Memorials of two sisters, Susanna and Catherine Winkworth (1908), p. 326; G. E. Russell
(ed.), *Malcolm Maccoll, memoirs and correspondence* (1914), p. 147.
[81] *The Leader*, 11 February 1869; *The Buteman*, 13 February 1869.
[82] Ibid., 6 February 1869; D. H. Blair, op. cit., p. 79.

political campaigning. His political influence at Cardiff was wielded on the initiative of his fanatically Tory lawyer, Shirley, and the marquess took no part in the most overtly political act of the Bute estate in the second half of the nineteenth century, the foundation of the *Western Mail*. He did not address the House of Lords until 1894, and when he did so, he spoke exclusively on the affairs of the University of St. Andrews, of which he was then rector.[83]

The Court and London society were as unattractive to the marquess as was political activity. It was reported when he came of age that his parents had left written instructions to him to ignore the royal family because of the queen's treatment of his aunt, Lady Flora Hastings. By the 1880s, a reconciliation must have taken place for, in that decade, the marquess visited Victoria at Balmoral and entertained Prince Leopold at Mountstuart. Although he was a member of seven London clubs, owned St. John's Lodge overlooking Regent's Park and rented Chiswick House from the duke of Devonshire, he did not care for metropolitan life. In society he was morose and awkward, given to remarks such as 'Isn't it monstrous that St. Magnus hasn't got an octave', ejaculations which puzzled and bewildered his companions.[84]

The third marquess of Bute's fame in society rested upon the fact that he was the hero of Disraeli's best selling novel, *Lothair*. Disraeli, who had links with Glamorgan through his wife Mary Ann, the widow of the Glamorgan lawyer and industrialist Wyndham Lewis, was acquainted with the marquess and had been present at his coming-of-age celebrations in Cardiff. The delineation of the marquess's character in the novel, which was published in 1870 when he was twenty-three, has a high degree of veracity: Lothair's over-intense religiosity, his fondness for religious paraphernalia and his desire to escape from the burden of wealth were all characteristics of the third marquess of Bute, although Disraeli was less than just in portraying him, in the person of Lothair, as the uncritical repository of conflicting ideologies. Like Lothair, he never had the experience of creating wealth, a

---

[83] *Parliamentary debates*, fourth series, XXV, p. 273. See below, pp. 135, 141–45.
[84] D. H. Blair, op. cit., pp. 51, 118; *Truth*, 18 October 1900; Lady Bute to Bruce, 26 August 1851 (Scot. P.R.O., H.B. MSS., 197); *W.M.*, 15 December 1884.

matter which exercised his father throughout his life. 'He did not have to turn his thoughts to the accumulation of wealth', noted the *Western Mail*; 'this flowed into his coffers unsought and unbidden.' During the long minority, a vast income accumulated and, like Lothair, he 'came into everything ready made'.[85]

When he came down from Oxford, the marquess was among the most eligible bachelors in the British peerage. After entanglements with the daughter of the duke of Abercorn and with Maria Fox, adopted daughter of Lady Holland,[86] he married, in 1872, Gwendoline Fitzalan-Howard, whose father, the first Baron Howard of Glossop, was a leading Catholic and a former Liberal Member of Parliament. Lord Howard was the second son of the thirteenth duke of Norfolk; the marriage thus linked the Stuarts with the most eminent Catholic house in Britain and also brought together the Scottish and English branches of the Fitzalan family which had diverged in the eleventh century. The marchioness bore her husband four children: Margaret, born in 1875, John, the fourth marquess, born in 1881, Ninian, born in 1883 and Colum, born in 1885.

Catholicism and liturgical scholarship were the abiding interests of the third marquess of Bute, but he was in addition a fervent Celt, an enthusiastic builder and an inveterate traveller. Much to the annoyance of the *Western Mail*, Scottish causes benefited greatly from the wealth which the marquess received from Glamorgan. He published extensively on Scottish history and bore most of the expense of the publications of the Grampian Club. In 1888 he bought the *Scottish Review* and subsidised it heavily; it died with him in 1900. He made strongly nationalistic speeches to bodies such as the Edinburgh Philosophical Institution and, as the devoted rector of St. Andrews, he sought to instil in the students a loyalty to Scotland. He unveiled a monument to Wallace and used the *Scottish Review* to advocate home rule, the Scottish parliament being for him a symbol of the 'national, Catholic and feudal'

---

[85] Ibid., 10 October 1900; B. Disraeli, *Lothair* (ed. 1927), pp. 25, 91; W. F. Monypenny and G. E. Buckle, *The life of Disraeli* (1929), II, 292.
[86] G. W. E. Russell, *Portraits of the seventies* (1916), p. 259; Lord Ilchester, *Chronicles of Holland House, 1820–1900* (1927), p. 434.

period of his country's past. As a patriotic Scots peer, he had interests in common with Lord Rosebery who had been his contemporary at Oxford. In 1894, when Rosebery became prime minister, the marquess gave a dinner for him at which Rosebery was most indiscreet. Following his friend's death, the statesman paid a touching tribute to him at a meeting of the Scottish History Society.[87]

The factors which made him a patriotic Scot also led the marquess to take a sympathetic interest in the culture of Wales. David Howell, vicar of St. John's, Cardiff, and a leading patriot, gave him Welsh lessons and he learnt to speak the language fairly fluently and to write it accurately. He gave his church livings to Anglo-Catholics who were Welsh enthusiasts, and he provided a pension for that weird druid, Evan Davies of Pontypridd. An ardent Celticist, he spoke at length on Eisteddfod platforms of the mission of the Celts, and it was claimed that his passionate advocacy of the Welsh language at the Cardiff National Eisteddfod of 1882 led directly to the formation of the Welsh Language Society, the body responsible for obtaining a measure of recognition for the language in education.[88] The marquess made a study of Welsh history, urged that a monument should be erected in memory of Llywelyn the Last and called for the re-establishment of the Council of Wales, whose abolition, together with that of the Scottish parliament, he attributed to the antinationalism inherent in Whiggery. T. E. Ellis suggested him as a possible member of the Royal Commission on Land in Wales, but he shrank from so controversial a task. In 1890 he was elected president of the Honourable Society of Cymmrodorion, an office which he held until his death. He was generous in assisting the society to publish Welsh records, paid

---

[87] D. H. Blair, op. cit., pp. 55, 68, 129, 247–48; A. Westcott, op. cit., II, 43; Lord Crewe, *Lord Rosebery* (1931), II, 474, 603; *The Atheneum*, 13 October 1900; *Scottish Review*, October 1889; W. Knight, *Some nineteenth century Scotsmen, being personal recollections by William Knight, Professor of Philosophy in the University of St. Andrews* (1903), p. 406; *W.M.*, 23 November 1893. The *Scottish Review* was revived in 1914.

[88] *W.M.*, 10 and 13 October 1900; N.L.W., MS. 2340C; *Transactions of the National Eisteddfod of Wales*, Cardiff, 1883, pp. 16–21, Rhyl, 1892, p. xxiii; O. M. Morgan, *The history of Pontypridd and Rhondda valleys* (1903), p. 84; G. A. Jones, J. W. Ward and H. H. Coe, *Father Jones of Cardiff* (1907), p. 59.

for the printing of the *Liber Landavensis* and gave £1,000 to the
Cardiff Central Library to buy the Sir Thomas Phillipps
manuscripts.[89]

Equally characteristic of the man was the way he indulged
his passion for building. The urge to build was inherent in
most of the Butes and in the third marquess it bordered upon
mania. When Mountstuart House burnt down in 1877, he
engaged Sir Rowand Anderson to rebuild it and the new
mansion, an incredible pile of sandstone in Italianate gothic,
cost £600,000. His interest in Scottish history led him to buy
many ancient monuments, including Falkland Palace, the
Old Place of Mochrum, the abbey and castle of St. Andrews,
the site of Whithorn Abbey, Pluscarden Abbey and the
Crichton Tower at Sanquhar, and to spend vast sums on their
preservation. 'He preferred', noted the *Western Mail*, 'to
restore an old chapel where there was no congregation rather
than provide an odious modern building in an industrial
town.'[90] His building activities were not confined to Scotland;
in Glamorgan he redecorated Cardiff Castle in a style of
overwhelming splendour, while at Castell Coch he created
what is perhaps the most delightful landmark in Wales.[91]

Although he spent freely upon rebuilding and redecorating
his houses, the marquess appears to have been happiest when
travelling. While at Oxford he bought the yacht of his
spendthrift cousin, the marquess of Hastings, and in it he
spent his vacations cruising around Scotland and in the North
and Baltic Seas. France, Germany, Italy and Greece he knew
intimately, but his great love was Palestine. During his first
visit in 1865 the Holy Land captured his imagination and
Palestine became something of an obsession with him. He
spent the winter of 1874 at Nazareth, the walls of his sitting
room at Cardiff Castle were covered with water-colours of the
Palestinian scene and he subscribed liberally to the Palestinian
Exploration Fund. He purchased considerable estates in

---

[89] N.L.W., Rendel Papers, 9, 94; *S.W.D.N.*, 10 October 1900; *Cymru*, III
(1892), 169; *W.M.*, 15 October 1900.
[90] Ibid.; D. H. Blair, op. cit., pp. 215–23; J. M. Crook, 'Patron extraordinary,
John, third marquess of Bute, 1847–1900', in *Victorian south Wales, the seventh conference report of the Victorian Society* (1969), pp. 3–22.
[91] See below, pp. 139–41.

Palestine and Syria and directed that his heart should be buried on the Mount of Olives.[92]

EPILOGUE, 1900–1947

The third marquess of Bute died in October 1900. The links between his successors and the family property in Glamorgan became increasingly tenuous. Under his will the estate was unequally divided between his eldest son John, the fourth marquess, and Colum his youngest.[93] Although a more robust character than his father, the fourth marquess inherited many of the tastes and attributes of the third. He spoke Welsh fluently and patronised Welsh cultural activities; an enthusiastic traveller, he visited India for the Delhi Durbar; a fervent Catholic, he continued his father's charitable gifts to Catholic causes. He was a compulsive builder, completing his father's work on Cardiff Castle and initiating a large-scale restoration of Caerphilly Castle; as an accumulator of houses he acquired Cottesmore Hall in Rutland, a house in Edinburgh, a place in Chile and an estate in Spain. Above all he was a patriotic Scot, being president of the Scottish History Society and chairman of the Records Committee for Scotland while also seeking to revive the traditional culture and industries of the Scottish islands.[94] During his lifetime the Bute family lost in turn their interests in their collieries, their agricultural land, their docks, their mineral reserves and their urban land in Glamorgan, and when the fourth marquess died in 1947, his son's inheritance in the county consisted of little more than Cardiff Castle and its park.

Four months after his father's death, the fifth marquess presented the castle and its 434-acre park to the city of Cardiff. On 10 September 1947, the standard of the Butes was lowered for the last time and, as aeroplanes flew overhead in salute, the marquess expressed his great satisfaction in presenting to the city the castle from which it had sprung.[95]

[92] D. H. Blair, op. cit., pp. 52, 55, 68; *W.M.*, 10 October 1900; J. C. A. Hare, *The story of my life*, IV, 269; *A list of paintings at Cardiff Castle* (1893).
[93] Will of the third marquess of Bute (N.L.W., B., 137, 5).
[94] *W.M.*, 3 May 1909; A. Fitzroy, *Memoirs* (n.d.), p. 447; Lady Gordon, *The winds of time* (1934), p. 51; Lady Norah Bentinck, *My wanderings and memories* (1924); *Times*, 16 January 1932, 26 and 29 April 1947, 25 August 1956; J. A. Jones, 'Dysgu Cymraeg i'r ardalydd Bute', *Y Gwrandawr (Barn)*, Awst 1965, pp. v–vi.
[95] *Times*, 7 August and 11 September 1947.

II

THE CARDIFF CASTLE ESTATE, 1766–1947

THE ESTATE AND THE FIRST MARQUESS, 1766–1814

The Cardiff Castle estate, that 'prudential consideration' which was Lord Mountstuart's motive for matrimony, when surveyed following the marriage of 1766, was found to consist of 11,211 acres of enclosed land together with rights over a vast area of common land within the manors of east and mid-Glamorgan. The enclosed land fell into four sections: within the town of Cardiff there were 711 acres; encircling the town, in the parishes of Roath, Llanishen, Llandaf, Llandough, Leckwith, Cogan and Lavernock, were a further 2,150 acres; in the border vale of Glamorgan, centred upon Llantrisant, lay 3,400 acres, while in the uplands of the county, extending in an arc from the Rhymney to the Neath valley, there were 4,100 acres, and the total was made up by an outlying 850 acres around Cowbridge and Llantwit Major. It was far from being a compact estate, scattered as it was 'in a space twenty-four miles by fourteen', its dispersed nature indicative of the fact that it represented by the 1760s merely a remnant of the vast possessions formerly owned by the Herbert family. Charlotte, last of the Herbert proprietors, had owned extensive lands in Monmouthshire as well as in Glamorgan and her father 'could have passed through his own manors almost the whole of the way from the vicinity of Monmouth to Newton Down beyond Cowbridge . . . a distance of nearly sixty miles'.[1] By the 1760s, a large proportion of the Glamorgan estates had been disposed of, while in Monmouthshire all the manors and lands had been sold. Alienation by sale was not the only cause of the shrinkage. In the 1820s, the second marquess's surveyor wrote of agents and local landowners who, in the seventeenth and eighteenth centuries, had usurped estate property and

---

[1] C.C.L., B., IX, 19; Valuation, 1774 (N.L.W., B., 104); E. Davies (ed.), *Coxe's historical tour through Monmouthshire* (1934), pp. 129, 137; D. Williams, *The history of Monmouthshire* (1796), Appendix, p. 10; C. Wilkins, *The history of Merthyr Tydfil* (1867), p. 189.

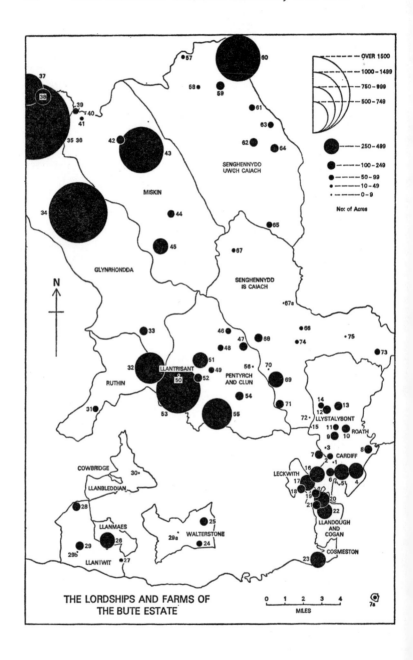

THE LORDSHIPS AND FARMS OF
THE BUTE ESTATE

The farms and lands of the Bute Estate in Glamorgan as listed in David Stewart's Atlas, 1824 (G.R.O., D/OB E. 1).

1. Cardiff Castle grounds, Cooper's Fields, Blackfriar's Fields, etc. 61 acres
2. Lands within the town of Cardiff 6 acres
3. Fields and cottages on the Merthyr road 2 acres
4. The Cardiff Moors 440 acres
5. Adamsdown with Spittle and Whitmoor 397 acres
6. Cardiff Moors, west of the Taff 181 acres
7. Plasturton 147 acres
7a. Flat Holme Island 49 acres
8. Dean's Farm and Pengam Moors 166 acres
9. Crwys bychan, Penywaun and Ysgubor fach 102 acres
10. Penylan 115 acres
11. Fair Oak and Merry Hill 143 acres
12. Cefnycoed and Celyn 224 acres
13. Rhydypennau and Rhydyblewyn 215 acres
14. Heol hir and Tir Sion Gruffydd 67 acres
15. Tiryfillog, etc. 7 acres
16. Leckwith Moor 407 acres
17. Farms at Leckwith, including Leckwith Bridge, Ynyston, Church farm, Hill farm and Well Spring 486 acres
18. Fferm wen 114 acres
19. Cedfin or Ty Mawr 140 acres
20. Llandough and Cogan Pill 324 acres
21. Corners Well, Green Seyes and Lower Cogan Pill 206 acres
22. Cogan 323 acres
23. Cosmeston and Swanbridge 485 acres
24. Cournix 80 acres
25. Walterstone 153 acres
26. Farms and lands at Llanmaes 307 acres
27. Battslays 37 acres
28. Lands at Llantwit Major 199 acres
29. Sheeplays 116 acres
29a. Cottages at Llanbleddian 3 acres
29b. Encroachments at Llantwit Major 7 acres
30. Cottages at Aberthin 3 acres
31. Lands at Trallwyn 51 acres
32. Ynys y Maerdy, Garth Maelog and Tir Christopher y Gof 692 acres
33. Gilfach Ithel, Tir Llewelyn foel, Tir Ton Addaf, Gwern Hebog, Gwaun yr Arglwydd and Cefn Tilcha 124 acres
34. Abergorci, Ystradfechan, Glynmoch, Pentwyn, Tyla du and Glyn coli 1237 acres
35. Farms at Rhigos, including Gwrelych Mill, Hendre fawr, Rhyd, Bailyglas, Blaengwrelych, Blaengwrangon, Gwrangon ganol, Gwrangon fawr and Gwrangon isaf 1685 acres
36. Sheep walks, acreage included in 35
37. Farms at Rhigos, including Llwyn y gwin, Ynyscambwl, Nant Gwna, Pencaedrain and Carnygist 550 acres

38. Farms at Rhigos, including Tir y castell, Nant llecha, Bryn y gaer and Tynewydd 280 acres
39. Lands at Rhigos and Hirwaun, including the Hirwaun Furnace ground, Bryn y Maerdy, Bryn y Cnapa and Tir Ifan y Gof 120 acres
40. Building ground at Hirwaun 7 acres
41. Scattered land adjoining Hirwaun Common 11 acres
42. Cwmdare Fechan, Tir Fryd and building ground at Aberdare 120 acres
43. Farms at Aberdare including Gwryd Uchaf, Craig y Gilfach, Tir y Gwryd and Pantygorddinan 836 acres
44. Fforch Don 217 acres
45. Clun y felin 273 acres
46. Lands at Llantwit Faerdre including Ynys y wern and Tir Penygraig 63 acres
47. Maesbach 115 acres
48. Bryn yr eglwys and Tir porth Dowlais 58 acres
49. Cae'r Dyon and Coed Cae Arglwydd 66 acres
50. Llantrisant castle and market place 2 acres
51. Cloddiau caban, Gwaun Miskin, Llwyd cae mawr, Coed cae canol and Gwaun y Stent 259 acres
52. Caerau and Gwern y Moel 172 acres
53. Lands near Llantrisant including Maes Harrill, Pontyparc, New Park, Fenalog and Felinfawr 810 acres
54. Lands at Pentyrch, including Llwyn yr eos 141 acres
55. Henstaff and Parc Coedmachen 510 acres
56. Cottages on the Garth 1 acre
57. Blaenmorlais 46 acres
58. The Dowlais Furnace ground 24 acres
59. Marchnad y Waun and Bryn y caerau 137 acres
60. Blaen Rhymni, Pidwell, Carno, Bryn glas, Penfedw, Blaencarno and Coed cae du 830 acres
61. Hafodiestyn 94 acres
62. Lands at Ysgwyddgwyn 161 acres
63. Tir ferch Gronw and Cae canol 84 acres
64. Tir y coli and Cae glas 190 acres
65. Melindre Gilla and Bryn Owen 54 acres
66. Caerphilly Castle 14 acres
67. Cefn y coed and Cae tir dinas 46 acres
67a. Cottages at Eglwysilan 3 acres
68. Ty'n y wern and Heol y Bwnshy 124 acres
69. Castell Coch and forest 419 acres
70. Cottages at Eglwysilan and Whitchurch 3 acres
71. Fforest isaf 112 acres
72. Cottages at Whitchurch 2 acres
73. Cefn porth or Coed y gwina 55 acres
74. Cottages on Caerphilly common 11 acres
75. Cottages on Rudry common 7 acres

rights. 'Many', he reported, 'are in possession of lands which belonged to Lord Bute's ancestors and to which they can show no title but quiet possession for a length of time.'[2]

The first marquess regarded himself as an able estate manager. 'Experience has taught me', he informed his son, 'that without being excessively attentive, accurate and watchful, an estate must suffer essentially.' Evidence available regarding the marquess's life, activities and temperament, however, does not suggest that he possessed such attributes. His brother Frederick told Boswell that he did not believe that Lord Mountstuart 'would ever be a man of business for that he would not persist'.[3] His life in the 1760s and 1770s as a man-about-town flirting with politics, his diplomatic career in the 1780s and 1790s, and the ceaseless wandering of his last years can have left little time for earnest application to estate management. In Glamorgan, his position was weakened by his lack of clear undivided authority and responsibility. Following the death of Lord Windsor in 1758, Lady Windsor held the estate as life tenant until her death in 1776; from 1776 to 1800 it was held by Lady Bute with her husband enjoying rights *iure uxoris*; from 1800 to 1814, one moiety belonged to the first marquess as life tenant and he administered the other in trust for his grandson, the future second marquess. But the situation was, in fact, more complicated than this. Lady Windsor's right to the two moieties after her husband's death was uncertain; the legal estate was never vested in her and her husband's will had given her no authority to grant leases. Furthermore, Charlotte, by marrying a Scotsman, had defied a major stipulation in her father's will and her right to the estate was therefore impugnable. The first marquess's entitlement to the guardianship of his heir was somewhat suspect and his right to one moiety of the estate after his wife's death was far from secure. The advisers of the second marquess affirmed that before his succession in 1814, no one had been entitled to the fee simple since 1738 and that the legal estate had been outstanding since the private Act of

[2] C.C.L., MS. 4.850; Survey and valuation, 1825 (N.L.W., B., 104); ibid., 126 and 132; G.R.O., D/DB, E 2.
[3] Bute to Mountstuart, 28 August 1793 (Sandon Hall Archives, XX); C. Ryskamp and F. A. Pottle (eds.), *Boswell, the ominous years, 1774–76* (1963), p. 130.

Parliament of 1696. It is hardly surprising that under the second marquess the neglect of the past was ascribed to 'the peculiar circumstances of . . . the family'.[4]

The lack of an active landowner with undivided authority is reflected in the confused administration of the estate under the first marquess. From 1758 to 1778 the estate was under the supervision of a Mr. Edwards, who received no formal wages but was especially active in matters relating to manorial rights and rents. He was succeeded by Thomas Thomas, a local attorney who disappears from the records in 1784, when Henry Hollier, who was the leading figure in the management of the estate until his dismissal in 1815, emerged as chief agent.[5] In addition to his estate duties, Hollier was, by the turn of the century, Cardiff's town clerk and collector of customs as well as receiver-general of taxes and clerk of the peace for the county of Glamorgan. He was also intent upon building up a landed estate for himself, acquiring several tracts of Cardiff's Great Heath together with the farms of Penylan, Rhydypennau and Adamsdown. In none of these enterprises did he distinguish himself. His record as estate agent was lamentable and there is at least a suggestion that he swindled his employer; as receiver-general, he became a very considerable defaulter and legal action was taken against him by the crown; he was removed from his office as alderman in 1818 for neglect and bad government, and his entire landed estate was impounded and sold.[6]

Despite his misfortunes, Hollier remains a shadowy figure. A far clearer personality is John Bird, whose diary is the main source of information on estate matters and indeed on the history of Cardiff as a whole at the end of the eighteenth century.[7] The founder of the extensive Bird clan in Glamorgan settled at Cardiff in the early-seventeenth century; by the end

[4] Will of Lord Windsor, 1755, case as to the construction of Lord Bute's will, suit 1795, suit 1802, statement 1825, action 1826 (N.L.W., B., 137, 1); Richards to Farrer, 6 August 1824 (G.R.O., D/DA 11).

[5] C.C.L., B., IX, 16, 17, 18 and 19; X, 11; N.L.W., B., 58, 126 and 132.

[6] C.C.L., MS. 2.716, 26 August 1793; J. Bird, *The directory of Cardiff* (1794), p. 15; J. H. Matthews, *Cardiff Records, materials for a history of the county borough* (1898–1911), IV, 338, V, 1; C.C.L., B., X, 11; case 1807, particulars of the estate of Henry Hollier, 1818, statement 1825, King against Hollier (N.L.W., B., 31).

[7] C.C.L., MS. 2.716. It covers the years 1790–95, 1797–1803 and 1826.

of the century the Birds had become hereditary agents to the lords of Cardiff Castle, residing at the castle itself, where John Bird was born in 1761. Bird entered Bute employment in about 1780 and in the directory he published in 1796 he described himself as the clerk of the marquess of Bute. He was a substantial citizen. In the 1790s the first marquess provided him with a house and paid him a salary of £40 16s. a year, but this represented but a small proportion of his earnings for he was, in addition, post master, shop-keeper, coach-owner, insurance agent, printer and tax collector. He retired from Bute employment in 1824 at the age of sixty-three and the second marquess awarded him a pension of £150, which was a drain upon the estate for many years, for Bird lived until 1840.[8]

Bird was the channel of communication between the first marquess and his Glamorgan estate. His diary is in fact a letter-book, most of the entries being copies of letters sent at irregular intervals to the first marquess. It contains nothing to suggest that the letters were answered or that the landlord conveyed any instructions to his estate officials. On 31 January 1801 Bird noted remarks made to him by Col. Capper, a Bute tenant: ' "Lord Bute asked for ye, Bird, he says he hears from ye *sometimes*", with particular emphasis on the latter word. I feel greatly at a loss for a proper construction on that sentence not being able to determine whether it means that I should be more communicative than I had been (which was only from fear of giving offence) or whether I should do right in transmitting a monthly or weekly journal of occurrences . . . I should rejoice at having a line of conduct marked out in that respect.' If remonstrances had to be conveyed to an employer through a mutual acquaintance, it would appear that the link between the landlord and his estate was indeed tenuous.

Apart from the part-time ministrations of Hollier and Bird, vouchers and accounts give the names of other men employed by the first marquess. Brown of Luton was the paymaster for the estate, other members of the Bird family were employed

[8] Ibid., *passim*; J. I. Jones, *A history of printing and printers in Wales and Monmouthshire . . . to 1923* (1925), pp. 92–94; J. Bird, op. cit., p. 15; J. H. Matthews, op. cit., IV, 373; V, 305; declaration of John Bird, 1838 (N.L.W., B., 140); vouchers 1796, 1822, 1832 (G.R.O., D/DA 56–117).

from time to time and the Wood family looked after some aspects of legal affairs at Cardiff. Bailiffs of the manors were employed and some of the estate tenants were engaged occasionally on specific projects.[9] The evidence available suggests a lack of co-ordination and of sustained administration. Although the Glamorgan estate was far larger than that of Luton and potentially far richer than the Scottish lands, unlike the agents of those estates, none of the marquess's employees at Cardiff was considered worthy of receiving bequests and annuities under his will. The maze of personal and local influences underlying the administration of the Bute estate in Glamorgan infuriated David Stewart, the second marquess's surveyor, in the 1820s. 'The Bedford estate', he wrote, 'is in much less danger of mismanagement than the Welsh estate . . . because [the agents] are complete strangers in Bedfordshire while all the persons who have influence over the Welsh property are directly connected with the people on the estate, being cousins and second cousins beyond the reach of calculation. You should not', he informed his employer, 'allow an estate of the size and consequence of your lordship's Glamorgan property to continue under its present miserable management.'[10]

Virtually the only tasks undertaken by the first marquess's agents were the biannual audits, the assessment of new levels of rent, inquiries relating to land for sale and the enforcement of manorial rights and dues. There was a degree of active management in the immediate neighbourhood of Cardiff, where some repairs were undertaken and where intermittent attempts were made to regroup farms into more efficient units, but the farms, great commons and rich mineral land of northern Glamorgan received minimal supervision. As the second marquess later admitted, 'My grandfather's agents were negligent in seldom visiting the mineral districts'.[11] The absence of any sustained effort to improve and modernise the estate gave it an archaic air. Professor Hughes writes of primitive estates in northern England whose lands had never been surveyed and where heriots were still being demanded in

[9] Ibid., 1790-1810 (ibid.); N.L.W., B., 58.
[10] C.C.L., B., IX, 19.
[11] Ibid., 17.

the mid-eighteenth century.[12] This remained the condition of the Bute estate until the second marquess embarked upon a programme of reform in the 1820s. Until then, there was uncertainty about the size of the estate and estimates of the extent of the great Senghennydd Common leased to the Dowlais Company varied between 9,000 and 18,000 acres. A *cymortha*, a payment specifically forbidden by the Act of Union of 1536, was received in Ystradyfodwg in 1777, while mises were claimed after the death of Lord Windsor in 1758 and of Lady Bute in 1800. Copyhold survived in the manor of Pentyrch and Clun and the old Welsh practice of *cyfran* (partible inheritance) still lingered. Heriots were demanded and Bird recorded with pride the success of his various stratagems to secure the best beasts of deceased landowners within the manors. The circumstances of the deaths of manorial residents were checked lest there should be a claim for deodands, efforts were made to maintain the ancient prisage of wine and the right of wreck was jealously guarded.[13] In 1774 chief rents, paid by the freeholders of the manors, and other manorial dues represented 12 per cent of the total receipts of the estate. They were considered 'a poor profit, half the sums go in collection', yet Bird's diary shows that the agents expended more energy in seeking to collect them than on any other aspect of estate business.[14]

Such a system of administration led to wholesale alienation of rights and to vast unchecked encroachments. The lease to the Dowlais Company of the minerals lying beneath the common of the manor of Senghennydd uwch Caiach for ninety-nine years at £23 a year was the crowning folly of the eighteenth century owners of the Cardiff Castle estate, but their foolishness was compounded by the absence of any attempt to supervise the activities of the company. Investigations

---

[12] E. Hughes, 'The eighteenth century land agent' in H. A. Cronne, T. W. Moody and D. B. Quinn (eds.), *Essays in English and Irish history in honour of J. E. Todd* (1949), p. 189.
[13] Accounts, 1815-17 (N.L.W., B., 140); Survey of Miskin, 1638, Survey of Pentyrch and Clun, 1666 (ibid., 88); C.C.L., MS. 2.716, 2 May 1792, 6 December 1793, 9 August 1799; Richards to Bute, 3 December 1831 (ibid., 4.713); ibid., 16 March 1842 (N.L.W., B., 70, L. 7); C.C.L., B., IX, 16 and 17; J. H. Matthews, op. cit., II, 5-7.
[14] Valuation, 1774 (N.L.W., B., 104); record of manorial rents, 1820-60 (ibid., 47); C.C.L., MS. 2.716 *passim*.

completed in 1823 brought 'to light the hidden mysteries of that den of iniquity', including wastage of minerals, destruction of surface soil, and the mining by the company of minerals not leased to them to the value of £102,000.[15] The Dowlais lease was not the only example of the almost gratuitous granting of valuable estate rights. 'Another proof of the utter inattention to the interests of the estate' was Lady Windsor's lease of 1765 granting the water and the fishing of the river Taff 'from Newbridge to Pontarsticill' to Lord Plymouth for ninety-nine years at an annual rent of £2 2s. at a time when 'the manager of Lord Plymouth's adjoining property was well aware of the value of water power'. It was through this lease that the Plymouth Iron Company obtained water for their works, a highly profitable transaction as far as they were concerned. In 1768, when James Harford began a mineral work at Melingriffith, he was granted a 200-year lease of the 105-acre farm of Fforest Isaf at £60 *per annum* and he proceeded, unchecked by his landlord, to denude the land of its timber, although this was specifically forbidden by the agreement.[16] Indeed, every industrial development in east Glamorgan seemed to carry with it a diminution of the rights and possessions of the lords of Cardiff Castle. Thus, the Glamorganshire Canal Company, which in 1794 had purchased twenty-five acres of Bute land, was found by 1815 to have taken advantage of the fact that its obligation 'to maintain a proper boundary fence . . . appears to have been waived by my grandfather's agents', to have usurped a further five acres in the parish of St. Mary, to have taken over large parts of the Senghennydd Common and to be throwing rubbish on Bute land.[17] The complex and lengthy litigation which followed was only partly successful and by 1824 Tyndall, the second marquess's adviser, was lamenting: 'When will that miserable ditch cease to bother us?'[18]

In addition to the loss of rights to major industrial enterprises, the Cardiff Castle estate also suffered from the activities of

[15] J. Davies, 'The Dowlais lease, 1748–1900', *Morgannwg*, XII (1968), 37–66.
[16] C.C.L., MS. 4.850; lease 1765, note on the Plymouth lease, 1840, case on the lease to James Harford (N.L.W., B., 31).
[17] Note on the Glamorganshire Canal (ibid.); Bute to Smyth, 13 July 1839 (ibid., 70, L. 6); C. Hadfield, *The canals of south Wales and the border* (1960), p. 91.
[18] Tyndall to Richards, 10 August 1824 (G.R.O., D/DA 11).

humbler citizens. On the great commons of the lordships of Senghennydd, Miskin and Glynrhondda, the practice of 'squatting' reached such alarming proportions in the late-eighteenth century that 'it seemed as if an Irish estate had been transferred and filled in as patchwork amongst the Welsh mountains'.[19] The first marquess's agents converted some of the squatters at Hirwaun into tenants without the consent of other landowners owning rights of common, thereby arousing the anger of the parishioners of Aberdare, who in 1788 demolished the buildings of thirty-five of the squatters and instituted legal proceedings against the marquess. Squatting continued, however, and Stewart's survey of 1824 shows that encroachment upon the waste, not only by landless squatters but also by freeholders whose lands adjoined the common, proceeded unchecked during the later years of the first marquess's lifetime. Such encroachments could be on a suffi-cient scale to create a barrier between the common and Bute freehold land, a serious matter, for although the minerals of the waste were the property of the lord of the manor, lack of access would render them unworkable; the second marquess was later obliged to expend much effort and money on re-establishing rights of access to the commons, rights which had been lost by his grandfather.[20]

Only in one sphere did the first marquess make a significant contribution to the Cardiff Castle estate. By making substan-tial purchases of strategic land at Cardiff and within the coalfield, he considerably enhanced the position of the Bute family in east Glamorgan. The Windsor estate had included little land in the immediate neighbourhood of Cardiff. Only a small proportion of the extensive ecclesiastical property around the town came into the possession of the earls of Pembroke in the sixteenth century and of the manors near the town, Roath alone had always been part of the estate.[21]

    [19] C. Wilkins, *The history of the iron, steel, tinplate and other trades of Wales* (1903), pp. 124–25; *P.P.*, XXXIV (1896), 210.
    [20] Opinion of G. R. Cross, 1824, note on a farm belonging to the British Iron Company, lists of encroachments at Hirwaun (N.L.W., B., 31); A. C. Davies, 'Aberdare, 1750–1850, a study in the growth of an industrial community' (unpublished University of Wales M.A. dissertation, 1963), pp. 15–18; D. W. Jones, *Hanes Morgannwg* (1874), pp. 190–91; C.C.L., MS. 4.850.
    [21] W. Rees, *Cardiff, a history of the city* (1962), pp. 21–23, 46, 48, 50–53; J. H. Matthews, op. cit., II, 1–10; note on the manors of Glamorgan (N.L.W., B., 141, 3).

Between 1780 and 1814 the first marquess purchased lands whose rental on his death amounted to £1,415, equivalent to almost a quarter of the receipts of the original estate. The most important purchase was that made in 1793 when, for £19,000, the marquess bought from Calvert Richard Jones, a descendant of Mathew Herbert of Swansea, the Friars estate which included the manors of Kibbor, Cogan and Leckwith, the advowsons of Llandough, Cogan, Leckwith and Roath, the Crwys, Cathays, Spittal, Whitmore, White Friars and Grange lands in Cardiff, several farms at Cogan and Roath, the farm of Henstaff in the vale of Glamorgan and the Ystradfechan and Abergorci estates in the Rhondda. Other significant additions to the estate included some of the properties of Robert Jones of Fonmon, sold following his bankruptcy in 1782, the Cardiff Arms Hotel and lands bought in 1788, the 450-acre Maendy estate of Wyndham Lewis purchased in 1804, Adamsdown House and lands acquired from Hollier in 1811 and, through various transactions, much of the land of the corporation of Cardiff.[22]

Further acquisitions were made at the beginning of the nineteenth century following the enclosure of the common lands of the Heath, north of Cathays. Squatting had been proceeding apace on the Heath during the 1790s and, when they were sued in 1798, the encroachers suffered judgement to go against them by their own default. The ejection of the squatters and the demolition of their buildings, undertaken in the summer of 1799, was accompanied by the attacks of 'Amazonian women armed with pitch forks' and the intervention of the cavalry.[23] In 1801 the Heath lands were enclosed by Act of Parliament, the marquess of Bute and the earl of Windsor, as joint lords of the manor, obtaining one-eighteenth of the land, the remainder being divided between the corporation of Cardiff and those owners of land with rights of common.[24] At least half the land enclosed, however, found its way into Bute hands. The corporation had borrowed £452

[22] Rentals (ibid., 73); note on Robert Jones of Fonmon, 1781 (ibid., 47); schedule of title deeds, 1881 (ibid., 137, 6); case of Elizabeth Jenkin, particulars of the estate of Henry Hollier, 1818 (ibid., 31); C., 2 November 1804.
[23] C.C.L., MS. 2.716, 24 February, 20 July, 23 August 1798, 11 June, 30 July 1799, 31 January 1801; W. Rees, op. cit., pp. 11, 133–34.
[24] 41 George III, cap. 113; J. H. Matthews, op. cit., III, 261.

from the marquess in 1789; this sum, secured upon a mortgage of corporation lands, had grown to over £750 by 1803, and to repay the loan the land obtained by the corporation through enclosure was sold; most of it, either immediately or subsequently, became part of the Bute estate. The first marquess had already shown an appetite for corporation land. In 1798 he bought all the small properties on the north-eastern side of the castle and in 1803 he and the corporation exchanged lands worth £1,240, the marquess gaining valuable property in the neighbourhood of the castle and Cathays. In the 1840s, when the Bute estate owned nearly 1,300 acres within the parishes of St. John and St. Mary, the total property of the corporation within the confines of the town amounted to sixty-two acres, a situation which, in the late-nineteenth century, was to give rise to rumours of underhand dealings.[25]

The Windsor estate had been strictly settled and its ownership after his death was outside the control of the first marquess. The purchases, however, were his absolutely and he saw no reason to bequeath them to his heir-at-law. In his will, drawn up in 1812, he left his entire personal estate to his second wife and her heirs, while almost all the land purchased in and around the town of Cardiff was also bequeathed to Lady Bute with remainder to her son, Lord Dudley Coutts Stuart. If this arrangement had endured, Cardiff would have heard much of Lord Dudley, champion of the Poles, and of his son, Paul Amadeus, great-nephew of Napoleon. In the event, however, the second marquess purchased his stepgrandmother's estate, a delicate and intricate transaction which cost him £32,000.[26]

THE ESTATE AND THE SECOND MARQUESS, 1814–48

To the second marquess of Bute, the condition of the Cardiff Castle estate which he inherited in 1814 could not but be a challenge. 'I never saw an estate in a more neglected condition',

---

[25] Ibid., II, 28; IV, 345, 359; V, 278, 360–61; W. Rees, op. cit., pp. 134–35, 138–39; N.L.W. Commutation of tithe, apportionment, parishes of St. John and St. Mary.

[26] Note on the 1824 rental (N.L.W., B., 74); will of Lord Bute, 1812 (ibid., 137, 1). The bequest to his second wife included the first marquess's personal papers which went to Lady Bute's daughter, Frances, who married the earl of Harrowby. The papers are now in the Harrowby collection at Sandon Hall.

wrote his surveyor following a visit to Glamorgan in 1818. 'The neglect of centuries cannot be corrected in two or three years and the marquess will not, during his life, be able to repair the consequences of the neglect of his predecessors.'[27] The task was one peculiarly suited to Bute's temperament, for the profession of landowner was his delight and to it he dedicated himself with unremitting zeal. In this, the contrast between the first marquess of Bute and the second is striking and may be indicative of changing aristocratic values and habits, for similar contrasts between generations have been noted in other noble families.[28] Writers such as J. S. Mill and James Caird commented sarcastically on the assumption that the profession of landowner was the only one for which neither training nor aptitude was considered necessary.[29] The second marquess had received no formal training in his profession but aptitude he had in plenty; he spent his time talking to agents, surveyors, engineers and lawyers and was recognised among his peers as an expert in estate management.

As the owner of extensive landed property, the marquess conceived it to be his duty to exalt the prestige of his family and to augment the income and enhance the viability of his estates. Unlike many of his fellow landowners, he saw his estates not as possessions to be enjoyed but as possessions whose possibilities should be exploited to the full. His dock building venture is, of course, the outstanding proof of this, but it is not an isolated example. Bute did not wait for industrialists to make an offer for his coal, for surveyors to discover exploitable seams and for speculative builders to promote housing schemes. He initiated such developments by offering mineral leases, organizing experimental borings and mapping out new urban expansion. Indeed, his plans for estate exploitation outstripped his achievements, considerable though these were. Among the Bute papers are elaborate schemes to harness the water power of the Taff, to establish markets and to build railways, schemes which never came to fruition.

[27] C.C.L., B., IX, 18.
[28] D. Spring, *The English landed estate in the nineteenth century: its administration* (1963), p. 53; W. A. Maguire, *The Downshire estates in Ireland, 1801–1845* (1972), p. 7.
[29] W. J. Ashley (ed.), J. S. Mill, *Principles of political economy* (1929), pp. 231–32; G. E. Mingay (ed.), J. Caird, *The landed interest and the supply of food* (1967), pp. 103–4.

On inheriting his estates, the second marquess became not the life tenant but the owner in fee simple of almost the whole of his landed possessions, a situation rare among the great landowners of the nineteenth century. His father having died before signing his will and his marriage articles, Bute had full power to dispose of his estates exactly as he wished.[30] In 1818, on the occasion of his marriage to Lady Maria North, he restricted his own freedom of action by granting all his estates in Wales and England to Sir Charles Stuart and the bishop of Lincoln to hold in trust for the eldest son of the marriage and to raise portions for the other children and a jointure for the marchioness.[31] Extensive purchases of land caused the proportion of Bute property in Glamorgan subject to the trust to fall to about three-quarters by the late-1820s but the inclusion of such rapidly developing land in settlement was irksome, for it restricted the owner's freedom to mortgage, lease or sell. In 1825 the marquess was urged to relieve the land in the vicinity of Cardiff from the bonds of settlement and this was done through Acts of Parliament in 1827 and 1837. The first vested the entailed parts of the Dumfries estate in the marquess in fee simple and the second granted the Dumfries estate to the trustees in lieu of dock and urban lands at Cardiff.[32]

The marriage settlement of 1818 became void when the childless marchioness died in 1842. On the occasion of Bute's second marriage in 1845, a new settlement was drawn up which excluded the Glamorgan estate. Instead, that estate became subject to a 'trust subservient to my settlement' whereby the marquess vested it in his brother, Lord James Stuart, his friend, O. T. Bruce, and his wife's relation, J. M. McNabb, not 'with any intention of divesting himself of absolute control . . . but only with providing for management . . . in the event of his being prevented by illness or absence from attending thereto'.[33] Two years later, when the marchioness was pregnant, Bute drew up an elaborate will

---

[30] The only exception was part of the Dumfries estate, held under a perpetual entail, a peculiarity of Scots law.

[31] Marriage settlement, 1818 (N.L.W., B., 137, 2).

[32] 7/8 George IV, *cap.* 25; 1 Victoria, *cap.* 42; Bute to Richards, 10 February 1825 (G.R.O., D/DA 12); decree of the Court of Session, 1838 (N.L.W., B., 26).

[33] Trust deed, 1845 (C.C.L., B., IX, 15); indenture, 1845 (N.L.W., B., 140); Bute to Richards, 25 June 1845 (ibid., 70, L. 1844–46).

bequeathing his Glamorgan estate to the heir of his body and giving full power to Bruce and McNabb to act as trustees. It was under these powers that the estate was administered during the long years of the third marquess's minority.[34]

Although the Glamorgan estate was potentially by far the richest part of the landed possessions of the Bute family, it was in acreage hardly one-sixth of the entire Bute estate. The marquess himself was virtually the only link between his far-flung properties, and in order personally to supervise his affairs, he undertook during most of his adult life a twice-yearly circuit of his estates which usually brought him to Cardiff for some weeks in the spring and again in the autumn. Only to one other man did Bute divulge matters relating to all his estates. That man was O. T. Bruce, the marquess's 'dearest and most intimate friend', to whom estate officials were authorised to talk 'without reserve on any point of my affairs'.[35] Bruce was that most exalted of estate administrators, the barrister-agent, although he appears in the Bute correspondence as a friend and confidant rather than as a paid official. Born Onesipherus Tyndall, son of a Bristol banker, he had been at Eton with the marquess and had joined him on his tour of Russia in 1813. In 1828 he married Margaret Stewart Bruce, heiress of Falkland Palace, whose surname he adopted. Moving to Fife, he established himself as a landed proprietor, renovating the ancient palace and becoming a respected figure in local affairs. Although he acquired estate responsibilities of his own, his service to his friend did not cease and in the period of confusion which followed the second marquess's death, Bruce was the final authority on estate matters. When he died in 1855, Falkland Palace passed to his son from whom, in his passion to acquire Scottish historical monuments, it was purchased by the third marquess of Bute in the 1880s.[36]

Apart from Bruce and the marquess himself, no one had the oversight of the Bute estates as a whole. The second marquess viewed his various estates as autonomous units and was anxious

[34] Will of Lord Bute (ibid., 137, 1); abstract of a deed of management, 1856 (ibid., 140).
[35] Lady Bute to Bruce, 10 May 1853 (Scot. P.R.O., H.B. MSS., 198); Bute to Richards, 24 March 1829 (G.R.O., D/DA 15).
[36] M.G., 31 March 1855; death certificate of O. T. Bruce (N.L.W., B., 140); D. Spring, op. cit., p. 78.

that each unit should pay its own way. The affairs of the Scottish properties were kept rigidly distinct from those in Wales and England, the Bute papers deposited at Aberystwyth and Cardiff containing virtually no references to the ancestral lands of the Stuarts and the Crichtons. The estates in Wales and those in England, coming as they did within the purview of the marquess's secretary, Thomas Collingdon, and of his London lawyers, did have a degree of common administration. Collingdon, born in 1791 the son of an army officer, was appointed Bute's secretary in 1817. He resided at Luton which thereby became the centre of the administration of the Bute estate in Wales and England, estate records being kept there and estate accounts being sent there for verification. The sale of Luton in 1845 deprived him of his base and, moving to Cardiff, he became secretary to the Bute trustees, an office which he held until his death in 1885 at the age of ninety-four.[37] The marquess's London lawyers were Farrer and Company who, as legal advisers to Coutts Bank, had a close association with the Bute family. It was Farrers who arranged mortgages and who drew up wills and family settlements. On other matters, particularly from the late-1820s onwards when the range of his activities widened, the marquess employed Roy, Blunt, Duncan and Co., solicitors to the London and Westminster Bank. Robert Roy, whom Bute described as 'my man of business', was in almost daily correspondence with the marquess in the 1840s, arranging loans, advising on dock and railway matters and negotiating with the Dowlais Iron Company.[38]

Six widely scattered estates formed a cumbersome inheritance, expensive and time-consuming to administer, and it was Bute's ambition to reduce them to a more viable entity. He believed that it was his duty to remain in possession of those properties which were his inheritance from his forefathers, the Bute estate of the Stuarts, the Ayrshire estate of the Crichtons, the Durham estate of the Claverings and the Glamorgan estate of the Windsors; had his first wife had issue, he would

[37] *W.M.*, 13 May 1885; *Weekly Mail*, 16 May 1855; affidavit of Collingdon, 1870 (N.L.W., B., 140).
[38] R. M. Richardson, *Coutts and Co., bankers, London and Edinburgh* (1901), p. 162; letter-book to Messrs. Coutts, Messrs. Farrer and Messrs. Roy, letter-books of Messrs. Roy, 1840–43 and 1844–46 (N.L.W., B., 70).

undoubtedly have felt the same about the Cambridgeshire estate of the Norths. Luton, a purchased estate, was not a 'family property' and Bute felt no conscientious obligation to retain possession of it. 'If I sell the [Luton] estate within £20,000 of the valuation (£200,000)', wrote Bute in 1821, 'I should, after establishing my library and pictures at Mountstuart or Cardiff and, after relieving myself from every encumbrance, have as large a landed income as at this moment, if the residue of the purchase money were laid out in Glamorgan..[39] None of the offers received came near the reserve price and in 1824 Bute abandoned his attempt to sell. In the 1840s, on the grounds that 'I should better be able to discharge my duties by concentrating my estates', Luton was again put on the market and by 1846 most of the Bedfordshire estate was sold. The sale of Luton and the reversion of the Kirtling lands to the North family after the second marquess's death reduced the number of estates to four and simplified the administrative problems faced by his successor's trustees.[40]

Although administratively and financially Bute sought to keep the affairs of his various properties as distinct as possible, the fact that estates in widely separated and diverse parts of the United Kingdom were owned by the same landlord was of considerable significance. A channel existed for the movement of ideas and men between western Scotland, county Durham, Cambridgeshire, Bedfordshire and Glamorgan. A link was thereby created between the Durham coalfield and that of Glamorgan which was of importance in the development of the south Wales coal industry. Advice from the Clydeside ports was acted upon at the Cardiff docks, the advanced farming of East Anglia was an inspiration to the agriculture of south Wales, the management of the woods at Durham, grown for pit props, was adopted in its entirety in Glamorgan, and the experience of bilingual parishes on the Isle of Bute aided the marquess in dealing with bilingual parishes in Wales.[41] Bute leant especially heavily upon the

[39] C.C.L., B., IX, 19; notes on the attempt to sell Luton, 1815-17 (N.L.W., B., 140).
[40] Bute to Chase, 17 April 1845 (ibid., 70, L. 1845-46); C.C.L., B., IX, 17; H. Cobbe, *The history of Luton church* (1899), p. 248.
[41] E.g., Collingdon to Gray, 18 July 1839 (N.L.W., B., 70, L. 3); Bute to Smyth, 14 August 1839 (ibid., L. 6); ibid., 29 May 1841 (ibid., L. 7); Bute to Corbett, 13 January 1844 (ibid., L. Corbett 1841-45).

advice of John Clayton, town clerk of Newcastle-upon-Tyne, whose family had been advising the Claverings and the Stuarts on their Durham affairs since the late-eighteenth century. Clayton's wealth was enormous, while his experience of town planning, the finances of dock building, the complexities of mineral leases and the fine art of corporation management was unrivalled.[42] Under Bute aegis, industrialists moved from Newcastle to Glamorgan, colliers and mineral surveyors from Ayrshire to south Wales, and servants from Luton to Cardiff. Galloway cattle and tree seedlings were sent from Ayrshire to Glamorgan, the mansion at Luton was heated by coal brought from the Bute pits in county Durham, pigs at Dumfries House were fed with acorns collected at Llanishen, and Bute would have been pleased to know that the trees shading his grave at Kirtling had been raised at Cardiff.

The second marquess of Bute first visited Glamorgan in the spring of 1815 and immediately arranged for his estate to be minutely surveyed. His deteriorating eyesight having forced him to give up his administrative duties in midsummer, he placed the supervision of his Welsh and English estates in the hands of P. T. Walker, a clerk in the office of the exchequer. Walker engaged David Stewart of Edinburgh to conduct a survey, which was clearly intended to be a thorough one for Stewart was to be paid 1¼ per cent of the capital value of the estate for his work. Stewart worked on the survey and upon the reformation of the estate until 1825 and then claimed a total of £26,745 in commission and expenses. An undignified wrangle followed. Bute examined the reports in great detail, complaining of their inadequacy, of the delays in producing them and of the many injudicious acts which Stewart was alleged to have committed.[43]

Yet, however deficient Stewart's work was considered to be, it was of crucial importance to the development of the estate. It was he who stimulated Bute's enthusiasm for dock building;

[42] See below, pp. 113–14, 199, 224–25.
[43] C.C.L., B., IX, 11–12, 16–20 and 34; proposals for a survey (N.L.W., B., 140).

it was he who discovered the encroachments of the Glamorganshire Canal Company and who first pointed out the enormous
potential of the land Bute owned between the town of Cardiff
and the sea. He uncovered the malpractices of the Dowlais
Company and provided the marquess with the evidence for
his long battle with John Guest. He fully appreciated the
value of mineral land and he paved the way for the consolidation and extension of Bute's hold over land within the
coalfield. Through the Pontlotyn lease he brought the upper
Rhymney valley under Bute control and negotiated the very
profitable leases with the Aberdare and Bute–Rhymney Iron
Companies. He valued the estate, reformed its tenurial system,
reorganised the rental, began the rebuilding of neglected
farms and initiated the improvement of the estate woodlands.
He was also responsible for several land purchases of importance, including the Cathays estate of the dowager Lady Bute,
the Aberdare and Llanishen estates of Wyndham Lewis and
the Rhondda estate of Sir John Wood. However much Bute
abused Stewart's efforts, and he did so in a most offensive
manner, it is not too much to claim that the history of the
estate under the second marquess is the history of the
fulfilment of Stewart's plans and suggestions.[44]

While the survey was being undertaken, the administration
of the estate fell into confusion. In 1816 Messrs. Farrer made
inquiries 'to see whether the Persons who have care of [the
estate] are such as may be confided in'.[45] By then Hollier,
the chief agent, had been dismissed following the discovery
that he had defaulted in his payments as receiver-general of
Glamorgan. In 1817 the Wood family, the estate solicitors,
having assumed the leadership of the anti-Bute faction on the
Cardiff corporation, ceased to handle Bute business.[46] Between
1819 and 1824, several agents undertook, and then gave up,
the administration of the Glamorgan estate, but little is known
of them beyond the fact that the accounts record that they
were paid salaries. In 1824 John Bird and his nephew resigned

[44] Ibid.; C.C.L., MS. 4.850; survey and valuation (N.L.W., B., 104); G.R.O.,
D/DB E 1 and 2.
[45] Messrs. Farrer to ?, 11 March 1816 (C.C.L., MS. 329.51).
[46] See below, pp. 116–19; king against Hollier (N.L.W., B., 31).

from Bute employment; by then Walker had left Cardiff and Stewart's commission was coming to an end.[47]

Out of this confusion emerged the man who was to be the central figure in Bute affairs in Glamorgan for the next forty years: Edward Priest Richards, the co-architect with the second marquess of the fortunes of the Bute estate, and for a generation the most powerful citizen of Cardiff. Born in 1792, the son of John Richards of Plasnewydd and Llandaf Court, he was a member of Cardiff's leading gentry family. In 1810 he was articled to the office of Powell, the Brecon attorney, and returned to Cardiff in 1814 to take over the legal practice of Wyndham Lewis.[48] He soon made his appearance on the Cardiff corporation, being elected a capital burgess in 1817 and an alderman in 1818. He was under-sheriff of Glamorgan in 1817 and in the same year stood for the office of county treasurer. His defeat by Nichol Wood confirmed him in his dislike of the Wood family, and during the struggle for the control of the corporation of Cardiff which began in 1817, he emerged as leader of the Bute party. When Wood retired from the treasurership in 1825, Richards stood again and was elected. His reason for wanting the office was characteristic of the man. 'The emolument is not worth seeking', he informed the second marquess, 'but the respectability of the situation makes it a desirable one to possess.'[49] In 1825 he was appointed clerk to the militia, the general meeting of deputy-lieutenants and the justices of Glamorgan. Having obtained key offices in the county, he turned his attention to the corporation of Cardiff. By 1833 he was its solicitor and the first action of the reformed corporation was to appoint him town clerk, while his own clerk, John Lloyd, was appointed corporation treasurer.[50]

Having come to the marquess's notice during the Wood dispute, Richards soon began transacting legal business for the Bute estate and assisting with estate accounts. It was not until

[47] Accounts, 1818–24 (ibid., 60); note on the surety of Thomas le Breton (ibid., 47).

[48] C., 21 June 1867; Bute to Richards, 14 September 1836 (N.L.W., B., 70, L. 6).

[49] Richards to Bute, 24 September 1824 (C.C.L., MS. 4.713).

[50] J. H. Matthews, op. cit., IV, 373, 375, 401 and 419; M. Elsas, *Iron in the making* (n.d.), pp. 223–24.

1824, however, that he became a regular estate official. In that year, he was described as the permanent agent and receiver of rents to the marquess of Bute, offices for which he was paid £450. In addition, he received an annual salary of £100 as steward of the Bute manors and after 1834 £100 as cashier to the Bute Dock, while his law expenses seldom fell below £500 a year. Although employed by the Bute estate, the corporation of Cardiff and the county of Glamorgan, Richards also found time to be agent to three small local estates, to conduct his law practice and to be the Glamorgan representative of the National Provincial Bank. After his half-brother's death in 1819, he managed his nephew's property, a seven-thousand-acre estate owned jointly with Lord Dynevor, which included the site of the Cyfarthfa iron-works.[51]

These multifarious activities brought Richards a substantial fortune. He became a landowner in his own right, acquiring several valuable properties at Crockherbtown where he built himself a large house and, although unmarried, maintained a considerable establishment. He was in a position to lend money to the marquess and during the period of Bute's heavy expenditure on the dock, Richards gave his employer significant assistance.[52] Opinions of his character varied: on his death the *Cambrian* described him as 'for forty-five years the sagacious and enlightened leader of the castle party', while the *Star of Gwent* considered him 'an eccentric character of uncertain temper and of forbidding exterior'. George Robinson, a Cardiff radical, remembered him as 'reserved and silent', whereas 'his *alter ego* Johnny Lloyd' was 'smiling and suave'. 'Their quaint half-timbered offices', wrote Robinson, 'were old and stuffy and from them one looked to see a trunk-hosed burgher emerge.'[53] Richards wholly identified himself with his employer's political and religious opinions and prejudices. 'I have been told by more than one respectable person', he complained during the parliamentary reform crisis, 'that my

[51] Accounts, 1818, 1821, 1825–26 (N.L.W., B., 60); affidavit of Richards, 1830 (ibid., 140); Roy to Richards, 24 November 1834 (G.R.O., D/DA 19).
[52] Richards to Bute, 29 January 1829 (C.C.L., MS. 4.713); Bute to Richards, 20 July 1833 (N.L.W., B., 70, L. 6); C., 21 June 1867.
[53] Ibid.; *Star of Gwent*, 22 July 1867; *S.W.D.N.*, 25 March 1910; J. H. Matthews, op. cit., V, 113; J. Winstone, 'Reminiscences of old Cardiff', Cardiff Naturalists' Society, *Report and Transactions*, XV (1883), 82.

opinions are merely the echo of your lordship's.'[54] In his letters
to the second marquess he appears as a dour and deeply
conservative man, but in his correspondence with O. T. Bruce
he is revealed as a witty and even effusive character.

The range of Richards's activities suggests a magisterial
competence and an inordinate capacity for hard work, yet by
the 1840s charges of dilatoriness were frequently levelled
against him. In 1855 when he was sixty-three, John Boyle, one
of the third marquess's trustees, declared that 'it is simply
impossible for me to manage the property with him as agent';
Boyle maintained that the second marquess had 'felt strongly
on the subject of [Richards's] inadequacy as an agent to whose
charge were entrusted to large and so growing interests' and
suggested that Bute 'would fain have had another to represent
him could he have had the heart to separate himself from an
old, trusted and devoted friend'.[55] In the 1840s the second
marquess did reduce the range of Richards's responsibilities;
agricultural and dock matters were taken away from him and
Collingdon took charge of building land and mineral accounts,
decisions which inspired in Richards a deep loathing towards
Collingdon, the ensuing quarrel adding to administrative
problems at Cardiff. The third marquess's trustees forced
Richards to seek assistance in his practice in 1853 and although
he remained in Bute employ almost until his death in 1867, his
duties after 1853 were increasingly undertaken by his partner
and great-nephew, W. C. Luard.[56] Yet, whatever criticisms
were made of Richards in his later years, he did in the prime of
his life provide the Bute estate with a vigorous and coherent
administration unlike anything it had previously experienced,
and the second marquess's debt to his 'old, trusted and devoted
friend' was a heavy one.

Although Bute made full use of his brief visits to Cardiff,
getting to know his tenants, associating with the members of
Cardiff corporation and visiting the local gentry, his long
absences enhanced Richards's importance. While the marquess

[54] Richards to Bute, 9 November 1832 (C.C.L., MS. 4.713).
[55] Boyle to Bruce, 24 January 1855 (Scot. P.R.O., H.B. MSS., 197).
[56] Richards to Bute, 20 May 1848, McNabb to Bruce, 1 July 1848 (ibid.,
196); Lady Bute to Bruce, 18 August 1849 (ibid., 197); Boyle to Bruce,
6 February 1853 and 24 January 1855 (ibid., 198); C.C.L., B., IX, 27, 21;
declaration of Luard, 1870 (N.E.W., B., 140).

corresponded with other leading Glamorgan figures and read the local newspapers with care, his picture of county affairs was essentially that given to him by Richards, while Glamorgan's picture of the marquess was essentially that created by Richards's activities. Richards was of higher social and professional rank than any previous agent of the estate and his appointment is an example of the increasing prestige of the estate agent in the early-nineteenth century. His status, his opinions and his zeal in the Bute cause made him appear as a proxy for the marquess himself and he came to embody the Bute system. 'Coming to Cardiff as an absolute stranger [in 1859]', wrote George Robinson, 'the personage who, more than any others, impressed himself upon my mental retina was Mr. Edward Priest Richards—no undignified shortening of his name could be dreamt of. Tall, reserved, silent and singularly difficult of access, he was the central pivot round whom revolved the whole Bute planetary system.'[57]

By the mid-1820s, Richards and Bute had evolved a system for the administration of the estate. All decisions, large and small, were to be made by the marquess; Richards had full powers of execution and full control over the subordinate officials of the estate, but he was given no freedom of decision whatsoever. 'I will not', he promised Bute in 1831, 'spend a shilling without your express directions.'[58] Bute's meticulous supervision extended to the most trivial matters. The books to be placed in the castle housekeeper's room, the tieing up of the castle dog, the buttons to be sewn on the uniforms of Llantrisant school-children and the use to be made of a broken flag pole are typical of issues upon which the marquess felt obliged to make a personal decision. Yet Bute's administrative practice did not deprive the agent of powers of initiative. The owner's absenteeism meant that it was Richards who brought matters to his notice while the topics raised and the information proffered concerning them had undergone a process of selection by Richards before Bute heard of them. Furthermore, Richards's freedom to suggest was infinite. It was he who indicated which farmhouses should be repaired, which contractors should be employed, which charities should be

[57] *S.W.D.N.*, 25 March 1910.
[58] Richards to Bute, 13 August 1831 (C.C.L., MS. 4.713).

subscribed to and which tradesmen should be patronised, and although the final decision was always that of the marquess, he usually followed the advice of his agent. The citizens of Cardiff considered that Richards was the real ruler of the Bute estate. When Bute policies were unpopular, it was upon the 'damned dirty lawyer', 'the rogues of lawyers and agents', that Cardiffians vented their spleen.[59]

Nevertheless, such a system made heavy demands upon the second marquess, especially when it is remembered that he had other estates where a similar system operated. The whole structure would have collapsed had not Bute possessed the taste and the aptitude for the work it involved. He insisted upon strict timetables; all monthly estimates had to reach him by the 26th of the previous month. 'You have made it impossible for me,' he wrote to an erring agent in 1842, 'to supply you with funds for paying the wages . . . I have so many things to attend to that unless estimates are sent to me in full time, I shall get confused.'[60] The key to the system was the letter. Bute and Richards exchanged up to four letters a week throughout the period of their association and these were all copied into letter-books. Those who did business with the Bute estate were often annoyed at the delay caused by the need to refer every matter to the marquess in Scotland or elsewhere. In 1826, William Crawshay, who was anxious to build houses at Hirwaun, pointed out that 'this week [I could] cut the foundations for twenty houses and begin and finish before I should get an answer from his lordship'.[61] When the marquess was at Cardiff, letters of course were unnecessary; indeed, material on the history of the estate would have been meagre had Bute been a resident landowner.

By the 1840s, the increasingly diverse activities of the estate made it desirable to divide its administration into departments. A move in this direction had been made in 1827, when the appointment of Robert Beaumont as mineral agent had led to the separation of mineral matters from general estate affairs.

---

[59] Routh to Crawshay, 21 May 1824 (N.L.W., Cyfarthfa Papers, 260b); Richards to Forrest, 23 August 1842 (G.R.O., D/DA 26).
[60] Bute to Corbett, 27 November 1842 (N.L.W., B., 70, L. 7).
[61] Crawshay to Bute, 11 April 1826 (ibid., 47).

After Beaumont's dismissal in 1833 Richards had resumed responsibility for the mineral estate, which did not again become an autonomous department until the appointment of W. S. Clark in 1845. The dock building operations of the 1830s had from the beginning been under the supervision of the resident engineer, but Richards had responsibility for the legal and financial aspects of the work until the appointment of Captain Smyth as dock manager in 1839.[62] In 1841 the range of Richards's duties was narrowed further following the division of the estate into 'country' and 'Cardiff' departments. As head of the 'Cardiff' department, he retained his position as chief agent, but the farms of the estate ceased to be under his care.[63]

The man chosen to administer the agricultural estate was the marquess's kinsman, John Stuart Corbett, son of the archdeacon of York and great-grandson of the third earl of Bute. Corbett was the first of the agents of the estate to have received agricultural training; following an apprenticeship during which he gained 'acquaintance both with machinery and farming', he was sent in 1840, at the age of twenty-three, to J. W. Poundley, the architect and agriculturalist who conducted training schemes for agents at Ceri in Montgomeryshire. A year later, when he moved to Cardiff, Corbett was considered to be 'an observant clear-sighted young man and really competent to manage the general business connected with Land Agency'.[64] Initially his duties were solely concerned with agricultural matters, but during his long period of service to the estate, which continued until his death in 1894, he became increasingly involved in general administrative duties. His growing usefulness to the estate is reflected in his salary, which rose from £300 a year in 1842 to £500 in 1849 and to £700 in 1873. He brought up three sons to serve the Bute estate. The eldest, J. S. Corbett, junior, a distinguished antiquarian, became solicitor to the estate in 1890, an office held in the 1880s by his brother, J. A. Corbett, also an antiquarian, while

[62] See below, pp. 252–53.
[63] Bute to Richards, 10 August 1842 (N.L.W., B., 70, L. 7). The division left 355 acres of land at Cardiff under Richards's supervision (ibid., 65).
[64] Roy to Bute, 26 and 28 September and 5 October 1840, 18 August 1841 (ibid., 70, L. Roy, 1840–43).

a third brother, E. W. M. Corbett, became estate surveyor and architect.[65]

The departmentalisation of administration meant that no one at Cardiff had responsibility for estate affairs as a whole. By the mid-1840s, the marquess, instead of discussing all matters with Richards, was corresponding directly with his mineral agent, his dockmaster, his agricultural agent and the agent of the 'Cardiff' estate. Thus, in the last years of his life, the cohesion of the Glamorgan estate and the efficiency of its administration depended more upon the person of the marquess than it had ever done before. The estate ceased to have one single office at Cardiff. The estate records, stored at Luton until the mansion was sold, were moved to Cardiff Castle in 1846. In the 1820s and 30s, all aspects of estate business had been conducted at Richards's office in Duke Street. In the 1840s dock business was conducted at the dock offices in Bute Crescent, agricultural business at the 'country' office opposite the town hall, 'Cardiff' business at Richards's office, and mineral business at Clark's office at Aberdare. Each office was autonomous and by 1845 Richards was complaining that he had no right of access to the dock offices to examine records.[66]

Expenses of management on the Bute estate were low. In 1823-24, when the gross receipts were over £14,000, they totalled £771; in 1847-48, when the gross receipts of the 'Cardiff' and 'country' departments stood at £16,000, the administrative costs of those departments were £802. The marquess was as parsimonious as possible over administrative expenditure. When Richards was in sole control, the provision of an office was his responsibility and when Corbett took up his duties he was allowed a one room office and the services of a clerk on one day a week. Richards's salary as agent was reduced from £400 to £150 in 1842 when much of his work was taken over by Corbett, a drop almost sufficient to cover Corbett's salary.[67]

[65] Accounts (ibid., 72 and 73); *S.W.D.N.*, 7 January 1889; *W.M.*, 15 March 1921; D. R. Patterson, op. cit., pp. 10-13.
[66] Roy to Collingdon, 24 November 1845 (N.L.W., B., 70, L. Roy, 1844-46); Corbett to Bute, 31 July 1843 (ibid., L. Corbett 1841-45); C.C.L., B., IX, 41; W. L. Jenkins, *A history of the town and castle of Cardiff* (1854), p. 26.
[67] Bute to Collingdon, 11 July 1846 (N.L.W., B., 70, L. 1845-46); accounts (ibid., 60).

The sums spent on estate management included the wages of several under-agents as well as the salaries of Richards and Corbett. The marquess employed, at £65 a year, a superintendent of woods and farms; Edward Edmunds, who held the office until 1842, was considered the repository of much of the unwritten lore of the estate and his beautifully written farm reports show that he was a man of considerable ability. Apart from an assistant woodman and a labourer, the only other permanent employees, other than those working at the castle, the dock and on mineral matters, were the bailiff of the manor of Senghenydd, the bailiff of the manors of Miskin, Ruthin and Glynrhondda, and, from the mid-1840s, the clerk of works of the Cardiff building ground. Some use was made of the services of tenants: the tenant of Swanbridge was obliged to supervise the raising of stone at the nearby beach and the tenant of Adamsdown expected his rent arrears to be viewed with indulgence because he occasionally acted as bailiff.[68]

As under the first marquess, a considerable proportion of the costs of management and of the energies of agents was expended upon manorial matters. Richards's salary as steward of manors and the wages of manorial bailiffs accounted for almost a quarter of the administrative expenses. Twice a year Richards travelled to nine different centres of the estate to hold 'the Court Leet and View of Frankpledge of our Sovereign Lord the King, with the Court Baron of the . . . Marquess of Bute, Lord of the Manor'. At the courts, absent resiants and tenants were amerced and affeered, constables and haywards were appointed, new tenants were admitted, and the cleaning of ditches and the marking of boundaries were arranged.[69] More time-consuming was the checking of encroachments upon the commons. Even after the enclosure of the Hirwaun and Coedpenmaen commons in the 1860s, the Bute manors contained over 11,000 acres of waste and the tracking down of those who 'build embankments in the night' absorbed much of the energies of the Bute agents.[70] In addition, they collected

[68] Ibid.; vouchers (G.R.O., D/DA 56–117); Edmunds to Richards, 20 November 1829 (N.L.W., B., 141, 5); Richards to Bute, 12 January 1828 (C.C.L., MS. 4.713).
[69] N.L.W., B., 82–99.
[70] Note on the manors of Glamorgan (N.L.W., B., 141, 4); Strawson to Bute, 23 February 1842 (G.R.O., D/DA 26).

manorial rents, claimed heriots, maintained rights of wreck, defended Bute lordship of the river Taff and the foreshore, and investigated unauthorised markets and fairs, thus confounding Cobden's proposition that the aristocracy 'cannot have the advantage of commercial rents and retain [their] feudal privileges too'.[71] Manorial courts were still being held at the end of the nineteenth century and it was not until the early-1930s that arrangements were made to extinguish feudal incidents.[72] There were compelling reasons for the Bute estate to maintain its manorial rights. Rights of lordship at Cardiff and Llantrisant were, before 1832, the key to Bute political influence. Lordship over the Taff and foreshore was crucial to the defeat of the hostile schemes of the Glamorgan Canal and Taff Vale Railway Companies and was the basis of Bute rights over reclaimed land needed for dock expansion. Unchecked encroachers could become the owners of the freehold of the common, and thus deny the marquess mineral rents and royalties.[73] Squatters were a potential burden upon the parish, and the unrestricted building of cottages on the waste would reduce the demand for houses built upon Bute freehold land for which ground rents were paid. Furthermore, squatters had no political rights, while freeholders, who disliked them, did, and at least part of Bute's concern for the boundaries of the common stemmed from a desire to placate the county vote.[74]

Despite the time-consuming demands of manorial business, the chief duties of the Bute agents were the holding of the twice-yearly audit and the drawing up of the estate account. Up to 1824 this had been the work of Bird and Hollier and the haphazard arrangement of the accounts suggests that they had no clear rules to guide them. In 1824 Richards took over and the record immediately assumed a more orderly appearance. The financial year was fixed as 1 August to 31 July and

[71] Quoted in J. D. Chambers and G. E. Mingay, *The agricultural revolution, 1750–1860* (1966), p. 160.
[72] *P.P.*, XXXVI (1894), 42; agreements extinguishing manorial incidents, 1931–36 (N.L.W., B., 88); G.R.O., D/DB M 1–22.
[73] C.C.L., MS. 4.850; ibid., B., IX, 18; case 1823, opinion 1824 (N.L.W., B., 31); see below, pp. 108–9, 215–17, 261.
[74] Corbett to Bute, 9 November 1844 (N.L.W., B., 70, L. Corbett 1841-45); the parishioners of Gelligaer to Richards, 1 April 1834 (G.R.O., D/DA 19); N.L.W., B., 82–99.

clear categories of receipts and expenditure emerged.[75] In theory, all receipts were to be sent to the marquess and all expenditure was to be paid for with money sent by him, but in practice the agents spent a considerable proportion of the rents and profits as soon as they were received. If the monthly estimate proved to be too small or if audit receipts were lower than had been expected, agents used their own money to make up the difference, Richards, for example, paying estate bills amounting to £589 in 1828 and to £976 in 1829.[76]

Accounts were not examined by professional auditors until after the second marquess's death, when the trustees employed Quitter, Ball and Co. of London to undertake the work. Neither did the financial affairs of the Bute estates as a whole come under the surveillance of a single bank. The family bankers were Messrs. Coutts, but after the establishment of the London and Westminster Bank Bute made increasing use of his account there. The Luton estate bankers were Sharples of Hitchin and Bute also had an account with Barclays, the London agents of the Hitchin bank. For his Scottish business, he dealt with Sir William Forbes and Company at Greenock and with the Royal Bank of Scotland at Edinburgh.[77] The marquess used one bank against another, borrowing from the London and Westminster in order to pay Sharples and from Coutts in order to pay the Royal Bank of Scotland. Remittances from Cardiff might be sent to any of these banks in accordance with Bute's convenience.

Banking facilities at Cardiff in the early-nineteenth century were highly unsatisfactory. In 1814 the estate bankers were Messrs. Wood, but when his relations with the Wood family became strained, the marquess ceased to have any dealings with them and Bird was obliged to send remittances in divided bank notes, one half by one post and one by another.[78] When Wood's bank failed in 1823, it was taken over by John Guest; this hardly endeared it to Bute who was then initiating legal action against the Dowlais Iron Company. In the 1820s Bute

[75] Accounts (ibid., 60 and 72); Bute to Richards, 14 December 1825 and 29 January 1833 (G.R.O., D/DA 12 and 18).
[76] Richards to Bute, 16 August 1828 and 30 May 1829 (C.C.L., MS. 4.713).
[77] E.g., Bute to Roy, 4 December 1832 and 18 December 1834 (N.L.W., B., 70, L. Coutts etc.).
[78] E.g., Bird to Coutts, 14 July 1823 (ibid., L. A).

agents made use of Savery, Towgood and Co., Cardiff's other bank, but the marquess considered the company to be unco-operative and disliked being obliged to assist in the circulation of its notes. Use was made of the Bank of England's branch at Swansea, but this was both inconvenient and hurtful to the pride of agents based at Cardiff. In 1835 the National and Provincial Bank established a branch at Cardiff; a general estate account and a dock account were opened there on the understanding that if there were a balance in one, no interest was to be charged upon a deficit in the other.[79]

In the annual accounts, no attempt was made to isolate the net yearly profit of the estate. The cheques sent by the marquess were included under the heading of miscellaneous receipts, along with casual profits, interest on loans and money received for land sold; cheques sent to him were included under the heading of miscellaneous remittances, along with a wide range of diverse payments. The sums paid to the marquess included not only the net income but also moneys raised through the realisation of capital assets and often the only sum given under 'miscellaneous remittances' is the total, along with a note stating that it included 'various sums paid to your lordship of which you have a record'. Thus, it is difficult to establish the second marquess's net income from the Glamorgan estate. In the mid-1840s Corbett sought to isolate the profit of the 'country' estate and established that the net proceeds of his department were between £4,000 and £5,000 a year; at the same time, Richards's 'Cardiff' estate, which was responsible for the charities, subscriptions and taxes paid by the estate as a whole, was, if anything, incurring a slight loss. For the year 1848–49, following the second marquess's death, a full estate account is available for the first time. It shows that the net receipts were £27,403, of which £23,050 represented mineral royalties and dock profits.[80] An estimate of Bute's total net receipts from Glamorgan between 1814 and 1848 can be suggested. A net average income of £4,000 from the 'country' and 'Cardiff' estates over thirty-four years would amount to

---

[79] Richards to Bute, 8 February 1831 (C.C.L., MS. 4.713); Bute to Richards, 20 July 1836 and 5 July 1837 (N.L.W., B., 70, L. 6); T. M. Hodges, 'Early banking at Cardiff', *Economic History Review*, first series, XVIII (1948), 48–91.
[80] Accounts (N.L.W., B., 60, 72 and 73); C.C.L., B., X, 2.

£136,000; a net mineral income rising gradually from about £750 in 1825 to £10,000 in 1848 would produce a further £80,000 and a net dock income rising from nothing in 1839 to £12,000 in 1848 would yield £60,000, giving a total of £276,000. In the same period, the second marquess spent £250,000 on dock building and laid out over £150,000 on land purchases in Glamorgan. Thus, the Glamorgan estate cost him at least £124,000 more than he received from it.

The land purchases were part of a planned reorganisation of the estate. As Brown had pointed out in 1776, the estate was extremely scattered and inconvenient. There was a distance of sixteen miles from Cardiff to the Bute land at Llantwit Major, twenty-seven to the Bute land in the upper Rhymney valley and thirty-one to the Bute land in the upper Neath valley. Stewart advised the marquess to dispose of all outlying lands except those bearing minerals and to embark upon a policy of land purchase. His advice was accepted and a total of 1,399 acres situated in the central and western parts of the vale of Glamorgan was sold between 1824 and 1842.[81] After 1842, the Bute estate owned no non-mineral land west of the parish of Llantrisant. A few more farms were sold in the mid-1840s but thereafter, apart from sales to public corporations and utilities, no further land was sold in the nineteenth century and estate policy on this matter became well known in Glamorgan.

When advising Bute to buy land, Stewart was thinking in terms of the purchase of an entire great estate rather than the piecemeal acquisition of farms. 'If Lord Plymouth offers his Glamorgan estate to your lordship', he wrote, 'you would then have an object in view sufficient to induce you to part with your Bedfordshire and Durham properties.'[82] No property approaching the size of the 16,000-acre Plymouth estate came on the market in east Glamorgan in the course of the nineteenth century, however, and Bute had to content himself with buying land farm by farm. He investigated every rumour of land for sale at Cardiff and within the coalfield. His friends considered

<hr>

[81] Valuation of land to be sold in Glamorgan, 1824 (N.L.W., B., 47); particulars of land to be sold, 1835 (ibid., 141); Corbett to Bute, 4 February 1843 (ibid., 70, L. Corbett 1841–45).
[82] C.C.L., B., IX, 19.

it their duty to inform him of impending sales, and freeholders, anxious to oblige him, frequently offered him first refusal when they considered selling their land. When an especially coveted property came on the market, Bute urged that 'some friend [should] make the purchase for me without its being supposed that I am concerned', for a display of interest by the Bute estate inflated land prices.[83]

The second marquess's most important acquisition in Glamorgan was the 496-acre Cathays estate, which included much of the land bought by the first marquess at Cardiff and which had been bequeathed by him to his second wife. This purchase made the second marquess the leading landowner on the northern outskirts of the town, while purchases from the corporation added to his overwhelming dominance within the ancient borough itself. Sales in 1823 to liquidate corporation debts and auctions arranged by Richards as town clerk in 1835 to raise money to build a new market further benefited the Bute estate.[84] Other significant purchases were made from financially-embarrassed middle-class landowners. The 280-acre estate of the former Bute agent Hollier, including Penylan and Rhydypennau, was bought in 1818 for £9,000, the 958-acre Rhondda estate of Sir John Wood was bought in 1824 for £5,550, and the 1,750-acre Llanishen and Aberdare estates of Wyndham Lewis, lawyer and industrialist, were bought in 1826 for £34,340. Purchases were also made from the freeholders of east Glamorgan, whose need to sell was dictated by their practice of partible inheritance. Thus, in 1838 Bute bought the 100-acre farm of Llandaf Mill from the family of John Pride, the vendors including the widow, who had a life-interest in the property, together with her two sons and two daughters who were to share it equally after her death, and in 1845 he bought Cwmsaerbren from William Davies, who was moved to sell his farm in order to divide the purchase money among his sons.[85]

[83] Bute to Richards, 29 March 1835 (G.R.O., D/DA 20).
[84] J. H. Matthews, op. cit., IV, 405-8, 434; P.P., XXIII (1835), 187-94; indenture, 1835 (N.L.W., B., 26).
[85] Indenture, 1827 (ibid., 21); indenture, 1838 (ibid., 26); Bird to Bute, 15 February 1824 (ibid., 70, L. A); Corbett to Bute, 27 March 1845 (ibid., 70, L. Corbett 1844-46).

Land prices were rising rapidly at Cardiff and within the coalfield in the nineteenth century. In 1837, £100 was paid for an acre of land for the Cardiff workhouse; by 1841, after the opening of the dock, the marquess was demanding £200 an acre for land for a cavalry barracks and in the 1890s his son was to receive £2,800 an acre for Cathays Park. The 53-acre farm of Blackweir lying to the north of the castle changed hands at £1,000 in 1807; Bute deemed it a satisfactory purchase at £5,000 in 1838. Agricultural rent bore little relevance to the price paid for potential urban land or for mineral-bearing property. Blackweir was bought at sixty years' purchase and Cwmsaerbren at 183 times its annual rent.[86] Most of Bute's major purchases were made between 1814 and 1826, before the marked rise in prices and before heavy expenditure on the dock began. By 1835 he was announcing that 'I feel it impossible to make any more purchases until my debt is reduced'.[87] Thereafter, only land of the utmost strategic importance to the estate was purchased and in the 1840s he allowed several important properties at Llanishen, Llantrisant, Rhymney and elsewhere to be purchased by others. In all, the second marquess acquired about 4,600 acres of land in Glamorgan, most of it potentially highly valuable mineral and urban land; he sold about 1,800 acres, most of it indifferent agricultural land. This was his contribution to the growth of the Bute estate in Glamorgan, from the 11,211 acres of 1774 to the 22,000 acres of 1884.[88]

The marquess's expenditure in Glamorgan outstripped his income from the county to a degree far in excess of that which could be covered by his personal wealth or through subventions from his other estates. Recourse to borrowing was therefore inevitable. At his death, Bute left debts amounting to £493,887.[89] Not all the debt had been incurred by direct expenditure upon estate improvement and enlargement. The second marquess had inherited his great-grandfather's Luton

[86] Indenture, 1838 (ibid., 26); Bute to Richards, 15 May 1837 (ibid., 70, L. 6); Richards to Bute, 27 May 1829 (C.C.L., MS. 4.713); memorandum, 28 January 1843 (ibid., D 305.51).
[87] Bute to Richards, 24 April 1835 (G.R.O., D/DA 20).
[88] Valuation, 1774 (N.L.W., B., 104); J. Bateman, *The great landowners of Great Britain and Ireland* (1883), p. 60.
[89] C.C.L., B., X, 1.

mortgage of £43,500 and his grandfather's £19,000 mortgage of the Welsh and English estates, while in 1818 he himself had obtained, on the occasion of his marriage, a mortgage of £20,000 secured upon the Glamorgan estate.[90] These mortgages, instituted to raise portions for younger members of the family under marriage settlements, were not heavy by comparison with those of other aristocratic families. Indeed, in many ways, the financial history of the Bute family was an enviable one. The second marquess's grandmother and his mother had died long before he inherited his estates; hence, jointures for dowagers, notoriously a source of aristocratic indebtedness, were not a burden on him.[91] He had inherited his estates at the age of twenty-one and he died when his only child was a baby; the family finances were therefore not embarrassed by an adult heir drawing a large income or by the need to raise portions for daughters. The marriage to Lady Maria North was profitable; she brought with her a fortune of £44,000 and a claim to estates worth over £100,000. As his father had died before signing his marriage articles and before drawing up a will, Bute was under no obligation to make any provision for his brother, Lord James Stuart. Family feeling was strong in the marquess, however, and his treatment of his brother was generous. He financed Lord James's political career, placed Cardiff Castle at his disposal, and paid him an annual annuity from the Glamorgan estate which rose from £500 in 1829 to £1,000 in 1845, making no attempt to cease payment when serious political differences divided the brothers in 1832. Furthermore, he executed a bond of £10,000 in favour of his brother's children and in 1845 arranged that £50,000 should be given to Lord James's eldest son when he came of age.[92]

---

[90] Will of the third earl of Bute, 1789, marriage settlement, 1818 (N.L.W., B., 137, 1); deeds, 1797 and 1826 (ibid., 140); Richards to Messrs. Farrer, 31 December 1824 (C.C.L., MS. 4.713).

[91] Compare the Ailsbury and Leeds families (F. M. L. Thompson, 'English landownership: the Ailsbury Trust, 1832–56', *Economic History Review*, second series, II (1958–59), 121–32; A. Goodwin (ed.), *The European nobility in the eighteenth century* (1967), p. 8).

[92] Richards to Bute, 12 November 1829 (C.C.L., MS. 4.713); ibid., 7 January 1843 (N.L.W., B., 70, L. 1842–44); ibid., 29 March 1845 (ibid., L.1844–46); Roy to Bute, 4 October 1844 (ibid., L. Roy 1844–46); indenture, 1869 (ibid., 140).

Thus, family charges, though not negligible, accounted for only a proportion of the total Bute debt. In the mid-1820s, the marquess began to borrow heavily for purposes other than portions and jointures. That decade saw many land purchases in Glamorgan and an expensive programme of rebuilding at Luton. In 1826, Bute bought the Wyndham Lewis estates, which were encumbered with a mortgage of £9,000; at the same time he borrowed a further £12,000 from Lewis's mortgagees and before the end of the decade had obtained on loan an additional £32,000 from various sources.[93] This, however, was merely the beginning. In 1827, when plans for the dock project were being formulated, Farrer informed Richards that 'we are about to make a pecuniary arrangement of an extensive description for Lord Bute in which it may be necessary to comprise all the property he is entitled to in fee simple'.[94] In 1830, the entire Glamorgan estate was mortgaged to the Pelican Life Assurance Office for £100,000, and this was followed by a series of mortgages to the Equitable Life Assurance Society which, by 1846, amounted to £185,000. Furthermore, during the 1830s and early-1840s, at least £30,000 was borrowed from other lenders, while members of the family assisted with an additional £33,000.[95]

With his indebtedness increasing so rapidly, Bute became concerned about levels of interest. Five per cent had been charged on the mortgage loan of 1818 and upon the mortgage taken over with the Wyndham Lewis estate in 1826. By 1827, however, the marquess had succeeded in reducing the latter to $4\frac{1}{2}$ per cent and in 1836 it was transferred to a new lender at 3 per cent. In 1830, in order to attract mortgages, the Equitable linked their interest rates to the price of consols: when consols were ninety or over, interest was at $3\frac{1}{2}$ per cent and when under seventy it rose to 5 per cent. Bute found this a satisfactory arrangement and sought to persuade the Pelican Company, with whom he had a loan at a fixed 4 per cent, to

[93] Indentures, 1827 (ibid., 21 and 140); Bute to Roy, 28 August 1830 (ibid., 70, L. Coutts, etc.).
[94] Farrer to Richards, 21 September 1827 (G.R.O., D/DA 13).
[95] Bute to Roy, 28 August 1830, 14 January 1831 (N.L.W., B., 70, L. Coutts, etc.); indentures, 1837, 1838, 1839, 1846, 1850 (ibid., 140); Roy to Richards, 11 July 1842; Richards to Roy, 7 September 1846 (G.R.O. D/DA 26 and 30); C.C.L., B., X, 1.

charge 'a Rate of Interest regulated by a scale adapted to that of the Public funds'.[96] In the mid-1830s and again in the early-1840s, the marquess refused to borrow at 4 per cent because in Scotland loans at 3 per cent were considered imminent. Such vigilance was necessary, for landowners lacking business sense paid at least 5 per cent on their loans in the 1820s, 1830s and 1840s.[97] On the second marquess's death in 1848, the Bute estate was making annual payments of £16,625 on a debt of £493,887, suggesting that the level of interest charged was in the region of $3\frac{1}{2}$ to 4 per cent.[98]

The evidence available is too diffuse to allow a categorical assertion that these mortgages, bond debts and loans include all the money raised by the marquess to finance his dock building venture. He was constantly reorganising and re-arranging his debts so that it is impossible to be sure that the debts mentioned were all held at the same time.[99] The total debt outstanding in 1848, the first year for which a full list is available, was certainly less than it had been in the early- and mid-1840s. In 1842, when debts to the Equitable were approaching £200,000, the company became worried about its security and insisted that it should receive the proceeds of any sale of mortgaged land. When Bute's indebtedness was at its height the Glamorgan estate's total net income was un-doubtedly smaller than the interest charges on the debts which had been incurred in the main to develop it. Thus, if the marquess had been obliged to rely solely upon his Glamorgan lands and if the income from those lands had remained stationary, he would have overstepped the limits of indebted-ness. He was aware of the danger and spoke of 'stripping

---

[96] Bute to Coutts, 12 December 1828 (N.L.W., 70, L. Coutts, etc.); Roy to Bute, 19 June 1844 (ibid., L. Roy 1844–46); indenture, 1830 (ibid., 21); M. E. Ogborn, *Equitable Assurance, 1762–1961* (1962), p. 214.

[97] Bute to Richards, 24 July 1835 (G.R.O., D/DA 20); Bute to Roy, 10 March 1843 (N.L.W., B., 70, L. Coutts, etc.). Compare the interest paid by the duke of Buckingham (F. M. L. Thompson, 'The end of a great estate', *Economic History Review*, second series, VIII (1955), 36–52).

[98] C.C.L., B., X, 2.

[99] There were certainly other short-term debts, such as the £10,000 borrowed from Bruce and the £30,000 from Clayton, both in 1827, the £15,000 from Coutts in 1828 and the overdraft of up to £20,000 at the London and Westminster Bank in 1835 (Bute to Clayton, 30 April and 17 July 1827, Bute to Forbes, 7 June 1827: N.L.W., B., 70, L. 2; Bute to Coutts, 18 July 1828: ibid., L. Coutts, etc.; memorandum, 1835: ibid., 140).

expenditure' until the Glamorgan estate could pay for itself.[100] The 1840s were for him a period of retrenchment: he sold his house at Camden Hill and rarely visited London; land buying was virtually suspended, expenditure upon estate improvement was scrutinised more carefully than ever before and the marquess's attitude to the Taff Vale Railway and Dowlais Companies, from which he had high hopes of financial gain, stiffened.

The difficulties of the London money market in the mid-1840s created severe embarrassment. The Equitable ceased lending in 1843 and began to press for repayment, while the London and Westminster Bank refused to oblige with short-term loans.[101] The situation was eased by the sale of most of the Luton estate in 1845 for £160,000. The £50,000 received as a deposit was immediately applied to debt reduction, and Bute's anger knew no bounds when the purchaser showed a marked reluctance to pay the balance.[102] More important, however, was the steady growth in the income from the dock and the mineral estate, coupled with the confidence instilled by the knowledge that the lease of the great Dowlais ironworks was nearing its end. By the late-1840s some impact had been made upon the debt. By 1848 the £100,000 debt to the Pelican had been halved and a number of other debts had been repaid. In the year 1848-49, with the interest charges on the Welsh and English debts running at £16,000 a year, the net annual income of the Glamorgan estate exceeded £27,000 and was rising rapidly; all danger of insolvency and foreclosure had passed.[103] By then, however, the marquess was dead. He had written in 1844: 'I am willing to think well of the prospects of my income in the distance'.[104] His optimism was fully justified, but that 'income in the distance' was not to be enjoyed by him.

[100] Bute to Richards, 7 April 1842 (ibid., L. 7); 26 September 1842 (ibid., L. 1842-44).
[101] Roy to Bute, 13 March 1843 (ibid., L. Roy 1842-44); Bute to Roy, 10 May 1847 (ibid., L. 1847-48).
[102] Ibid., 28 June 1845 (ibid., L. 1845-46); letters by Roy in ibid., L. Roy 1844-46. Bute also received £9,650 for the advowson of Luton (C.C.L., B., V, 51, 19).
[103] C.C.L., B., X, 1 and 2; indenture, 1846 (N.L.W., B., 140); Bute to Roy, 5 and 11 March 1845 (ibid., 70, L. 1845-46).
[104] Ibid., 26 December 1844 (ibid., L. Coutts, etc.).

THE THIRD MARQUESS OF BUTE, 1848–1900

The death of the second marquess in March 1848 at the age of fifty-four was a severe blow to the Bute system of estate management, dependent as it was upon the ceaseless participation of the owner. 'My feeling', wrote Lady Bute, 'is that the entire fabric of our affairs has been shivered to its foundation by Lord Bute's death! and the hope of all knitting together again depends mainly on the fewest possible changes of what *He* established, being made'.[105] In the absence of an adult heir, the maintenance of the system in its entirety was, however, a vain hope and even the creation of an alternative working arrangement proved difficult, for the second marquess, despite his punctiliousness, had failed to make adequate preparations for a minority. In his will he had vested his Glamorgan lands in Bruce and McNabb to hold in trust for his heir, but it soon became obvious that the powers they had been granted were not sufficiently explicit and that on a number of important matters the trustees had been given no guidance whatsoever. Their power to grant mineral leases was insufficient, a matter of pressing importance in view of the imminence of the renewal of the Dowlais lease. The will, while vesting the docks in the trustees, had not specified how they were to be administered and the trustees doubted their competence to appoint a manager. The second marquess, after making certain bequests, had directed that the residue of his personal property should be used to pay his debts but the trustees felt that this should not entail the sale of the family collection of books and paintings.[106] Estate officials at Cardiff wondered whether their employment terminated at Bute's death and Richards complained: 'I really know not the position in which I stand or in which the trustees wish to consider me'.[107] Among the officials deep antagonisms arose as the marchioness and Lord James Stuart sought to create their own partisans amongst them.

The position of members of his family in relation to the estate had not been clearly defined by Bute's dispositions. No

[105] Lady Bute to Richards, 7 March 1849 (G.R.O., D/DA 33).
[106] Abstract of a deed of management (N.L.W., B., 140); minute book of the trustees of the marquess of Bute (ibid., 70); letters 1848–50 in G.R.O., D/DA 32–33, and Scot. P.R.O., H.B. MSS., 196–97.
[107] Richards to Bruce, 6 June 1848 (G.R.O., D/DA 32).

direction had been given concerning rights of occupancy of the family's residences and no provision had been made for the guardianship of the infant marquess. Lady Bute's position with regard to her son was vague and although she had a jointure of £3,500 a year, she had no allowance for his maintenance and no funds with which to pay estate pensions and annuities. 'I am wearied out', she wrote in June 1848, 'by not knowing who to apply to or what to say to those who apply to me.'[108] Lord James Stuart's position was particularly anomalous. Since the early-1840s, he had been living at Cardiff Castle and had long received a rent charge from the Glamorgan estate, but both arrangements ended with his brother's death. Until the last six months of the marquess's life, Lord James had been heir to the Bute titles and, he had assumed, heir also to the Bute estates. He received nothing under his brother's will and proceeded frantically to ransack bureaux in search of codicils. As tutor-at-law he had certain powers over the Scottish estates but the marquess's provisions had excluded him from any influence in Glamorgan. Lady Bute, who loathed her brother-in-law, accused him of 'speculating on the poor Child's death' and declared that she had 'a superstitution not to give *him* anything marked with the coronet and cipher'.[109]

Under the guidance of Robert Roy, vigorous attempts were made to amplify the powers of the trustees and to clarify the position of Lady Bute. In 1848 and 1853 acts of Parliament were obtained giving the trustees authority to lease mineral land, to appoint a dock manager and to postpone the sale of the family collection until the third marquess came of age. In 1848 the court of Chancery appointed the marchioness guardian of her son and directed that the estate should pay £5,000 a year for his maintenance. Lady Bute gave Lord James Stuart an ultimatum to vacate Cardiff Castle by the summer of 1849 and, after a bitter wrangle, he ceased to have any connection with Glamorgan. The trustees agreed to continue the subscriptions and annuities to which the second marquess had committed himself, while the agents at Cardiff were

[108] Lady Bute to Richards, 15 June 1848 (ibid.).
[109] Lady Bute to Bruce, 20 April 1848 and 1 May 1853 (Scot. P.R.O., H.B. MSS., 196 and 198); letters of Lord James Stuart in ibid., and G.R.O., D/DA 32-33.

confirmed in their employment and their duties were closely defined.[110]

The trustees, Bruce and McNabb, were overwhelmed by the immensity of the task with which they were confronted. 'You and I', wrote McNabb to Bruce in May 1848, 'have already seen enough of our new office to satisfy us that it is to be no sinecure, nor its duties a pastime. I should less regret the almost Entire Occupation of my time, if I could feel myself more competent to the undertaking . . . The anxiety of mind which the duties of the Trust involve, shake my hope of being enabled to persevere in their performance.' 'If there were a speedy prospect of an end of all this', wrote his wife, 'I would wait quietly, but that cannot be.'[111] Ill health forced McNabb to abandon any active role in October 1848, although he did not resign until 1852 when he was replaced by John Boyle of Calder Hall, near Glasgow, a friend of Lady Bute's family. Bruce, under severe strain, threatened to resign in May 1853, Lady Bute urging him to continue as nominal trustee. 'Let Mr. Boyle do the work', she wrote, 'He benefits from the Education in Life it gives'.[112] Bruce died shortly afterwards and was replaced by Charles Stuart, a great-grandson of the third earl of Bute. Stuart, who was military secretary to his relation, Lord Canning, the first viceroy of India, was absent from the United Kingdom for long periods and after standing in for him in 1859–60, his kinsman William Stuart permanently replaced him in 1868.[113]

Since no letter-books relating to the estate exist for the second half of the nineteenth century, it is not possible to obtain as full a picture of the trustees' system of management as it is of that of the second marquess. The evidence available suggests that every attempt was made to adhere to the practice of the second marquess. Bruce and McNabb, advised by Roy and by Clayton, 'whose attention and assistance in all our

[110] 11/12 Victoria *cap.* 20; 16/17 Victoria *cap.* 22; Lady Bute to Richards, 7 February 1853 (C.C.L., B., IX, 27, 21); letters 1848 and 1849 in G.R.O., D/DA 32 and 33 and Scot. P.R.O., H.B. MSS., 196 and 197.

[111] McNabb to Bruce, 10 May 1848, Mrs. McNabb to Bruce, 29 May 1848 (ibid., 196).

[112] Lady Bute to Bruce, 10 May 1853 (ibid., 198); Lady Bute to Brown, 26 November 1852 (N.L.Scot., MS. 2881, ff. 145); Lady Bute to Richards, 14 May 1849 (G.R.O., D/DA 33).

[113] Based on the names of the grantors of Bute mineral leases.

concerns cannot be overvalued', acted as the marquess in commission, although in a far more hesitant way.[114] By the mid-1850s Boyle had emerged as the chief figure in estate administration. As active trustee and as manager of the Bute Docks, by the 1860s he was receiving a salary of £1,000 a year and in addition was chairman of the Bute-sponsored Rhymney Railway Company.[115]

At Cardiff, the agents inherited from the second marquess continued to run their respective departments under the supervision of the trustees. Corbett managed the agricultural department throughout the minority and beyond, the net profits of his department, at around £4,000 a year, remaining much as they had been in the 1840s. Richards, increasingly truculent in the 1850s, continued to handle legal matters and to administer the 'Cardiff' estate. From his gross receipts, which by the early 1860s were approaching £10,000 a year, he paid most of the general estate costs, including legal and parliamentary expenses, and in consequence his annual remittances to the central account at Coutts rarely exceeded £2,000.[116] Richards died in 1867 at the age of seventy-six, having resigned from Bute service a few months before his death. His successors as solicitors and as managers of the 'Cardiff' estate were his great-nephew, W. C. Luard, and Luard's partner L. V. Shirley, who were to play a leading role in Bute affairs until the 1880s.[117] Collingdon managed the dock account, and during the minority the net receipts of the dock and its subsidiary enterprises rose from £12,285 in 1848–49 to £38,346 in 1867–68. The mineral department was under the control of W. S. Clark until his death in 1864, when he was succeeded by his assistant W. T. Lewis. Net income from minerals grew rapidly during the minority, rising from £10,765 in 1848–49 to £44,700 in 1867–68.[118]

[114] Boyle to Richards, 22 January 1853 (G.R.O., D/DA 35).
[115] Indenture, 1879 (N.L.W., B., 137, 4); C.C.L., B., X, 6, 2; see below, pp. 286–87.
[116] Estate accounts (C.C.L., B., X, 1–6 and MS. 4.937); accounts of Corbett (N.L.W., B., 72); Cardiff rentals, 1849–67 (ibid., 65).
[117] Boyle to Bruce, 6 February 1853 (Scot. P.R.O., H.B. MSS., 197); Lady Bute to Richards, 1 March 1853 (C.C.L., B., IX, 27, 21); declaration of Mr. Luard, 1870 (N.L.W., B., 140).
[118] Declaration of Mr. Collingdon, 1870 (ibid.); Weekly Mail, 16 May 1885; C.C.L., B., X, 1–6 and MS. 4.937.

The early years of the minority were propitious for the fulfilment of the primary duty with which the second marquess had charged the trust, namely that of debt reduction. Income from minerals and the docks was rising rapidly and Bute's death had brought £36,075 in life assurance; sales of land to railway companies were profitable and those traditional burdens of the landowning class, family charges and the maintenance of establishments, were very light. One of the first actions of the trustees was to clear the estate of all that remained of the family charges which the second marquess had inherited from his forefathers. At the same time, outstanding bills, debts to banks and all loans apart from those secured by mortgage were repaid. Between 1848 and 1852, the total debt, excluding that secured upon mortgages in Scotland, was reduced from £398,636 to £271,000 and annual interest payments fell from £16,625 to £9,300. In 1852, however, work on the East Bute Dock began and the repayment of large sums ceased. In 1855 further loans had to be made to finance the new dock; by 1861 the debt had risen to £380,980 and interest charges to £15,375.[119]

In the 1860s, however, no large-scale additions to the dock were made and the business of debt reduction was renewed. When the third marquess came of age in 1868, the total indebtedness of the Glamorgan estate had been consolidated into two long-term mortgage loans, one of £190,000 to the Equitable Assurance and the other of £45,000 to John Clayton, while interest charges had been reduced to £9,343. Furthermore, in the 1860s the trustees invested nearly £150,000 of the substantial surplus of the Glamorgan estate in consols. In addition, large bank deposits were made and considerable sums were invested in local companies, including over £100,000 in the Rhymney Railway Company. By 1866-67 the return on investments and deposits, standing at £7,260, was only £2,000 less than the total interest charges. In 1868, when the trustees came to give an account of their stewardship, they had reason to be proud. The 'income in the distance' had materialised and, from the Glamorgan estate alone, the third marquess in

---

[119] Ibid., memoranda of agreement, 1848-52 (N.L.W., B., 137).

the year of his majority could look forward to an annual income approaching £100,000.[120]

The coming of age of the third marquess made little difference to the system of administration in Glamorgan. It was within his power to wind up the trust established by his father, but he chose to allow it to continue and throughout the 1870s the estate was administered as it had been during the minority. Boyle remained dock manager and chief trustee, his salary rising to £2,000 a year after 1868, and under him the agents of the various departments continued to operate. A marked feature of the 1870s was the increasing prominence of the mineral agent, W. T. Lewis, who in that decade became an industrialist and a public figure in his own right.

By 1880, however, the system was under strain. Tension had arisen between the marquess and his trustees over attempts to disentangle the marquess's personal finances from those of the dock and also over his right to dispose of family heirlooms at will. Boyle's administration of the docks was the cause of some dissatisfaction and, as a ready substitute was available in Lewis, he was under pressure to resign. The local press assumed that the conflict was evidence that the marquess was resolved upon personal management of his estates but, in fact, he was anxious to lighten his responsibilities and to broaden the trust by including in it a representative of his wife's family. In November 1880 Boyle retired as dock manager, the pill being sweetened for him by an annuity of £3,000. He was succeeded by Lewis, who also became manager of the estate as a whole and, as such, the only channel of communication between the marquess and his employees in Glamorgan. In 1881 Boyle and Stuart resigned as trustees and the trust was reconstituted with three members—H. Dudley Ryder, a Bute kinsman and a director of Coutts bank, E. B. Talbot, a relation of Lady Bute's mother, and Frederick Pitman, writer to the Signet at Edinburgh. It continued in existence until 1902, when it was declared that as the duties imposed upon the trustees under the will of the second marquess had been fulfilled, it should be wound up.[121]

[120] C.C.L., B., X, 1–6 and MS. 4.937.
[121] C., 3 December 1880; C.T., 11 December 1880; C.C.L., B., X, 29–33, 19, 20 and 23 November, 10 December 1880, 28 January 1881, 29 October 1884; indenture, 1902 (N.L.W., B., 137, 6).

On his appointment as dock manager and chief estate administrator, Lewis retained his position as mineral agent. Under his overall control, the estate was administered by Shirley, the Bute solicitor, who was followed on his death in 1886 by J. A. Corbett who, in turn, was succeeded in 1890 by his brother, J. S. Corbett, junior. Under these arrangements the trustees had little beyond formal duties to perform until the incorporation of the Bute Docks in 1887 gave them a further function as company directors. In theory, all major decisions were the marquess's responsibility, but in fact his role was that of a reigning, rather than a ruling, monarch.[122] Indeed, the constitution of the estate evolved in the course of the nineteenth century from the absolute monarchy of the second marquess, when there had been no distinction in finance or personnel between domestic and estate matters, to the figure-head monarchy of the third marquess, with Lewis, sole spokesman for his 'cabinet', in the role of prime minister and the marquess in receipt of a civil list.

That the government of the Bute estate should have evolved in such a way was not solely the result of the third marquess's distaste for administration. It was also a reflection of the increased complexity of estate business and of the vastly increased income from Bute properties. In the year of the second marquess's death, the dock produced £10,765 and mineral royalties £12,284, while the gross rentals of the 'country' and 'Cardiff' estates were £8,859 and £3,485 respectively; miscellaneous proceeds brought in a further £1,500, making a total of £36,893. In 1880, the figures were as follows: minerals £48,900, dock £111,005, country estate £11,238, Cardiff estate £20,789, miscellaneous £4,000, making a total of £195,932. Thereafter, precise figures are not available, but the increase in the trade of the Bute docks, the expansion of coal mining in east Glamorgan and the continuing urbanization of Bute land in the late-nineteenth century all indicate that the income of the estate had by no means reached its peak in 1880.

In the later-nineteenth century, the demands of the various departments absorbed over half the gross income of the estate.

---

[122] C.C.L., B., IX, 32.

Most of the income of the 'country' estate was spent as it was received and frequently the department made a net loss. Legal and parliamentary expenses amounted to between £4,000 and £8,000 a year in the 1870s and were to rise very considerably during the fight against the Barry dock scheme in the 1880s. Expenses of management for the estate as a whole were low but other charges, including charities, annuities and periodic losses on Bute-owned collieries, made significant inroads. Above all, the dock proved insatiable in its demands. During the 1870s interest upon loans raised to finance dock building fluctuated between £20,000 and £40,000 a year and these payments, together with estate income spent on new works, amounted in most years to at least 60 per cent of the net dock receipts. Thus in 1880, of the £195,932 produced by the estate, only £84,000 was transmitted to the Bute account in London.[123]

A major item of expenditure listed in the general account was the purchase of land. The policy of buying land in and around Cardiff and within the coalfield was continued at least until the end of the century. The estate was permanently in the market for any freehold plots in central Cardiff, acquiring, for example, the Crockherbtown estate of E. P. Richards in 1869 and, in subsequent decades, buying lots sold by, amongst others, the Great Western Railway Company and the County Roads Board.[124] The estate persevered with its policy of purchasing leasehold houses in the vicinity of Cardiff Castle and a similar strategy, initiated at Caerphilly Castle, came to fruition under the fourth marquess when in the 1920s he was able to demolish all the buildings obscuring that magnificent ruin.

With almost a monopoly of land in the centre of Cardiff, the Bute agents turned their attention to the fringes of the town. During the minority the trustees had purchased 130 acres in the parish of Llandaf, including the demesne of the old mansion of Gabalfa and the farm of Llystalybont, and later in the century further land was bought in parishes adjoining Cardiff, a particularly valuable acquisition being the farm of Llandaf Bridge, bought from the sons of Lord Romilly in 1882. Consolidation was also pursued in the industrial valleys, where a

---

[123] Ibid., **X**, 1-6 and MS. 4.937; see below, pp. 272-77.
[124] Conveyances (N.L.W., B., 27, 28 and 141).

considerable acreage of Mynydd Maio, much of the land
enclosed under the Hirwaun Common Enclosure Act and
valuable mineral properties near Llantrisant were acquired.
Between 1872 and 1885 the estate invested nearly £90,000 in
the purchase of mineral land in the Rhymney valley; over a
thousand acres were bought, including the farms of Bedlinog
Isaf, Bedlinog Uchaf, Brithdir, Ysgwyddgwyn and Maerdy
Bach. By the end of the century the minerals beneath these
farms were being extensively mined by the Rhymney, Dowlais
and Powell Duffryn Companies, and the investment proved
very profitable.

In the second half of the nineteenth century the Bute estate
spent £200,000 on land purchases in Glamorgan.[125] In the
same period, a similar amount was received from land sold.
These sales consisted of £159,323 received for fifty-seven acres
of Cathays Park, sold to the Corporation of Cardiff in 1898,
and over £40,000 received for land sold to railway companies
and other public utilities.[126] Although the sums spent and the
sums received were roughly equal, the acreage of the estate
rose considerably. One reason for this was that what was sold
consisted largely of small areas of highly valuable urban and
commercial land, while much of what was bought consisted of
large tracts of mountainside valuable only for their minerals.
There was, however, another reason. In 1870 the third
marquess received a gift of over a thousand acres of land in
south-east Wales worth at least £100,000. In that year, W. E.
Williams, squire of Pwllypant, near Caerphilly, died, and
apparently inspired by Mathew 25, 29, he bequeathed his
entire possessions to the young marquess. The bequest included
the mansion of Pwllypant, later the home of John Stuart
Corbett, junior, the Pwllypant quarry, which produced much
of the stone used to construct the Bute docks, several valuable
farms, the Energlyn colliery, mineral land near Caerphilly and
£11,949 in personal estate. Williams, a bachelor, was survived
by numerous relations with whom he was on friendly terms
and his will seems quite unaccountable.[127] It was rumoured

[125] Ibid.; the figure excludes the price paid for the Glamorganshire Canal.
[126] J. H. Matthews, op. cit., V, 170; *S.W.D.N.*, 12 January 1898; C.C.L., B.,
X, 1–6 and MS. 4.937.
[127] Will of W. E. Williams; note on the personal estate of W. E. Williams
(N.L.W., B., 124); C.C.L., MS. D 296.51.

that the marquess would decline the bequest, but he accepted the real property and divided the personal estate among the testator's relations. The Pwllypant bequest helped to raise the acreage of the Cardiff Castle estate by the late-nineteenth century to 22,000 acres and to make it among the richest estates of its size in the United Kingdom.

EPILOGUE, 1900–1950

Following the death of the third marquess in 1900, his estates were divided. Under his will his daughter, Margaret, inherited all the lands he had acquired in Syria and Palestine, while his second son, Ninian, received the remnant of the Durham estate of the Claverings and the extensive property in Fifeshire bought from the Bruces of Falkland. To his third son, Colum, went part of the Stuart inheritance on Cumbrae, the abbey of Pluscarden and its estate and most of the Bute property in the vale of Glamorgan. The bulk of the third marquess's property, however, followed the title and thus John Crichton-Stuart, the fourth marquess, became, at the age of twenty, the major shareholder in the Bute Docks and the owner of his father's lands and rights at Cardiff and within the coalfield.[128]

Although it was rumoured that he did not care for Cardiff, the fourth marquess spent considerable periods of his adulthood there and showed an intelligent interest in Welsh cultural affairs. His father, in addition to his real property, had left personal estate worth £1,142,246, but death duties, family charges and substantial bequests to the younger children meant that the fourth marquess was far less wealthy than the third.[129] The professionalisation of administration, which had begun under his father, continued under him and, in the first decade of the twentieth century, W. T. Lewis retained full authority over all estate matters. In 1909 Lewis, soon to be elevated to the peerage as Lord Merthyr, resigned as manager of the dock. By then the complexities of administration, the low yield of the

[128] Will of the third marquess of Bute (N.L.W., B., 137, 5).
[129] W.M., 19 October 1900; P.P., XII (1919), 656; note on the decease of the marquess of Bute; indenture, 1902 (N.L.W., B., 137); inventory of the personal estate of the marquess of Bute, deposited at the Sheriff Court, Rothesay (letter of the Sheriff Court Depute, 5 January 1978).

dock investment, the virtual extinction of the political influence of landed property and the need to realise capital assets and to diversify investments were all inducements to the fourth marquess to dispose of his Glamorgan possessions. Urban land in the industrial valleys was first put on the market in 1909, and this began a process which culminated in a large series of sales at Aberdare, Treorci and Treherbert in 1919 and 1920.[130] Between 1915 and 1919 the Bute collieries were disposed of, and in 1923 and 1924 a considerable proportion of the farms and other freehold property within the coalfied was sold. In 1922 the Bute docks were absorbed by the Great Western Railway Company thus relieving the Bute estate of its greatest responsibility.

In 1926 surviving Bute property, largely mineral land under lease and urban land at Cardiff, was incorporated under the private family company of Mountjoy Ltd.[131] In 1938 Mountjoy sold its interests in leaseholds to the Western Ground Rents Company, and in the same year mineral reserves became the property of the state. By the second world war, therefore, all the major departments of Bute estate administration had been extinguished.

The gift of the castle to the corporation of Cardiff in 1947 was followed in 1950 by the deposit at the National Library of Wales of most of the papers relating to the Bute estate in Glamorgan, an act which brought to a close the period during which Bute administration had played an important role in the life of Cardiff and Glamorgan.[132]

[130] W.M., 30 July and 1 August 1924; N.L.W., Sale catalogue collection, sub Bute; maps of Bute property in the south Wales coalfield (Coal House, Llanishen, Claim Files: see chapter VI, note 5); Estates Gazette, 1 January 1921, 7 July 1923, 27 December 1924.
[131] Ibid., 9 October 1926; files relating to the Mountjoy Company (Companies House, Cardiff).
[132] B. G. Charles, 'The marquess of Bute collection', National Library of Wales Journal, VII (1951–52), pp. 246–58.

III

THE MARQUESSES OF BUTE AND THE COMMUNITY IN GLAMORGAN

GLAMORGAN AND THE FIRST MARQUESS, 1766–1814

The centre of the estate which became linked with the Bute family through the marriage of 1766 was a small, decayed market town. In the thirteenth century, Cardiff had been the largest borough in Wales but it had declined sharply in the fourteenth and early-fifteenth centuries, and despite a period of growth in the late-sixteenth and early-seventeenth centuries, its population in the high middle ages was probably as great as the 1,870 recorded in 1801.[1] In the 1760s the borough, described as having 'more of the furniture of antiquity about it than any town we had seen in Wales', covered much the same area as it had when John Speed mapped it in 1610. It was a walled, T-shaped town; the horizontal consisted of narrow parallel streets extending from the Taff water meadows at the west gate to the extramural suburb of Crockherbtown in the east and the vertical of the wider and more dignified St. Mary's Street which terminated at the south gate, beyond which lay a waterlogged moor extending from the town to the sea.[2]

Cardiff's chief feature was its castle, occupying nine acres and extending along almost the whole of the northern side of the town. It stood within a Roman fortification, the auxiliary fortress of Cardiff, built in the first century A.D. and strengthened in the third. In about 1093 Robert Fitzhamon, the Norman conqueror of Glamorgan, built a motte-and-bailey castle within the derelict fortress; his wooden building was

---

[1] M. Beresford, *New towns of the middle ages* (1967), pp. 527–74; D. G. Walker, 'Cardiff', in R. A. Griffiths (ed.), *Boroughs of mediaeval Wales* (1978), pp. 103–30; D. R. Paterson, *Early Cardiff* (1926), p. 22; L. Owen, 'The population of Wales in the sixteenth and seventeenth centuries', *Transactions of the Honourable Society of Cymmrodorion* (1959), p. 99.

[2] W. Gilpin, *Observations on the river Wye and several parts of south Wales, etc., made in the summer of the year 1770* (fifth edition, 1800), p. 130; J. Evans, *Letters written during a tour through south Wales in the year 1803 and at other times* (1804), p. 71; W. Rees, *Cardiff, a history of the city* (1962), plates XI, XII, XIX.

reconstructed in stone in the middle of the twelfth century and in the fifteenth Richard Beauchamp erected new domestic quarters along the western curtain wall. In the late-sixteenth century, the outer ward became the site of the Glamorgan shire hall and Beauchamp's buildings were extended. Cardiff Castle was then frequently used by the Herberts as a residence but in the following century, their Wiltshire estates and their seat at Wilton becoming more congenial to them, the castle was neglected and fell into ruin. By the eighteenth century, the Bird family, hereditary agents to the lords of Cardiff Castle, had made their homes within it while the medieval fortifications crumbled around them.[3]

Nothing was done to make the castle a suitable home for a great magnate until 1776, when Lord Mountstuart, later the first marquess, decided it should be the seat of his eldest son, heir to the Windsors and the Pembrokes. Mountstuart removed the walls of the inner ward, demolished the shire hall and built along the western wall a mansion which, contemporaries considered, harmonised ill with the ancient fabric and which was left uncompleted when his son died in 1794. On no occasion did the first marquess or any member of his family reside at the castle; the total establishment during his lifetime appears to have consisted of a housekeeper and a porter, and when the marquess visited Cardiff he was accommodated at the Cardiff Arms inn. 'The Castle', noted an anonymous opponent of the Bute interest in 1818, 'has been and is still without an occupant, its chambers untrod, its portals desolate.'[4]

In consequence of the non-residence of the lord of Cardiff, the economic life of the borough was not dependent upon the home of an aristocrat as were, for instance, the towns of Alnwick or Arundel. Annual household expenses at Welbeck in the late-eighteenth century averaged £18,000; at Cardiff Castle they hardly exceeded a few hundred pounds. Still

[3] V. E. Nash-Williams, *The Roman frontier in Wales* (1954), pp. 94–96, 139, plates XXV–XXXVIII; J. A. Corbett (ed.), *Rice Meyrick's Booke of Glamorganshires antiquities* (1887), pp. 96–100; papers relating to Cardiff Castle (N.L.W., B., 141, 5).

[4] *C.*, 19 June 1818; J. P. Grant, *Cardiff Castle, its history and architecture* (1923), pp. 38–39; T. Rees, *Description of south Wales* (1815), p. 614; vouchers, 1795–97 (G.R.O., D/DA 56); C.C.L., MS. 2.716, 2 June 1800; opinion of W. E. Taunton (N.L.W., B., 21).

essentially part of the economic organisation of its rural hinterland, Cardiff's modest prosperity in the mid-eighteenth century arose from its position in the fertile coastal lowlands of southern Wales and its main economic activity was the export of agricultural produce to Bristol, upon whose position as emporium and entrepôt it was heavily dependent. Cardiff had been recognised in the sixteenth century as one of the three head ports of Wales, the coastline of Monmouthshire and Glamorgan being placed under its jurisdiction. Vessels of up to eighty tons could navigate the tortuous two-mile channel of the Taff to trade at the town quay, which was situated near the present entrance of Cardiff Arms Park.[5]

In the last quarter of the eighteenth century the town obtained a new role as the port for Merthyr Tydfil. Iron had been shipped from Cardiff since the sixteenth century but the development, from the 1760s onwards, of the great ironworks of Merthyr brought a vast increase in trade and by the end of the eighteenth century over 10,000 tons of iron a year were being shipped from the port. Until the 1790s, the iron was carried to the coast by cart. Such a laborious method of transport caused the export from Cardiff of coal, a far less valuable commodity in relation to its bulk than iron, to be an uneconomical proposition. In a much-quoted comment, the Cardiff customs officer stated in 1782: 'No coal is exported from this port nor ever will be because of the expense of bringing it down from the interior part of the country'.[6] In 1794 the Glamorganshire Canal was opened, linking Cardiff with the ironworks of Merthyr, and four years later the canal was extended a mile and a half south of the town to a sea-lock basin which could accommodate vessels of up to two hundred tons. The construction of the canal gave a 'most notable impulse to the commerce of Cardiff', bringing a wave of enthusiasm and optimism to the town. In the last decade of the eighteenth century, Cardiff was provided with a racecourse and a new bridge over the Taff; it obtained for the first

---

[5] A. S. Turberville, *Welbeck Abbey and its owners* (London, 1938–39), II, 307–8; G. Williams (ed.), *Glamorgan County History*, IV (1974), 311–75; A. H. John, *The industrial development of south Wales, 1750–1850* (1950), pp. 10–13; E. A. Lewis, *The Welsh port books, 1550–1603* (1927), p. xv.
[6] J. H. Matthews, *Cardiff records, materials for a history of the county borough* (1898–1911), II, 393.

time a printing press, a bank and a daily mail-coach to London; the Cardiff Coffee Room and Philanthropic and Sociable Societies were established, the church was repaired, improvements were made in street paving and the sea-defences were completed.[7]

Yet, despite this new vitality, the impact upon the town of its new economic opportunities should not be exaggerated. At the turn of the nineteenth century Cardiff was no match for those centres of polite society, Carmarthen and Brecon; within Glamorgan, Swansea was a far more dynamic focus of trade and industry and the vale of Glamorgan still looked to Cowbridge as its capital. East Glamorgan, which became in the nineteenth century one of the pivots of the world's industry and in the twentieth one of the storm centres of British politics, was, when the Cardiff Castle estate first became linked with the Bute family, less vigorous, economically, socially and intellectually than the western parts of the county. The east was certainly markedly more agricultural than the kingdom in general in the early-eighteenth century when all Glamorgan's owners of substantial non-agricultural wealth dwelt in the western half of the county. The vigorous revival of Welsh literary culture was a phenomenon largely rooted in the west, where the literary campaign of Griffith Jones, Llanddowror, and support for the older dissent and the newer Methodism were also more prevalent. Nevertheless, Glamorgan as a whole, during the lifetime of the first marquess, experienced a remarkable explosion of intellectual activity allowing one historian to write of 'the rich and literate Glamorgan of the late-eighteenth century, one of the nurseries of the democratic ideology of the Atlantic World'.[8]

Cardiff was only on the fringes of this activity, springing as it did from among the older dissenters, the independent freeholders of the uplands and the semi-industrial communities of the west. Iolo Morganwg, an astounding product of

[7] Ibid., III, 477; W. H. Smyth, *Nautical observations on the port and maritime vicinity of Cardiff* (1940), p. 9; C. Hadfield, *The canals of Wales and the border* (1960), pp. 90–94; J. Bird, *The directory of Cardiff* (1794); C.C.L., MS. 2.716, 6 March 1790, 27 January 1795, 24 February 1798; S. Lewis, *A topographical dictionary of Wales* (1833), I, *sub* Cardiff.

[8] G. A. Williams, *The Merthyr rising of 1831* (1978), p. 73; G. Williams (ed.), op. cit., IV, 313–75; G. J. Williams, *Traddodiad llenyddol Morgannwg* (1948), pp. 228–318; C. Price, *The English theatre in Wales* (1948), pp. 40–45, 80.

Glamorgan's culture, looked to Cowbridge for his intellectual stimulation, despising Cardiff, that 'obscure and inconsiderable' town, as an alien community which aped English manners. Iolo's lifespan coincided broadly with that of the first marquess and extended over a period during which Cardiff did not become significantly less 'obscure and inconsiderable'.[9] Its growth in population kept pace almost exactly with that of the small port and cathedral town of Bangor and was greatly exceeded by that of such ports as Llanelli and Pembroke. By 1821 Cardiff, with its 3,579 inhabitants, had slipped from twenty-fifth to twenty-seventh place among the towns of Wales. The estuary of the Taff, which Gilpin considered in 1771 to be 'the finest estuary we have seen in Wales', had hardly changed twenty years later when Bird talked of 'prodigious quantities of salmon being caught in the river'; a generation later still, in the 1820s, so rural were the lands between the town and the sea that the sea-lock pond and its iron-laden wharves were, to many of the townspeople, no more than a passing obstacle to the cattle driven from their back-street byres to graze the salt pastures.[10]

Cardiff was governed by a corporation consisting of a constable, two bailiffs, twelve aldermen, twelve burgesses, a steward and two serjeants-at-mace. They held office under the terms of the charter granted by James I in 1608, which declared that Cardiff was a free town and which invested the corporation with wide powers. This charter was modified by that of James II, granted in 1687, a document the validity of which is in some doubt. While the charter of 1608 gave the lord of Cardiff Castle no specific powers to influence corporation affairs, that of 1687 strengthened the role of his appointee, the constable of the castle, before whom every official of the corporation was to be sworn into office. The charter of 1687, with its emphasis upon the office of the constable and, by implication, upon the influence of the lord of the castle who appointed him, became in the course of the eighteenth century the constitutional basis of the government of Cardiff. Thus the corporation, while in theory enjoying

[9] G. J. Williams, *Iolo Morganwg*, I (1950), 30–33.
[10] W. Gilpin, op. cit., p. 130; C.C.L., MS. 2.716, 14 September 1790; Stewart to Richards, 25 February 1822 (G.R.O., D/DA 9).

independent powers, was little more than the creature of the castle. 'The Council Chamber in the Guildhall', noted J. H. Matthews, the editor of Cardiff's records, 'became an office for the transaction of castle business and the rarely held meetings were occupied with little more than the formal installation of the Bailiffs and Aldermen who were nominees of the Lord and devoted to his service'.[11]

This was the situation which the first marquess of Bute inherited. The marquess, with his 'imperious, proud and haughty carriage', hardly had the inclination or the talent for tactful corporation management.[12] He contributed to the restoration of the tower of the church of St. John and established a Bute mausoleum at the church of St. Margaret; he refurbished and embellished the castle and its grounds and paid subscriptions to institutions such as the Cardiff Coffee Room and the Cardiff races. His visits to the town were, however, infrequent and his channels of communication with the townspeople were tenuous. In the economic and social changes which Cardiff experienced during his lifetime the lead was taken by others. The system of corporation control endured not because it was assiduously cultivated by the marquess, but because of the natural deference and conservatism of the small borough. The estate's rental from lands in and around Cardiff vastly exceeded the total income of the corporation, the marquess's land purchases had made him the only landowner of consequence within the borough and his loans to the corporation made it financially dependent upon him. The dividing line between the business of the estate and that of the corporation remained vague and the officials of the two organisations were often identical. Hollier, the estate steward, was regularly one of the bailiffs of Cardiff; Wood, the marquess's solicitor, held, among other offices, that of town clerk and the Bird clan provided burgesses and aldermen. From 1792, the constable of the castle was John Richards, half-brother of E. P. Richards and head of the leading local dynasty at Cardiff

[11] J. H. Matthews, op. cit., II, 113; W. Rees, op. cit., p. 43; J. Bird, op.cit., p. 12; S. and B. Webb, *The manor and the borough*, I (1908), 254–56; *P.P.*, XXIII (1835), 186–94.
[12] Letter to Lord Mountstuart, 1789, quoted in L. B. John, 'The parliamentary representation of Glamorgan, 1536–1832' (unpublished University of Wales M.A. dissertation, 1934), pp. 115–18.

whose fortunes were closely linked with those of the Bute estate. Under the first marquess, therefore, economic interest and family ties served to buttress the influence of the castle; the threat posed to that influence by organisations such as the Glamorganshire Canal Company which were outside the castle complex was as yet unrealised and when the bells of St. John rang for three days in celebration of the birth of the marquess's grandson in 1793, there were no dissenting voices.[13]

To the marquess, the main advantage resulting from his domination of the corporation of Cardiff was the opportunity this afforded of controlling a parliamentary seat. Although he possessed far-flung estates, only at Cardiff did he have a base for establishing enduring control over a constituency. His ascendancy over the Buteshire seat, perhaps the most corrupt in Scotland, was absolute, but as the county was only represented in alternate elections it provided an unsatisfactory basis for sustained political influence. Bossiney, the constituency he himself had represented, was an appanage of the Wortley estate which passed to his brother James Stuart Wortley in 1792, and the borough of Poole, which at great expense had been brought under the control of the Highcliffe estate, passed to another brother, Sir Charles Stuart. Following the death of Lord Dumfries in 1803, the marquess, as manager of his grandson's estates, had control of thirteen of the 205 votes in the county of Ayr, together with some influence in the Ayr boroughs, but the Dumfries estate offered no preponderance in any constituency. The town of Luton had no member and the influence of the Luton estate in Bedfordshire was used to support the ducal house.[14]

The lords of Cardiff Castle had a long tradition of influence in the electoral affairs of south Wales. In the sixteenth and early-seventeenth centuries the earls of Pembroke had virtually nominated the members of parliament for Glamorgan and

[13] J. H. Matthews, op. cit., III, 408–9, 477, IV, 330–73; vouchers, 1790–1810 (G.R.O., D/DA 56–117); C.C.L., MS. 2.716, 12 August 1793.
[14] L. Namier and J. Brooke, *The House of Commons, 1757–1790*, I (1964), 205, 223, 464, 471, 474; T. H. B. Oldfield, *The representative history of Great Britain and Ireland* (1816), VI, 141, 206–7; Mrs. Stuart Wortley, *Highcliffe and the Stuarts* (1927), p. 17; letters on Luton, 1802–10 (G.R.O., now transferred to the Bedfordshire Record Office).

Monmouthshire and the influence of the castle had been revived by the Windsors in the early-eighteenth century. Thomas, Lord Windsor was the member for Monmouthshire from 1709 to 1712, his kinsman, Andrews Windsor, represented Monmouth from 1720 to 1722 and his son, Herbert Windsor, represented Glamorgan boroughs from 1734 to 1738. But, following the death of the insolvent Lord Windsor in 1758, the Monmouthshire lands were sold, the castle was left unoccupied and the political influence of the estate reached its nadir.

To seek to reimpose the Cardiff Castle nominee upon the Glamorgan boroughs was no small task. The constituency consisted of eight boroughs, Cardiff, Cowbridge, Llantrisant, Aberafan, Kenfig, Neath, Swansea and Loughor, and in each the right to vote was vested in the burgesses at large. Those claiming the freedom of Cardiff through birth, marriage or apprenticeship were confirmed in their privileges by the chief burgesses, while freedom by gift could, at the bailiff's discretion, be granted to applicants, resident or non-resident alike. Thus, control of the corporation meant control of the admission of burgesses. At Llantrisant the Bute-controlled court leet admitted those claiming by birth, marriage or apprenticeship, while others could be elected freemen if approved by the constable, himself a Bute nominee. Bute influence was also predominant at Cowbridge, but the number of burgesses there was small and included several of the independent gentry of the vale who resented the intrusion of a non-resident noble family.

A nominee of Cardiff Castle was, therefore, assured of the support of the three eastern boroughs, but to be certain of success he would need the support, or at least the acquiescence, of the patrons of the other five boroughs. To increase the number of burgesses by gift was more difficult in the western boroughs, where burgess-ship carried with it substantial material benefits. The most populous borough was Swansea, but the number of its burgesses was small and the patron, the duke of Beaufort, who had more amenable constituencies elsewhere, had not cultivated his influence assiduously. Yet the Beaufort interest there and at Loughor had to be secured, as had the Margam interest at Kenfig and Aberafan and the Gnoll estate interest at Neath.

To seek to impose a nominee of Cardiff Castle upon the county of Glamorgan was an even more formidable task, for the county, where the earls of Pembroke had once held almost undisputed sway, had a political structure more complex than that of any other constituency in Wales. As a result of land alienation, the Cardiff Castle estate was no longer the largest in the county, a position appropriated by the Margam estate which directly controlled over a fifth of the total electorate. The prestige of the Herberts had not been inherited by the Windsors. Indeed, the second Viscount Windsor had aroused deep enmity in the county, for when he was collector of duchy rents in the Lancaster lordship of Ogmore, it was rumoured that he had embezzled the money and that, after he had died insolvent, the tenants had been obliged to pay them again. 'The honest feelings of the injured', wrote a Glamorgan Whig in 1789, 'glow with indignant detestation at the very name of Windsor.' The eighteenth century had seen the rise in the county of a coalition of resident gentry prepared to contest the influence of aristocratic families, and although later in the century the duke of Beaufort established a temporary ascendancy, suspicion of non-resident noblemen was intense.[15]

The first marquess did play some part in the life of the county. In 1772 he was appointed lord-lieutenant and by 1780 was being accused of 'stuffing the commission of peace with low characters'. As lord-lieutenant, he considered himself *locum tenens* for his son and knowing that 'he is popular [while] I am not, which is no indifferent matter', he yielded the office to his son in 1793. The young man died the following year and his father was reappointed.[16] At the turn of the century, the marquess applied himself to his duties with some vigour. In the face of a threat of invasion, he was active in 'putting the county in a defensive state from foreign foes', and the Swansea *Cambrian*, never a champion of the Butes, paid tribute in 1804

---

[15] W. R. Williams, *The parliamentary history of Wales* (1895), pp. 108, 128, 137; R. D. Rees, 'The parliamentary representation of south Wales, 1790–1850' (unpublished University of Reading Ph.D. dissertation, 1962), pp. 9–12, 198–248; G. Williams (ed.), op. cit., IV, 415–29; G. Roberts, *The municipal development of the borough of Swansea to 1900* (1940), pp. 10–21; L. B. John, op. cit., pp. 115–18.
[16] 'A calm address to the ... gentry ... of Glamorgan, 1780' quoted in ibid., pp. 103–8; A. Aspinall (ed.), *The later correspondence of George III* (1963–68), II, 3–4; University of Nottingham Library, Portland Papers, Pwf. 8628; *Gentleman's Magazine*, LXIV (1794), ii, 1210.

to his 'indefatigable attention to the duties of the important office of Lord Lieutenant'. Yet his attention to those duties was intermittent. In 1801, when food shortages were giving rise to great distress and to revolutionary talk, there were complaints that the 'county was without a head' and in the later years of his life the marquess hardly ever visited Glamorgan. When he died in 1814, the *Cambrian*, then Glamorgan's only newspaper, recorded the event in a curt four-line obituary and his memory was not revered in the county.[17]

Despite the electoral complexities of Glamorgan's constituencies, the 1780s saw an attempt by Lord Mountstuart (as he then was) to bring both the county and the borough seats under his control. In preparing the ground he had, in the election of 1780, supported the Beaufort nominee for the county, Charles Edwin of Dunraven, hoping in return for the duke's future support in the boroughs. By 1789 he had persuaded the duke to jettison Edwin in favour of Thomas Windsor, a member of the Plymouth branch of the Windsor family, a conspiracy of the aristocracy which was condemned by the country gentry and which aroused deep antagonism amongst them towards Mountstuart. Edwin, refusing to acquiesce, brought forward his son, Thomas Wyndham, as county candidate. A 'general union' of resident gentry, led by Margam, forced Windsor's withdrawal and Wyndham lethargically represented Glamorgan until 1814.[18] Wyndham's victory taught the Bute family that, even with powerful backing, it could not impose its own nominee upon the county, a constituency the nature of which demanded that it should be held by a representative of a coalition of interests and families; even at the height of his prestige, the second marquess of Bute never sought directly to dictate the representation of the county.

There were grounds for greater optimism in the boroughs, where in 1790 Mountstuart brought forward his son, John, then aged twenty-two. With the burgesses of Cardiff 'his most subservient creatures' and with the support of the duke of Beaufort, he was confident of success. The boroughs had, since

[17] *C.*, 28 January and 10 February 1804, 9 December 1814; M. Elsas, *Iron in the making* (n.d.), pp. 207, 209; C.C.L., MS. 2.716, 31 January 1799, 21 April 1801, 28 January 1804; vouchers, 1795 (G.R.O., D/DA 56–117).
[18] L. B. John, op. cit., pp. 103–8, 115–18; G. Williams (ed.), op. cit., IV, 422–29; R. D. Rees, op. cit., pp. 191–202; C.C.L., MS. 2.716, 21 April 1801.

1739, been represented by members of the Mackworth family of the Gnoll estate at Neath, and the burgesses of the western boroughs sought to oppose the displacement of Sir Humphrey Mackworth by a Cardiff-based aristocratic nominee. At Cardiff, 101 new burgesses were created, thus materially increasing the town's electoral importance. The precaution proved unnecessary for neither Neath nor Swansea felt strong enough to force a contest and, at a cost of £289, John Stuart was elected. In 1791, Mackworth died and, there being no clear alternative candidate, Bute control was riveted on the boroughs. Oldfield reported in 1816 that 'The marquess is allowed to have the control and his nomination is implicitly obeyed'.[19] John Stuart died in 1794 and was succeeded by his brother, Evelyn; Evelyn retired in 1802 and was succeeded by his brother William; William died in 1814 and Evelyn took up the seat again. The expense and trouble of maintaining control became almost negligible; there were no more marked increases in the number of burgesses and the cost of the election of 1802 was less than £50.[20] But the ease of victory was fraught with danger. Assured of their position, the Stuarts did nothing to conciliate Glamorgan opinion or to bring forward in the Commons matters of vital interest to the county. Both Evelyn and William were on active service in the war with France and neither addressed the House. The antagonism produced by their negligence came to the surface after the death of the first marquess and threatened to destroy the political influence of the Cardiff Castle estate.

GLAMORGAN AND THE SECOND MARQUESS, 1814–48

'Weep, sons of Cambria', wrote T. E. Clarke on the death of the second marquess of Bute, 'weep at the loss of such a benefactor and may the lasting monuments of his genius and beneficence, his boundless generosity, high character and philanthropic mind excite a nation's feeling of admiration and regret.'[21] Such adulation of an aristocrat was characteristic of mid-nineteenth century society, but there is ample evidence

[19] T. H. B. Oldfield, op. cit., VI, 74; J. H. Matthews, op. cit., IV, 342–44.
[20] W. R. Williams, op. cit., p. 109; C.C.L., MSS., D 299.51.
[21] T. E. Clarke, *Guide to Merthyr Tydfil* (1848), p. 82; J. H. Matthews, op. cit., IV, 434.

that Clarke's tribute was more than conventional eulogy and that the people of Cardiff and Glamorgan saw the death of Bute as the removal of an unusually powerful and beneficent personality from their midst.

The years of Bute's marquessate were among the most momentous in the history of Glamorgan and its county town. Between 1811 and 1851 the county's population rose from 85,000 to 232,000, while that of Cardiff rose from 2,457 to 18,351. When Bute inherited his estates, agriculture was still the mainstay of Glamorgan's economy; when he died it could only claim one in seven of the working population of the county. Cardiff, in 1814, was still a small market town with no premonition of its future greatness; by 1848 the foundations from which it grew to become the most populous town in Wales and the greatest coal port in the world had been laid. In the wake of this expanding society came social and administrative problems, political tension, cultural revival and religious realignment and in these momentous changes the second marquess of Bute played a significant role. To initiate, to influence or to obstruct change, he built up a structure of power and influence in Glamorgan in fulfilment of his concept of the landowning aristocrat as the natural leader of society. He assumed that it was his right to direct the affairs of the corporation of Cardiff, to use the borough seat for family ends and to have a dominant voice in the ordering of county affairs. Leadership, however, involved obligations to those led and the marquess also assumed that he was obliged to support charitable institutions, to succour and defend the church and to protect the interests of the lower classes.

As the marquess learnt to his cost, such a benevolent despotism needed his constant personal involvement. As he spent no more than a few weeks of the year in Glamorgan, his castle at Cardiff was not a great household whose purchasing power, employment opportunities and hospitality could radiate Bute influence throughout the town and the surrounding countryside. As a noble residence, the castle was wholly inadequate; Bute begrudged expenditure upon it and apart from the removal of some of the houses which obscured the curtain-wall, the buildings inherited by his son were essentially those left uncompleted by the first marquess in 1794. The moat stank, there were no stables and the domestic offices were virtually non-existent. Only four full-time domestic servants were employed and in comparison with other aristocratic households, the annual cost of the establishment was miniscule, averaging in the 1830s a mere £291 a year. For visits of a few days' duration, meals were carried from the Cardiff Arms Hotel, while for longer stays Bute brought his own servants with him as he did on his last and fatal visit in March 1848.[22]

To compensate for his non-residence, the second marquess briefed himself on all aspects of Glamorgan affairs during his absences and used his short visits to maximum effect. His knowledge of the county came to be phenomenal, his letters showing awareness of even the most obscure details of the kinship, financial circumstances and religious affiliations of its leading inhabitants. At Cardiff he was remembered as 'a kindly and far-seeing nobleman, father of the town and loved by the townspeople . . . [who] would listen to the longest tale of woe with exemplary patience'. When in residence, the event of the week was his progress to St. John's church, where the whole of the south aisle was his, an eyewitness remembering that 'as the captain of the militia towed his lordship along Church St. every man doffed his hat and every woman "bobbed" '. Bute used his social influence consciously and gave much thought to who should be invited to dine at the castle. Such invitations were much sought after and to John Bird they were the highlight of the year. 'Delightful evening at the castle', he noted in his diary in October 1826, 'talking French.'[23]

It is his philanthropic activities which demonstrate most clearly the second marquess's sense of obligation to the local community. Between 1821 and 1848, such activities in Glamorgan cost him a total of some £25,000, representing 7 to 8 per cent of the gross rental, a rather higher proportion than was usual among aristocratic landowners.[24] Richards was dismayed by his employer's obligations. 'I have long thought', he

[22] Accounts (N.L.W., B., 60); papers relating to Cardiff Castle (ibid., 141, 5); Bute to Richards, 15 March 1836, 16 March 1839 (ibid., 70, L. 6), 11 March 1848 (G.R.O., D/DA 32); C.C.L., B., IX, 17.
[23] J. Howells, 'Reminiscences of Cardiff', Red Dragon, V (1884), 221; C.C.L., MS. 2.716, 11 October 1826.
[24] Accounts (N.L.W., B., 60, 72 and 73); F. M. L. Thompson, English landed society in the nineteenth century (1963), p. 210.

wrote in 1826, 'a large fortune . . . and all the hangers-on
attendant upon it a great evil . . . If I were called to pay out
of the little pittance it has pleased providence to bestow upon
me in the same proportions to my means as his lordship, I fear
St. Lukes would be my resting place.'[25] A considerable proportion of the marquess's donations consisted of subscriptions
to various charitable societies; in 1840, for example, he
subscribed to Cardiff's Infirmary, Reading Room, Dorcas
Society, Sympathetic Society, Auxiliary Bible Society, Visiting
Society and Literary and Scientific Institution, to the
Glamorgan branch of the S.P.C.K. and the S.P.G., to the
county's Agricultural Society and Clergy Widows Charity
Fund, to the Swansea Infirmary and to the Bristol Eye Dispensary. In other years he contributed to Cardiff's Merciful Society,
Midwifery Society, Loan Society, Dispensary, Society for the
Prosecution of Felons, its Jewish Relief Fund, its races, its
harriers, its hunt, its bellringers and its Mechanics Institute, to
the Glamorgan Prison Charity Fund, the Glamorgan and
Monmouth Horticultural Society, the Society for the Improvement of the Working Population in Glamorgan, the Llandaf
Diocesan Board of Education, the Widows and Orphans Fund
of the Society of Oddfellows, the Society for the Suppression of
the Profanation of the Lord's Day, the Merthyr Auxiliary
Bible Society, the Bridgend Dispensary, the Neath Library,
the Bristol Asylum for the Blind and the Cambrian Geological
Society. Many of these societies sought the marquess as their
president and arranged their annual meetings to coincide with
his visits to Glamorgan. The marquess's patronage was essential
to a society's success, for other subscribers took their cue from
him; thus, 'the non-appearance of the "castle subscription"
from the list . . . [was] more injurious than the loss of the
money'.[26]

Such subscriptions did not exhaust Bute's philanthropic
activities. He distributed coal, blankets and shoes to the poor at
Cardiff and Llantrisant each Christmas, giving special consideration to those who 'struggle honestly against applying for
poor relief'. Gifts were often explicitly linked with the family,

[25] Richards to Tyndall, 15 October 1826 (Scot. P.R.O., H.B. MSS., 196).
[26] Pryce to Bruce, 13 June 1850 (ibid., 197); accounts (N.L.W., B., 60); Bute
to Richards, 22 November 1841 (G.R.O., D/DA 25).

donations being doubled in 1841 because 'the poor have behaved so well over Lady Bute's death'.[27] In years of unusual hardship extra assistance was given; in 1820 and again in 1822 the marquess established a fund for those made destitute by the depression, and during the hardship of the 1840s he bombarded his agents with suggestions for varying the diet of the poor. In addition to succouring the poor as a class, Bute paid attention to the plight of individual persons and families. Instructions to Richards to pay for the funerals of indigent tenants, to give 'Edward Williams's wife £5 to enable her to have the benefit of sea bathing at Swansea', to pay £10 a year 'to Mrs. Roderick for the maintenance of her idiot son', to pay £1 per month 'to the post boy who broke his leg' are typical of the charity bestowed upon individuals and it was this form of charity, above all, which made the second marquess such a well-loved figure among the poor of Glamorgan.

In addition to assisting the poor through donations and subscriptions, Bute considered himself their shield against the power of the new industrialists, particularly that of the great ironmasters whose rapacity, pretensions and hostility towards him were frequently the subject of his correspondence. He exulted in his power over them, keeping Sir John Guest on tenterhooks over the renewal of the Dowlais lease, punishing Fothergill of the Aberdare Company for his political opposition and reminding Hill of the Plymouth Company of what he owed to Bute goodwill. The Glamorganshire Canal and the Taff Vale Railway Companies were, the marquess considered, combinations of ironmasters bent upon his destruction. 'I have ample security over the Taff Vale Railway Company', he wrote in 1845, 'both from the property they are investing in my land and from the strong measures which I could resort to against the individual directors' credit and property.'[28] He expected industrialists to treat him not as a fellow businessman but as an aristocrat to whom special deference was due. The action of the Taff directors in bringing forward a railway bill at the time of his second marriage he considered 'very

[27] Bute to Richards, 27 January 1825, 22 November 1841, 25 December 1846 (ibid., 12, 25 and 30).
[28] J. Davies, 'The Dowlais lease, 1748–1900', *Morgannwg*, XII (1968), 41–59; Bute to Roy, 24 June 1845 (N.L.W., B., 70, L. 1845–46).

ungracious' and 'an insult to Lady Sophia'.[29] It is significant that among the occupants of the thirty-one carriages which escorted his coffin from the castle to the dock there were no leading ironmasters.

In his antagonism towards the ironmasters, Bute was not solely motivated by his own interests. He was also concerned at the degree to which whole communities were within their power, a power which he sought to restrict by means of his reluctance to nominate them to the bench of magistrates. The great ironmasters who used his dock were, in Bute's opinion, seeking to squeeze out the smaller freighters and, as the leading shareholders in the Taff Vale Railway Company, they were, he believed, robbing the smaller investors. William Crawshay's eccentricities he viewed with amused condescension, but when some of the younger members of the family caused annoyance to his woodman, Bute considered instituting proceedings against them, believing that 'exposure at the assize' was the only means of curbing their arrogance. The epitome of the capitalists' abuse of power was to him the practice of truck, that 'artificial, atrocious and cruel system'. He conducted an enquiry into the prevalence of the practice, denouncing it as the main cause of unrest in the Llynfi valley and exerting pressure upon the Rhymney Iron Company to abandon their extensive truck system. Equally obnoxious to him was the laxity with which employers enforced safety regulations in mines, while the knowledge that some ironmasters kept private policemen and imprisoned strikers in private lock-ups strengthened his determination to secure a county police force for Glamorgan.[30]

There was nothing romantic in Bute's view of the poor and his attitude to the working classes was untouched by egalitarianism. He supported the main provision of the Poor Law Amendment Act because 'it was calculated to benefit the honest and industrial classes'. He regarded such classes, which were in his opinion especially numerous in Scotland, with

[29] Bute to Richards, 24 March 1845 (ibid., L. 7).
[30] Bute to Peel, 25 April 1826 (P.R.O., H.O. 52/4), to Richards, 27 August 1825 (G.R.O., D/DA 12), 12 January 1841 (ibid., 25), to McDouall, 4 December 1831 (N.L.W., B., 70, L. 1), to McNabb, 14 July 1845, to Nicholl, 17 September 1845, to Napier, 18 and 24 September 1845, to Collingdon, 4 November 1846, to Stuart, 25 November 1846 (ibid., L. 1845–46).

warm approval, but the idle poor received no indulgence from him. 'Do not set any able-bodied man to work', he told the vicar of Luton, 'except in the character of hard labour, who cannot bring proof that he has applied unsuccessfully at twenty places in the neighbourhood . . . we must induce young men to go out of their parish and endeavour to better their condition in the world . . . this has been the effect of education in Scotland and if the same does not follow the introduction of education in England, it is clear there is something wrong in the system.'[31] He was impatient with the 'state of the nation' issue which aroused such concern in the late-1820s and believed that the Chartist agitation of the late-1830s was caused by high wages and periods of idleness among colliers.[32] Any indulgence towards farmers was, he believed, ill-advised. 'If they get a better house', he argued, 'they almost without exception let part of it to lodgers. Give them strong plain offices with a humble dwelling house.'[33] Towards the most depressed class in Glamorgan, the Irish immigrants, who in the 1830s and 1840s were pouring into Cardiff 'with pestilence on their backs and famine in their stomachs', he showed scant sympathy, urging the government to bring the Irish local authorities to 'a proper sense of their duties' and to enforce the act for the removal of Irish paupers. His exhortations were ineffective and by mid-century Cardiff had received, in proportion to her population, more Irish immigrants than any other port in Britain.[34]

Closely allied with Bute's philanthropic activities was his concern for the welfare of the established church. He considered state churches, whether English or Scottish, to be the chief bulwarks of the social order and his political opinions were largely determined by his conviction that they should be maintained at all costs. An adjunct of the estate was the patronage of eight livings, Merthyr, Gelligaer, Neath, Roath,

[31] Bute to McDouall, 23 May 1831 (ibid., L. 2); *Parliamentary debates*, third series, 25, p. 274.

[32] Ibid., second series, 22, p. 998; Bute to Melbourne, 28 April 1832, to Normanby, 17 October 1839 (P.R.O., H.O. 40/46, 52/21).

[33] Bute to Corbett, 26 January 1843 (N.L.W., B., 70, L. 7).

[34] Bute to Lewis, 15 April 1847 (ibid., L. 1847–48); C.C.L., B., XXI; T. W. Rammell, *Report on a preliminary inquiry into . . . the sanitary condition of the inhabitants of the town of Cardiff* (1850), pp. 13–14, 41.

Llanmaes, Llandough, Leckwith and Cogan. With the exception of Merthyr, they were of little use in furthering the careers
of clerical relations, their low income causing them to be
valuable only 'to a Gentlemen . . . whose rank in life would
not preclude his immediate connections from accepting such
situations'.[35] Merthyr, whose rectory was worth £675 a year,
was the richest living in the diocese of Llandaf and Bute
bestowed it upon his tutor, Maher, who left it entirely in the
hands of curates. The marquess regretted this false step and
found that the responsibility for nurturing the church in the
town fell upon him rather than upon the incumbent. When
Maher died in 1844, the living was given to the Bute kinsman,
T. C. Campbell, later bishop of Bangor, who presided over a
revival of Anglicanism in mid-nineteenth century Merthyr.
The less lucrative livings were bestowed upon members of those
Glamorgan gentry families whom Bute considered his political
allies. He took pains to assure himself of the ability and
qualifications of his presentees and his policy towards his
advowsons was warmly praised.[36]

The second quarter of the nineteenth century, characterised
as it was in Glamorgan by the growth of politicised Nonconformity, provided Bute with ample opportunity to fulfil his role
as champion of the church. Concerted opposition to church
perquisites, increasingly common in the 1830s, he considered
especially insidious. 'The promoters of the attack upon church
rates', he wrote, ' . . . are, I suspect, desirous to give footing
to the spirit of universal suffrage, besides the desire of saving
their own pockets. It is very obvious to me that the church
will require the interference of lay Patrons in many instances
to maintain its property. When will the friends of the church
discover that unless they awake, arise and Act for themselves,
they will be forever fallen.'[37] An opportunity to act came
in the late-1830s and 1840s, when commissioners toured
Glamorgan to carry out the commutation of the tithe. Fearing

[35] Valuation of the Cathays estate, 1823 (N.L.W., B., 140).
[36] G. A. Williams, op. cit., p. 42; W. D. Wills, 'Ecclesiastical reorganisation
and church extension in the diocese of Llandaf, 1830–50' (unpublished University
of Wales M.A. dissertation, 1965), pp. 46–47; G. A. Wilkins, Wales, past and
present (1870), p. 350.
[37] Bute to McDouall, 23 November 1834 (N.L.W., B., 70, L. 2); Richards to
Bute, 25 December 1846 (ibid., L. 1844–48).

that this could lead to a fall in the income of the church, the marquess conducted a voluminous correspondence with the commissioners and threatened to challenge their valuations in court. As a result, the tithe of most of the parishes where he was landowner or patron rose following commutation, Laver-nock's valuation of £56, for example, being replaced by one of £73.[38]

To the marquess, the school provided the crucial battlefield between Nonconformity and the establishment. 'The education of the people', he informed the vicar of Luton, 'is a charge inherent to the Established church . . . I am familiar with this principle in Scotland and I regret it is not so fully established in England.' Richards, characteristically, was wholly partisan, warning that 'unless education . . . is attended to by the exertion of clergymen and Conservatives . . . the time will come when Wales will be the seat of dissent and radicalism'.[39] Bute had exerted himself at Cardiff as early as 1815, when he gave a site, an initial grant of 120 guineas and an endowment of twenty guineas a year to a school whose object was 'to educate the poor in suitable learning and works of Industry and the principles of the Christian Religion according to the estab-lished church.'[40] In 1826 he provided Llantrisant with a school, assuming the responsibility for paying all its expenses and for clothing and apprenticing the poorer pupils. He also gave significant assistance to schools at Aberdare, Llanbleddian, Cowbridge, Hirwaun, Rudry, Bridgend, Fochriw, Llandough, Treherbert, Pentyrch, Aberafan, Baglan, Neath, Loughor and Llandaf.[41] By the 1840s donations to schools accounted for about a fifth of his total philanthropic disbursements, such donations assuming the appearance of weapons in the fight against the rising tide of Nonconformity. 'Last Tuesday', wrote Richards in March 1845, 'there was a meeting at the Town

[38] Corbett to Bute, 31 January 1844 (ibid., L. 1841–45); Bute to Corbett, 8 September 1847 (ibid., L. 1847–48) and a mass of correspondence in the letter-books of the 1840s.
[39] Bute to Lockwood, 26 December 1839 (ibid., L. 2); Richards to Bute, 25 January 1840 (C.C.L., MS. 4.860).
[40] J. H. Matthews, op. cit., III, 494; S. Lewis, op. cit., sub Cardiff; Walker to Richards, 7 March 1818 (C.C.L., B., IX, 27, 21).
[41] Bute to Richards, 22 November 1824, Rickards to Richards, 28 August and 1 September 1825 (G.R.O., D/DA 11 and 12); Y Diwygiwr, April 1846, p. 120; accounts (N.L.W., B., 60, 72 and 73); Corbett to Bute, 5 January 1843 (ibid., 70, L. Corbett, 1841–45).

Hall on Universal Education called by the Baptists . . . It is therefore advisable that we should proceed as quickly as possible with our new school in St. Mary's parish.'[42]

Equally pressing was the need to expand church accommodation for Anglican worshippers in the rapidly growing urban areas of Glamorgan. Again the activity of Nonconformists was the crucial stimulus. By 1851 Merthyr Tydfil had a religious seating capacity which compared not unfavourably with ancient Anglican centres such as Oxford, but in the feverish building which had created this situation the church had lagged far behind. 'What are one church and two ministers for 20,000 people', wrote Archdeacon Thomas Williams to Bute in 1839: 'whole families have become dissenters and not from choice.' 'I see no prospect of preventing a further increase [of dissent]', warned Richards in 1835, 'but by increased accommodation for the supporters of the establishment.'[43]

In its attempt to compete with Nonconformity, the church was gravely handicapped by the restrictions inherent in an establishment, as Bute found to his cost when planning new churches for St. Mary's, Cardiff, and for Aberdare, the most rapidly growing parishes on his estate. Since the collapse of its church in 1607, the parish of St. Mary had been linked to that of St. John. The realisation that the construction of a dock in the parish would cause a rapid increase in population led the marquess to make plans for the separation of the parishes of St. John and St. Mary and for the building of a new St. Mary's church. He made himself largely responsible for the £5,700 spent on the church and provided it with an endowment of £380 a year. Discussions on the division of the parishes and the granting of the patronage of St. Mary's to the marquess, initiated in 1835 with the dean and chapter of Gloucester, patrons of St. John's, proved long and complex; the vicar of St. John's, fearing a diminution of his income, raised every possible objection and the matter was not settled until 1846.[44]

[42] Richards to Bute, 18 March 1845 (ibid., L. 1844–46); Bute to Smyth, 25 July 1840, to Richards, 10 December 1842 (ibid., L. 7).
[43] Williams to Bute, 16 December 1839 (C.C.L., B., XX, 132); Richards to Bute, 24 January 1835 (ibid., MS. 4.713).
[44] N.L.W., B., 70, letter-books 6, 7 and 13, passim; W. D. Wills, op. cit., pp. 61–62.

The dean and chapter of Gloucester were also the patrons of Aberdare, a perpetual curacy attached to the living of Llantrisant. In the early-1830s Bute made plans to rebuild the inadequate church at Aberdare, endow the parish and transfer its patronage to himself. Again there were lengthy discussions; again the obstacles raised by an interested cleric, in this case the vicar of Llantrisant, had to be overcome, and fourteen years elapsed between the inception of the scheme and its completion. The result of Bute's work and that of a succession of devoted incumbents would have delighted him, for in the late-nineteenth century Aberdare became the most lively Anglican parish in Glamorgan.[45]

Elsewhere in Glamorgan, Bute proved a generous benefactor to the church and churchmen considered his death a calamity to the establishment. It was to him rather than to the ironmasters that the Anglicans of Merthyr looked for succour. When Dowlais was constituted a separate parish, Bute compensated Merthyr with a donation of £300 and in addition paid £30 a year to provide a weekly lecturer in the town, hoping, in vain, that the ironmasters would assist him in converting the lecturer into an additional curate. In the parishes of which he was patron, church restoration was largely financed by him and in other parishes where he owned land his contribution to building costs bore the same relationship to the total as did his land to the total acreage of the parish.[46] During his lifetime, the marquess gave some £15,000 towards extending the accommodation and increasing the endowment of the Anglican church in Glamorgan, almost all his gifts being aimed at maintaining the hold of the establishment over the working classes. Expenditure upon pretentious churches made no appeal to him. Hearing in 1846 that large sums were to be spent upon Llandaf cathedral, he wrote: 'I cannot go into the notion of laying out many thousands of pounds on an attempt to restore the cathedral before the populous districts of the

[45] Bute to Dynely, 21 November 1833 (C.C.L., MS. 4.713), to Griffiths, 16 July and 5 August 1846 (N.L.W., B., 70, L. 1845–46); E. T. Davies, *Religion in the industrial revolution in south Wales* (1965), p. 137.
[46] W. D. Wills, op. cit., p. 106; Williams to Bute, 16 December 1839 (C.C.L., B., XX, 132); Bute to Richards, 6 August 1840 (G.R.O., D/DA 24); accounts (N.L.W., B., 60); Bute to Webb, 12 November 1843 (ibid., 70, L. 1840–44).

county are much better provided with churches than they are at present'.[47]

In supporting church extension, Bute was concerned that adequate provision should be made for the needs of Welsh-speaking worshippers. Industrial Glamorgan was overwhelmingly Welsh-speaking in the first half of the nineteenth century, a fact recognised by the marquess when he urged that the proclamation threatening the Merthyr insurrectionists with charges of high treason should be promulgated in Welsh.[48] The marquess was familiar with the problems of a bilingual church on the Isle of Bute, where he was also faced with the reluctance of the establishment and the readiness of secessionists to provide services in a Celtic tongue. 'The Welsh people', he informed Campbell, 'like to go to the church service on Sunday and if they do not find two services in their language in the Established church, they will go to a chapel of any denomination of Christians which will give them two services.' When an additional church was erected at Merthyr, Bute insisted that all services at the parish church should be in Welsh. '[To have two churches] as all persons who are familiar with Wales well know', he wrote, 'is the only arrangement agreeable to the feelings of the Welsh people. The system of having one service in Welsh and the other in English will not do.' At St. John's church, Aberdare, the marquess insisted that all the services should be in Welsh and he also intended building a Welsh church at Cardiff, a plan fulfilled by the widowed Lady Bute.[49]

A similar concern was reflected in the marquess's choice of incumbents. 'The Welsh language', he noted in 1828, 'is . . . called for in almost every piece of patronage I possess.' Campbell, before being presented with Merthyr, was boarded out with a Welsh-speaking family until Bute was satisfied that he was capable of holding Welsh services. Hely Rickards, whose family was the mainstay of Bute influence at Llantrisant, was refused the living of Aberdare because he had 'not made much progress to fit himself for taking a Welsh living . . . [as

[47] Bute to Richards, 21 December 1846 (G.R.O., D/DA 30).
[48] G. A. Williams, op. cit., p. 161; J. H. Matthews, op. cit., IV, 415; W. Rees, op. cit., p. 161; Richards to Bute, 1 August 1830 (C.C.L., MS. 4.713).
[49] Bute to Campbell, 10 January and 10 March 1845 (N.L.W., B., 70, L. 1845–46); Griffiths to Lady Bute, 7 January 1850 (Scot. P.R.O., H.B. MSS., 197); E. T. Davies, op. cit., p. 117.

he is not] really familiar with the tongue.[50] Lady Bute was appalled that the Lord Chancellor had presented Llanilid, where 'hardly anyone speaks English', to 'a man *without Welsh*', and was active in seeking a fluent Welsh speaker for the living of Llanmaes. The marquess followed the same policy over the appointment of teachers at the schools he founded or aided. 'Welsh children', he wrote, 'should begin by being taught to read in the Welsh language', and he urged that at least one of the school inspectors appointed by the Privy Council should be 'a gentleman familiar with colloquial Welsh'.[51]

In other spheres, too, the second marquess showed a close interest in Welsh affairs. Although his commitment to Wales was but a pale shadow of his commitment to Scotland, it is clear that when he wrote of meetings of 'Welsh gentlemen' in London, he was including himself among them. He interested himself in the workings of the Court of Great Session, discussed its future with Peel, spoke in favour of its abolition in the House of Lords and attended a meeting on the matter at Sir Watkin Williams Wynn's London house, a meeting which sealed the fate of the Welsh judicature.[52] He was vice-president of the Royal Cambrian Society and subscribed generously to the Cymreigyddion and the Welsh Manuscripts Society. Patron of the Cardiff Eisteddfod of 1834, he bought tickets worth £37 8s. and his donation of £100 was by far the largest, *eisteddfodwyr* acknowledging his generosity in verse. From the Eisteddfod platform he waxed eloquent on the value of the Welsh language, 'the great storehouse of the people's long treasured recollections and the distinctive barrier of their nationality'.[53] He bought copies of the Tory anglican monthly *Yr Haul* for free distribution to his tenants and in 1833, much to Richards's disgust, for Richards believed that 'the continuance of the language is of no benefit to the country and . . . is kept up . . . to keep the dissenters together', he considered

[50] Bute to Richards, 27 November and 13 December 1845 (N.L.W., B., 70, L. 1845–46), 17 August 1843 (G.R.O., D/DA 27); Mrs. Rickards to Richards, 3 June 1848 (Scot. P.R.O., H.B. MSS., 196).
[51] Lady Bute to Bruce, 3 and 9 June 1848 (ibid.); Bute to Phillips, 10 August 1846, to Sinclair, 5 October 1846 (N.L.W., B., 70, L. 1845–46).
[52] Bute to Richards, 11 May 1829 (G.R.O., D/DA 15); *Parliamentary debates*, second series, 25, p. 1292.
[53] *M.G.*, 6 July 1833, 18 January and 23 August 1834; *Greal y Bedyddiwr*, IX (1835), 17; Bute to Richards, 22 July 1834 (N.L.W., B., 70, L. 6).

launching his own Welsh magazine 'to counteract one with which we are threatened by the Useful Knowledge Society'.[54] There were limits to the marquess's enthusiasm, however. 'J. B. Pryce', he wrote in 1833, 'has hinted that I might show [the tenant of Pantygorddinan] some indulgence as, it seems, he belongs to the classic race of Bards . . . I must say this is not a ground to be recognized in the management of an estate.'[55]

In addition to the duties which Bute felt obliged to undertake as a landowner, there were others which fell to him as lord-lieutenant of Glamorgan, an office to which he was appointed in succession to his grandfather in May 1815. As the representative of the crown in the county, he had a role to play in the administration of justice, while matters of internal and external security were also his concern. Furthermore, the lord-lieutenant was the channel of communication between the government and the county and was the acknowledged head of county society. In the hands of an indolent man in a stable rural community, the position could be of little significance, but the social upheavals in Glamorgan in the first half of the nineteenth century and the character of the marquess himself made it inevitable that during his tenure of the office the lord-lieutenant should be a central figure in the history of the county.

A primary duty of the lord-lieutenant was to recommend to the Lord Chancellor the names of suitable candidates for the bench of magistrates, which in Glamorgan was some one hundred strong. For the vale of Glamorgan with its numerous landed families this was a simple task, but the rapidly expanding industrial areas with their dearth of resident gentry posed considerable problems. There Bute's reluctance to nominate ironmasters left the Anglican clergy as the most obvious candidates, but he was also reluctant to nominate these, for 'not only would it break in unfairly upon their time but would weaken them in their religious position'.[56] Tradesmen-magistrates he abhorred; 'I refused to recommend

[54] Ibid., 11 December 1833 (ibid.); Richards to Bute, 19 December 1833 (C.C.L., MS. 4.713); accounts (N.L.W., B., 60).
[55] Bute to Richards, 7 October 1833 (ibid., 70, L. 6).
[56] Bute to Dalton, 20 November 1846 (ibid., L. 1845–46).

Mr. E. L. Richards', he wrote, 'because he is a brewer at Merthyr'. Richards, in advising Bute, was particularly exclusive in his views, urging the rejection of the Merthyr surgeon-turned-squire, William Thomas of the Court, who 'although a man of some property . . . was not of the class of individuals whom I think your lordship would introduce into the Commission of Peace' and opposing the nomination of Merthyr's wealthiest lawyer because 'there is something unsavoury about Mr. Meyrick's household'. The marquess, however, was obliged to be more circumspect; Thomas reached the bench, becoming 'a bluff and racy Tory magistrate' and of Meyrick Bute wrote 'I cannot refuse [him] if he is recommended by District magistrates [for] he is amply qualified by estate'.[57]

As lord-lieutenant, Bute had a deciding voice in appointments other than those of magistrates. The clerkship to the justices was within his gift and to it he appointed Richards, who used the office and that of county treasurer to buttress Bute influence. Richards's many roles, public and private, caused some confusion; in the 1850s it was discovered that his salary as justices' clerk had been for years a charge not upon the county of Glamorgan, but upon the Bute estate.[58] The choosing of deputy-lieutenants was also the marquess's prerogative, while in the election of the chairman of the Quarter Sessions and in the selection of the high sheriff his wishes were paramount. In making such appointments Bute had to tread warily, for there was much antagonism between the western and eastern wings of Glamorgan. Cardiff's position as county town was resented by the western magistrates and by the citizens of Swansea, whose town was, in the early-nineteenth century, three times the size of Cardiff. As his estate lay almost entirely in the eastern half of the county and as Richards was known to be fanatically in favour of Cardiff, the westerners were suspicious of the marquess's every move, and in his successful opposition to the recognition of Bridgend as county town the utmost discretion had to be employed.[59]

[57] Richards to Bute, 1 April 1843 (ibid., L. 1842–44), 12 January 1828 (C.C.L., MS. 4.713); Bute to Richards, 31 March 1843 (G.R.O., D/DA 27), 8 April 1843 (N.L.W., B., 70, L. 7); G. A. Williams, op. cit., p. 57.
[58] McNabb to Richards, 25 May 1848 (G.R.O., D/DA 32).
[59] Richards to Walker, 21 March 1818 (ibid., 6), to Bute, 9 December 1829, 12 May 1832, to Lyon, 14 September 1832 (C.C.L., MS. 4.713); N.L.W., Calendar of the diary of L. W. Dillwyn, passim.

Responsible as lord-lieutenant for the internal and external security of the county, Bute was also from 1825 colonel-in-chief of the Royal Glamorgan Militia, an organisation he regarded with warm affection, considering its adjutant to be one of his closest friends. He took his duties seriously, organising training schedules, paying the band's expenses of some £150 a year and insisting upon the appointment of Welsh-speaking officers. The militiamen acted as family retainers; their band played in the castle yard when the marquess was in residence and, on retirement, some of them donned the Bute livery and manned the castle lodges.[60]

Under the second marquess, no external danger arose to test the mettle of the militia. There was, however, an internal threat. From the mid-1820s, Bute was concerned about the inflammable nature of the industrial society of northern Glamorgan. Richards, who had the true Cardiffian's suspicion of the people of the 'hills', fed his anxiety, although it must be admitted that Richards's prejudice and perspicacity had deserted him when he stated in 1830 that 'I do not think there is the least chance of riots at Merthyr'.[61] When tension in Merthyr reached crisis point in the late spring of 1831, the marquess was at Cardiff. His presence there was probably a consequence of the unrest, for this was the only occasion for him to visit Glamorgan during the month of May. During the Merthyr rising, Bute played a central role. He authorised the deployment of troops, received from the beleaguered authorities of Merthyr a stream of reports, among them a letter which a distinguished historian has described as 'perhaps the most dramatic that I have ever read in the public records' and sent detailed dispatches to London for the guidance of the Home Secretary and for perusal by the king.[62] The marquess left for London to attend parliament in late June and was, therefore, not present at the Cardiff Assizes which condemned Richard Lewis (Dic Penderyn) to death in July. Unlike his brother,

[60] Note on the militia (ibid., B., 47); C.C.L., B., XXI; J. H. Matthews, op. cit., V, 317; Bute to Richards, 30 September 1830 (G.R.O., D/DA 16); L. V. Evans, 'The Royal Glamorgan Militia', *Glamorgan Historian*, VIII (n.d.), 146–66.
[61] Richards to Bute, 19 January 1830 (C.C.L., MS. 4.713).
[62] G. A. Williams, op. cit., p. 128; accounts, 1830–32 (N.L.W., B., 60); letters, 1831 (C.C.L., MS. 4.713).

Bute took no part in the agitation against the sentence and although he informed Melbourne that the judge favoured commutation, there is no evidence that he influenced the Home Secretary's decision to allow the execution to proceed. On 13 August 1831, Dic was hanged at Cardiff; Richards informed the marquess that 'Richard Lewis was executed this morning without the slightest noise or disturbance . . . I showed the undersheriff your letter concerning the body which he promised to communicate to the Sheriff'. That letter, which has not survived, could have a bearing upon the decision to bury Dic, not at Cardiff gaol, but in his native parish of Aberafan.[63]

From the Merthyr rising onwards, Bute kept a close watch upon events in the industrial areas. The magistrates were asked to inform him of any untoward developments, the marquess collating their intelligence and passing it on to the Secretary of State.[64] When Chartist unrest assumed serious proportions in 1839, Lady Bute was ill at Walmer and Bute was unable to visit Glamorgan until December. In the weeks leading up to the march on Newport in November 1839 he received almost daily letters from a variety of correspondents describing the situation in Glamorgan, and when transmitting them to Whitehall he called for a military presence in the county and for the establishment of a police force in the 'hills'. He considered that it was he who had aroused the Glamorgan magistrates to a realisation of the dangers of Chartism and who had arranged for the military to be immediately available. Nevertheless, during the disturbances Cardiff felt far from secure. 'It is fortunate for us', wrote Richards, 'that the Chartists did not come as we were so wholly unprepared to meet them. I fear that had they visited us, we could not have resisted them as, by the aid of the soldiers, the Newport magistrates were able to do so satisfactorily.'[65]

[63] Richards to Bute, 13 August 1831 (ibid.); G. A. Williams, op, cit., pp. 182, 187.
[64] P.R.O., H.O. 40/46, 52/51, 52/25; note on a meeting, 13 June 1834 (N.L.W., B., 47).
[65] Ibid.; Richards to Bute, 19 November 1839 (C.C.L., MS. 4.860); C.C.L., B., XX; G.R.O., D/DA 22-23; C.C.L., MS. 4.860; N.L.W., B., 70, L. 6.

Following the events at Newport, Bute was determined that a police force should be established in Glamorgan, for although he hoped 'that there is an end for the present of the public meetings of the Chartists', he recognised that 'the revolutionary spirit is far from extinguished'.[66] He made a study of police matters and drew up a scheme for dividing the county into four districts, each under a superintendent. The rural areas were hostile to his plans but the industrial areas welcomed his initiative and, despite the antagonism between him and the ironmasters, there was harmonious co-operation. Indeed, during the social unrest of the 1830s and 1840s the new capitalists found increasing common ground with those traditional guardians of stability and property, the aristocratic landowners. The marquess attended the Easter Quarter Sessions of 1841 in order to move a resolution that a Glamorgan police force should be established. Thereafter matters moved quickly; in June Bute's scheme was accepted by the magistrates, in July the location of stations and the wages of constables had been decided, and by August a chief constable had been appointed and a headquarters established at Bridgend. Bute followed these developments with close interest, befriending the chief constable, Captain Napier, investigating requests for more constables and advising on station sites.[67]

THE SOURCES OF POLITICAL INFLUENCE

Benevolent and altruistic although the second marquess's activities as landowner and lord-lieutenant may appear, it would be naive to assume that he was motivated solely by a desire to do his duty, by concern for the needy and the defenceless and by solicitude for public order and the general weal. Underlying much of his activity was the desire for political power. Central to his purpose in Glamorgan was the maintenance of his hold over the corporation of Cardiff and his influence over the borough's representation in the House of Commons. Such influence was important to him as it had

[66] Bute to Stuart 3 September 1842 (ibid. L. 1840–44).
[67] C.C.L. B. XXII; Bute to Richards 11 September 1839 (N.L.W., B., 70, L. 6); Bute to Nicholl 7 January and 25 September 1845 (ibid. L. 1845–46); note on the police (C.C.L. MS. D 300.51); E. R. Baker 'The beginnings of the Glamorgan County Police' *Glamorgan Historian* II (1965) 40–52.

been to the first marquess, for until 1832 it was only at Cardiff
that he had a base for a permanent electoral interest. Through
his first marriage he gained an ascendancy over the borough
of Banbury but such ascendancy was temporary, for under the
North Estate Act, Wroxton with its electoral appendages was
allotted to his sister-in-law. The electoral influence of the Luton
estate was zealously upheld but although a Bute kinsman,
William Stuart, founded a political dynasty in Bedfordshire in
1830, the Luton interest was too small to give the marquess a
dominant voice in the county's politics. In 1832 Buteshire was
granted a member in every Parliament and the three hundred
voters then enfranchised proved as amenable to the influence
of the Mountstuart estate as had the twenty-one voters of
the old régime.

Bute had many reasons for seeking political influence.
Having members of the Commons who were loyal to him
emphasised the temporal glory of the house of Bute and
enhanced the marquess's prestige in London political circles.
He also had specific tasks for a client member to perform, in
particular to scrutinise and amend bills which might contain
clauses hostile to the interests of his dock. Furthermore, the
marquess was profoundly loyal to the Conservative cause.
Despite his deep-seated family attachments, he refused to
further the political career of his radical uncle, Lord Dudley
Coutts Stuart, and he preferred to break with his brother
rather than allow Cardiff to be represented by a reformer.
'Every inch of my estates, except a portion of my Dumfries
property', he wrote in 1835, 'is in my own absolute power. To
cut off my brother is certainly one of the last acts I should like
to carry through . . . but I should have little hesitation in
reducing him and myself to the Dumfries estate in order to
prop the conservative cause.'[68]

A proprietary borough has been defined as 'so much under
the control of one proprietor that the electors would return . . .
anyone whom he chose to put forward in his interest'.[69] The
Glamorgan boroughs before 1832 and the Cardiff boroughs
thereafter were not in this sense a Bute proprietary seat.

[68] Bute to Richards 18 April 1835 (G.R.O., D/DA 20), 22 November 1830
(C.C.L., B., IX, 27, 21).
[69] N. Gash, *Politics in the age of Peel* (1963), p. 193.

Richards fully appreciated the distinction between control and influence. 'I do not think', he wrote in 1831, 'any non-resident (except one of your lordship's family) could be elected for these boroughs.' When organising an anti-reform petition at Cardiff he noted: 'The omission of the statement that the Boroughs are not under the control of any individual arose to prevent the possibility of objection as, although it is well known they are not under control, I should have had difficulty in making some of our worthy burgesses understand the difference between control and influence'.[70]

While control could be exercised without undue exertion, influence was only effective through the tactful employment of a variety of different forms of power, pressure and patronage. The power to ensure that those enfranchised at Cardiff, Llantrisant and Cowbridge were virtually the nominees of the lord of Cardiff Castle and to add to the electorate there if opposition from the other five boroughs materialised, a power which had allowed the first marquess to dominate the parliamentary representation of the Glamorgan boroughs, remained operative until 1832. Thus, in 1818, when Swansea threatened resistance, 123 new burgesses were created at Cardiff and eighty-two at Llantrisant, while between 1824 and 1830 Cardiff's burgesses were increased by 239 and Llantrisant's by at least seventy. The numbers could, in theory, be increased without limit but there were severe practical limitations. A large body of burgesses was expensive, for it was necessary not only to pay the fees of the poorer claimants but also to reward the entire electorate with regular dinners and charitable gifts.[71] Admission of unreliable burgesses could defeat the whole object. At Llantrisant, where the population was in a 'dreadful state of ignorance, depravity and barbarism' and was 'dissolute and venal to a high degree', indiscriminate admissions had caused the borough to be 'the most tiresome part of our election business'.[72] A lavish expansion, even of reliable burgesses, could also be damaging, for a cheapening of the privilege was offensive to those already admitted. The

[70] Richards to Bute, 11 March and 23 July 1831 (C.C.L., MS. 4.713).
[71] R. D. Rees, op. cit., p. 14; P.P., XXIII (1835), 186–94, 221–24, 313–17; accounts (N.L.W., B., 60).
[72] Bute to Richards, 11 November 1825 (G.R.O., D/DA 12); Richards to Bute, 16 October 1824 (C.C.L., MS. 4.713).

Cowbridge burgesses, 'whose ideas on most subjects are notoriously confined' and who 'so pique themselves on their respectability and independence . . . that it is a rather delicate matter to have any communication with them', resisted attempts to admit non-resident freemen in the Bute interest and in consequence the electorate there was less than a sixth of what it was at Llantrisant.[73]

The 1832 Reform Act enfranchised men occupying a house of a yearly value of £10 and above, while at the same time it preserved the existing rights of resident freemen. Thereafter, virtually no new freemen were created, but in 1832 so rare were £10-houses in the Bute-dominated boroughs that voters qualifying under the old system exceeded those qualifying under the new. As death thinned the ranks of freemen, the number of voters at Llantrisant fell and, in the short term, the new system proved less 'democratic' than the old. Freemen voters had an ingrained loyalty to the lord of the borough but the same deference could not be expected of the £10-house-holders. However, as Cardiff had hardly outgrown its ancient boundaries before the middle of the nineteenth century, Bute owned most of the building land of the town and was ground-landlord to the majority of the new voters, a position which his agents urged him to use for political ends, Richards preparing abortive plans for letting the building plots for the full ninety-nine-year term while letting the gardens on an annual tenancy.[74]

In the county, where he could not hope to control representation, the marquess had need of some votes at his command since, before the Reform Act, he was obliged to offer his interest in the county to the Margam estate in exchange for Margam's interest in the western boroughs. This obligation ceased in 1832 but the leftward shift in the county's representation and Guest's hold upon Merthyr made Bute anxious to cultivate his interest in both constituencies. Before 1832 the votes which Bute could command in the county arose largely from his power to create freehold leases, for while tenants on fixed term or annual leases did not qualify for a vote, those

[73] Ibid., 9 February 1828, 5 January 1831 (ibid.).
[74] M.G., 25 October 1833; I. G. Jones, 'Franchise reform and Glamorgan politics in the mid-nineteenth century', Morgannwg, II (1958), 47–64; H. J. Hanham, Elections and party management (1959), p. 29.

holding under life leases did, a factor which goes far to explain the survival of life leases on the Bute estate well into the nineteenth century.

The Reform Act opened up new opportunities to enlarge the Bute interest in the county. The enfranchisement of the £50-annual tenant gave the vote to all the larger Bute agricultural tenants. In 1844–45, among the Glamorgan county voters, there are thirty-seven who can with certainty be identified as Bute tenants, but the imprecise descriptions of property in the list probably mask many more. There is no suggestion that such tenants defied the marquess's voting instructions and attempts by opponents to canvass them were roundly denounced. Borough dwellers with county qualifications could also vote in county elections, and in 1844–45 almost a third of Glamorgan's county voters claimed their votes on property situated within a borough. They included 163 voters whose entitlement was based upon property within the Bute-dominated boroughs and among them were holders of leases drawn up by Richards, who in 1843 asked the marquess 'if you wish leases of building ground in Bute St. to be so prepared as to entitle the lessees to vote in the county . . . This can easily be done by the insertion of a life or lives before the form of ninety-nine years . . . There would be no control over the tenants but the majority would, no doubt, vote with their landlords.'[75]

Until the passage of the Municipal Corporation Act in 1835, control over the corporation of Cardiff was assured as long as the burgesses admitted were loyal Bute supporters. In 1835, when all who were rated for poor relief became burgesses, the power which Bute had enjoyed as lord of Cardiff Castle disappeared. His power as landlord of most of Cardiff, however, did not and when elements on the corporation proved recalcitrant, Richards urged him to make that power explicit. 'It is not a matter of Whig, Tory, Conservative or Radical politicks', he wrote in 1840, 'but whether your lordship . . . should have the legitimate interest [your] property ought to command . . . It is wholly impossible for any agent of your lordship's here to

[75] Richards to Bute, 11 January 1843 (N.L.W., B., 70, L. 1842–43), 1 August 1837 (G.R.O., D/DA 21); *The register of persons entitled to vote at any election of a member or members to serve in parliament for the county of Glamorgan* (1844).

keep up your interest if on every occasion he is not upheld by your lordship's tenants, or at any rate not opposed by them. There is still time, by notices to quit, to remind the parties that your lordship expects your property to have the weight it ought to possess.'[76]

The power which stemmed from his ownership of an estate was not the only source of Bute's political influence in Glamorgan. As lord-lieutenant, he assumed that all members of the militia would vote as he wished, and when some of them defied him in 1832 their action was described as mutiny.[77] The marquess could not control the political activities of magistrates and was indeed obliged to recommend for the bench men who were hostile to him politically; yet in the face of such announcements as that of 1820: 'The Marquess of Bute's good wishes are in favour of Sir Christopher Cole. His tenants and friends know it and will act accordingly', there can be little doubt that those who aspired to the bench or to a deputy-lieutenancy, but whose claims to such offices were not incontrovertible, knew where their interests lay. Above all, a deferential society was reluctant to challenge the prestige attached to the office of lord-lieutenant. When L. W. Dillwyn considered standing for the Glamorgan boroughs in 1818, he recorded in his diary: 'Mr. Bruce addressed the Neath corporation . . . and expressed his astonishment that a man who had been in business should presume to oppose the Brother of the Lord Lieutenant'.[78]

Furthermore, much of Bute's activity as a conscientious public figure could be used to strengthen his political influence. Although it would be unjust to assume that there were no altruistic motives behind his philanthropy, much of it was explicitly aimed at furthering his electoral interest. When Lord James was member for the Glamorgan boroughs, the marquess subscribed to borough, but not to county, charities in his name, and after the boroughs were divided in 1832, organisations in the western boroughs ceased to receive Bute contributions. The marquess subscribed to the Cardiff Reading Room,

[76] Richards to Bute, 21 and 27 July 1840 (C.C.L., MS. 4.860).
[77] Ibid., 15 December 1832 (ibid., 4.713).
[78] C., 20 February 1820; Bute to Richards, 19 January 1825 (G.R.O., D/DA 12); N.L.W., Calendar of the diary of L. W. Dillwyn, 9 June 1818; cf. R. Grant, *The parliamentary history of Glamorgan, 1542–1976* (1978), p. 135.

established specifically as a rallying point for Bute supporters; assistance given to Methodist chapels was aimed at capturing the Methodist interest, and Lady Bute, in 1825, was urged to make a crippled girl her protegée so that 'all her family would be secured'. Charities to individuals ceased if the recipients proved politically disloyal and Richards was active in obtaining evidence of such treachery.[79] Bute considered that the permanent nature of his philanthropy was a telling argument against the largesse of a carpet-bag opponent. 'It is most desirable', he wrote in 1825, 'that my acts show . . . a character of permanence corresponding to my property . . . to let the permanent character of my measures . . . be held out in contrast to the temporary measures of my opponents.' The establishment of a school with an estate endowment would, he believed, emphasise that permanence, for voters were 'more thankful for what is done for their children than for themselves'. 'Much political good', wrote Richards, 'will arise from a uniform clothing of twelve or twenty-four children. They would be considered the objects of your lordship's bounty and the parents of other children in the school would be looking forward to vacancies.'[80]

Estate policy could be dictated by political considerations. Bute was anxious that his rents should be known to be lower than those of neighbouring landowners and there can be no doubt that the lot of a tenant on an estate whose landlord was politically active was better than that of a tenant whose landlord viewed his estate solely in economic terms. Improvements were sometimes undertaken for political ends. 'Richard Morgan wants his house repaired;' Richards was informed in 1825, 'there are a great many votes in the family and if you will accommodate him, he will be active amongst them.'[81] The employment provided by an estate was a further political weapon. In 1824, when constructing a colliery pond at Llantrisant, despite Richards's warning that 'employing burgesses

[79] Tyndall to Bute, 2 December 1825 (Scot. P.R.O., H.B. MSS., 196); Richards to Walker, 13 October 1818 (G.R.O., D/DA 6); letters of Richards, December 1832 and January 1833 (C.C.L., MS. 4.713).
[80] Richards to Bute, 29 January and 26 February 1825 (ibid.); Bute to Richards, 3 February 1825 (G.R.O., D/DA 12).
[81] Rickards to Richards, 10 September 1825 (ibid.); Bute to Richards, 11 February 1835 (N.L.W., B., 70, L. 6).

will increase the expense tenfold [for] they . . . will only work at extravagant prices', Bute ordered him to 'take care to have workmen selected who will vote for my brother'.[82] The marquess's dock building activities were to Richards the basis of a significant expansion of political influence. 'The commencement of the work', he wrote on the eve of the 1832 election, 'would work wonders. It would act as a charm upon our poorer burgesses who may thus derive employment through the winter.' The dock project was partly inspired by political motives, the marquess hoping that the 'increased good feeling towards me' that it would engender would promote 'Conservative feeling'.[83] Anxious to employ Cardiff people at his dock, he gave priority to those whose families had been loyal to his. 'The post of assistant tide waiter at Cardiff is vacant', he wrote in 1845. 'Who has claims on me for that sort of job?' In answering, Richards commented upon one of the applicants: 'Mr. Riches certainly has [no claims]. He and his family have done all in their power to promote discontent in the town.'[84] Rapid urban and industrial growth is generally considered to have hastened the decline of aristocratic influence. At Cardiff, however, the growth of the town, following the construction of a dock wholly under the marquess's control, strengthened rather than weakened Bute influence, at least in the short term.

In the art of political management, landed possessions, social prestige, philanthropy and patronage were not in themselves enough. They had to be married to a skilful handling of men, a thorough understanding of electoral mechanics and an appreciation of the importance of propaganda. The need for tact Bute had learnt from the disastrous consequences of Walker's rule at Cardiff between 1815 and 1821.[85] His success in handling the corporation of Cardiff owed something to his experience at Luton and Banbury and he undoubtedly learnt much about the methods of corporation control through his

[82] Bute to Richards, 22 December 1825 (G.R.O., D/DA 12); Richards to Tyndall, 15 May 1826 (Scot. P.R.O., H.B. MSS., 196).

[83] Richards to Bute, 8 and 9 October 1832 (C.C.L., MS. 4.713); Bute to Smyth, 9 August 1839 (N.L.W., B., 70, L. 6).

[84] Ibid., 23 April 1839 (ibid.); Bute to Richards, 29 September 1845 (ibid., L. 7); Richards to Bute, 1 October 1865 (ibid., L. 1845–46).

[85] See below, pp. 116–20.

long association with that acknowledged master of the technique, John Clayton of Newcastle-upon-Tyne, a list of whose public offices fills a page of the *Archaeologia Aeliana*. Before the Commission on Municipal Corporations Clayton gave 'such a case as . . . has rarely been made out for any old and close corporation and his skilful fencing, frank avowal, ingenuous excuse and ready justification earned recognition and applause'. He was town clerk of Newcastle from 1822 to 1867 and 'his power was greater in the new corporation than in the old'.[86]

By the mid-1820s Bute, ably assisted by Richards, had mastered all the intricacies of electoral mechanics. It was Richards who planned politically advantageous charities, retained lawyers and selected reliable burgesses. He was responsible for that 'groundwork of political management, the compiling of electoral lists', making the registration of voters his special province, buying books on electoral law and scrutinising the lists compiled by the opposition.[87] He kept a tight rein on electoral expenditure, for the marquess disliked extravagance at election time and considered the £2,037 spent at inns in 1818 to be lamentably excessive. Overt corruption Bute deplored and he was sensitive to charges that as a peer he was interfering in elections to the Commons. Among the estate accounts, however, there are a few entries which appear to be direct money bribes and in 1824 Tyndall Bruce commented that 'elections dress many a burgess in a little brief authority which is frequently sold at a price far beyond its worth'.[88]

Bute and Richards understood the value of propaganda. A major item of election expenditure was the publication of Welsh and English broadsheets, songs and leaflets, some of them very scurrilous, for distribution to the voters. The marquess and his agents were active in inspiring favourable articles in the press, Bute noting in 1840 that 'Mr. Mallalieu

[86] L. Wilkes and A. Dodds, *Tyneside classical: the Newcastle of Grainger, Dobson and Clayton* (1964), pp. 50–52; *Archaeologia Aeliana*, third series, X (1913), 183.
[87] Bute to Richards, 19 February 1824 (G.R.O., D/DA 11); letters, 1824, 1825 and 1832 in C.C.L., MS. 4.713, and 1825–26 in Scot. P.R.O., H.B. MSS., 196.
[88] Tyndall to Bruce, 25 November 1825 (ibid); Walker to Richards, 10 June 1818, 20 and 23 February 1820 (G.R.O., D/DA 6 and 8); vouchers, 1826 (ibid., 56–117); accounts, 1818–19 (N.L.W., B., 60).

writes in the *Morning Herald* and the *Courier* . . . He also has some connection with the *Newcastle Journal*, with *Blackwoods Magazine* and with the Canada Press; Mr. Shaw . . . is now editor of *Felix Farley*; so we can work the press'.[89] During the reform crisis, Bute felt handicapped by Glamorgan's lack of a Conservative newspaper and the numerous press attacks he then suffered made him determined to start his own. Richards encouraged him. 'A good County paper', he wrote, 'would be the means of promoting your lordship's political influence and interest throughout the county . . . the proprietors should be of the old Tory, Church and King, Conservative or any more fleeting name of the day Party . . . and the paper would, I think, clearly pay its way in a very few years.'[90] The marquess's correspondents were told to burn all the letters which referred to his connection with the project, but enough disobeyed to provide ample evidence that east Glamorgan's first weekly newspaper, the *Glamorgan, Monmouth and Brecon Gazette and Merthyr Guardian*, launched on 17 November 1832, was a Bute creation. It was the marquess who insisted that it should be published at Merthyr and it was he who appointed the editor and underwrote its substantial losses. The paper proved a burdensome undertaking; other Tory land-owners gave little support, Bute was still helping to finance it in the mid-1840s and, in the mid-1850s his son's trustees were faced with unpaid bills relating to it. Its quality proved disappointing, its offices at Merthyr were ransacked, and of its frequently changing editors one was arrested and another became bankrupt. Nevertheless, Bute was proud of his venture. Although its Toryism proved too virulent even for him, leading articles on such matters as the church and the ballot, copied from more responsible newspapers, had 'an effect in the Pot-Houses'.[91] The *Guardian* always spoke respectfully of the marquess, gave prominence to his personal and charitable activities, championed him in all his disputes and, when he died, dedicated black-edged editions to his memory.

[89] Bute to Smyth, 21 July 1840 (ibid., 70, L. 7).
[90] Richards to Bute, 31 August 1832 (C.C.L., MS. 4.713).
[91] Ibid., 11 January 1833 (ibid.); G.R.O., D/DA 17–24; C.C.L., B., XX, 13 and 81; R. D. Rees, 'Glamorgan newspapers under the Stamp Acts', *Morgannwg*, III (1959), 72–76.

THE EXERCISE OF POLITICAL POWER

When the second marquess of Bute inherited his estates in November 1814, the political influence of his family in Glamorgan seemed secure. The corporation of Cardiff had long been content to be little more than an appanage of the Bute estate and scions of the Stuarts had succeeded each other as member for the Glamorgan boroughs for a generation. Beneath the surface, however, there was much discontent. The family was entirely non-resident, the estate had been neglected and the borough members had paid no attention to their parliamentary duties. Nevertheless, there was general rejoicing when in June 1815 the young marquess made 'his first appearance in this Borough as Lord thereof'.[92]

At Cardiff the new lord discovered that the town, which had long been untrammelled by any direct Bute supervision, had fallen under the sway of the estate's country bankers and solicitors, the Wood family. John Wood, senior, the banker, and his solicitor sons, John and Nichol, had gathered into their hands most of the key offices in the corporation of Cardiff and the county of Glamorgan. Their entrenched power was galling to the ambitious young solicitor, E. P. Richards, who hinted to the marquess that the Woods had abused their trust, particularly in relation to Cardiff's educational charities. In the autumn of 1815, Bute, who was then obliged because of his deteriorating eyesight, to retire from active supervision of his affairs, placed his estates in Wales and England under the superintendence of P. T. Walker, a clerk in the Exchequer, who had no previous connection with Glamorgan. In 1816, Walker became an alderman of Cardiff and in the following year was appointed constable of the castle, his rapid promotion constituting an obvious challenge to the position of the Woods. Towards the citizens of Cardiff Walker was haughty and arrogant, demanding that they 'should show proper and respectful behaviour towards Lord Bute and those in whom his lordship had been pleased to place confidence'.[93] In 1817, shortly after the death of John Wood, senior, he began an investigation into corporation finances, making allegations

[92] J. H. Matthews, op. cit., IV, 270–71, 366–67; C.C.L., IX, 17; L. Hargest, 'Cardiff's "spasm of rebellion" in 1818', *Morgannwg*, XXI (1977), 69–88.
[93] Walker to Richards, 18 October 1820 (G.R.O., D/DA 6).

'grossly reflecting upon the memory of John Wood' and 'calculated to excite a strong prejudice against [the family] in the town'.[94]

The Woods' reaction was to create an anti-Bute faction within the Cardiff corporation. As a result, the Woods were no longer employed as estate solicitors and bankers and in July 1817, Walker, acting in the marquess's name, dismissed Nichol Wood from the office of town clerk, replacing him with Richards. Wood, however, refused to give up his office. 'I proceeded', wrote Walker, 'to point out to [the Woods] how prudent it would be for them to return onto the path of propriety from which they had deviated, by throwing themselves on Lord Bute's clemency. The Town Clerk set me at defiance and began to get into a Welsh fever . . . You must therefore prepare for eternal war.'[95] Walker and Richards sought to pack the corporation with Bute supporters as Wood manoeuvrings had placed the Bute majority in jeopardy. Litigation in the King's Bench was instigated against Walker, who as constable had refused to swear in anti-Bute officers, and Walker retaliated by bringing a case against Nichol Wood to compel him to hand over papers relating to corporation affairs. The court ruled in favour of the Woods on both issues, giving them the opportunity to pose as champions of freedom against aristocratic control. Nichol Wood, who remained town clerk of Cardiff until 1835, received a tumultuous welcome on returning victorious from the court proceedings, the celebrations leading to the calling out of the militia and to charges of riot and assault.[96]

The dispute dragged on into the 1820s, the Woods keeping it alive through their publications, the *Cardiff Reporter* and the *Cardiff Recorder*. The importance of the episode should not, however, be exaggerated. It was a factional squabble rather than a determined attack upon privilege. Used by the Woods

[94] King against Wood, statement for Messrs. Taunton (N.L.W., B., 31); C., 20 June 1817.
[95] Walker to Richards, 5 July and 28 August 1817; Richards to the bailiffs of Cardiff, 3 July 1817 (G.R.O., D/DA 5).
[96] King against Wood, statement for Messrs. Taunton, opinion of Taunton, the corporation of Cardiff against Thomas Morgan (N.L.W., B., 31); G.R.O., D/DA 5–7; C., 8 August 1817, 20 February and 23 May 1818; L. Hargest, op.cit.; J. H. Matthews, op. cit., II, 116–20; S. and B. Webb, op. cit., p. 256.

to divert attention from their mismanagement of Cardiff's affairs, the campaign faded away especially after the prestige of the family was further dimmed by the failure of their bank in 1822. Throughout the controversy there was no serious danger that the marquess would lose his majority over the corporation and, even if he had, his influence over Cardiff's affairs would still have been great. The corporation, deeply in his debt, had an income of less than one-sixteenth of that of the Bute estate and the acreage of land it owned within the corporation was less than one-twentieth of that owned by the marquess. Perhaps the most important result of this 'spasm of rebellion' was that it taught Bute to be circumspect in the exercise of political power. By 1820 he was 'fully aware that a different management would . . . have been better for his real interests'.[97] Walker was dismissed and the long reign of Richards began.

When the Wood controversy was at its height, the general election of June 1818 was held. It was arranged that Bute's uncle, Lord Evelyn, would stand down and be replaced by the marquess's brother, Lord James Stuart, then aged twenty-two. It had been hoped that the substitution would occur as peacefully as had previous arrangements of the kind but with dissidence at Cardiff and resentment in the western boroughs with their growing industrial interests, the marquess's intentions could not avoid being challenged. 'The burgesses want no sons of lords to represent them', stated an advertisement in the Swansea *Cambrian*. 'They want a man of business to do so, a man on the spot to communicate with and who will be at his post in the House of Commons when his duty requires it.'[98] The problem of the opposition was to find a candidate of sufficient status, for among the gentry of Glamorgan there were few, even among the opponents of the Butes, who wished to associate with the rabble-rousing Woods. Approaches were made to John Homfray and L. W. Dillwyn, both respected men with an industrial background, but Homfray was obliged to refuse because of ill health and Dillwyn because he could

[97] Thomas to Richards, 5 July 1820 (G.R.O., D/DA 8).
[98] *C.*, 29 May 1818; Walker to Richards, 21 October 1817, 22 May 1818 (G.R.O., D/DA 5 and 6); N.L.W., Calendar of the diary of L. W. Dillwyn, 5 June 1818.

not free himself of the office of high sheriff without compro-
mising his independence. As a result, Frederick Wood, brother
of Nichol and a man of little standing, was chosen as the
candidate of the 'Wooden interest'. The election proved lively;
indecent broadsheets were published and Lord James was
twice physically attacked by Wood supporters. The result was
never in doubt. Lord James secured the Margam interest and,
after one day's voting, Frederick Wood retired having gained
seventeen dubious votes to Lord James's forty-five.[99]

The election of 1818 was a salutary experience for the
marquess. Although the opposition proved feeble, the election
cost Bute £5,132 and Lord James was obliged to make amends
for the neglect of his predecessors by promising to reside in the
county and 'neither to think of anything night or day but his
parliamentary duties and the interests of the boroughs'.[100]
Nevertheless, in the election of 1820, Lord James was withdrawn against his will from the Glamorgan boroughs after he
had begun his campaign, and was elected instead for the
county of Bute. The probable reason for the switch was the
marquess's reluctance, in the absence of a firm understanding
with the patrons of the western boroughs, to face the expense
of a contest when, at virtually no cost, he could find a seat for
his brother in Scotland. To replace Lord James, the Bute and
Margam estates brought forward, as their joint nominee,
Wyndham Lewis, Disraeli's future wife's first husband and a
partner in the Dowlais Iron Company. The choice suggested
that the marquess's will, although not absolute, was still
paramount for, as L. W. Dillwyn noted, 'As a large proprietor
in the Dowlais ironworks [Lewis] is so obviously under the
thumb of the marquess that I cannot consider him much more
than a *locum tenens*'.[101] The burgesses of Swansea nominated
Ludlow, the duke of Beaufort's auditor; after a six-day poll
Lewis, with a considerable number of votes in hand, defeated
Ludlow by 354 votes to 245.

[99] Ibid., May and June 1818; G.R.O., D/DA 6; R. D. Rees, 'Parliamentary
representation', pp. 208–15; J. Ballinger, 'Elections in Cardiff and Glamorgan,
1818–32', *Cymru Fu*, I (1889), 348–59; C.C.L., Box labelled Posters, etc.
[100] *C.*, 19 June 1818; note on election expenses, 1818 (N.L.W., B., 60).
[101] *C.*, 4 March 1820, 17 June 1826; Bute to Knight, 9 July 1824 (G.R.O.,
D/DA 11); N.L.W., Calendar of the diary of L. W. Dillwyn, 7 March 1820.

Bute's first excursions into political management had produced disappointing results. Stewart, reviewing the marquess's experience, noted that 'large sums spent on elections are spent in the worst way possible and the true mode to acquire the command of a solid political influence is to acquire the command of a preponderating landed property . . . that may carry all before it'.[102] The second marquess did add significantly to the size of his Glamorgan estate, but his success in politics after the early-1820s was the consequence of his growing awareness of the diverse forms of his political influence and of his determination to wield it with energy and circumspection. In July 1821 Bute resumed active management of his estates and immediately set about relaxing the tensions created by Walker. Nichol Wood, although remaining town clerk, resided abroad and Richards, as solicitor to the corporation and as alderman, led the 'castle party' with consummate skill. Walker was replaced as constable of the castle by Lord James Stuart, and in 1829 the marquess's intimate friend, O. T. Bruce, was appointed corporation steward. Bute ascendancy was restored in its entirety. Richards sent the marquess lists of possible aldermen and capital burgesses and asked for instructions, the annual election of bailiffs was carried out according to Bute wishes, and corporation officials whom the marquess considered unsuitable resigned.[103]

While the corporation of Cardiff proved compliant, the borough member proved less so. Bute assumed that by consolidating his interest, he could without opposition bring back his brother as member for the Glamorgan boroughs. Central to his plans was the assumption that Wyndham Lewis would retire when required to do so. By 1824, however, it became clear that Lewis had no intention of resigning, the marquess interpreting his refusal as an extension into the political field of the dispute which by then had arisen between the Bute estate and the Dowlais Company. 'It is an attempt', he wrote, 'to bully me into submission to a most destructive fraud which they have committed upon my property . . . I shall

---

[102] C.C.L., B., IX, 19; Tyndall to Bute, 30 September 1825 (Scot. P.R.O., H.B. MSS., 196).
[103] C.C.L., MS. 4.713; N.L.W., B., 70, L. A; J. H. Matthews, op. cit., IV, 384, 394.

certainly increase their fine for renewal in proportion to any expense they may put me to.'[104] From 1824 until the election of June 1826, Bute, Richards and O. T. Bruce dedicated themselves to the task of strengthening the Bute party machine in the Glamorgan boroughs and did not flinch from using the most unscrupulous methods to bludgeon the other patrons into supporting Lord James. Such machinations proved successful and, twelve days before the poll, Lewis withdrew from the contest. Lord James was returned unopposed and his election 'passed off most admirably . . . before a crowd of about seven thousand'.[105]

Bute's show of strength in 1826 gave him undisputed sway and, in the election of 1830, no attempt was made to oppose Lord James. 'We met in the hall at ten o'clock', wrote Richards, 'and Lord James was proposed by Colonel Morgan and seconded by Mr. Richards . . . about four hundred dined at three o'clock . . . and the whole party separated by eight as orderly and soberly as it is possible for free and independent burgesses to do.'[106]

Such unanimity proved short-lived. The poor markets of the late-1820s, the near-bankruptcy of many farmers and the depression in the ironworks led to considerable hardship and poverty. In the winter of 1830 there were rick burnings on farms near Cardiff; in January 1831 four thousand men were rumoured to be marching on the town to pull down the gaol and five months later came the enormous upheaval of the Merthyr rising. Rural and industrial unrest merged with the agitation over parliamentary reform. 'The language of the opponents of the late ministry', wrote Richards in August 1830, 'has raised opposition to the existing order of things throughout the county . . . The distress of the county has certainly quietened those who would otherwise have been ready to come forward with addresses of loyalty . . . I very much fear till our agricultural and commercial interests are improved we will not see a reaction.'[107]

[104] Bute to Richards, 19 February 1824 (G.R.O., D/DA 11); Richards to Bute, 16 October 1824 (C.C.L., MS. 4.713).
[105] C.C.L., MS. 4.716, 12 June 1826; C., 17 June 1826; extensive correspondence 1824–25 in G.R.O., D/DA 11 and 12, C.C.L., MS. 4.713 and Scot. P.R.O., H.B. MSS., 196.
[106] Richards to Bute, 1 August 1830 (C.C.L., MS. 4.713).
[107] Ibid., 4 December 1830 and 11 March 1831 (ibid.).

During the reform crisis of 1831–32 there were among the
six thousand inhabitants of Cardiff representatives of all
the diverse elements which played a part in the struggle and,
through Richards's letters, the town can be seen as a microcosm
of the kingdom as a whole.[108] The marquess considered that
the electoral system in parts of the county was 'incorrect in
principle but not injurious in practice' and believed that
reform would lead to 'ten times more bribery and corruption
than at present'.[109] To Richards, the likely consequences
of reform were far more menacing: 'Reform', he wrote,
'will be the ruin of the country and the subversion of the
monarchy'. Landed gentry who supported the bill he abhorred,
considering Jones of Fonmon, the descendant of Colonel
Philip Jones, the Cromwellian, as 'a good example of a
reformer, having spent his paternal estate . . . he probably
thinks any turn may be of benefit to him'. The Cardiff agents
of the great iron companies and the officials of the Glamorganshire Canal Company, whom Richards contemptuously
referred to as 'wharf gentry', were all reformers, as were most
of Cardiff's shopkeepers and professional men. Many of these
were dissenters, all of whom, with the exception of the
Methodists, were ardent advocates of the bill. 'That the mob
is in favour of the bill', wrote Richards, 'is quite clear, but
this is the order of the day . . . The Reformers have certainly
numbers to boast of but if *property* is to be considered, their
followers would cut but a sorry figure.' Lady Bute was insulted
by a mob at Rothesay and, following the Bristol riots of
October 1831, Bute arranged for Cardiff Castle to be guarded
against attack.[110]

Richards's fear was that the Cardiff reformers would obtain
'respectable leaders', a fear which materialised when, in March
1831, Lord James voted in favour of the first Reform Bill. His
brother, who was actively supporting the duke of Wellington
and other anti-reformers, was mortified and prepared to
replace Lord James at the forthcoming election. Richards
convinced him, however, that such an upheaval should be

---

[108] In C.C.L., MS. 4.713 and G.R.O., D/DA 16–17.
[109] *Parliamentary debates*, third series, 7, pp. 1015–18.
[110] Richards to Bute, 8 October and 16 November 1831, 24 January, 17 April,
28 May, 20 October and 10 November 1832 (C.C.L., MS. 4.713).

avoided and in May 1831, Lord James's popularity as a
reformer and Bute's reluctant support secured an unopposed
return. 'Everything went off yesterday as we wished', wrote
Richards on 3 May, ' . . . very little was said of reform. Both
Monmouthshire and Carmarthenshire are in a ferment and
happy ought we to consider ourselves as not exposed to a
contest.'[111] Lord James went his own independent way,
informing the Commons that Cardiff supported reform and
voting in favour of the second and third Reform Bills.

The Reform Act, as the *Times* pointed out, strengthened
Bute's political position, for the division of the Glamorgan
boroughs into an eastern and a western division relieved the
marquess of the need to conciliate the patrons of the western
boroughs where he had little direct influence. The act also
increased the county representation to two and gave a member
to Merthyr Tydfil, a provision of which the marquess approved
for he had feared that Merthyr would have been added to the
eastern boroughs, thus overwhelming his interest.[112]

Before the election of 1832, Bute sought an assurance from
his brother that he would never again oppose him publicly.
This Lord James refused to give, preferring to resign his seat
rather than vote against his conscience. Richards sought to
remonstrate with him. 'Lord Bute's interest and your own
must be the same', he wrote in September 1832. 'Do not
therefore allow your present political feeling . . . to warp your
own good sense and judgement and destroy an Interest here
which nothing but disunion between Lord Bute and yourself
can ever shake.'[113] Lord James, however, was adamant and in
October 1832 announced that he would not be standing again
for Cardiff. Richards recommended the able barrister, John
Nicholl of Merthyr Mawr, as the most eligible Tory candidate
and on 8 October 1832 Nicholl agreed to stand. To the Whigs
and radicals the split in the house of Bute was a heaven-sent
opportunity. 'The Reformers would make use of his lordship',
wrote Richards to Bute, 'to serve their own views . . . Those
always opposed to your lordship's Interest are now the loudest

[111] Ibid., 11 March and 3 May 1831 (ibid.).
[112] Ibid., 9 April 1831 and 21 January 1832 (ibid.); *Times*, 22 October 1832;
Parliamentary debates, third series, 5, pp. 828, 866, 1139, 1151; 11, pp. 73, 231, 239.
[113] Richards to Stuart, 26 September 1832 (C.C.L., MS. 4.713).

in upholding Lord James against your lordship.'[114] The matter was given wide publicity in an article published in the *Times* on 22 October. 'It is notorious throughout Glamorgan', it wrote, 'that the Marquess of Bute prefers the substitution of a Tory member for his own brother . . . The Tories themselves speak of it with deep regret and condemnation.' The paper advised Glamorgan reformers to nominate Lord James and to accept no refusal.

The advice was accepted and a committee was set up at Cardiff to further Lord James's candidature. Richards was at his wits' end; most of those who had promised their votes to Nicholl had done so on the understanding that Lord James would not stand and, despite the publicity given to the differences between the brothers, there were many who believed they were obliging Bute by supporting Lord James. Bute declared that his brother was annoyed with those who had brought forward his name and demanded, through Richards, that Lord James, who was also a candidate for Perth, should state that, if elected, he would not take his seat. 'Nothing on earth', wrote Lord James, 'would have induced me to comply with Lord Bute's most extraordinary and most improper and unconstitutional demand . . . I learn that he took it upon him to say . . . that I was disgusted with the efforts of my friends. How so, what authority had he and how could I be disgusted with those who stood by me . . . such conduct created in me the very opposite feeling of disgust.'[115] Bute ceased to pay any subscriptions on behalf of his brother and required him to resign from the offices of captain in the Glamorgan militia and constable of Cardiff Castle.

The Cardiff election of 11 December 1832 was strenuously fought. The reformers of the three boroughs were active on behalf of Lord James as were the Whigs of Swansea, the dissenting leaders of Glamorgan and powerful interests in London, but they were handicapped by their candidate's absence from the campaign. Bute made use of every form of political pressure and on the first day's poll it became clear

---

[114] Richards to Bute, 10 October 1832 (ibid.); *C.*, 13 and 20 October 1832.
[115] Bute to Richards, 16 January 1833, Stuart to Richards, 29 February 1833 (G.R.O., D/DA 18).

that the marquess's influence had overcome his brother's popularity. The election ended on the second day with Nicholl having won 342 votes to Lord James's 191, making Cardiff almost the sole constituency where a sitting reformer was defeated by an anti-reformer in the election of 1832. Richards was proud of his success in stemming the reformist tide. 'The Conservatives', he wrote, 'are beat in all quarters in this neighbourhood. Mr. Morgan at Brecon, Jones at Carmarthen, Lord Worcester at Monmouth and Blakemore at Hereford.'[116] The *Merthyr Guardian* rejoiced that 'the attempt, insidiously and unworthily made, to sow dissension between two noble brothers has failed', while the *Cambrian* considered that the lesson of the election was that reform was incomplete without the ballot, and the *Silurian* wrote of the 'poor rotten borough of Cardiff . . . lonely since its kindred spirits, Galton and Old Sarum, died'.[117] Bute's control over the representation of Cardiff continued inviolate until his death. Nicholl had a moderately distinguished parliamentary career, holding office as a Lord of the Treasury in 1835 and as Judge Advocate General from 1841 to 1846. Bute warmly approved of his political conduct and at each election he was unopposed. In 1835 his attendance at Cardiff for the election was considered unnecessary and in 1841 the chairing of the victor and the victory dinner were abandoned.[118] Bute's support for the repeal of the Corn Laws made the Whigs and radicals less anxious to oppose and, electorally, the 1840s at Cardiff were a period of outward calm.

Secure in the boroughs, Bute turned his attention to the county and Merthyr seats. Some attempt was made in 1832 to oppose Dillwyn and Talbot, the county's Whig candidates, but as the marquess was preoccupied with Cardiff they were elected unopposed. Of the five Glamorgan seats, Cardiff alone returned a Conservative in 1832, much to the disgust of the 'scurrilous ultra-Tory' paper, the *Age*, which found it 'melancholy to witness the way in which the Liberals ride rough-shod over a county hitherto famed for its loyalty and constitutional

---

[116] Richards to Bute, 15 December 1832 (C.C.L., MS. 4.713).
[117] *M.G.*, 15 December 1832; *C.*, ibid.; *Silurian*, 17 December 1836.
[118] Bute to Richards, 30 December 1834, 6 September 1841 (G.R.O., D/DA 19 and 25); Richards to Bute, 22 July 1837 (C.C.L., MS. 4.860).

principles'.[119] At Merthyr in 1832, Sir John Guest was elected unopposed, but by the mid-1830s Bute was active in rallying anti-Dowlais and Tory sentiment there in the hope of undermining Guests's 'industrial feudalism'. Anthony Hill, strongly supported by the marquess, made a bid for Merthyr in 1835, but 'he only made a shew of light and did not come up to the Scratch'.[120] In 1837, Tory interests at Merthyr and Aberdare, led by Bute, brought forward Bruce Pryce to oppose Guest; he did well at Aberdare but failed to win a single vote at Dowlais and was beaten by 309 votes to 135. Having failed to oust him by electoral means, the marquess tried to make Guest's resignation a condition for the renewal of the Dowlais lease. Guest ignored this blackmail and by 1846, in preparation for the general election of that year, Bute was searching for a candidate who would stand on a 'church and king' platform at Merthyr. Richards convinced him that such a platform would have little appeal to the radical or even republican voters of Merthyr, and Guest was left undisturbed in his constituency until his death.[121]

In the county, Bute found that Dillwyn and Talbot proved less radical than he had feared and he did not oppose their re-election in 1835. Dillwyn decided not to stand in 1837 and, to the marquess's annoyance, Guest came forward in his place. The Glamorgan Tories nominated Lord Adare, heir to the Dunraven estate and, in the summer of 1837, the entire energies of the Bute estate were dedicated to securing Adare's return. Richards's labours over registration and Bute's pressure upon the voters to plump for Adare made the Cardiff area the stronghold of Conservatism in Glamorgan. Adare headed the poll with 2,009 votes, followed by Talbot with 1,791 and the unsuccessful Guest with 1,590.[122] Emboldened by success,

---

[119] *The Age*, August 1832; A. Aspinall, *Politics and the press* (1949), p. 342; Richards to Bute, 31 July, 26 August, 3 and 8 September 1832 (C.C.L., MS. 4.713).
[120] Letters of Richards, 1834 (ibid.) and of Bute, 1834 (N.L.W., B., 70, L. 6); N. Gash, op. cit., p. 173; M. Elsas, op. cit., p. 227.
[121] Letters, June and July 1837 (C.C.L., MS. 4.860); Bute to Richards, 13 October 1841, 26 August 1846 (G.R.O., D/DA 25 and 30); Richards to Bute, 27 June and 27 August 1846 (N.L.W., B., 70, L. 1845–46); Lord Bessborough, *Lady Charlotte Guest; extracts from her journal, 1833–52* (1952), pp. 121–22.
[122] Ibid., pp. 51–55; letters, December 1834, July and August 1837 in C.C.L., MSS. 4.713 and 4.860 and in N.L.W., B., 70, L. 6; note on the election of 1837 (ibid., 47).

Bute made plans to put up two Conservatives at the next election. Richards, however, advised caution. 'In the peculiar situation in which this county is placed in respect to Mr. Talbot and the Margam interest', he wrote in 1839, 'I doubt whether it would be advisable to start two candidates without losing both.'[123] Richards's advice was accepted and Talbot and Adare remained unopposed as members for Glamorgan until 1852.

The Reform Act of 1832, which had obliged Bute to find new methods of influencing parliamentary elections, was soon followed by the Municipal Corporations Act of 1835, which obliged him to find new methods of controlling the corporation of Cardiff. The commissioners appointed to enquire into the state of the municipalities visited Glamorgan in the autumn of 1833 and Richards was questioned for seven hours at Cardiff and for two at Llantrisant. The report portrayed Llantrisant as corrupt and dissolute and the act did not grant it full borough status. The corporation of Cardiff was described as having no identity of interest with the inhabitants and to be among those where everything was subordinated to political purposes. Bute resented these attacks and talked in the Lords of corporations which had felt aggrieved by the allegations of the commissioners and which were ready to refute them. He followed the passage of the act with close attention, co-operating with Wellington in preserving aldermen and other life interests.[124]

The act gave Cardiff a corporation consisting of a mayor, six aldermen and eighteen councillors, elected by all the occupiers of buildings rated to the relief of the poor. In some towns the act led to the transfer of power to new classes and new interests. Matthews seeks to invest the change in Cardiff with the character of a revolution, talking of the abolition of 'the last remnants of feudalism' and of Cardiff becoming 'suddenly . . . a municipality in the modern sense'. The evidence available hardly sustains his argument. Among the first acts of the new corporation was the appointment of Richards as its town clerk and although Nonconformists were increasing in

[123] Richards to Bute, 20 and 25 May 1839 (C.C.L., MS. 4.860).
[124] *P.P.*, XXIII (1835), 186–94, 221–24, 313–14; *Parliamentary debates*, third series, 29, p. 1422; Richards to Bute, 28 September and 2 October 1833 (C.C.L., MS. 4.713); Bute to Richards, 15 and 23 July, 19 and 21 August 1835 (G.R.O., D/DA 20).

number rapidly at Cardiff, the act did not lead, as it did for example at Leicester, to Nonconformist control of municipal affairs.[125]

The lack of any revolutionary change was exactly what Bute desired. He advised Richards to treat the act 'as of little consequence . . . I should hope that we may ultimately be able to bring the people to think as little of this as they do of the election of parish officers. The nearer we can bring them to this on the present occasion, the better.' The election of the new corporation took place in December 1835. Bute had made preparations for it since the previous August. 'You must endeavour', he told Richards, 'to keep good watch so that we are not surprised by the Radicals getting promises . . . it is advisable that we should put into our lists some of the most substantial among those persons whom we might generally be disposed to call *the other side* . . . You may depend upon it these substantial men are not sorry in the bottom of their hearts to find themselves separated from their pauper tail. I adopted this course in the election of the Guardians for Luton . . . I put the wealthiest Baptist in the Town, the most moderate of the Quakers and a friendly Methodist on my list. The radicals had a meeting for the express purpose of getting up a contest but the list was admitted to be so respectable that they were obliged to give up their intended agitation.' The same policy of 'making a virtue of necessity' was pursued at Cardiff and the list prepared by Bute and Richards was, with few exceptions, the list of those elected.[126]

The new corporation began energetically, drawing up plans for an improvement act and setting up a committee to investigate borough funds and lands. Bute was amused by its zeal. 'I am not surprised by the activity of your new town council', he wrote, 'but if they begin to make rates in proportion, they will soon become unpopular.' Within a few years, the vigour of the corporation had been dissipated and in many meetings in the late-1830s and the 1840s a quorum was not obtained.[127]

[125] J. H. Matthews, op. cit., V, p. 413; A. Briggs, *Victorian cities* (1963), p. 382.
[126] Bute to Richards, 19 and 20 August and 25 November 1835 (N.L.W., B., 70, L. 6). Compare J. H. Matthews, op. cit., IV, 471, with 'List of town councillors to be recommended' (N.L.W., B., 47).
[127] Bute to Richards, 21 January 1836 (ibid., 70, L. 6); J. H. Matthews, op. cit., IV, 418; 7 William IV, *cap.* XVIII.

Energetic or lethargic, the corporation continued to act according to Bute's wishes. 'Our six town councillors', wrote Richards in 1836, 'have been re-elected as your lordship determined', and in 1839 the marquess was informed that 'Mr. Davies, the surgeon, offered himself as a councillor and I have stated that your lordship would have no objection to his election and I therefore expect he will be elected without opposition.'[128] When the marquess died in 1848 his influence over the corporation of Cardiff, as well as over the town's parliamentary representation, seemed as secure an inheritance for his son as the estate itself.

Yet, it would be misleading to suggest that all that happened during the thirty-four years when the second marquess of Bute played a dominant role in the affairs of Cardiff was that, despite some difficulties and temporary embarrassments, his power and influence as a landed aristocrat were maintained and enhanced. Although he spent much time, money and energy on strengthening his interest, his efforts were, to a considerable extent, being counteracted by the forces which, during his lifetime, were transforming Glamorgan society. It was not solely the loss of his guiding hand which caused the web of influence which he had woven with such care to be unravelled so soon after his death. His own activities helped to undermine the political power of Cardiff Castle. Aristocratic control of small boroughs survived until the late-nineteenth century but, largely because of Bute's initiative in providing Cardiff with dock facilities superior to those of her neighbours, the town, by mid-century, was ceasing to be a small borough. Although the dock strengthened the Bute interest, the growth of Cardiff and its port gave rise to new interests, independent of the castle; most particularly, an assertive middle class arose with sufficient confidence to challenge aristocratic pretensions. As the town expanded, its income increased and as the sphere of the corporation's activities widened, it was inevitable that disputes would arise between it and the Bute estate. When

[128] Richards to Bute, 11 November 1836, 13 August 1839 (C.C.L., MS. 4.860); Bute to Richards, 5 November 1838, 11 November 1839 (N.L.W., B., 70, L. 6).

Cardiff expanded beyond its ancient boundaries and building took place on the land of other landowners, the shadow of the castle began to pale. Even the Anglican church and the Conservative party, on whose behalf the marquess had made such efforts, were soon to show that they found Bute benevolence irksome. Above all, opinion was turning against the whole concept of the rightful influence of landed possessions and of the deference due to aristocratic birth. Tentative beginnings can be seen in the revolt of the Cardiff burgesses in 1818. Thereafter, there was an undercurrent of opposition to the Butes; it came to the surface in 1832 and then was submerged again. Although Bute was sincerely mourned at Cardiff, his death marks the beginning of the end of Cardiff's tutelage.

GLAMORGAN AND THE THIRD MARQUESS, 1848–1900

In September 1849 the widowed marchioness of Bute brought her infant son to Cardiff for the first time since he had inherited his titles and estates. The visit was designed to make the greatest possible impact, for Lady Bute and the trustees were concerned to maintain the prestige and influence of the house of Bute in Glamorgan. From 1849 until her death in 1859, the marchioness, having succeeded in prising the castle from the grasp of her hated brother-in-law, spent lengthy periods at Cardiff where she sought to assume the role her husband had played in Glamorgan.[129] Although her establishment at the castle was modest, she fulfilled her duties as aristocratic patroness of Cardiff, presiding at the ball held to celebrate the opening of the new town hall in 1854 and regularly entertaining Sunday-school children to tea and presenting them with flannel and hymn books. She interested herself in the relationship between the estate and the industrial community in Glamorgan, urging that the freighters of Cardiff should have ample accommodation at the docks and ardently advocating the renewal of the Dowlais lease, fearing that failure in the negotiations would lead to an attack on the castle.[130] Acutely aware of the

---

[129] Lady Bute to Richards, 21 September 1849 (G.R.O., D/DA 33); letters, 1848–50, in ibid., 32 and 33, and Scot. P.R.O., H.B. MSS., 196–98.
[130] Accounts (N.L.W., B., 60); Lady Bute to Lloyd, 24 December 1853 (G.R.O., D/DA 36); *M.G.*, 9 June 1854.

deficiencies of the castle as a residence, she made some modifications to it and in 1854 began laying out a large garden on part of Plasturton farm on the west bank of the Taff. Between 1854 and 1863 some £1,500 was spent on what became known as the Sophia Gardens and in 1858 the public was granted free accesss to them.[131] The marchioness continued her husband's policy with regard to the Anglican church, concerning herself with the completion of All Saints, the Welsh church he had promised to build at Cardiff, subscribing generously to the costs of St. Andrew's church and showing strong feelings on the presentations to family livings. Like her husband, she considered a concern for the culture of Wales to be proper in an aristocrat, making plans to learn the Welsh language and seeking 'a Welsh-speaking companion for myself . . . to try in that manner to get on with that luckless language'. She subscribed to Iolo Morganwg's monument at Flemingston, assisted the Welsh college at Llandovery and was anxious to finance the publication of the works of Thomas Stephens and other Eisteddfod competitors.[132]

Yet, although Lady Bute patronised religious and cultural activities in Glamorgan, she could not from her own resources perpetuate the second marquess's structure of philanthropy, a structure which the trustees, doubtful of their authority to continue any subscriptions not secured by deed, also proved unable to sustain. It was a matter on which they felt vulnerable; 'the most successful issue of our Exertions', wrote McNabb, 'will be to accumulate wealth for parties whose wealth will at any rate be enormous while we are denied the compensatory comfort . . . of promoting the spiritual and intellectual improvement of the people residing on the Estates under our charge'. Later during the minority, the accumulation of wealth and the conviction that the heir would 'not tax them' for acts of generosity made them more confident.[133] In the 1860s, when Anglicans were feverishly seeking to complete

[131] Ibid., 15 March 1855; W. J. Trounce, *Cardiff in the fifties* (1918), p. 74; accounts (N.L.W., B., 73); Lady Bute to Bruce, 14 February 1850 (Scot. P.R.O., H.B. MSS., 198).
[132] Lady Bute to Richards, 29 October 1848, 17 August 1857 (G.R.O., D/DA 32 and 37); 30 May and 11 June 1853 (C.C.L., B., IX, 27, 21).
[133] McNabb to Bruce, 22 May 1848, Stuart to Bruce, 25 March 1850 (Scot. P.R.O., H.B. MSS., 196).

their network of national schools in order to forestall the
threatened provision of secular ones, the trustees gave several
thousan ls of pounds to the campaign. They were also generous
patrons of the church building boom of the third quarter of
the nineteenth century, subscribing almost £20,000 to the
building of new churches, the sums ranging from the £6,000
given to St. German's, Roath, to the £25 given to Christchurch,
Cyfarthfa. In addition, they built a home at the Bute Docks to
accommodate 110 seamen in order 'to keep them out of the
hands of land sharks'. Between 1853 and 1859, £7,500 were
spent on the home and, thereafter, its annual losses of £300
were covered by the trustees.[134] Nevertheless, during the
minority, donations to individuals ceased, subscriptions to
local societies were drastically reduced and the trustees declined
all invitations to preside at local festivities. By the 1860s, the
personally-administered philanthropy of the second marquess
had ebbed away and symptomatic of the contrast between his
relationship with the local community and that of the trustees
is a note written by General Stuart to Richards in 1863: 'Here
is another beg. Pray advise me on it'.[135]

Following Lady Bute's death in 1859, the castle ceased to
be used as a regular residence. Boyle, the most active of the
trustees, made lengthy visits to Glamorgan, but by the 1860s
there was no focus of Bute influence at Cardiff. The absence
of a castle establishment in that decade is indicated by a letter
of General Stuart: 'My carriage will arrive on Monday . . .
my butler with another man and my cook and kitchen maid
will arrive by steamer on Tuesday, a groom with my own
horse . . . and two riding horses from London on Wednesday.
We arrive on Thursday.'[136] Even if the second marquess had
lived until his son's majority, it is unlikely that the Cardiff of
the 1850s and 1860s would have bowed to his wishes as had
the Cardiff of the 1830s and 1840s, but the marked decline of
Bute political influence after the second marquess's death is
certainly in part attributable to the replacement of a conscientious and popular aristocrat by rather anonymous and alien

[134] C.C.L., B., X, 1–6 and MS. 4.937; accounts (N.L.W., B., 60 and 65);
W. J. Trounce, op. cit., pp. 26, 51; W. Turner, *The port of Cardiff* (1882), p. 84.
[135] Stuart to Richards, 20 and 22 November 1863 (G.R.O., D/DA 43).
[136] Ibid., 4 April 1863 (ibid.).

trustees. During the minority, the parliamentary representation of Cardiff was captured by interests hostile to the castle, Bute ascendancy over the town's corporation was eroded beyond recall and even the burgesses of Llantrisant threw off their old allegiance.

Within less than a year of the second marquess's death there were fears that castle domination of the representation of Cardiff was in danger. For health reasons, Nicholl had spent most of the late-1840s in Italy and in 1849 he informed the trustees that he wished to give up his parliamentary duties. The news caused consternation. 'There are no grounds for resigning the seat;' wrote Bruce, 'gratitude to Lord Bute and consideration for those left in charge of the family property ought to decide him not to put the family interest to hazard by opening the seat unnecessarily.' 'I beg you will ask Mr. Nicholl as a favour to our family', wrote Lady Bute, 'to abandon his idea of resigning if he has no other reason for doing so than conscientious motives towards his constituents.' Nicholl was prevailed upon to change his mind and in 1851, when it became obvious that the Bute interest would be challenged in the forthcoming election, he agreed to stand again.[137]

The challenge came from Cardiff's growing middle class. In 1851, four hundred of the town's thousand electors petitioned Walter Coffin, coalowner, unitarian and chairman of the Taff Vale Railway Company, to stand for parliament in the 'commercial interest'. Coffin had once been a close ally of the castle party and his acceptance of the invitation made him appear something of a renegade. In the Cardiff election of July 1852, while the ballot was mentioned and protestant prejudice was stirred by Nicholl's residence at Rome and his son's 'perversion to catholicism', the avowed aim of Coffin's supporters was 'to destroy the Bute interest in the Borough'. Those supporters included the 'wharf gentry', the radicals among Cardiff's professional and middle class and the increasingly influential Nonconformists of the town. Sir John Guest, although close to death, roused himself to instruct the Dowlais agents at Cardiff and the officials of the Taff Vale Railway Company to support Coffin and similar action was taken by

---

[137] Bruce to Richards, 27 February and 24 March 1849; Lady Bute to Richards, 7 March 1849 (G.R.O., D/DA 33); *Times*, 16 June 1851.

Crawshay with regard to the Cyfarthfa agents and the
employees of the Glamorganshire Canal Company. Bute
officials were reported to have used 'much intimidation and
undue influence' and the election proved lively; Nicholl was
attacked on the steps of the town hall and the chief constable,
coming to his aid, was wounded.[138] Coffin won by 498 votes
to 461. Cowbridge gave Nicholl the overwhelming majority of
eighty-seven to six and Llantrisant the ample one of 115 to
sixty-two, but Cardiff, 'Lord Bute's own Town', repudiated
the castle nominee by 410 to 259, causing the marchioness to
lament 'the ascendancy of revolutionary principles and the
abasement of the family'.[139] The new member proved inactive
and resigned the seat in 1857. In the Commons 'he declined
to risk his reputation as a speaker' and 'in opening the borough,
he felt he had fulfilled his mission'.[140]

With the loss of the seat in 1852, the Bute trustees made no
further attempt to sponsor a candidate at Cardiff until the end
of the minority. Apprehension concerning their intentions
remained strong, the founders of the *Cardiff Times* in 1857
declaring that they were establishing the paper 'to deliver the
borough from the degrading position of being a mere appanage
of the Bute estate'.[141] In that year, on the retirement of Coffin,
Colonel J. F. D. Crichton Stuart, who had inherited the
Liberal views of his father, Lord James Stuart, was elected
unopposed and was re-elected, again without opposition, in
1859 and 1865. Although dismayed by the increasingly radical
position into which Stuart was manoeuvred by the Liberals of
Cardiff, the trustees, uncertain of what the political opinions
of the young marquess would be when he reached manhood,
were reluctant to oppose the heir presumptive to the estate.

In 1868, the knowledge that the third marquess was a Tory
and the enthusiasm generated by the coming-of-age celebrations gave the trustees an opportunity to challenge Stuart. By
then, however, the population of Cardiff and its suburbs was

---

[138] Richards to Bruce, 14 March 1851 (Scot. P.R.O., H.B. MSS., 198);
I. Humphries, 'Cardiff politics, 1850–74', *Glamorgan Historian*, VIII (n.d.), 108;
C., 18 June and 10 July 1852; M. Elsas, op. cit., pp. 230–33; W. J. Trounce,
op. cit., p. 23.
[139] Lady Bute to Bruce, 8 August 1853 (Scot. P.R.O., H.B. MSS., 198).
[140] C. Williams, *A Welsh family* (1893), p. 185; I. Humphries, op. cit.,
pp. 108–9.
[141] *Merthyr Express*, 21 January 1888.

approaching 60,000 and to be successful a Conservative candidate needed to represent a wider segment of the town than that represented by the Bute estate alone. Nevertheless, the initiative in bringing forward H. S. Giffard, the future Lord Chancellor Lord Halsbury, as Stuart's Conservative opponent was that of the Bute trustees and agents. The election cost the Conservatives £10,000 and was fought with much bitterness, the Liberals making specific allegations of intimidation against Bute employees. Giffard lost by 2,055 votes to 2,501, and the trustees' ambition of presenting the young marquess with a client member of parliament as a twenty-first birthday present was foiled.[142]

A by-product of the 1868 election was the foundation of the *Western Mail*. Convinced by Giffard's argument that the Conservative campaign in 1868 had been 'hampered by the fact that we had no powerful press support', the trustees launched, on 1 May 1869, the first daily newspaper in Wales. Thus, just as the second marquess had established the *Merthyr Guardian* following electoral conflict with his brother, so his son's trustees established the *Western Mail*, following electoral conflict with his brother's son. Ostensibly the proprietor was L. V. Shirley, a partner in the legal practice of Luard and Shirley, successors to E. P. Richards, but the expenses of the venture were met by the Bute estate. The accounts show that £19,800 was spent on the paper between 1868 and 1871 and the third marquess later claimed that it had cost him a total of £50,000. It continued in Bute hands until 1877, when Shirley arranged for it to be sold to the editor, Lascelles Carr.[143] Under its new owner it continued to advocate the causes which had been championed by the Bute estate since the time of the second marquess, combining staunch Conservatism and support for the Anglican establishment with a wide coverage of Welsh cultural and national affairs.

Bute control of the corporation of Cardiff had survived the constitutional changes brought about by the reform of the

[142] I. Humphries, op. cit., pp. 109–17; *The Buteman*, 23 January 1869; *C.T.*, 30 March 1907.
[143] Lord Riddell, *The story of the Western Mail* (1927), p. 1; S. W. Allen, *Reminiscences, being a few rambling recollections of some people and things I have met with* (1918), pp. 94–95; C.C.L., B., X, 6; ibid., MS. 4.459; D. H. Blair, *John Patrick, third marquess of Bute, K.T., 1847–1900, a memoir* (1921), p. 80.

municipalities. What it did not survive was the greater self-assertion of the corporation which was a consequence of the widening of its activities and responsibilities. It was the issue of sanitary reform in particular which led to a breach between the estate and the town authorities for, at Cardiff as elsewhere, 'economic individualism in the hour of its triumph over the Corn Laws, found itself challenged by a sanitary doctrine that involved innumerable interferences with private property, often in fields in which it was strongly and profitably entrenched'.[144] The split began in the summer following the second marquess's death when over three hundred of the people of Cardiff died of cholera, the disease battening upon the squalor caused by the absence of an adequate sanitary system. Following a petition from the more radical element among the citizens, T. W. Rammell visited the town to enquire into its sanitary condition. Richards, as town clerk, did all in his power to impede Rammell's work, in particular resisting the suggestion that the Public Health Act of 1848 should be applied to Cardiff. The report, published in March 1850, drew an appalling picture of the town's sewerage and drainage systems, its water supply, its working-class housing and its burial grounds and urged that a local board of health should be constituted at once.[145]

Despite Richards's obstruction, the board was established in September 1850 and a medical officer of health appointed. Immediately, pressure was placed upon the trustees. They were ordered to cover drains, mend sewers, fence the dock feeder, cease depositing dock dredgings within the borough and expedite the drainage of new streets. In 1853, the trustees made plans to raise the level of the weir near the castle; the tone of the reaction of the board of health, when compared with the corporation's quiet acceptance, thirty years earlier, of the dock feeder which the second marquess had driven through the town, is some measure of the change which had taken place in the relationship between the town authorities

---

[144] G. M. Young and W. D. Handcock (eds.), *English historical documents, 1833–1874* (1956), p. 78.
[145] T. W. Rammell, *Report . . . on a preliminary inquiry into . . . the sanitary condition of the inhabitants of the town of Cardiff* (1850).

and the Bute estate.[146] In 1857, Richards came to the conclusion that his duties as Bute agent could no longer be combined with the office of town clerk. In resigning the clerkship he gave as his reason that 'circumstances have . . . arisen where the Council and the trustees are antagonistic to each other', and, he added ruefully, 'when I was appointed there was no Board of Health'.[147]

During the minority, antagonism did not lead to party political conflict, for council elections at Cardiff were not fought on party lines until the 1870s. The trustees lacked the second marquess's skill in corporation management and by the 1860s were standing aloof from the council's affairs, the *Cardiff Times* noting in 1864 that they 'have never yet been known to make use of their "interest" in this town to advance one side or another in a municipal contest'. Yet, despite this diffidence and despite recurrent tension, so closely entwined were the fortunes of the town and those of the owner of the docks that there were on the corporation men who would willingly uphold the cause of the family whose 'interest in the welfare of the town of Cardiff and the extension of its commercial progress is one and indivisible with the general weal'.[148] Nevertheless, the notion, so assiduously cultivated by the second marquess, that the interests of the Bute estate and those of the town were identical was rejected, and long before the minority was over Bute control over the corporation had been eroded beyond recovery.

In September 1868, the minority came to an end. The trustees saw the third marquess's coming of age as an opportunity to emphasise the prestige, power and benevolence of the Bute estate and staged celebrations on an enormous scale. Disraeli, who witnessed them, sought in his novel *Lothair* to interpret the motives of the trustees. ' "What I wish to effect", said Mr. Giles [Lothair's solicitor], "is to produce among all

---

[146] Letters, 1849–56 in G.R.O., D/DA 33–37, C.C.L., B., XI, 43, and Scot. P.R.O., H.B. MSS., 197–8; J. H. Matthews, op. cit., IV, 540–44.
[147] *M.G.*, 23 May 1857.
[148] *C.T.*, 14 October 1864; W. J. Trounce, op. cit., p. 47

classes an impression adequate to the occasion. I wish the lord and the tenantry alike to feel they have a duty to perform".[149] Celebrations lasted for a week and included balloon ascents, school fêtes, two concerts, two balls, two regattas, three public dinners and a firework display, the cost to the estate in Glamorgan exceeding £14,000. Special trains brought tenants and well-wishers from the Rhondda, Aberdare, Merthyr, Rhymney and the vale of Glamorgan; ministers of all denominations assisted in a lavish display of philanthropy and the corporation of Cardiff provided illuminations and triumphal arches. Similar rejoicings were held in Scotland, and Bute-men resident even in Australia marked the occasion with celebrations.[150]

To a man of the temperament and tastes of the third marquess of Bute, Cardiff with its expanding docks, its aggressive coal freighters and its booming industrial hinterland made little appeal. 'Athens and Assisi', he wrote, 'have spoilt me for anything else.'[151] It was rare during his adult life for him to spend any length of time at Cardiff and by the late-1870s his long absences from the town which was the source of the bulk of his wealth were strongly criticised. He played some part in the public life of Glamorgan and accepted office in a number of local organisations. At Cardiff he was president of the Provident Dispensary, the Savings Club and the Cricket Club, and chairman of the Benefit and Annuitants Society; in addition, he was a trustee of the Monmouthshire and South Wales Miners Permanent Benefit Society and Honorary Colonel of the Glamorgan Artillery Volunteers. He played a leading role in the National Eisteddfod held at Cardiff in 1883 and in 1888 was chairman of the Cardiff Chamber of Commerce. The climax of his public career came in 1890, when he was elected mayor of Cardiff, the first peer to be mayor of a major British town since the sixteenth century.

---

[149] B. Disraeli, *Lothair* (Bradenham edition, 1927), p. 90; *W.M.*, 10 October 1900.
[150] *M.G.*, September 1868; *Illustrated London News*, 19 and 26 September 1868; C.C.L., Box labelled Posters, etc.; MS. D. 321.51; B., IX, 27, 20, and X, 6, 3; *The Buteman*, September 1868 and 23 January 1869; J. H. Matthews, op. cit., IV, 458–60; D. H. Blair, op. cit., p. 57.
[151] M. E. Grant Duff, *Notes from a diary, 1851–72* (1897), II, 201.

These offices, however, were largely honorary, and apart from his philanthropic activities the third marquess's contribution to the community life of late-nineteenth century Glamorgan was slight. During his lifetime, he gave away many hundreds of thousands of pounds, most of the money, much to the *Western Mail's* annoyance, going to Scottish causes. Nevertheless, his benefactions in Glamorgan were numerous and impressive, although it is doubtful whether, in proportion to his gross income from the county, they approached the 7-8 per cent which his father had given to charities there. Among his major donations were £13,000 to rebuild the Hamadryad Hospital, £10,000 to University College, Cardiff, £10,000 to the drill hall, £5,000 to alleviate the distress caused by the failure of the Cardiff Savings Bank and almost £5,000 to the Monmouthshire and South Wales Miners Permanent Provident Society. He was generous to Catholic causes at Cardiff; he defrayed most of the expenses of Nazareth House and of the Convent of the Good Shepherd and made large donations to Catholic churches and schools. Despite his dislike of schismatics, he also assisted in the restoration of historic Anglican churches on condition that his subscription would not be used to provide 'the auxiliaries of Anglican worship'. His gifts of land at Cardiff included the site of the University College and the presentation to the town of Cardiff Arms Park, much of Roath Park and many squares and open spaces. He employed an almoner to deal with smaller charities and although details of these contributions are not available, the total disbursement was undoubtedly considerable. Such donations allowed him free rein to express his own tastes. In 1897, on the occasion of his silver wedding, he instituted a £1,000-fund to assist poor girls in Cardiff to marry, stipulating that the first eleven chapters of the Gospel of St. John should be read to the recipients.[152]

At Cardiff, the most impressive evidence of the third marquess's taste is the castle. Aware, even before coming of age, 'that the Castle is very far indeed from setting anything like an example in art', he had in 1865 commissioned Burges,

---

[152] *W.M.*, 10 and 21 October 1900; D. H. Blair, op. cit., pp. 219 and *passim*; *Cardiff tide tables and almanack* (1893), p. 133; J. H. Matthews, op. cit., V, 119, 136, 343–44; C.C.L., B., IX, 29.

the distinguished architect, to prepare a thorough report on its possibilities. From 1868 until his death in 1881, Burges was employed not so much to restore as to recreate the castle; the aristocrat and his architect, each dedicated to the same ideals of scholarship and romance, stimulated each other towards an extraordinary achievement, 'massive, learned and glittering'. The great clock tower with its luxurious summer smoking-room, the opulent oratory, the Chaucer Room and the Arab Room, executed in Burges's exquisite workmanship, all bear the strong impress of the marquess's personality, reflecting as they do his absorption in mediaevalism, orientalism, occultism and ecclesiasticism. The third marquess's work at Cardiff and his vast building activities elsewhere make him the most prodigious patron of architecture in nineteenth century Britain. 'I have', he wrote, 'a considerable taste for art and archaeology and happily the means to indulge them.' Those means came primarily from the Glamorgan estate, although evidence of the extent to which the profits of the estate were diverted into non-productive building is lacking. Corbett's accounts for 1872–73 list £4,417 spent upon the castle, but this is the sole item of such expenditure listed in the estate accounts.[153] The marquess's building programme was largely financed from his personal funds, themselves composed of an accumulation of the estate's surpluses; thus, much of the money transmitted from Glamorgan to the central Bute account in London returned to Cardiff to pay for the work of craftsmen and artists.

While the castle itself was being refurbished, its curtain walls were cleared of their accretions and the buildings of Angel Street, huddled between it and Duke Street, were demolished, thus allowing visitors to Cardiff, such as the young George Santayana, to appreciate the incongruity of a nobleman's seat at the heart of the world's coal metropolis, 'the living survival of mediaeval features, material and moral, in the midst of [modernity]'.[154] In 1887 the remains of the

[153] *M.G.*, 19 December 1868; accounts (N.L.W., B., 72); J. M. Crook, 'Patron extraordinary, John, third marquess of Bute, 1847–1900' in *Victorian south Wales, seventh conference report of the Victorian Society* (1970), pp. 6–10; M. Girouard, *The Victorian country house* (1971), pp. 125–30; W. Rees, op. cit., p. 170.

[154] G. Santayana, *Persons and places, the background of my life* (1944), pp. 137–38; 'Cardiff before 1890', *Glamorgan Historian*, I (1963), 104; J. H. Matthews, op. cit., V, 48; N.L.W., B., 27.

Franciscan friary, later the home of one of the branches of the Herbert family, were excavated and the outlines of the Dominican friary near the Taff were marked with low walls in 1888; in the 1890s the ruined north curtain wall of the castle was demolished and the foundations of the Roman fort laid bare. North of the castle, parts of five farms were thrown together to enlarge the park, thus providing Cardiff with the most extensive central parkland of any British city.[155] The third marquess's passion for building also found expression outside Cardiff. Between 1874 and 1888 Burges and Frame rebuilt the ruined Taff valley fortress of Castell Coch, an achievement of which it has been said that 'besides its integrity, the more famous restorations by Viollet-le-Duc at Pierrefonds and Carcassonne appear rather harsh and obviously modern'.[156] On a south-facing slope adjoining Castell Coch, the marquess laid out a vineyard and vines were also planted on the walls of Cardiff Castle and at Swanbridge. The 1893 vintage of forty hogsheads was considered superb and the experiment brought the marquess much renown and some profit.[157]

Although a staunch Tory, the third marquess's diffident personality and his preoccupation with travel, scholarship and architecture caused him to have little inclination or time for active intervention in local politics. He did, however, support the trustees' sponsorship of a Conservative candidate at Cardiff in 1868 and in the 1870s he allowed Shirley, his solicitor, publicly to commit the estate's interest to the Conservative cause. In 1868 Shirley established a Constitutional Association at Cardiff which, according to the *Cardiff Times*, 'kept alive in the town a bitter political feeling and by its interference with elections . . . its fêtes, mountebank performances and open debauchery in the Sophia Gardens has become obnoxious to all members of the community. Its object is to reduce Cardiff to a mere appanage of the house of Bute'.[158] The association

[155] J. Ward, 'Cardiff Castle, its Roman origin', *Archaeologia*, LVII (1901), 335–53; 'Roman Cardiff', *Archaeologia Cambrensis*, VIII (1908), 29–64, XIII (1913), 159–64, XIV (1914), 407–10; A. Pettigrew, *The public parks and recreation grounds of Cardiff* (1926).
[156] H. R. Hitchcock, *Architecture, eighteenth and nineteenth centuries* (1958), p. 188; G. T. Clark, 'Castell Coch', *Archaeologia Cambrensis*, IV (1850), 241–50.
[157] A. Pettigrew, 'The vineyard at Castell Coch', Cardiff Naturalists Society, *Report and Transactions*, XVI (1884), 6–11; D. H. Blair, op. cit., p. 120.
[158] *C.T.*, 31 January 1874; *W.M.*, 11 February 1874; Bradley to Shirley, 28 August 1871 (G.R.O., D/DA 48).

brought party organisation into the town's municipal elections, an example quickly followed by the local Liberals, causing the corporation by 1870 to be divided for the first time along partisan lines. The revival of an open coalition between the castle and the Conservative party, initiated in the general election of 1868 and sustained by Shirley's association, galvanised the opposition and the consequent controversy aroused the corporation from its previous 'culpable indifference and neglect'.[159]

By the mid-1870s, there were elements among the Conservatives of Cardiff who considered that too close an entanglement with the castle interest was harmful to their party's cause. At the 1874 election, however, that interest remained sufficiently powerful to insist that Giffard, rather than the Cardiff alderman preferred by many local Conservatives, should again be the candidate for Cardiff. By then, the Ballot Act of 1872 protected voters from open coercion, but the *Western Mail*, a powerful addition to the Conservative arsenal, believed that Cardiffians would support the Bute-sponsored candidate uncoerced in order to demonstrate their approval of the estate as 'the principal promoter of the prosperity of the town'.[160] Giffard succeeded in 1874 in reducing Stuart's majority to nine votes, but this was more a tribute to the revived fortunes of the Conservative party than to the influence of the Bute estate.

By the late-1870s, most Bute officials had come to believe that it was indiscreet to commit the Bute estate to public support of the Conservative party. Although Shirley continued to be active, the party had by 1880 emancipated itself from Bute domination, and its nomination of Sir John Guest's son Arthur as candidate for Cardiff in that year found little favour with the marquess's advisers. Nevertheless, their reluctant support of Guest was considered sufficient to make the result of the election doubtful.[161] In the event, the Liberal, E. J. Reed, a naval architect, defeated Guest by 3,831 votes to 3,483. After 1880, the Bute estate was only one of many

---

[159] M. J. Daunton, *Coal metropolis, Cardiff, 1870–1914* (1977), pp. 167–68.
[160] *W.M.*, 27 January, 11 and 14 February 1874; *C.T.*, 31 January 1874.
[161] Ibid., 9 October 1880; *W.M.*, 13 March 1880; *S.W.D.N.*, 13 March 1880; C.C.L., B., IX, 31; G.R.O., D/DA 50 and 51.

concerns at Cardiff supporting the Conservative cause, and although Reed made much of sinister Bute influence, this ceased to be a major factor in determining the town's parliamentary representation. In the December election of 1910, the seat was won by the third marquess's son, Lord Ninian, but his victory was that of the party and his link with the castle gave no more than an added lustre to his candidature.

Parallel with the erosion of the castle's sway over parliamentary representation was the decline of Bute influence over Cardiff's corporation. Between the coming of age of the third marquess and his death the population of Cardiff and its suburbs rose from 60,000 to 160,000. In the 1870s it won a decisive lead over all its Welsh rivals and this lead was confirmed and strengthened in the last decades of the century. The rapid growth in the population and wealth of Cardiff exhilarated its citizens. 'The rise of Cardiff', wrote one of them, 'more nearly resembles that of an American city . . . than that of a British. Its rapidity has probably been without parallel in the United Kingdom.' 'Cardiff', stated the corporation when congratulating Queen Victoria on her diamond jubilee, 'proudly terms itself a Victorian town.'[162] In 1888 the town was recognised as a county borough, in 1890 it received its own quarter sessions, in 1897 monuments to its civic greatness were begun at Cathays Park and in 1907 it became a city. In consequence, Cardiffians were imbued with pride and self-confidence, and although they acknowledged that their town's growth owed much to the initiative of the second marquess of Bute, they became increasingly impatient of any suggestion of castle dictation.

Bute control of the corporation had been lost in the 1850s, and by the 1880s it could not be assumed that even Conservative councillors or the *Western Mail* would automatically champion Bute interests. In the later-nineteenth century, few members of the corporation apart from McConnochie, the dock engineer, considered themselves apologists for the estate, yet there were among the forty councillors a number who were, particularly on issues relating to the dock, broadly sympathetic to the castle viewpoint. The corporation was

---

[162] J. Howells, op. cit., p. 218; J. H. Matthews, op. cit., V, 246.

dominated not by the commercial elite of shipowners and coal freighters, but by men drawn from the small business and professional classes. The former had no major investments within the town and their trade could, if necessary, be accommoted elsewhere, but the latter had an abiding concern for the prosperity of Cardiff and its docks and therefore a common interest with the Bute estate. The attitude of the corporation became a matter of central importance in the 1880s, when the estate was seeking support for the Bute Docks Bill of 1882 and allies in its fight against the Barry dock scheme. The Chamber of Commerce, dominated by the freighters, was opposed to the bill of 1882 and, in opposing plans for rival docks, the Liberals were lukewarm, their newspaper, the *South Wales Daily News*, established in 1872 as a counterweight to the *Western Mail*, commenting: 'It is not to be supposed that the coal trade of South Wales would be fatally injured . . . if Cardiff should come to a full stop'.[163] With the estate sponsoring dock candidates, the 1880s saw an effective revival of the Bute-Conservative coalition which led, in the middle of of the decade, to the capture of the corporation by the Conservatives. Their period of control was brief and when the party again won power at Cardiff in 1904, that power had no Bute dimension. Attempts to ensure that there would be a spokesman for Bute interests in the corporation continued into the twentieth century. The grounds upon which such influence was claimed had changed markedly since the time of the second marquess; it was as a major ratepayer rather than as lord of Cardiff Castle that the fourth marquess demanded a voice in the affairs of Cardiff.[164] Yet long before the third marquess's death, Bute influence over the corporation was a lingering remnant rather than a dynamic force. When the corporation invited him to be mayor in 1890 the unanimity of the decision suggests that even the radicals considered that there was no political danger in placing the leadership of the corporation in the hand of the marquess of Bute. It was only when aristocratic influence was a spent force that the prestige

---

[163] M. J. Daunton, op. cit., pp. 155–59; *S.W.D.N.*, 26 February, 5 March, 26 June and 16 August 1884; *Weekly Mail*, 18 February 1882; *C.T.*, 1 July 1882, 24 February 1883, 1 November 1884.
[164] M. J. Daunton, op. cit., pp. 169–71; *P.P.*, XII (1919), 654.

of the peerage could be exploited to further civic dignity. The marquess understood his position: 'They only elected me', he wrote, 'as a kind of figure-head'.[165]

In the course of the nineteenth century, there was a reversal of roles between the Bute estate and the corporation of Cardiff. The first and second marquesses had coveted the property of the corporation; the property of the third marquess was coveted by the corporation. At the same time there were those at Cardiff who were prepared to question his right to his estate. These attacks took an antiquarian turn and much energy was spent on researching into the existence of a manor of Cardiff, into the precise intention of Edward VI's grant to William Herbert and into the fate of the corporation lands. Local Liberal newspapers took a close interest in these investigations and insinuated that the Bute estate owed its origins to fraud. In 1893 the corporation resolved that all documents relating to its lands should be collected and published and it appointed J. H. Matthews to undertake the task. The result, which owed something to the academic assistance of the third marquess, was the six large, handsome and confused volumes of the *Cardiff Records*.[166] The publication did little to resolve the controversy which continued to agitate Cardiff until the First World War. By the twentieth century, however, the attack upon the Bute estate had developed beyond its antiquarian phase, and the calculated rudeness which the fourth marquess suffered at the hands of the Sankey Commission proved beyond doubt that the age of deference was dead.[167]

---

[165] D. H. Blair, op. cit., p. 174; J. H. Matthews, op. cit., V, 151; cf. D. N. Cannadine, 'From "feudal" lords to figure-heads', *Urban History Yearbook*, 1978, pp. 23–35.

[166] J. H. Matthews, op. cit., V, 176, 189, 194–96, 205, 212; case in the high court (N.L.W., B., 83); *S.W.D.N.*, 24 October 1892, 20 and 28 June 1894, 11 May 1895, 23 June 1907, 25 March 1910, 20 June 1914.

[167] *P.P.*, XII (1919), 653–58.

IV

AGRICULTURE AND THE BUTE ESTATE

INDUSTRY AND AGRICULTURE

When the Cardiff Castle estate first became linked with the house of Bute it was overwhelmingly agricultural. Brown's valuation of 1774, undertaken when the estate consisted of 11,211 acres, showed that of the total receipts of £2,797, some £400 represented cottage rents, manorial dues and miscellaneous payments; the rest, 84 per cent of the gross income, constituted farm rents. Fifty years later, on an estate of 16,700 acres, the situation was broadly similar. In 1822, total receipts were £9,417, of which £7,577 were farm rents and a further £1,082 were the proceeds of the sale of timber, wheat and hay. By the late-nineteenth century, however, the estate had undergone a profound transformation. When the third marquess came of age in 1868, the gross earnings of the estate stood at £109,659 and farm rents amounted to £8,450, a mere 7.6 per cent of the total. By the early-twentieth century, when mineral royalties alone produced over £120,000 a year, income from agriculture could hardly have been more than 4 per cent of the gross receipts.[1]

This change in the role of agriculture from a dominant position to a subsidiary, indeed almost a negligible, one has few parallels among the great estates of the United Kingdom.[2] But, although agriculture ceased to be of central importance to the estate, it did not suffer on that account. The massive growth in non-agricultural income allowed agriculture to be subsidised: rents were kept low, expenditure upon improvements continued throughout the depression of the late-nineteenth century and, when attacks upon the Bute estate gathered momentum in the 1880s, no mention was made of the agricultural estate.

[1] Valuation, 1774 (N.L.W., B., 104); schedule, 1868 (ibid., 140); accounts (ibid., 60).
[2] Compare the Lambton, Fitzwilliam and Devonshire estates (F. M. L. Thompson, *English landed society in the nineteenth century* (1963), pp. 256–58).

Industrialization and urbanization, in addition to being the sources of subsidies for agriculture, had other profound effects upon the farms of the Bute estate. By the 1820s, it was clear that land within the coalfield was destined in the near future for workers' cottages, surface mining operations and the disposal of industrial refuse. A substantial amount of Bute land in the valleys of northern Glamorgan was of considerable fertility but, in discussions on its future use, its agricultural value was discounted, Stewart in his survey recommending that no land improvement schemes should be undertaken within the coalfield. The withdrawal of Bute land from agricultural use was the most striking consequence of the growth of industry. It had been happening since the late-eighteenth century at the heads of the valleys, where many acres had been destroyed by industrial refuse and where the standard of farming on the large tracts of land leased by the ironmasters was notoriously bad. With the southward drift of industry and the urbanization of the valley floors in the mid- and late-nineteenth century further depredations took place. The rent of the farm of Pantygorddinan, Aberdare, for example, was reduced from £41 to £28 in 1848, when a third of its land was leased to Messrs. Wayne; in 1874, it disappeared from the rental altogether. Cwmsaerbren in the upper Rhondda valley, the site of the first pit to reach the steam coal seams, was whittled away until it consisted in the 1880s of a few mountain pastures.[3]

The construction of railways and the growth of Cardiff led to similar developments in the richer land of the coastal plain. While high prices were paid to landowners for land sold to railway companies, such payments were not all profit. The construction of the Taff Vale Railway ruined the 127-acre farm of Maendy which in 1844 was split up into accommodation land, and equivalent disruptions followed the building of the Rhymney and South Wales Railways. More far-reaching were the consequences of Cardiff's craving for land. The 405-acre farm of Adamsdown, let in 1826 for £504, had its rent reduced by £44 in 1827, £32 in 1847, £40 in 1860, £150 in 1870 and £20 in 1878; by 1880 only the rump of the holding

[3] C.C.L., MS. 4.850; rentals (N.L.W., B., 58, 74, 75 and 101).

remained. Plasturton Farm, let at £225 until 1830, was re-let at £155 in 1833, and by 1864, after the construction of Cathedral Road, the building of the Poor House and the laying-out of Sophia Gardens, it had ceased to exist as an agricultural unit and its remnants were divided into allotments. The proportion of the estate which was farmed declined sharply in the second half of the nineteenth century. In 1842, the agricultural estate consisted of 16,636 acres. Several thousand acres of land were acquired by the third marquess, yet in 1893 the total area let to agricultural tenants was 12,500 acres.[4]

The developments which were causing the withdrawal of Bute land from farming were also creating an enormous local market for agricultural produce. As early as 1796 John Fox had noted that the growth of Merthyr Tydfil was creating a demand for 'great quantities of the necessities of life', and by the 1830s Glamorgan, whose northern industrial districts had by then a population exceeding 100,000, had ceased to be self-supporting in basic foodstuffs. There were complaints that Irish corn was undercutting local produce and that 'the labourers in the works are not consuming the produce of the country', for seaborne corn from Ireland or indeed from west Wales, often shipped initially to Bristol, could, before the coming of the railways, be conveyed to Merthyr via Cardiff and the Glamorganshire Canal more cheaply than could the produce of the farms of the vale of Glamorgan.[5] Thus, at least in the first half of the nineteenth century, high transport costs restricted the impact of the new industrial markets upon those Bute farms, including some in the richer lands of the vale, which lacked easy access to the canal and the ports. Nevertheless, local meat and dairy produce commanded a ready market in the industrial areas, and in the second half of the nineteenth century the move towards the production of such commodities and away from corn growing was particularly marked in Glamorgan. The coalfield provided a steady market for local dairy products, the colliers remaining loyal to salt butter and farm-produced Caerphilly cheese long after tastes elsewhere

[4] Ibid.; *P.P.*, XXXVI (1894), 209; report, 1842 (N.L.W., B., 140).

[5] J. Fox, *General view of the agriculture of Glamorgan* (1796), pp. 7, 11; *P.P.*, V (1833), 10–23; *P.P.*, VIII (1836), 198–212; *P.P.*, V (1837), 69, 74–75, 133–36.

had turned to more standardized and packaged foodstuffs. 'Large colliery districts have sprung up', stated E. W. M. Corbett in 1893, 'requiring quantities of milk, cheese and so on; . . . this has to some extent counteracted the general depression.' The rise in the population of Cardiff, from 6,187 in 1831 to 18,351 in 1851, led the second marquess in the 1840s to raise the rents of farms in its vicinity on the grounds that the town was 'one of the most improving markets in the Kingdom'.[6] Market gardening, a rare occupation in nineteenth century Wales, was stimulated by Cardiff's growth. By 1836, the farm of Dobbin Pits, fertilized by town manure, provided the town with much of its fresh vegetables. Town manure (or night soil) provided a useful by-product of urbanization and, before Cardiff's sewerage system was completed in the 1850s, its availability was taken into consideration when fixing levels of rent. The growth of industry also created a market for hay and straw for colliery horses. By 1842, 8,000 tons of hay a year were being sent to Merthyr, and the impoverishment of the land resulting from its removal from the farm was frequently condemned by Bute agents. The collieries were even more insatiable in their demands for pitwood; the trade proved highly profitable and Bute woods were adapted to its needs.[7]

The availability of employment at the pits and furnaces of north Glamorgan ensured on the Bute estate the perpetuation of holdings which were incapable of providing a livelihood; at Llantrisant, Aberdare and Rhigos, in particular, there were many smallholdings whose tenants were industrial workers as well as small-time farmers. On the other hand, competition from relatively well-paid industrial employment created an acute shortage of agricultural labour in Glamorgan and caused the wages of farm workers in the county to be the highest in Wales and the third highest in Britain.[8] Farming in Glamorgan, therefore, was comparatively more costly than elsewhere, but

[6] Bute to Webb, 22 January 1845 (N.L.W., B., 70, L. 1845–46); *P.P.*, XXXVI (1894), 210; *P.P.*, XVII (1896), 302–10; C. S. Read, 'The agriculture of south Wales', *Journal of the Royal Agricultural Society of England*, X (1849), 132; D. W. Howell, *Land and people in nineteenth century Wales* (1978), pp. 118–20.
[7] Report, 1842; reports on Dobbin Pits, Maendy, and Cogan Pill (N.L.W., 140); J. D. Chambers and G. E. Mingay, *The agricultural revolution, 1750–1860* (1966), p. 64; see below, pp. 182–84.
[8] J. H. Clapham, *An economic history of modern Britain* (1950–52), II, 282; *P.P.*, XXXIV (1896), 620–31.

this was undoubtedly offset by the greater availability of markets. It has been claimed that non-cereal farms in the vicinity of large concentrations of population suffered little from the agricultural depression of the late-nineteenth century, a claim which the stability of rent and the low level of arrears on the Bute estate in the late-nineteenth century may help to corroborate. Yet, the difficulties which the second marquess encountered in seeking to modernise his estate must cast some doubt upon the degree to which Bute tenants, enmeshed in traditional practices and hampered by lack of capital, were able to take full advantage of the vast new markets created by industrialization and urbanization.

THE CONDITION AND ORGANISATION OF THE AGRICULTURAL ESTATE

East Glamorgan, within the confines of which lay the scattered Bute estate, offered a wide variety of farming terrain. While Adamsdown was situated virtually at sea level, Bute farms at Blaenrhymney contained large tracts lying at altitudes of over 1,500 feet. The annual rainfall at Swanbridge was thirty-five inches while at Bailyglas near Rhigos it approached a hundred inches. Of the estate as it existed in 1824, some 30 per cent, about 5,000 acres in all, lying around Cardiff and in the vale of Glamorgan, came within what the Land Utilisation Survey defined as good quality farmland. Of such land, none was of first class character but the 2AG general purpose category of the Survey was well represented, consisting largely of clay loams derived from lias limestone. Natural drainage on the whole was good, although the Cardiff and Leckwith Moors were of a character closer to that of the Gwynllŵg and Caldicot levels, whose agricultural usefulness depended upon the efficiency of their drainage systems. Up to the mid-nineteenth century this part of Glamorgan concentrated heavily upon the growing of wheat, although as early as 1801 its crop combination patterns were such as to allow Professor Thomas to define it as one of the few regions of ingressive agriculture in Wales.[9]

[9] L. D. Stamp, Land Utilisation Survey of Britain, Map, Great Britain, sheet 2 (1944); D. Thomas, *Agriculture in Wales during the Napoleonic Wars* (1963), pp. 93–94; J. F. Rees (ed.), *The Cardiff region, a survey* (1960), *passim*.

About a third of the estate lay within the category of medium quality land. Farms within this classification included those of the border vale around Llantrisant where land, although ill-drained, was often of high potential fertility. This was a dairying district but it contained farms such as Henstaff and New Park, where over a third of the land was under the plough in the 1820s. Areas of medium quality land also extended in elongated tongues up the valleys of the Taff and the Cynon and included meadows on the valley floors which, although liable to waterlogging, yielded up to three crops of hay a year. The rest of the enclosed estate, some 6,500 acres, consisted of poor quality mountain land, the coarse pastures of its leached soil sustaining a sparse population of sheep and store cattle. By the mid-nineteenth century, much of this land, particularly between Merthyr and Rhymney, had been ruined by industrial refuse; elsewhere such despoliation had not yet begun, a traveller writing of the Rhondda in 1848: 'The people of this solitudinous and happy valley are a pastoral race, almost entirely dependent on their flocks and herds for support . . . The air is aromatic with wild flowers and mountain plants—a sabbath stillness reigns'.[10]

The agricultural land of the Bute estate was not a unit of production. Apart from the great enterprise of dock-building, the marquesses of Bute were loath to exploit their estates directly. There was a Bute home farm in the late-eighteenth century and the farm of Mynachdy, bought in 1804, was kept in hand until 1814, but the first marquess's interest in direct farming was minimal.[11] The second marquess was adamant in his refusal to farm his own land. Richards, whose interests were legal rather than agricultural, agreed with him, but Corbett, the trained agriculturalist, was eager to establish model farms 'in order to obtain the most beneficial mode of cropping suitable to the soil and climate'. He did not, however, succeed in persuading Bute to accept his plan of taking the farms of Swanbridge and Parc Coedmachen in hand, and during the second marquess's lifetime the amount of land in

[10] G.R.O., D/DB E 1 and 2; C. F. Cliffe, *The book of south Wales, the Bristol Channel, Monmouthshire and the Wye* (1847), p. 85; D. W. Jones, *Hanes Morgannwg* (1874), p. 189.
[11] C.C.L., B., X, 11; report on Mynachdy (N.L.W., B., 140); Cardiff Castle day bills (G.R.O., D/DA 56–117).

hand, excluding the woodlands, consisted of little beyond the immediate environs of the castle.[12] The third marquess extended the castle grounds until they consisted of several hundred acres but, although the pastures of the park were grazed, the function of the cattle was decorative rather than economic.

Thus, in common with the vast majority of the landowners of the United Kingdom, the marquesses of Bute were, with regard to their agricultural land, rentiers rather than entrepreneurs. In 1774 there were, within the 11,211 acres of enclosed land of which the estate was then constituted, a total of 145 tenancies over five acres. By no means all of these were farms in any meaningful sense. In parts of the vale of Glamorgan, in particular, Bute lands consisted of unconnected and fragmented fields. Many of the tenancies were of tracts of land rented by a tenant who, in some cases, held his house and main farm of another landlord.[13] In addition to such by-takes, about 10 per cent of the rented acreage of the estate was specifically let as accommodation land. Such had always been the use made of the Cardiff and Leckwith Moors, some thousand acres in all, which in the mid-eighteenth century had been leased almost in their entirety to the Mathews family of Llandaf, and had, through neglect, become overgrown and waterlogged. The second marquess bought out the leases, draining and subdividing the land in order to have something to offer the people of Cardiff, an action which underlines the essential rurality of the town in the 1820s.[14] The burgesses of Llantrisant were similarly provided for when the dilapidated 193-acre farm of New Park was divided into small plots in 1824.[15] When, in the early-1830s, allotments came to be seen as the answer to rural destitution, Richards was asked to seek suitable sites in all parts of the estate. At Rhigos, where there

[12] Vouchers (ibid.); C.C.L., B., IX, 59, X, 11–13; Bute to Corbett, 6 April 1842 (N.L.W., B., L. 7); Corbett to Bute, 15 March 1842, 1 and 9 May 1844 (ibid., L. Corbett 1841–45).
[13] Valuation, 1774 (ibid., 104); report, 1842 (ibid., 140); G.R.O., D/DB E 1; The National Farm Survey of England and Wales, A summary report (1944), pp. 7–8.
[14] Rentals (N.L.W., B., 73–75); note on the repurchase of the Lequeth lease, 1824 (ibid., 74); Bute to Richards, 19 January 1825 (G.R.O., D/DA 12).
[15] Richards to Bute, 18 November 1831 (C.C.L., MS. 4.713); Edmunds to Bute, 10 February 1826 (N.L.W., B., 141, 5).

was a major rearrangement of farms, sixty acres were divided into two-acre plots for the poor of Hirwaun, and at Roath and Leckwith a number of twenty-perch allotments was created. Bute's interest in providing land for the poor won considerable renown and he was one of the three landowners singled out for special praise in a book on the subject by an Essex clergyman.[16] In the late-nineteenth century, the whole of the Cardiff Moors was swallowed up by the docks, but the proportion of the agricultural acreage of the estate let as accommodation land increased as urbanization and industrialization caused the progressive fragmentation of farms.

The evidence available for the late-eighteenth century makes it difficult to be precise concerning the size of the farms on the Bute estate. Acreages fluctuated, particularly in northern Glamorgan where some tenants were losing fields of old enclosed land which, through neglect of fencing, were reverting to the waste while others were adding to the acreage of their farms by surreptitious enclosure of the common. In the mid- and late-eighteenth century large areas of the estate were leased to tenants who then sub-let individual farms to the actual cultivators of the soil. The Mathews family, lessees of the Cardiff Moors, had in 1750 also leased five farms in the parish of Leckwith, while by 1801 Bradley, Bird's predecessor as Cardiff's post master, held the farms of Splott, Adamsdown and Whitmore, together with fields at Cathays and elsewhere. The Dowlais Company, in addition to its leases of the minerals of the Senghennydd Common, had leased most of the Bute farms in the upper Rhymney valley and had also sub-let farms from Bute tenants. The Aberdare Iron Company held 700 acres in the Cynon valley, and Messrs. Tappenden were tenants of numerous farms in the Hirwaun area. In the Rhondda, the Lewis family held five Bute farms while Thomas Edwards held three at Rhigos.[17] In consequence, there was on the estate as elsewhere in Glamorgan, a high degree of sub-letting, Murray claiming in 1833 that in the county the practice was two or even three deep. At Rhigos, in particular, some tenants had

---

[16] Ibid., 13 February 1828 (ibid.); Richards to Bute, 10 December 1830, 18 November 1831 (C.C.L., MS. 4.713); J. H. Clapham, op. cit., I, 472–73; A. Pearson, *Some account of a system of garden labour* (1831), p. iii.

[17] C.C.L., MS. 4.850; N.L.W., B., 73–75; Richards to Bute, 15 July 1830 (ibid., 141. 5).

sub-let their land by the field and had allowed the farmhouse and outbuildings to fall into ruin.[18]

For the 1820s, following the preparation of Stewart's superb atlas and terrier of the estate, it is possible to obtain a far clearer picture of the Bute farms. The terrier lists a total of 251 tenants renting tracts of land exceeding five acres in extent. Of these, 117 were holders of accommodation land varying from five to ten acres and situated upon the 1,025 acres of the Cardiff and Leckwith Moors. Of the remaining 134 tenancies, the plans of fifty-four of them do not indicate the existence of a farmhouse and these holdings must therefore be regarded as appendages to the farms of freeholders or to those of tenants of other landowners. Such by-takes were ill-regarded by the second marquess's agents, for the tenants usually carried all the crops away and their eradication was a central feature of Bute's programme of reform. Particularly prevalent around Llantrisant and Llantwit Major, they were often very extensive, five of them exceeding a hundred acres and one, the Clunyfelin sheepwalk at Llanwynno, consisting of 272 acres. Accommodation land on the Moors and by-takes elsewhere accounted in 1824 for 3,407 of the 15,245 acres of the rented land of the estate. The remaining 11,838 acres were divided among eighty tenants holding what may be considered to be farms in the full sense. Not all these tenancies were those of individual farms, for the practice of leasing large blocks of land, prevalent in the eighteenth century, had not been wholly discontinued by 1824. Thus, the eighty tenancies included the Rhymney Iron Company's lease of five farms extending over 829 acres at Carno and the Aberdare Iron Company's lease of eight farms extending over 836 acres in Cwm Cynon, both cases involving extensive sub-letting.

The remaining seventy-eight tenancies appear to have been held by the direct cultivators of the soil. These tenancies were not synonymous with farms, and farms were not synonymous with tenancies. A number of the farms listed in the rentals were, in fact, held by several tenants, Plasturton, Ynyston and Bailyglas, for example, each being rented in 1824 by two tenants apiece. On the other hand, a number of separately listed farms

---

[18] Note on Carnygist (ibid.); *P.P.*, V (1833), 10–13; C.C.L., MS. 4.850; Richards to Bute, 15 November 1834 (ibid., 4.713).

were held by a single lessee, the farms of Blaengwrelych, Blaengwrangon and Gwrangon Ganol at Rhigos, for example, being rented by the same cultivating tenant. Tenancies were more meaningful than farms; yet a Bute tenancy consisting perhaps of a number of farms did not necessarily constitute an entire unit of production. Mary Morgan, tenant of 311 acres of Cogan farm in the 1840s, also rented twenty-three acres of glebeland, forty-eight acres of the Cefn Mabli estate and seven acres belonging to Sir George Tyler, while elsewhere on the estate rights of pasturage on the waste could expand a tenant's farming activities far beyond that which could be sustained on the acreage of enclosed land he rented. Taking the seventy-eight Bute tenancies of 1824 which can be considered to represent the major part, if not in all cases the whole, of an agricultural unit, their average size was 132 acres. This average was swollen by the existence of five sheep holdings exceeding 400 acres, the median acreage of the seventy-eight tenancies being eighty-seven. The difference between the size of Bute farms in the uplands and the lowlands was not very marked. The average acreage of the thirty-seven farms lying to the north of Llantrisant was 146 acres while the forty-one to the south averaged 119 acres apiece.[19] Indeed, the Bute agents, while anxious that there should be some large prestige farms in the neighbourhood of Cardiff, sought to restrict the size of upland farms in the belief that it would be impossible to attract farmers with sufficient capital for a substantial farm to the remoter areas of northern Glamorgan.[20]

In common with most of the estates of south Wales, the Cardiff Castle estate clung to long leases for agricultural land after they had ceased to be granted elsewhere. Arthur Young believed that leases for a period of years were a necessary condition for investment by the tenant in his land and other agricultural writers of the eighteenth century agreed with his contention. The rapid rise in rents in the late-eighteenth century, however, made landowners reluctant to grant long leases at fixed rents and by 1800 a progressive estate, such as that of Faenol in Caernarfonshire, had converted all its

[19] G.R.O., D/DB E 1 and 2.
[20] Richards to Bute, 17 March 1829 (C.C.L., MS. 4.713); Corbett to Bute, 9 November 1844 (N.L.W., B., 70, L. Corbett 1841–45).

leaseholders into tenants-at-will.[21] When the Glamorgan estate became linked with the Bute family, only £997 of the total rental of £2,797 was paid by tenants holding by the year and two-thirds of the income from longer leases was paid by tenants who had leases of two or three lives or ninety-nine years. The marriage settlement of 1766 gave specific powers to grant such leases and these powers were used, for the last lease of three lives did not expire until the second half of the nineteenth century. In the late-eighteenth century, the Bute agents became increasingly reluctant to grant long leases, following the advice of Brown, the author of the survey of 1774, who pointed out that lands let from year to year produced 4 per cent return on their value while those on long leases produced only 3·2 per cent.[22] Stewart's terrier of 1824 provides detailed information on Bute tenurial arrangements; the most recent three-life lease of a substantial holding listed by him is that of the 454-acre farm of Abergorci in the Rhondda, granted in 1788. There were by the 1820s no farm leases for lives in the neighbourhood of Cardiff and only two in the vale of Glamorgan; in the uplands, however, there were thirteen three-life leases of extensive farms still in existence in 1824.[23]

Stewart urged a rigid adherence to annual leases within the coalfield in order to ensure maximum flexibility in dealing with mineral property, and he attacked the granting of life leases, which before 1832 was the main method available to a landowner wishing to manufacture county votes, as an example of the subordination of agriculture to politics. For the coastal plain Stewart advocated twenty-one-year leases and until the 1840s the marquess was prepared 'to allow a man of capital and a good agriculturalist a lease not under fourteen years or over twenty-one years', although he became increasingly reluctant to grant such leases in the immediate vicinity of Cardiff.[24] In 1842 Poundley recommended the abandonment of leases beyond a year on the ground that 'yearly tenure is

[21] J. D. Chambers and G. E. Mingay, op. cit., p. 46; D. Williams, *The Rebecca Riots, a study in agrarian discontent* (1955), pp. 62–67; D. W. Howell, op. cit., p. 59; report, 1842 (N.L.W., B., 140).
[22] Valuation, 1774 (ibid., 104); marriage settlement of Lord Mountstuart (ibid., 137, 1).
[23] G.R.O., D/DB E 1 and 2.
[24] Ibid.; C.C.L., MS. 4.850; ibid., B., IX, 37; Bute to Corbett, 20 January 1844 and 6 January 1845 (N.L.W., B., 70, L. 7).

better than long leases because it keeps up a friendly intercourse between landlord and tenant'.[25] His advice was heeded; by 1868 almost all the agricultural land was let on annual tenancies, suggesting that twenty-one-year leases had ceased to be granted at least by the late-1840s. All such leases had disappeared by the late-nineteenth century. The Royal Commission on Land in Wales was informed in 1894 that the whole of the Bute estate was held on yearly tenancy. No leases of lives of a whole farm were granted after the second marquess inherited his estates, although tenants continued to ask for them. Some tenants on long leases were bought out before their leases expired, while those who continued as life tenants until the end of their term almost invariably left their farms in a deplorable condition.[26]

Much has been made of the insecurity of tenure resulting from the substitution of annual tenancies for long leases. On the Bute estate, however, there is no evidence that the change led to a greater turnover in tenants. The Royal Commission on Land in Wales was informed in 1894 that there was practically hereditary succession among the agricultural tenants of the Bute estate.[27] The evidence of the rentals, however, suggests that hereditary succession over several generations was rare. Evidence is available on the succession of tenants on fifty farms from 1800 to 1886 and not one of them was held throughout the period by an unbroken succession of tenants bearing the same surname, although on a number of farms there was hereditary tenure in the male line for part of the period. Taking the fifty farms together, eighteen tenants of the same surname followed each other on one occasion, twelve on two occasions, four on three occasions and one on five occasions between 1800 and 1886; fifteen of the fifty farms have no example of a tenant being followed by another of the same surname. There was no marked difference in the prevalence of hereditary tenure between the uplands and the lowlands. Indeed, if anything, it was more prevalent in the neighbourhood of Cardiff. Blue House, Llanishen, purchased in 1826,

[25] Report, 1842 (ibid., 140).
[26] Schedule, 1868 (ibid.); Richards to Bruce, 6 January 1825 and 23 May 1829 (C.C.L., MS. 4.713); P.P., XXXVI (1894), 209.
[27] Ibid., p. 206.

remained in the hands of the Wride family thenceforward until the series of available rentals ends in 1886, an example which can hardly be matched by any upland farm. The high turnover of tenants and of families of tenants in the uplands of Glamorgan appears not to be typical of Wales as a whole. Almost all the Bute farms in northern Glamorgan were located near industrial undertakings and alternative employment for tenants' sons was readily available. The prevalence of continuity of tenure on the fertile and better-managed lowland farms may reflect the greater pride taken by the tenants in their holdings and consequently their stronger desire to keep them within the family.[28]

A concomitant of some degree of hereditary tenure was the existence of a number of female tenants. Listed in the rentals for the period from 1800 to 1886 are thirty-eight female tenants, representing about 16 per cent of the total. The woman generally succeeded a tenant of the same surname, presumably her husband, being in turn succeeded by a male tenant of the same surname, presumably her son. The average length of such tenancies was eight years, doubtless the interval between the death of the husband and the maturity of the son. There is some evidence that farms held by women were badly managed, and the second marquess bought back a number of such leases and gave pensions to widowed yearly tenants who gave up their holdings.[29]

Although tenants' sons may not have been over anxious to succeed their fathers, the evidence available suggests that most tenants continued in possession of their holdings until they died. Examples of eviction are rare and examples of capricious eviction non-existent. Where industry and urbanization had encroached upon a farm to such an extent that it could no longer provide a livelihood, the tenant was, of course, obliged to leave, but efforts were made to reduce the number of dispossessed farmers by drawing together the remnants of a number of farms into one or two viable holdings. In parts of northern Glamorgan afforestation caused the disappearance of several farms, while at Rhigos, where investment in the

[28] *P.P.*, XXXIV (1896), 290–97; N.L.W., B., 58, 74, 75 and 101.
[29] Reports on Hendre Fawr and Bailyglas (ibid., 140); Bute to Richards, 11 November 1839 (ibid., 70, L. 6).

numerous decrepit holdings was unlikely to bring a return, the second marquess was anxious to evict pauperised tenants. The coal-mine he sank there was established largely in order to draw tenants away from agriculture to industry.[30] Bute was an ardent advocate of emigration from distressed rural districts, and in 1832 he informed the officers of the parishes of northern Glamorgan that he would assist 'in sending out poor persons desirous of emigrating to America', promising to give up to sixpence per acre, according to his property in the parish, for that purpose.[31] Some farmers were evicted for flagrantly breaking their agreements. The agents of the first marquess proceeded against the tenant of Carnygist in 1790 because 'the undertenant for this year has sold part of his corn and sent all his cattle into Breconshire'. At Nantygwina in 1827 the tenant was evicted because he had under-let land at a profit and the tenant of Coedygwina suffered the same fate in 1843 because he had sold all his stock.[32]

The most common cause of eviction was inability to pay the rent. There were a number of insolvency cases among Bute tenants in 1820–23 and in 1823 Bird reported that 'there is scarcely any money to be got at present from persons of any description . . . nine out of ten of the debtors of Lord Bute would thank his lordship to order their incarceration that they might take the benefit of the Insolvent Act and begin *de novo*'.[33] In 1829–31, the problem again became widespread, Richards declaring that 'I have never before remembered such a depression amongst all classes; our town is nearly in a state of perfect insolvency'.[34] Matters improved in the mid-1830s, but isolated examples of insolvent tenants do occur later in the century.[35] Landowners always sought to obtain rent arrears before a tenant had reached a state of bankruptcy, for although the landowner had preferential claims upon the estate of a

[30] Rental of Celyn (ibid., 101); reports on Rhigos farms (ibid., 140); see below, pp. 218–19.

[31] Bute to Richards, 16 May 1832 (C.C.L., MS. 4.713), to Webb, 15 March 1844 (N.L.W., B., 70, L. 1840–44).

[32] C.C.L., MS. 2.716, 31 (sic)September 1790; note on the rental of Coedygwina (N.L.W., B., 74); Richards to Dalrymple, 30 January 1827 (ibid., 70, L. 1825–36).

[33] Bird to Collingdon, 13 February 1823 (ibid., L. A).

[34] Richards to Bute, 27 June 1829 (C.C.L., MS. 4.713).

[35] E.g., Cefn Tilcha, 1836, Cefnyporth, 1840, Llandaf Mill farm, 1876 (N.L.W., B., 74, 75 and 101).

debtor and could, by means of a distress, seize the goods of a defaulting tenant without legal process, delay could mean that only a proportion of the arrears would be recovered. This happened in the case of the tenant of Cefn Tilcha, where arrears of £33 were lost in 1836, while in 1833 the tenant of Clunyfelin, having been imprisoned for debt, was unable to pay more than 10s. in the £ of his arrears of £44 10s.[36]

Bute tenants were generally allowed to default on their rent for up to three years before action was taken, but the second marquess disliked this latitude and put pressure on his agents to demand prompt payment. He abided, however, by their advice that the issuing of notices to quit on a large scale after a poor audit in a depression year would result in widespread ruin. Thus, notices to quit as a preliminary to a distress were issued only as a last resort. 'I enclose a list of notices to quit I have served', wrote Corbett in 1843. 'I have chosen the worst. Many others are in arrears but they have made promises and I think they are honestly inclined. I trust your lordship will not think that I have done wrong by not serving them notices to quit considering the low prices tenants get for their produce.'[37] A reluctance to insist upon all that the law allowed was characteristic of the Bute agents when carrying out a distress. The tenant of Fferm Wen, whose arrears amounted to £99 in 1829 and whose stock was distrained, was allowed to retain goods worth £35 because 'he has behaved very well'; the entire possessions of the tenant of Ystradfechan were seized in lieu of rent in 1830 but he was allowed to keep his furniture as 'his family are in a wretched state'; the arrears of the tenant of Cogan exceeded the value of her stock by £93 in 1835, but on departing she was allowed to take her two best cows with her.[38]

New tenants were recruited by the estate either through direct application or through recommendation by neighbouring landowners. Applicants were often relations of existing tenants and the estate operated a form of promotion whereby tenants who had proved themselves on smaller farms

[36] Ibid.; *P.P.*, XXXIV (1896), 543.
[37] Corbett to Bute, 26 July 1843 (N.L.W., B., 70, L. Corbett 1841–45).
[38] Note on the rental of Fferm Wen (ibid., 74); Richards to Bute, 28 January 1831 and 14 February 1835 (C.C.L., MS. 4.713).

were encouraged to take over larger ones. Accommodation land was let by auction on occasion but there is no evidence that such a procedure was ever followed in the letting of farms.[39] Richards and Corbett went to great lengths to obtain full particulars of a prospective tenant and if satisfied they forwarded the name to the second marquess or, later, to the trustees for approval. In selecting tenants, Bute's main criteria were that they should be capable farmers and men of capital. Despite his staunch Toryism and his fervent attachment to the established church, there is no evidence that he rejected applicants on political or religious grounds. When arranging to let Llandaf Mill farm in 1836 he wrote, 'I must confess that [the applicant] is a radical who might do mischief if the great body of my tenants were not too sound to be corrupted'.[40] The proposed tenant was a capable farmer with some capital and was therefore accepted. The financial resources of applicants for larger farms were examined in some detail and if they were found to be insufficient, a surety who would guarantee the rent was demanded. These sureties were closely scrutinised and in some cases 'more responsible names' were demanded.[41] For the very largest farms the second marquess sought tenants from England, for his opinion of Welsh farmers was not high. In 1845 he asked the agents of the North estate at Kirtling to assist him 'in placing upon my farm of Swanbridge an English farmer of the best class'. On occasion, farms to let were advertised in 'the Bristol paper—such a paper being a good channel to obtain a desirable tenant'. The number of tenants recruited from outside Wales, however, cannot have been large; throughout the century Welsh surnames were in the overwhelming majority among Bute tenants.[42]

When a tenant left a Bute farm there was a well-established system of assessing the compensation due to him for any

[39] Notes on rentals (N.L.W., B., 58, 74, 75 and 101); Bute to Richards, 19 January 1825 (G.R.O., D/DA 12).
[40] Bute to Richards, 4 February 1836 (N.L.W., B., 70, L. 6).
[41] Richards to Bute, 20 February and 5 March 1828, 5 February 1829 (C.C.L., MS. 4.713).
[42] Bute to Webb, 22 January 1845 (N.L.W., B., 70, L. 1845–46). Of over 250 tenants listed in the rentals only twenty-two bear English surnames; all farmed in the immediate neighbourhood of Cardiff and most belonged to old-established Glamorgan families.

improvements he had undertaken, the value of which had not been exhausted. The Bute estate lay wholly within those areas of central and east Glamorgan where the Custom of Glamorgan prevailed. The authors of the report of the Royal Commission on Land in Wales believed that the Custom of Glamorgan, which was the only well-ascertained custom of compensation for unexhausted improvements in Wales, evolved during the first half of the nineteenth century.[43] By the 1890s there was in Glamorgan a complex system for payment of compensation by an incoming tenant to an outgoing tenant for a wide variety of unexhausted benefits arising from the latter's culti-vation of the soil. Both tenants appointed valuers, the compen-sation usually did not exceed two years' rent and did not cover construction, enlargement or repair of buildings. This was precisely the practice on the Bute estate from the 1820s onwards and the custom, whose eastern and western boundaries are virtually those of the Bute manors, may owe something to Bute practice. A typical agreement over crops was that made at Fferm ganol, Leckwith, in 1823, whereby the outgoing tenant was to have two-thirds and the ingoing tenant one-third of the crop of wheat in the ground; the latter was to pay the former the cost of reaping, the cost of clover seeds planted and one shilling an acre for harrowing them in.[44] The payments were an arrangement between the two tenants, and the land-lord was generally not obliged to interfere. The efficient operation of the system was, however, a matter of concern to him for, if the ingoing tenant refused to pay, the outgoing tenant could sue the landlord in court. Thus, in 1844, when the outgoing tenant of Swanbridge demanded compensation of £1,185 and the prospective tenant refused to give more than £650, Bute, having failed to get them to compromise, with-drew the offer of the farm. The custom of the Bute estate did not include compensation for buildings and the second marquess was unwilling to consider such claims, especially if the buildings had been erected without his express authority. On occasion, however, he was prepared to make an *ex gratia* payment if the outgoing tenant proved obdurate 'for the sake

[43] *P.P.*, XXXIV (1896), 483–85.
[44] Agreement, 1823 (N.L.W., B., 140).

of closing the final settlement . . . pleasantly'.[45] Bute approved
of the system, for he was anxious to attract farmers whose
standard of farming would deserve compensation. Incoming
tenants with little capital found it burdensome and in 1829
the marquess himself compensated the outgoing tenant of
Rhydypennau on the understanding that the new tenant
would make no claims when he left. Possibly in order to make
sure of their compensation, there was a tendency for tenants,
in the last years of their tenancy, to run up arrears equivalent
to their claims; in 1842, for example, the outgoing tenant of
Parc Coedmachen offset his arrears of £329 with claims for
compensation amounting to £350. When the Agricultural
Holdings Act came into operation in 1883, the Bute estate
contracted out, preferring the custom of Glamorgan, which
according to informed opinion in the county was superior to
the custom of Lincolnshire upon which the Act was based.[46]

The relationship between landlord and tenant was determined by the agreement. By 1823, Stewart had a printed form
of agreement prepared but it does not appear to have come into
general use in the 1820s. By the 1840s, however, a modified
form of Stewart's document governed most of the Bute agricultural tenancies and by the late-nineteenth century all
tenants had written agreements.[47] The agreement stipulated
what was to be let and what was reserved to the landlord, the
length of the tenancy, the rent to be paid and the duties of the
tenant. The Bute agricultural leases generally reserved
minerals, stone, game, fish and timber to the landlord; of the
items reserved, the Bute minerals were in the course of the
century progressively leased to industrialists, the stone was
worked by quarries which pitted the estate, the game and fish
were half-heartedly preserved and the woods were kept
in hand.

[45] Bute to Corbett, 17 March 1843, 7 May 1844 (ibid., 70, L. 7); Corbett to
Bute, 14 March 1843, 30 April, 1 and 6 May 1844 (ibid., L. Corbett 1841–45);
P.P., XXXIV (1896), 483–85.
[46] Richards to Bute, 5 March 1828 (C.C.L., MS. 4.713), 22 March 1842
(N.L.W., B., 70, L. 1842–44); P.P., XV (1881), 197; P.P., XXXVI (1894), 207;
P.P., XVII (1896), 303.
[47] Ibid., p. 206; P.P., XXXIV (1896), 287–89; agreements (N.L.W., B., 31);
note on Blue House farm, 1827 (ibid., 141, 6, T).

The tenant's primary duty to his landlord was, of course, the payment of rent. Rents in kind, which continued to be exacted in parts of Wales until the early-twentieth century, were ceasing to be a feature of the Bute estate by the early-nineteenth century. Vestiges of service rents did survive but rent on the Cardiff Castle estate under the marquesses of Bute meant, virtually exclusively, money payments.[48] All Bute agricultural tenancies began, as they did in most of Glamorgan, on 2 February. Rents due for the half-year from February to August were paid at the December audit and those for August to February at the June audit. Audits were held at Cardiff and Llantrisant, but it was usual for the agent to call to collect the rent of the more isolated farms. The December audit was followed by estate dinners at Cardiff and Llantrisant which, to judge from the liquor bills, were highly convivial occasions.[49] At the audit, the money which tenants had paid in the course of the year in property tax and, later, in road and police rates was returned to them, the annual cost to the estate of this practice varying between £300 and £600. Thus in 1851, on a rent of £160, the tenant of Llanishen House farm was allowed £5 1s. 2½d. property tax, 17s. 6½d. road rate and £1 police rate.[50] A few of the wealthier tenants, generally landowners who rented Bute land in order to round off their own estates, paid by cheque and the rest, by the 1820s, were paying in country bank-notes. The smaller tenants were the most prompt payers: 'The gentlemen here', wrote Bird in 1823, 'are much worse paymasters than the poorer farmers: I am sure of getting nearly their last shilling from the latter class but many of the former . . . are next to incorrigible.'[51]

During the first marquess's period of ownership, coinciding as it did with the Napoleonic Wars, rents rose rapidly. The rental of the original Windsor estate of 11,211 acres, standing at £2,778 in 1778, had risen to £3,713 in 1800, an increase of 32 per cent in twenty-six years; on the marquess's death in 1814

[48] Walker to Richards, 23 August 1817 (G.R.O., D/DA 5); Edmunds to Richards, 20 November 1829 (N.L.W., B., 141, 5).
[49] Franklen to Richards, 19 August 1817 (G.R.O., D/DA 5); vouchers (ibid., 56–117); letters of Bird, 1822–24 (N.L.W., B., 70, L. A); Richards to Tyndall, 8 October 1826 (Scot. P.R.O., H.B. MSS., 196).
[50] N.L.W., B., 74 and 75.
[51] Bird to Bute, 29 December 1822 (ibid., 70, L. A.).

the rental, excluding his purchases, amounted to £6,168, an increase of 70 per cent in fourteen years and of 120 per cent in forty years, a rather higher increase than was general on Welsh estates in that period. These overall figures mask widely differing changes in the rentals of individual farms. A large proportion of the tenancies, particularly in the remoter areas, was still on long leases and their rents could not therefore be increased. Thus, the 654-acre farm of Ystradfechan in the Rhondda remained at the absurdly low rent of £18 4s. until the lease expired in 1829 and the fifty-five-acre farm of Coedygwina was rented at £7 5s. until 1840. The farms whose leases had expired before 1800, which included most of those in the immediate neighbourhood of Cardiff, experienced very substantial increases in the period from 1800 to 1815. The farm of Adamsdown, whose rent was £75 in 1800, was re-let at £138 in 1814, and Penywaun, let at £57 in 1800, was re-let at £80 in 1811. The greatest increases were experienced by those tenants whose long leases expired during this period. The rent of the 204-acre farm of Blaengwrelych at Rhigos, standing at £8 in 1800, rose to £40 when the lease expired in 1814, and that of an 83-acre farm at Llanmaes rose from £36 15s. to £120 in 1809.

That these increases were beyond the paying capacity of the tenants is suggested by the high level of arrears in the later years of the Napoleonic Wars. Annual arrears stood at between £500 and £1,000 in the first few years of the nineteenth century and consisted largely of decades of unpaid manorial rents, long since irrecoverable. By 1808, however, rents of individual farms remained unpaid and the arrears of the estate, excluding new purchases, rose to £2,500. Matters worsened in subsequent years and on the first marquess's death in 1814 arrears on the original estate amounted to over £10,000. The tenant of Ynyscambwl paid none of his rent of £46 after 1808 and owed £322 by 1814; the tenant of Llanmaes farm, whose rent had risen so sharply in 1809, had arrears of £365 by 1814, while the tenant of Clunyfelin became insolvent with arrears of £44 10s. and found himself in gaol. In the face of the tenants' difficulties, annual allowances of around £500 were granted and some of the more sharply increased rents were reduced a little; the problems of the rental were, however, bequeathed by the first marquess to his grandson and were not satisfactorily solved until 1824.[52]

By 1815 arrears on the old and new estates together stood at £17,883, the equivalent of almost three years' receipts, and the second marquess's agents were obliged to attempt a readjustment of the rental. Land purchases caused the overall rental to continue to rise, but in 1815–16 and again in 1820–22 the rent of a large number of farms was reduced and considerable allowances were made to tenants. In 1817, of the arrears of £14,767, £1,648 were declared to be errors and £1,832 were abandoned as irrecoverable; by the end of 1818 vigorous debt collection had reduced the sum outstanding to £2,988. Thereafter, until the late 1820s, apart from the exceptional year of 1821, accumulated arrears as a proportion of the total rent were below 30 per cent. Meanwhile, Stewart was engaged upon a revaluation of the whole estate. He lowered the rent of most of the farms in the neighbourhood of Cardiff and increased that of many upland farms not on long leases. The new rental, which ranged from five shillings per acre in north Glamorgan to twenty-five shillings at Swanbridge, came into operation in 1824 and, in consequence, the total rental of the estate, from non-agricultural as well as agricultural sources, rose from £11,310 to £12,392. The estate as a whole was not valued again in the course of the nineteenth century.[53]

The depression of 1829–31 caused arrears to rise to 50 per cent and led to the revision of some of the rents fixed in 1824. 'There will be some deficiencies in the audit', warned Richards in June 1829, and in November he reported that 'Our fair this day, the largest of the year, has been badly attended and there was no sale whatever of stock of any description.' In 1830, Wride, one of the estate's best farmers and tenant of Blue House, Llanishen, a 226-acre farm let at £210, 'found himself sinking' and Edmunds, the farm supervisor, wrote: 'I am not an advocate for disturbing the rent roll, but the present time is such that some allowances must be made and not to him only'.[54] Great losses were suffered as a result of the foot-rot

[52] Valuation, 1778 (ibid., 104); D. W. Howells, op. cit., pp. 9-10; D. Williams, op. cit., p. 104; N.L.W. B., 58, 73–75, 93 and 101.
[53] Ibid.; survey, 1824 (ibid., 104); G.R.O., D/DB E 2; C.C.L., B., IX, 17.
[54] Richards to Bute, 27 June and 30 November 1839 (ibid., MS. 4.713); note on Blue House farm, 1830 (N.L.W., B., 140).

epidemic of 1829–30, the farm of Coston, for example, losing 150 sheep; in 1829 the tenant of Swanbridge, the richest of the Bute farms, became bankrupt, and in July 1830 a number of tenants petitioned for rent reductions. In the December audit the accumulated arrears rose sharply; cash allowances which had been made in 1829 'on account of the hard times' were continued in 1830, when most of the tenants also received an abatement of $7\frac{1}{2}$ or 10 per cent, and similar abatements were made in 1831.[55]

In the 1830s Bute became anxious lest it should be considered that his tenants were overburdened. 'I think that my Glamorgan estate like all other large estates', he wrote in 1835, 'ought to be let below its value, that is to say at a lower rate than adjoining estates belonging to smaller proprietors . . . but on the other hand, the condition is that the rent must be paid on the day appointed and will be rigidly insisted upon.'[56] In consequence, the marquess instructed his agents to re-assess the rents of a large number of farms. Edmunds considered that rents were too high and cited as an example that of the 167-acre farm of Mynachdy which was fixed at £240 'just before peace was made when stock and crops were sold for full double what they are selling now'.[57] Bute was reluctant to authorise permanent reduction, but by the mid-1830s it was becoming obvious that temporary allowances would have to be made permanent if tenants were to remain solvent. Thus, in 1835 the rent of Mynachdy was lowered to £200 and similar reductions were made in the rents of most of the lowland farms. The rental of the estate as a whole, including non-agricultural as well as agricultural receipts, fell from £13,178 in 1829 to £12,405 in 1837. Those years were ones during which non-agricultural receipts rose significantly but these figures suggest that the fall in farm rents on the Bute estate was of a rather lower order than the 25 per cent which Evan David claimed had been experienced in that period in Glamorgan as a whole.[58]

---

[55] Ibid., 74; note on Swanbridge, 1829, on Coston, 1830 (ibid., 141, 5) Richards to Bute, 9 July 1830 (C.C.L., MS. 4.713).
[56] Bute to Richards, 11 February 1835 (N.L.W., B., 70, L. 6).
[57] Note on Mynachdy, 1830 (ibid., 140).
[58] P.P., V (1837), 134–35; Richards to Bute, 24 January 1835 (C.C.L., MS. 4.713); N.L.W., B., 74.

In the 1840s a measure of prosperity returned. Arrears fell
to around 15 per cent and rents edged upwards. Farms around
Cardiff were re-valued in the light of the growing prosperity
of the town: in 1844 the rent of the 112-acre farm of Rhydypennau rose from £126 to £140 and that of the 154-acre
Llanishen House farm from £140 to £160. During the 1840s
also, as the commutation of the tithe was completed, farm
rents rose by a sum equivalent to the tithe. It has been
estimated that in the period 1836 to 1840, tithe amounted to
about 10 per cent of rent. On the Bute estate in the 1840s it
ranged from 7 per cent on the lowland farm of Swanbridge to
20 per cent on the upland farm of Tir ferch Gronw. In the
late-1840s, the combined sum of the rent and tithe was reduced
slightly to the nearest round figure.[59]

Thereafter until the end of the century, apart from reductions made for land lost through industrial and urban growth,
there was no movement of rent at all. Some allowances were
made in mid-century when arrears rose to 35 per cent and
when tenants petitioned the trustees for assistance in the face
of 'bad harvests, low livestock prices, the repeal of the Corn
Laws and increased taxation'. Corbett, noting that veal was
selling at 3d. to 4d. per pound in the June markets of 1850,
wrote: 'Farmers must be very much in want of money to sell
calves at such ruinous prices. For the sake of a few shillings of
ready money to carry on with for the present, they are parting
with that which is the only chance they have of making
anything of farming these days'.[60] The situation improved in
the mid-1850s, when arrears fell to below 20 per cent, at which
level, apart from a trough in the 1870s, they remained until
the series of available rentals ends in 1886. The Royal Commission on Land in Wales was informed in 1894 that over the
previous fifty years there had been no rent increases on the
Bute agricultural estate, a statement which the rentals confirm.
The rents of perhaps half the farms remained unchanged from
1848 to 1886 and in many cases the 1886 figure, apart from the
addition of tithe, was the same as that of 1835; of the rest, the
rentals record a steady decline as non-agricultural concerns
encroached increasingly upon agricultural land. Under the

[59] Ibid.; C.C.L., B., IX, 36; J. H. Clapham, op. cit., II, 258.
[60] Corbett to Bruce, 4 June 1850 (Scot. P.R.O., H.B. MSS., 197).

third marquess, income from non-agricultural sources rendered
unnecessary the management of the agricultural estate on
strictly commercial lines and thus there were no rent increases
during the agriculturally prosperous 1850s and 1860s. It was
acknowledged that the rents of the Bute farms were low and
there was no significant rise in arrears in the depression years
after 1878. The total rent of the Bute farms in 1893 was £6,600;
although the acreage of the estate had increased by 76 per cent
in the course of the nineteenth century, the agricultural rent
of 1893 was identical with that of 1809.[61]

THE IMPROVEMENT OF THE AGRICULTURAL ESTATE

To a man of the tastes of the second marquess of Bute, the
agricultural estate in Glamorgan could not but be a challenge
and throughout his life its improvement was one of his main
preoccupations. Faced as he was with a much neglected
inheritance and a deeply traditional tenantry, such improvement was a complex task and near the end of the marquess's
life it may well have been his opinions that his companion
de Grave reflected: 'In Celtic districts the course of Improvement bears some resemblance to the course of true love which
Shakespeare says "never did run smooth".'[62]

Tenancy agreements had much to say about the duties of
tenants but little about the duties of the landlord. Nevertheless,
on the Bute estate under the second marquess, an attempt was
made to establish a partnership between the two parties in
the interests of good farming. In those areas of the United
Kingdom where agriculture was progressive—and Bute, both
as a Scot and as the owner of an estate in East Anglia, knew
them well—there was a clearly defined economic role for both
landowner and tenant. The landowner supplied and maintained the permanent capital equipment, the land, the house,
the outbuildings, the fences and the drains, while the tenant
supplied the working capital, the stock, the seeds, the implements, the fertilisers and, of course, the labour. Under the first
marquess, Bute tenants themselves supplied almost all the
forms of capital, the landlord's contribution consisting merely

[61] N.L.W., B., 58, 74, 75 and 101; *P.P.*, XXXVI (1894), 209.
[62] De Grave to Bruce, 13 May 1847 (Scot. P.R.O., H.B. MSS., 196).

of supplying the land; indeed, some of the life leases specifically absolved the landlord from any responsibility towards the farm during the duration of the lease.[63] Under the second marquess, there was a groping towards a clear division between the function and capital of landlord and tenant and towards a system which would give the owner a far more active role in improving the standard of farming on his estate. The methods available to the second marquess to effect such improvements were many. He could influence the condition of agriculture through appointing well-informed and energetic land agents, through the level of his investment in permanent capital equipment, by rearranging farms into more viable units, evicting poor tenants and replacing them with capable ones, controlling the activities of tenants by means of covenants, giving premiums, providing examples of good husbandry and through introducing better stock, seeds, machinery and fertilisers. The second marquess made use of all these methods. Information relating to the administration of the agricultural estate after his death is meagre, but there is every reason to believe that the programme of improvement initiated by him was continued in the second half of the nineteenth century.

In seeking to improve the condition of his farms and the husbandry of his tenants, the second marquess's initial step was to appoint an energetic land agent to survey the estate and supervise reform. Between 1817 and 1825, these tasks were undertaken by David Stewart, who laid down the guidelines for the improvement of the Bute agricultural estate. Thereafter until 1841, although Stewart's policies were continued, there is no sign of new initiatives. From 1825 to 1841 the estate was under the management of Richards who, while not ignorant of farming, was primarily a lawyer and may be seen as an example of those solicitor-agents whom Professor Spring sees as retarding the agricultural development of great estates.[64] In 1841 Corbett, a trained agriculturalist, was appointed to take charge of the Bute farms and he began a programme of improvement which was intended to carry the

[63] *P.P.*, XXXIV (1896), 488, 479–81; Richards to Bute, 17 March 1829 (C.C.L., B., 4.713); report, 1830 (N.L.W., B., 141, 5).
[64] D. Spring, *English landed society in the nineteenth century, its administration* (1963), pp. 58–68.

estate into the era of high farming; for the rest of the century Bute farms were to be the special responsibility of the Corbett family.

Of primary importance in the modernisation of the estate was the improvement of farmhouses and outbuildings for, as Corbett pointed out in 1841, 'if you want to let your farms to a better class of farmer, the houses and buildings will require being put into repair'.[65] Those in the uplands were no more than hovels: the outbuildings were in ruins, the farmhouses had been constructed from 'lime, dung and mould mixed', and the second marquess, on his first visit to northern Glamorgan, was appalled to find that not one of them had glass windows. Even in the richer land of the vale the condition of farm buildings was deplorable. By the 1820s the buildings of the 245-acre farm of Swanbridge were 'in a perfect state of ruin' and the 357-acre farm of Parc Coedmachen, once the residence of Edward Somerset, earl of Glamorgan, was in such a neglected state that Bute chose to sell it rather than undertake the costly task of its restoration.[66] Where adequate buildings had been provided they had sometimes been abused by their occupants. In 1827 the tenant of Cogan gave up his holding, leaving the house 'in a shameful manner, hardly a pane of glass left, the doors all to pieces'. Many of the farmhouses had been built on exposed, damp or inconvenient sites, while the arrangement of farm buildings was often inconvenient and the layout of fields wasteful; in a group of farms at Leckwith consisting of 293 acres, thirteen acres were taken up by hedges.[67] There is nothing to suggest that the poor condition of Bute farms was in any way exceptional; Wyndham Lewis's farms, sold to the marquess in 1826, were in a wretched state, as were most of those purchased from small freeholders, and the Pwllypant lands inherited in 1870 were in dire need of improvement.[68]

The second marquess assumed that it was his responsibility to provide his tenants with sound, serviceable buildings and

[65] Corbett to Bute, 23 January 1843 (N.L.W., B., 70, L. Corbett 1841–45).
[66] Reports (ibid., 140); note on Parc Coedmachen (ibid., 31); C.C.L., B., IX, 18; Richards to Bute, 21 November 1829 (C.C.L., MS. 4.713).
[67] Report on the Lequeth property, 1841 (C.C.L., B., IX, 59); note on Cogan, 1827, on Hendy, 1829 (N.L.W., B., 141, 5).
[68] Note on Maesbach (ibid., 104); note on Llandaf Mill farm (ibid., 140); ibid., 124; C.C.L., B., IX, 17.

to repair them, assumptions not universally shared by Welsh landowners in the nineteenth century. Carrying out this responsibility proved a costly and protracted task. The scale of dereliction, the necessity to spread the expense over the years and the need to delay improvement schemes until life leases had expired meant that plans for renovation took at least a generation to fulfil and that, under the second marquess, well-managed farms existed side by side with the most dilapidated holdings. The estate rule that repairs to buildings were the landowner's responsibility was sometimes broken, for there were occasions when it was more convenient for the occupant to undertake the work himself. Thus in 1837, the tenant of Ystradyfodwg mill, because he lived 'in a District where repairs cannot be easily effected', rebuilt the mill himself at a cost of £120 and for so doing was given a rent abatement of £40 for three years.[69] When a new tenant took a farm whose buildings had not been made adequate at the marquess's expense, it was usual for considerable rent allowances to be made. In 1830 it was agreed that the tenant of Maendy should receive an allowance of £30 out of his rent of £220 for the first three years of his tenancy, while in 1842 the new tenant of Parc Coedmachen held the farm rent free for his first year.[70]

Nevertheless, under the second and third marquesses, most of the cost of erecting and renovating farm buildings was a charge upon the estate. Between 1817 and 1825, 30 to 40 per cent of the gross rents of the estate was spent on repairs and improvements, the proportion falling to 20 per cent in the late-1820s and to 10 per cent in the 1830s. Following the establishment of the 'country' department in 1841, the proportion of the rents of that department thus spent rose to 20 per cent and in the late-1840s to 30 per cent and above. The Land Commission was informed in 1893 that since 1888 expenditure on repairs and improvements had averaged £3,381 a year on an annual rental of £6,600 and that the proportion had been similar over the previous fifty years.[71] Apart from the low percentages of the late-1820s and the 1830s, when the agency lacked a dedicated agriculturalist and when expenditure on

[69] Note on Ystradyfodwg Mill farm (N.L.W., B., 140).
[70] Ibid., 58, 74, 75 and 101.
[71] Ibid., 60, 72 and 73; P.P., XXXVI (1894), 209.

the dock was at its height, the proportion of the gross rents spent on repairs and improvements by the Bute estate in the nineteenth century was remarkably high. During the 1820s and 1830s, on most of the great estates of the United Kingdom, such expenditure was between 5 and 15 per cent and only on exceptional estates, such as that of the dukes of Bedford, did it exceed 30 per cent. By the depressed 1890s, 15 per cent was generally the maximum spent, even by the most dutiful land-owners.[72] The Bute estate had both the need for a higher investment and, by the late-nineteenth century, the means to finance it.

Under the third marquess, the estate had the reputation of repairing liberally. The second marquess, however, was anxious that the strictest economy should prevail. 'I am a little frightened by your notions of expenditure on farm buildings', he informed Corbett in 1845, ' . . . we must build on a less expensive scale in future . . . Most of my farmers in Bute are superior to those in Wales and are content with less'.[73] Bute preferred to sell a farm rather than commit himself to excessive expenditure and he constantly questioned the price charged for materials and the wages paid to day labourers. The timber, stone and reeds used in building were provided by the estate itself and the marquess insisted that the tenant should be responsible for the haulage of materials, a rule abandoned in the late-nineteenth century.[74] Poundley maintained in 1842 that 6d. a yard could be saved if estate-made bricks were used instead of stone and thereafter, where suitable beds of clay were available, Corbett manufactured bricks for the estate building programme. Rebuilding by the use of such methods could be inexpensive. In 1829 the house and buildings of the fifty-one-acre hill farm of Tir Ralph were rebuilt in a rectangle fifty-eight feet by sixteen feet for a total cost of £170.[75] On the richer farms of the lowlands, the expense was greater; in 1832 £195 was spent on providing outbuildings for the 117-acre

[72] F. M. L. Thompson, op. cit., pp. 236, 313; duke of Bedford, *A great agricultural estate* (1897), *passim*.
[73] Bute to Corbett, 16 January 1845 (N.L.W., B., 70, L. Corbett 1845–46); *P.P.*, XXXVI (1894), 209.
[74] Ibid., p. 210; Bute to Richards, 31 May 1836 (N.L.W., B., 70, L. 6), to Corbett, 21 July 1842, to Richards, 13 April 1843 (ibid., L. 7).
[75] Report, 1842 (ibid., 140); Corbett to Bute, 7 March and 19 April 1842 (ibid., 70, L. Corbett 1841–45); note on Tir Ralph, 1829 (ibid., 104).

farm of Pontyparc and the houses of farms such as the 226-acre Blue House and the 153-acre Llanishen House cost at least £300 to rebuild for, as Corbett pointed out in 1842, at least five bedrooms were required 'where it is the custom for men servants to live in the house'.[76]

Apart from the erection and the repair of farm buildings, the main agricultural investment made by the second marquess was expenditure on drainage. In 1842 Poundley argued that most of the estate was in urgent need of drainage and prepared a scheme involving expenditure of up to £5 an acre. Bute preferred that tenants should do the work themselves and in the 1820s and 1830s gave rent allowances to those who did so, distributed leaflets on the subject among them and bought a swan-necked draining plough for the use of the farmers of the estate.[77] Corbett was a warm advocate of drainage and in the mid-1840s persuaded the marquess to undertake the scheme outlined by Poundley. In that decade the introduction of machine-made tiles resulted in a sharp decline in the cost of drainage and in 1845 Bute established a factory near the docks to manufacture tiles for the estate and for sale to neighbouring landowners. From 1847, when drainage was first listed as a separate item in Corbett's accounts, until 1863, when the series of available accounts ends, nearly £7,000 was spent on drainage, over and above the cost of running the tile factory. During the 1850s and 1860s, Glamorgan landowners borrowed considerable sums of money under the Improvement of Land Act to undertake drainage schemes, but the Bute authorities had no need to seek government assistance to finance their improvements. After the 1860s, estate spending on drainage declined; Corbett's accounts for 1872–73, the only year of that decade for which they survive, show an expenditure of £175, and in 1893 the Land Commission was informed that 'in recent years' the estate had not done much drainage.[78]

[76] Corbett to Bute, 9 April 1842 (ibid., L. Corbett 1841–45); note on Lower Hill farm, 1834 (ibid., 140); note on Pontyparc, 1832 (ibid., 141, 5).

[77] Report, 1842 (N.L.W., B., 140); notes on rentals (ibid., 74 and 75); Bute to Richards, 9 January 1836 (ibid., 70, L. 6); Bute to Richards, 19 January 1825 (G.R.O., D/DA 12).

[78] N.L.W., B., 72 and 73; Bute to Corbett, 15 and 19 November 1844 (ibid., 70, L. 7); J. H. Clapham, op. cit., I, 459–60; J. D. Chambers and G. E. Mingay, op. cit., p. 175; D. W. Howell, op. cit., p. 52; P.P., XXXVI (1894), 214.

The marquesses of Bute recouped themselves for their expenditure on drainage by adding a proportion, usually 5 per cent, of the outlay to the rent. Thus, in 1847 the rent of Mynachdy rose by £2 10s. and in 1860 by a further £8 19s. 6d., representing drainage costs of £229 10s. It was only with regard to tile drainage that the estate consistently followed a policy of seeking a return on investment through rent increases. E. W. M. Corbett stated in 1893 that it was unusual for the rents of the estate to be raised following expenditure by the owner and there are many examples in the first half of the nineteenth century of rents remaining at the same level although considerable sums had been spent on erecting new buildings.[79] Nevertheless, where a ruined farm had been renovated at great expense there is evidence that rent increases were made. When plans were drawn up to spend £200 on improving the wretched farm of Tir Ifan bach draws, Aberdare, the tenant resisted the proposal because his rent would be raised from £30 to £45, a sum which, he maintained, he could not afford.[80] Over the nineteenth century as a whole, however, the estate's return on investment through increased rents was negligible. If there were a clear economic motive behind the expenditure upon agricultural improvement, it arose from the desire to maintain rather than to increase the level of rent.

Almost as basic to the development of the agriculture of the estate as the landlord's investment in improvements was the question of the size and layout of farms. The work of bringing order to the rental and of rearranging the Bute farms into compact and viable units was a task of great complexity. Under the second marquess valiant efforts were made to rid the estate of unconnected and fragmented fields, to reduce the number of by-takes, to divide very large farms for which it was difficult to obtain suitable tenants, to unite very small farms in order to reduce the number of farm buildings needing maintenance, and to improve the layout of the farms themselves. By the second marquess's death, the scattered lands in the vale of Glamorgan had either been sold or had been linked to the

[79] Ibid., pp. 209–10; *P.P.*, XXXIV (1896), 715–20; N.L.W., B., 74, 75 and 101; report 1842 (ibid. 140).

[80] Note on Tir Ifan bach draws (ibid., 141, 5).

rest of the estate through purchase or exchange and the extensive acreages which the first marquess had let in blocks had been divided. When the lease of the 654-acre farm of Ystradfechan expired in 1829, its land was divided between four tenants and a major reorganisation of tenure at Leckwith produced a group of farms of between a hundred and two hundred acres apiece. At Rhigos, where there was a number of holdings of unsurpassed wretchedness, part of the land was taken for forestry, part for allotments and the rest was reorganised into three viable farms. This policy, allied with a strict prohibition of under-letting, had some success, and but for the encroachments of industry and urbanization, the layout of the Glamorgan estate would have approached, by the late-nineteenth century, the neatness which Stewart had admired in the Luton estate of the 1820s.[81]

Improving the internal layout of the farms themselves was more difficult. In the early-1820s, Stewart had rearranged the fields of Parc Coedmachen into regular squares but the experiment proved costly and was not repeated. When rebuilding occurred, the opportunity was taken of siting farmhouses in more suitable positions and of erecting the outbuildings around a convenient yard. It was estimated in 1842 that by re-siting the buildings of Llanishen Mill farm at the centre of its land the tenant would be saved one horse, and in the same year it was considered that the buildings of Parc Coedmachen should be moved in order to avoid the complications arising from their location on the boundaries of three parishes.[82] Most of the farm buildings of the estate were, however, inconveniently situated and badly arranged; the expense of re-siting them all was prohibitive and many of the defects which Poundley had condemned in 1841 still existed at the end of the nineteenth century.

Reform of the layout of farms and investment in building and drainage, while making Bute tenancies more attractive to capable farmers, were not in themselves sufficient to ensure that the standards of farming on the estate would improve.

[81] Reports on Ynyston, 1832, 1833 (ibid., 141, 6); notes on Rhigos farms (ibid., 141, 5); ibid., 58, 74, 75 and 101; Richards to Bute, 17 March 1829 and 18 March 1834 (C.C.L., MS. 4.713).

[82] Ibid., B., IX, 17 and 59; Corbett to Bute, 9 April 1842 (N.L.W., B., 70, L. Corbett 1841–45).

Evidence for the need for such improvement is extensive. In 1768, Arthur Young described the husbandry of the vale of Glamorgan as 'the most imperfect I have ever met with' and attacked the 'vile custom of sowing four white crops in succession'.[83] Poundley in the 1840s agreed with him, condemning in particular the ceaseless cropping of land 'with corn, year after year until almost exhausted', the practice of paring and burning 'which exhausts the soil of its permanent sources of fertility', and the sale of hay and straw which robbed the estate of thousands of tons of manure a year. It was the conservatism of the tenants which most disturbed Poundley, faced as he was with 'ancient prejudices to be contended with, old usages to be broken through and time-honoured customs to be innovated upon'.[84] Insufficient means prevented many tenants from availing themselves of new farming techniques and machinery, the Wynford Commission being told in 1837 that because of lack of capital there had been virtually no improvement in the farm implements in general use in Glamorgan between the 1790s and the 1830s. The flail and the wooden plough were still in use in the county in the 1840s and the ox survived as a draught animal in the neighbourhood of Cardiff until 1850.[85] The livestock carried by many Bute farms was inadequate in quantity and quality. In 1832 'it was wholly out of the power [of the tenant of Llandough farm] to stock his farm or to cultivate it with any success', and the total stock of the 654-acre farm of Ystradfechan consisted in 1831 of six 'poor little cows', four calves, one heifer, three old mares and 'about fifty poor sheep', with a total value of £51 10s.[86]

In the absence of institutions aimed at assisting tenant farmers financially, the second marquess, in seeking to improve the farming standards of his tenants, was faced with two alternatives: to evict impoverished, incapable tenants and replace them with solvent, efficient ones, or, through coercion

[83] A. Young, *A six weeks' tour through the southern counties of England and Wales* (1772), pp. 163, 167–68.
[84] C.C.L., B., IX, 59; report, 1842 (N.L.W., B., 140).
[85] *P.P.*, V (1837), 71; J. H. Matthews, *Cardiff records, materials for a history of the county borough* (1898–1911), V, 325.
[86] Richards to Bute, 14 January 1832 (C.C.L., MS. 4.713); note on Ystradfechan, 1831 (N.L.W., B., 141, 5).

or cajolement, to lead his tenants towards a more skilful husbandry. There were very serious objections to the former course; although a small minority of incorrigible tenants was evicted, wholesale evictions would have been disastrous to a politically active landlord, while the supply of men 'who had made farming a reasoned art' to replace 'old time peasants for whom it was an inherited habit' was severely limited.[87] In seeking to follow the latter course the covenant was the main weapon. Under the second marquess the clauses in tenancy agreements laying down the obligations of tenants increased in number and complexity, Bute declaring in 1845 that 'As a general rule, where tenants are less acquainted with what they ought to do, more stringent covenants are required than in an improved country, and the tenants should be bound to do certain things in return for outlays by the landlord'.[88]

In the 1820s the emphasis of the agreements was upon activities prohibited. Those brought into use in 1823 stipulated that tenants should not plough up old pasture, should not plant straw crops in the same land in two successive years and should not sell straw and hay unless two loads of dung were brought in for every load of straw or hay removed. In subsequent decades more positive action was demanded and, under the guidance of the agents of the North estate in Cambridgeshire, the marquess sought to impose the Norfolk system upon some of his tenants in the vale of Glamorgan, one of the few areas of Wales where such a system had any relevance. By the 1840s agreements relating to Swanbridge and the Leckwith farms were detailed documents directing, for example, that at least one-fifth of the arable land should be planted with turnips which were to be manured with fourteen cubic yards of dung to the acre, that fallow crops should be alternated with white straw crops and that a return of tillages should be sent to the agent by 21 December each year.[89] Bute was anxious to discourage wheat growing and to prepare his estate for the ending of protection. Precise evidence on the proportion of the

---

[87] J. H. Clapham, op. cit., I, 109.
[88] Bute to Corbett, 22 January 1845 (N.L.W., B., 70, L. 1845–46).
[89] C.C.L., B., IX, 59, 60 and 61; N.L.W., B., 31 and 33; Bute to Webb, 22 January 1845 (ibid., 70, L. 1845–46), to Richards, 10 February 1829 (G.R.O., D/DA 15).

estate under cereal crops is lacking. Stewart's survey of 1824, which gives the acreage of arable land on each farm, shows that such land constituted over half the area of almost all Bute farms in the neighbourhood of Cardiff and in the vale of Glamorgan, rising to 92 per cent of the acreage of Plasturton and to 99 per cent of that of Sheeplays.[90] The laments of the agents and earlier evidence from the Acreage Returns of 1801 suggest that of the arable land in those districts, well over half was planted with wheat and over 95 per cent with some form of cereal crop, the high incidence of cereal growing causing them to be the only districts in Wales to have a strong vested interest in the Corn Laws. Even in the uplands the amount of arable land was often significant, Ynyscambwl near Rhigos, for example, having 23 per cent of its land under the plough in 1824.[91]

Efforts by the landowner to restrict corn growing had little effect during the lifetime of the second marquess. Between the mid-1820s and the mid-1840s, the arable percentage on farms in the immediate vicinity of Cardiff declined, that of Plasturton, for example, falling from ninety-two in 1824 to seventy-one in 1846. Elsewhere, particularly on Bute farms around the estuary of the Ely, there was a considerable increase in that period, arable as a percentage of the total acreage of Cogan farm rising from fifty to seventy-five and on Llandough farm from thirty-eight to sixty. When, in the second half of the nineteenth century, a decline in the incidence of cereal growing occurred on the Bute estate as elsewhere in Glamorgan, it was the consequence not so much of pressure from the landowner as of more general factors, such as the fall in corn prices and the scarcity of labour.[92]

It is therefore difficult to attribute change and improvement in agricultural practice specifically to the provisions of leasing agreements. Such provisions were not popular among tenants; the tenant of Rhydypennau, for example, strongly objected in 1845 'to covenants which are usual in England where the

[90] Ibid., D/DB E 1; notes on Hendre House and Cornerswell (N.L.W., B., 140); note on Llandough farms (ibid., 104); Bute to Corbett, 11 June 1845 (ibid., 70, L. Corbett 1845–46).
[91] D. Thomas, op. cit., pp. 54–95; G.R.O., D/DB E 1.
[92] Ibid.; D. Howell, op. cit., p. 14; N.L.W., Tithe Award maps and apportionments, parishes of St. John, Cogan and Llandough.

highest cultivation is carried on by tenants'.[93] The provisions
may well have been ignored, for some Bute tenants, even of
sizeable lowland farms, were illiterate.[94] Most agreements
contained clauses stipulating that punitive rents were to be
charged if covenants were broken but among the Bute papers
there is no evidence that these clauses were ever implemented,
E. W. M. Corbett stating in 1893 that they were inserted not
'to find fault with the average tenant but as protection against
a thoroughly bad tenant who begins to ruin his farm as he is
leaving'. In the second half of the nineteenth century, on the
Bute estate as elsewhere, there was a movement away from
meticulous control of the activity of tenants; by the 1890s the
estate had ceased to demand any specific method of cultivation
and Bute agricultural agreements of that decade had returned
to the simple format current in the early-1820s.[95]

While a landowner could use covenants to coerce tenants to
adopt a better system of husbandry, there were also methods
open to him to cajole them into doing so. From the 1820s
onwards the second marquess issued handbills offering premiums to his tenants. No copies appear to have survived but
the Bute papers do include a list of premiums offered on the
Mountstuart estate and doubtless those offered in Glamorgan
were similar. At Mountstuart, prizes were offered for the best
field of turnips, for the best beasts in various categories and
for the best-kept ditches and hedges. The rewards were usually
money but could on occasion be iron ploughs or pairs of
harrows.[96] Bute believed that 'the only way to meet low prices
is to make the same piece of land produce double crops' and
considered that premiums could play an important part in
encouraging greater productivity. Corbett agreed with him,
declaring in 1845: 'Unless some inducement towards an
improved system be held out, agriculture must remain in its
present stationary position in this part of the country'.[97] The

[93] Bute to Corbett, 22 January 1845 (N.L.W., B., 70, L. Corbett 1845–46).
[94] Corbett to Bruce, 1 June 1849 (Scot. P.R.O., H.B. MSS., 197).
[95] P.P., XV (1881), 200; P.P., XXXVI (1894), 206, 215; J. H. Clapham, op.
cit., II, 274–75; W. Little, op. cit., p. 165.
[96] Richards to Bute, 27 November 1834 (C.C.L., MS. 4.713); note on premiums
(N.L.W., B., 137, 2).
[97] Bute to Richards, 11 February 1835, 21 January 1836 (ibid., 70, L. 6);
Corbett to Bute, 18 January 1845 (ibid., L. 1841–45).

marquess was depressed to find that his premiums did not evoke the same enthusiastic response in Glamorgan as they did in Scotland and the attention of tenants had to be drawn to them time and time again. The system of premiums on the Isle of Bute was administered by the Bute Farmers Society, which was run by the agent of the Mountstuart estate. An agricultural society had been in existence in Glamorgan since 1772, but its influence does not seem to have been significant; the second marquess paid a subscription to it but it is hardly mentioned in Bute correspondence.[98]

Although Bute was reluctant to undertake direct farming, he was anxious that his estate should be a channel for introducing new stock, implements and machinery to Glamorgan. He sent Ayrshire and Galloway cattle to the county from his Dumfries estate and gave Corbett every encouragement to bring the two great innovations of the 1840s, guano and machine-made drainage tiles, to the attention of Glamorgan farmers. In the 1840s also, at Corbett's prompting, he acquired a threshing-machine, a steam-engine and a sub-soil plough for the use of his tenants. The practice of offering such equipment and services was extended in the later nineteenth century, and by the 1890s the estate kept a pedigree bull and stallion to improve the stock of the tenants.[99]

ADJUNCTS OF THE AGRICULTURAL ESTATE

As lords of most of the manors of east- and mid-Glamorgan, the marquesses of Bute had rights of game not only over their freehold land but also over the extensive commons of the manors. Such rights could be a source of considerable profit and enjoyment, but to the second and third marquesses they brought neither. The second marquess's poor eyesight barred him from participation in blood sports and he considered the preservation of game to be uneconomical and likely to make a landowner unpopular. 'I cannot allow', he wrote in 1843,

[98] Bute to Richards, 7 January 1836 (ibid., L. 6); Richards to Bute, 20 August 1840 (C.C.L., MS. 4.860); J. Wilson, *Tourists' guide to Rothesay and the Isle of Bute* (1862), p. 139.
[99] Bute to Richards, 11 July 1825 (G.R.O., D/DA 12); Bute to Corbett, 19 March 1842 (N.L.W., B., 70, L. 7); C.C.L., B., IX, 51; J. H. Clapham, op. cit., I, 456; *P.P.*, XXXVI (1894), 210.

'any person to make my estate a preserve for game, thereby giving the tenants grounds to ask for a rent reduction.'[100] In the 1840s, expenditure on game, averaging £100 a year, was included in the accounts for the first time and in that decade two gamekeepers were appointed, largely to prevent poachers from annoying the tenants.[101] The third marquess, among whose delights were his colonies of beavers and wallabies at Mountstuart, considered blood sports to be objectionable, and although some game was preserved on the Glamorgan estate in the late-nineteenth century it did not assume the proportions of a major charge or a serious annoyance to tenants.[102] More attention was paid to manorial rights of fishing on the Taff and parts of the Rhymney, the Ely and the Ogmore for, although the profits they produced were minimal, their maintenance had an important bearing upon Bute rights of lordship over the rivers.

Both game and fish pale into insignificance alongside that other adjunct of the agricultural estate, the woodlands. All the woods on Bute farms were reserved to the landlord and such plantations varied in size from two acres on the twenty-two-acre farm of Llwynyreos to the eighty-four acres on the 219-acre farm of Llwynygrant. Although the vale of Glamorgan was noted for its bareness, the slopes of the low-lying parts of the estate at Leckwith, Llanishen and Castell Coch were well wooded and in the uplands large areas were taken in hand and planted in the course of the nineteenth century. Stewart's atlas lists a total of 1,383 acres of woodland on the estate in 1824. Other land planted in subsequent years would undoubtedly have caused the area under timber to rise to 2,000 acres by the mid-nineteenth century.[103] Bute attached great importance to his woodlands and showed a close interest in their administration. Until 1842 they were the responsibility of Edmunds, the farm manager, whose timber book listed every tree on the estate. Under his charge were the nurseries at

---

[100] Bute to Richards, 23 March 1843 (N.L.W., B., 70, L. 7).
[101] Corbett to Bute, 12 August 1843 (ibid., L. Corbett 1841–45); accounts (ibid., 72 and 73).
[102] W.M., 10 October 1900; P.P., XXXVI (1894), 207.
[103] G.R.O., D/DB E 1; C.C.L., MS. 4.850; ibid., B., XIV, 31; notes on farms (N.L.W., B., 104, 140 and 141).

Cathays, the planter and the fencer at Rhigos, and the forester at Aberdare.[104]

When the woods came into Corbett's care in 1842, Poundley recommended that the estate should employ eight additional woodmen and urged that large-scale plantings should be undertaken. He considered that timber was by far the most profitable crop for large areas of the estate and estimated that the woods planted at Rhigos in 1827 would be showing a profit of £18 an acre by 1842, or £1 4s. an acre over fifteen years, a much higher return in such a district than agricultural rent. His calculations were optimistic: he made no allowance for the lack of return on capital for at least fifteen years; he ignored the abatements granted to tenants as compensation for disturbance caused by timber cutting and made no mention of the misfortunes to which woodlands were often subject. Gross annual receipts from timber stood at between one and two thousand pounds in the early-1820s; they fell to around £700 in the late-1820s and early-1830s, rising in the 1840s and 1850s to an average of £1,500; in the early-1860s they fell to £300 but rose in the late-1860s to the level of the 1840s. Expenses, however, were high; in the late-1820s, during a heavy programme of replanting, they regularly exceeded the receipts, and in the 1850s they absorbed between a third and a half of the gross income. Between 1827 and 1862, the period for which full details are available, the total profit of the Bute woods amounted to £12,500; this represents a net annual return approaching £400 and indicates an income of four shillings an acre a year.[105]

The Bute woods contained a variety of trees. In 1824 Stewart recommended that 2,560 trees per acre should be planted, consisting of 840 oaks intermixed with larch, fir, pinaster, sycamore and ash, the oaks to be permanent and the others providing shelter for them when young. The old-established lowland woods consisted largely of oak but in the upland plantations there was an increasing tendency to plant

[104] Papers on timber (ibid., 141, 5); Bute to Corbett, 13 January 1844 (ibid., 70, L. 7).
[105] Report, 1842 (ibid., 140); accounts (ibid., 60, 72 and 73); report on Rhigos plantations (C.C.L., B., XVI, 4, 13).

larch and Scots pine. When planting or cutting, the ornamental value of the woods was taken into account and particular consideration was given to the appearance of the Aberdare woods, for the second marquess had intended to build a summer cottage for himself in the Cynon valley.[106]

There was a ready market for Bute timber. The second marquess hoped that the finer oaks would be purchased by the navy and in 1840 urged that the sale of 5,563 feet of oak from Llanishen, suitable for ship building, should have ample publicity. Much of the timber felled was used on the estate itself for rebuilding farmhouses and in making fences and gates, while most of that utilised in dock building had been grown on the estate. The bulk of the timber sold was bought by local collieries. In county Durham the Bute family owned woods whose management had been geared for generations to the pit-prop trade and the experience gained there proved useful in Glamorgan. The trees planted to shelter the young oaks were grown expressly for pit-props and plantations were established at Rhigos because there was a market at hand for their produce. The coalowners, who rarely had much surface land, proved more eager buyers than the ironmasters, who often had their own plantations. Thus, in 1836 Coffin paid £735 for trees from the Bute farms in the upper Rhondda and in 1839 Powell bought timber worth £900 from the farm of Llethrddu. Prices depended upon the state of the coal and iron trades, being low in the late-1820s but rising rapidly in the mid-1830s. The high cost of haulage caused the value of a plantation to be determined by the prosperity of a contiguous colliery and therefore prices varied from locality to locality as well as from year to year.[107]

Many aspects of the history of the Bute agricultural estate in Glamorgan have their parallels elsewhere. The rapid increase in rent and arrears before 1815, the remissions of the

[106] Ibid., IX, 18; report on plantations (N.L.W., B., 47); papers on timber (ibid., 141, 5).
[107] Ibid.; Bute to Corbett, 13 January 1844 (ibid., 70, L. 7); report on plantations (ibid., 47); Richards to Bute, 16 January 1828, 21 February 1829 (C.C.L., MS. 4.713), 22 February 1839 (ibid., 4.860); ibid., B., XVI, 4, 13.

early-1820s and the early-1830s, the development of the covenant, and the drive towards high farming in the 1840s and 1850s are the commonplaces of the history of nineteenth century agriculture. The enormous impact of non-agricultural factors, however, gives the history of the estate a special significance; the phenomenal decline in the relative importance of agriculture and the swamping of a large proportion of the farms by industry and urbanization reflect in an extreme form the generally declining position of agriculture in the economy as a whole. Landlordism in nineteenth century Wales is often portrayed as a system of oppression tempered by neglect, yet those responsible for the management of the Bute estate showed a solicitude for the welfare of the tenants and a concern for the improvement of agriculture. Admittedly, the surveys and correspondence of the estate were all written from the stand-point of the landlord and his agents, but that standpoint, although often arrogant, displays much benevolence and an earnest dedication to constructive improvement. In the late-nineteenth century, when anti-landlord agitation in Wales was at its height, many aspects of the activity of the Bute family were widely criticised; in those criticisms the farming tenants of the estate, 'a hard-working, thrifty people', did not partici-pate, E. W. M. Corbett claiming in 1893 that 'we have between them and us the very best of feeling'.[108]

---

[108] *P.P.*, XXXIV (1894), 210.

V

THE URBAN ESTATE

Associations with the Bute family are inescapable in urban east Glamorgan. Their castle and its park dominate the centre of Cardiff. The statue of the second marquess commands the access to the city's main thoroughfare and the statue of the third guards the entrance to Cathays Park. The names of the Cardiff district of Butetown and the township of Treherbert commemorate the family and its Pembroke ancestors, while Aberdare, Treorci and Treherbert have their Bute Street and their Stuart Street. The districts of Cardiff—Adamsdown, Penylan, Maendy, Mynachdy, Cathays, Rhydypennau, Black-weir and Pontcanna—recall Bute properties, and the names of major features of the city—Ninian Park, Cardiff Arms Park, Bute Park and Sophia Gardens—are memorials to the family. The names of the streets developed by the estate were chosen by the marquesses and their advisers, Collingdon commenting in 1850 that 'it is very desirable to have . . . the names written up to prevent any objectionable names being given by the occupiers of the houses'.[1] This provided abundant opportunities to commemorate the Butes and their associates. The titles of the family—Bute, Dumfries, Windsor, Mountjoy, Crichton and Mountstuart—appear on streets, places, crescents and squares. The names of their predecessors as lords of Cardiff Castle, among them Fitzhamon, Despenser, Clare and Tudor, are recalled in the streets of Riverside. In much of Cathays the streets bear the names of the manors and villages of the Bute estate in Glamorgan, while elsewhere are Sanquahar Street, Inchmarnock Street and others, named after Bute properties in Scotland. The first wife of the second marquess has a Guilford Street, his second a Sophia Street and a Loudoun Square. Glossop Terrace and Howard Gardens are named after the family of the third marquess's wife, and Colum Road, Ninian Road and Lady Margaret's Terrace

---

[1] Collingdon to Bruce, 27 July 1850 (Scot. P.R.O., H.B. MSS., 197).

after her children. Bute agents and advisers are also commemorated. E. P. Richards has a Priest Street and a Richards Terrace, O. T. Bruce a Tyndall Street and a Bruce Street, while Corbett, Ryder, Pitman, Talbot, Sneyd, Clark, Lewis and Collingdon all have at least one street apiece. The advisers of the second marquess on dock matters, Rennie, Stephenson and Smeaton, have streets in Riverside, as do the dock engineers, Hunter and Pomeroy, at Pierhead. Indeed, there can be few cities where the imprint of a single family is as legible as is that of the Bute family at Cardiff.

While the comparative importance of the Bute agricultural estate declined dramatically in the course of the nineteenth century, that of the urban estate rose even more dramatically. Ground-rents within the borough of Cardiff, which in 1830 had yielded £214, produced by 1894 a total of £28,348.[2] Over the estate as a whole the growth of income was even more marked, for in addition to their urban land at Cardiff, the Butes owned extensive suburban land outside the borough boundaries together with the sites of much of the townships of Aberdare, Treherbert, Treorci and Hirwaun, and those of more scattered settlements in the valleys of the Taff, the Ely and the Rhymney. In 1938 when the Bute family company, Mountjoy Ltd., sold its urban estate in Glamorgan for £5 million to Western Ground Rents, a syndicate headed by Lord Kennet, the sale included the leases of 20,000 houses, 1,000 shops and 250 public houses at Cardiff, as well as extensive leasehold property within the coalfield.[3]

In 1821, when Cardiff had a population of 3,579, most of the built-up area lay around St. Mary's Street and the church of St. John, land which belonged for the most part to the corporation of Cardiff and to a number of small landowners. At the same time, the urbanization of Bute land in the coalfield had hardly begun, Stewart's terrier of 1824 listing only two small groups of building plots, one at Hirwaun and the other at Aberdare.[4] In the late-1820s, work began on Bute Street, which was to extend from Cardiff's south gate to the sea, and

[2] C.C.L., B., XI, 20.
[3] *Estates Gazette*, 21 May and 9 July 1938; *Economist*, 31 December 1938.
[4] G.R.O., D/DB E 2; N.L.W., Tithe maps and apportionments, parishes of St. John and St. Mary.

in 1826 John Bird described a visit he had made to the improvements south of the town where the new streets were being laid out.[5] By 1841, the completion of the Bute Dock and the Taff Vale Railway had brought an influx of people into the town, and Cardiff's population stood at 10,077. Despite developments in Bute Street, most of the increased population had been accommodated, not in new housing on Bute land, but in the overcrowded courts which honeycombed the existing built-up area, and Bute income from ground-rents within the borough increased in the 1830s by a mere £44 to £258.

In the 1840s building activity between the town and the dock quickened, ground worth £123 a year being let in the first four months of 1848. Bute Street was completed and the marquess considered it worth his while to employ Sir Frederick Pollock to plead his case for compensation for the loss of building ground on the eastern side of the street which had been taken by the dock branch of the Taff Vale Railway. In the same decade, Cardiff began expanding eastwards as well as southwards, substantial houses being erected at Crockherbtown on land which the marquess shared with Richards and the Vachell family and, by 1850, Bute income from ground-rents within the borough amounted to £622.[6]

It was the second half of the nineteenth century which saw the dramatic expansion of Cardiff and the massive rise in the Bute ground-rental. Calculations based upon the number of house plans approved by the town authorities show that the 1850s were a period of vigorous building, with 200 to 400 plans a year being approved; in the 1860s the number dropped sharply, then rose to between 500 and 600 a year in the mid-1870s and to between 700 and 800 a year by the end of the decade. By the mid-1880s, at least 1,200 plans a year were being approved, but in the early-1890s the number fell to between 700 and 900, rising again to 1,200 in the late-1890s.[7]

[5] C.C.L., MS. 2.716, 16 June 1826.
[6] M.G., June 1839; Collingdon to Bruce, 26 June 1848 (Scot. P.R.O., H.B. MSS., 196); T. W. Rammell, *Report on . . . the sanitary condition . . . of the town of Cardiff* (1850), map 2; C.C.L., B., XI, 20.
[7] J. H. Richards, 'Fluctuations in house building in the south Wales coalfield 1851–1954' (unpublished University of Wales M.A. dissertation, 1956); J. H. Richards and J. P. Lewis, 'Housebuilding in the south Wales coalfield', *Journal of the Manchester School of Economic and Social Studies*, XXIV (1956), 289–301.

Not all of this building occurred on Bute-owned land, especially after the 1860s when the town burst out of the confines of the parishes of St. John and St. Mary, but the rise in Bute income from ground-rents at Cardiff does follow a pattern broadly similar to that of the growth of the town's housing stock. The decennial increases in income were noted by W. T. Lewis in a memorandum in 1894, but more detailed information is available in the annual rental of the 'Cardiff' estate.[8] That rental included income from freehold properties, accommodation land, ancient lights, wharfs, yards and warehouses within the town, but the most significant factor in its rise was the increase in ground-rents. Between 1850 and 1859, the total rent of the 'Cardiff' estate rose from £3,487 to £7,885, an increase largely accounted for by the ground-rents of the buildings erected in that decade in and around Bute Street and Mountstuart and Loudoun Squares. Between 1860 and 1870, a period which saw considerable building on the Tredegar estate at Cardiff, the Bute rental rose gradually from £8,180 to £10,708, the increase still mainly attributable to new building in the vicinity of the dock. By the 1870s, most of the land in the parish of St. Mary, 84 per cent of which was owned by the Bute estate, had been utilized either by building or by the docks; indeed, during that decade, the parish showed a slight fall in population. By then the areas of growth were north of the town, and extensive building took place in the 1870s on the land of the Bute farms of Plasturton, Maendy, Mynachdy, Crwys, Penywaun and Blackweir. By 1881, the Cardiff street rental stood at £17,874; in the 1880s it increased at a rate of £1,000 a year and in the mid-1890s at over £2,000 a year.[9] Complete rentals of the Cardiff estate are not available after 1894, but the evidence available suggests that the growth of Bute urban income declined sharply in the early years of the twentieth century, as did Cardiff's index of house-building. In the 1920s, however, much of the town's suburban development took place on the land of the Bute farms of Penylan, Rhydypennau, Tyglas, Llwynygrant and others, leading to further increases in the estate's receipts from ground-rents.[10]

[8] C.C.L., B., XI, 20; N.L.W., B., 65.
[9] Cardiff rentals, 1878–87, 1892–95 (ibid., 101 and 103); schedule, 1868 (ibid., 140).
[10] C.C.L., Cardiff supplementary rental, 1927–30.

Outside the Cardiff area, ground-rents were listed until 1841 in Richards's general account and thereafter in Corbett's 'Country' account. From 1845, Corbett divided his rental into 'Farms' and 'Cottages etc.'; the latter included manorial dues and rents of Bute freehold houses but the increase in the receipts in that category was almost entirely the consequence of the growth of leasehold building in the industrial valleys. In 1845 the cottage rents amounted to £802, of which some £300 were ground-rents from Hirwaun and Aberdare. The growth of Aberdare in the late-1840s and early-1850s caused the rental to increase by £50 to £100 a year in that period and by 1860 it stood at £1,750. Urbanization at Aberdare continued in the 1860s, when considerable building also took place on Bute land at Treherbert in the Rhondda. By 1870 the cottage rental amounted to £2,941, the coal boom of the early-1870s and the consequent demand for housing in the Rhondda raising it to £4,210 by 1875.[11] Figures relating to the Bute urban estate are not available in full after the 1870s, but income from that source undoubtedly continued to grow up to the First World War. Howard Street, Treorci, for example, was not built until 1889–91, while Luton, Stuart and Colum Streets in the same town were not completed until 1904–5. When the fourth marquess of Bute auctioned his urban property in the coalfield after the war, 1,662 items were sold in the Rhondda alone and a three-day sale of leaseholds at Aberdare in 1919 realised a total of £124,000.[12]

When it became clear in the 1820s and 1830s that Bute land, both at Cardiff and in the industrial valleys, would soon be in demand for urban development, the second marquess was faced with three possibilities: either to sell the land to those who wished to build houses, or to build houses himself, or to

[11] Rentals (N.L.W., B., 74, 75 and 101).
[12] N.L.W., Sale catalogues, 55, 213, 214 and 219; C.C.L., IX, 7; *Estates Gazette*, 6 December 1919, 3 January 1920. In these sales, the minerals were reserved to the seller. The maps in the Claim Files at Coal House, Llanishen, which indicate the pieces of land where the ownership of the surface had been divorced from the ownership of the minerals, provide precise evidence of the success of the sales.

lease land on building leases. The first possibility he did not consider. No building land was sold by the Bute estate to individuals in the course of the nineteenth century and Richards was instructed not to forward any such applications to the marquess.[13] It was with reluctance that the second marquess and his successors sold land to public institutions such as the Board of Guardians or the Army and, in each case, a clause obliging the purchasers, if and when they wished to sell the land, to give first refusal to the owner of the Cardiff Castle estate was inserted in the conveyance.[14]

The second possibility had little appeal. The Glamorgan estate did, of course, include some house property. The second marquess had inherited several hundred rural cottages together with houses at Cardiff, Cowbridge, Llantrisant and Usk. Such property he viewed with disfavour. A high proportion of the cottage rents was absorbed by repairs and expenses of management, and their arrears were higher than those of any other type of property. The houses at Cardiff consisted largely of 'ruins and paupers', while the Bute-owned inns in the town, including the Angel and the Cardiff Arms, made considerable demands on the marquess's time and money. By 1829, the Angel had become so expensive to maintain that consideration was given to selling it or dividing it into tenements.[15] A large number of the houses owned by the estate at Cardiff were demolished to enhance the appearance of the castle, while urban property at Usk, the last remnant of the vast Monmouthshire estates of the earls of Pembroke, was sold.

A reluctance to own house property went hand in hand with a reluctance to build. In the 1820s and 1830s, when land adjoining Bute Street was being laid out as building ground, Richards on several occasions urged the marquess to build some pattern houses in order to induce speculators to come forward to take leases. Bute had succumbed to such persuasion at Luton and had built 'superior houses' there in order to attract 'superior people' to the town. He regretted the venture

---

[13] Bute to Richards, 2 March 1838 (N.L.W., B., 70, L. 6).
[14] E.g., ibid., 15 May and 5 July 1837 (ibid.); Richards to Bute, 27 February 1838 (C.C.L., MS. 4.860); the Army to Richards, 1 February 1841 (G.R.O., D/DA 25).
[15] C.C.L., B., IX, 47; Richards to Bute, 8 May 1829 (C.C.L., MS. 4.713); N.L.W., B., 58, 74, 75 and 101.

and informed Richards that 'I have burnt my fingers in other places [by building] and, on every account, I believe, . . . houses should not appear as my speculation'.[16] He was prepared on occasion, however, to assist reputable speculators with a private guarantee or a supply of building material from the estate at reduced prices. Reputable builders were slow to come forward, and in the early-1840s the marquess was obliged to overcome his reluctance and to turn builder, partly in order to provide houses for key dock workers and partly to encourage the growth of a dignified residential district adjoining his dock. In 1840 he financed the building of eight houses and a dock office at Bute Crescent, a venture which cost £8,250; behind them he built seven houses for lockmen at £175 apiece.[17]

Similar motives impelled his son's trustees to become house-builders in the Rhondda in the 1850s. The reaching of the steam coal measures at Cwmsaerbren and the subsequent establishment of the Bute Merthyr colliery in a district hitherto almost totally uninhabited, created an acute demand for houses for miners. By 1857 some fifty houses had been built by the trustees at Treherbert, their standard being considered superior to the accommodation generally provided by coal companies in the mid-nineteenth century.[18]

Refusal to sell and a reluctance to build left only one course open to the second marquess if he wished to profit from the potential riches of his urban land. This was to lease his land on building leases. Under such a system the landlord leased a building plot for a term of years on the understanding that the tenant would erect a building upon it and enjoy the use of it for the duration of the lease. Initially, all that the landowner was obliged to provide was the plot of land itself; thus, the building lease bore a strong resemblance to the three-life agricultural leases which had been so prevalent in Wales in the eighteenth century and earlier, whereby the landowner provided none of the capital equipment apart from the land.

[16] Richards to Bute, 24 July and 3 September 1824 (C.C.L., MS. 4.713); ibid., 29 November 1837 and 13 January 1838 (ibid., 4.860); Bute to Jennard, 13 September 1833 (N.L.W., B., 70, L. 2); Bute to Richards, 1 December 1837, 17 January 1838 (ibid., 6).
[17] Lloyd to Richards, 10 October 1840 (G.R.O., D/DA 24); Roy to Bute, 13 January 1846 (N.L.W., B., L. Roy, 1844–46); C.C.L., B., XI, 27, 21; XII, 19.
[18] N.L.W., MS. 7458B, 1854; D. W. Jones, Hanes Morgannwg (1874), p. 284; E. D. Lewis, The Rhondda valleys (1959), p. 201.

The overwhelming predominance of the leasehold system in urban Wales may have been the result of the adaptation of the eighteenth century agricultural lease to an urban setting. But, if a pattern for the lease system were needed, there was one readily available in London, the great leasehold city, where the ninety-nine-year building lease had evolved in the late-seventeenth century following the Great Fire.[19] The second marquess was certainly aware of the London system; his town house at Camden Hill was held on lease and William Cubbitt, adviser to the marquess on dock matters, was the brother of Thomas Cubbitt, builder of Belgravia and Pimlico. Bute was also familiar with the leasing system in that other major leasehold area of England, the watering-places of the south coast. He was in touch with Sir George Jervis, who in the 1830s was 'endeavouring to get a new town or watering-place established upon his estate . . . about five miles beyond Christchurch', and obtained in 1838 copies of Sir George's 'system . . . for encouraging building there'.[20]

The building leases of the Bute estate conformed to the pattern which prevailed in almost the whole of Wales in the nineteenth century. The only freehold houses at Cardiff were those built upon the 110 acres of land purchased by the National Freehold Land Society at Canton in 1852. With that exception, the tenurial system in the town contained little variety, the other major estates, Plymouth and Tredegar in particular, following policies similar to those of the Bute estate.[21] The standard length of a lease of a dwelling-house at Cardiff was ninety-nine years, the maximum authorised by the chief mortgagees of the Bute estate. There were those at Cardiff who were willing to take shorter leases; in 1822, for example, Bird sought permission to build two houses at Crockherbtown on a sixty-one-year lease and in 1839 Richards received an application for a forty-year lease of a plot in Castle Street.[22] The second marquess disliked the notion of tying down

[19] J. Summerson, *Georgian London* (1948), pp. 23–24.
[20] Bute to Richards, 1 December 1837, 24 April 1838 (N.L.W., B., L. 6); the laying out of Bournemouth began in 1836.
[21] Map of the tenurial system in England and Wales (*P.P.*, XIII (1887), opposite page 816); M. J. Daunton, *Coal metropolis, Cardiff, 1870–1914* (1977), pp. 81–82.
[22] Bird to Stewart, 23 April 1822 (N.L.W., B., 70, L. A); Richards to Bute, 6 June 1839 (C.C.L., MS. 4.860).

his land for as long as ninety-nine years, especially if the houses built were of modest proportions, and he sought to establish sixty-three rather than ninety-nine years as the general length of a lease.[23] Such attempts met with resistance, and by the mid-nineteenth century all building leases for houses on the Bute estate were for ninety-nine years.

By the 1840s, the nature of the lease had been established and in 1849 forms were printed, gaps being left for the date, the rent and the names of the lessee and the premises. The initial agreement with the estate stipulated that if the prospective lessee completed within a specified time, usually twelve months, 'a dwelling house in such a manner and with such materials as shall be approved of in writing by the agent', he would be granted a ninety-nine-year lease of the property. Payment of ground-rent began, not with the signing of the agreement, but with the completion of the house and the signing of the lease, thus, the prospective lessee was not burdened with rent while building was in progress. The lessee covenanted to paint the outside woodwork every three years and the inside every seven, to insure the buildings at an insurance office chosen by the lessor and not to use the premises as a tavern or a butcher's shop. Other clauses covenanted against the assignment of the lease without the written consent of the lessor and some agreements allowed the Bute estate to repossess the property before the expiration of the lease if it were needed by the estate and if fair compensation were paid. No mention was made of any right of the lessee to buy the freehold or to renew the lease at its expiration.[24]

In determining the level of ground-rent, the location of the site, the nature of the building, the demand for plots and the charges made by neighbouring landowners were all taken into consideration. At Llanelli in the 1880s, the ground-rent was estimated to be equivalent to one-seventh of the rack-rent,

[23] Bute to Smyth, 27 October 1840 (N.L.W., B., L. 7); Bute to Corbett, 27 January 1845 (ibid., L. Corbett, 1845–46); Collingdon to Richards, 28 November 1846 (C.C.L., B., IX, 27, 21).
[24] N.L.W., B., 143; C.C.L., B., IX; McNabb to Bruce, 31 July 1849(Scot. P.R.O., H.B. MSS., 197); *P.P.*, XIII (1887), pp. 796–97.

so that a house which would let at £35 a year would carry a ground-rent of £5.[25] There is no evidence that this was the criterion which guided the administrators of the Bute estate. By the early-twentieth century, ground-rents at Cardiff were calculated by the square yard, but in the Bute correspondence of the first half of the nineteenth century, all such calculations are in terms of rates per foot of frontage. The estate's minimum size for a building-plot at Cardiff was fifteen feet by sixty feet, although the depth depended upon the site and could, even in modest housing schemes, be up to a hundred feet. In the 1820s, the normal charge for such a plot was calculated at the rate of 1s. a foot of frontage, but by the mid-1830s Richards believed that the increasing prosperity of Cardiff justified the raising of the rate in the Bute Street district to 1s. 6d. and in Crockherbtown to 2s.[26] By the late-1830s, Richards and Bute were seeking to establish 2s. a foot as the normal charge where the plot was under a hundred feet in depth, and 2s. 6d. where it exceeded a hundred feet, but lower charges were made if a number of plots were taken or if the marquess were particularly anxious to oblige the lessee.[27]

Rents rose rapidly in the 1840s; by 1846, both at Crockherbtown and Butetown, 3s. a foot had become the norm and by 1850 a charge of 4s. was not uncommon.[28] The rentals suggest that the 3s. a foot received for houses in the main thoroughfares in the 1840s had become the standard in the unfashionable back-streets by the late-nineteenth century. In 1884, terraced houses at Hirwaun Street, Cathays, with a frontage of some sixteen feet, were leased at £2 5s. apiece, indicating a ground-rent of 3s. a foot of frontage and of around 5d. a square yard. At the same time, rather larger houses in the pleasanter Ryder and Pitman Streets, near Cathedral Road, were leased at £4–£5 apiece, equivalent to 4s.–5s. a foot of frontage and to 7d.–9d. a square yard. Access to public gardens affected the

[25] Ibid., p. 185.
[26] N.L.W., Jevons Papers, IV, 122; Richards to Bute, 10 September 1836 (C.C.L., MS. 4.860); Vachell to Richards, 4 February 1835 (G.R.O., D/DA 20).
[27] Richards to Bute, 13 January 1838, 22 and 24 January 1839 (C.C.L., MS. 4.860); Bute to Richards, 17 January 1838 and 26 January 1839 (N.L.W., B., 70, L. 6).
[28] Richards to Bute, 5 and 10 September 1846 (ibid., L. 1845–46); T. W. Rammell, op. cit., p. 10.

level of ground-rent; the average charge for houses at Pen-hevad Street, Grangetown, in the 1890s was £3 10s., while for identical houses in the adjoining Pentrebane Street, which overlooked Grange Gardens, payments of £4 10s. were made.[29] The creation of 'squares or gardens which provide a little breathing space', a characteristic of Bute town-planning, and the subsequent presentation of the gardens to the public, a policy for which the estate was warmly praised, was therefore one which was not conducted wholly at a loss. Such a strategy was pursued on a large scale at Roath Park where, by presenting an extensive area of marshy land to the corporation to be laid out as a park, the estate was able to charge substantially higher ground-rents for the surrounding properties.[30]

By the first decade of the twentieth century, the ground-rents which the estate was charging in middle class, residential districts were equivalent to 6d. a square yard for the total area, including roads. Professor Jevons estimated in 1913 that the value of such suburban building land amounted, at twenty-five years' purchase, to £2,500 an acre, a figure which may be compared with the £2,800 an acre received by the third marquess in 1898 for fifty-seven acres of Cathays Park in the heart of the town. As the twentieth century advanced, ground-rents rose sharply. In the 1920s, £5–£6 was the standard rate for terraced houses in Grangetown, while houses in the neighbourhood of Roath Park were leased at £10–£15 apiece.[31]

Ground-rents of buildings other than dwelling-houses were negotiated individually. The charges made—£156 for Mar-ments the department-store, £52 10s. for the County Club and £150 for the Great Western Hotel, for example—suggest that for such buildings the location rather than the size of the plot was the most significant factor. Some of the agreements relating to public buildings made provision for graduated rents similar to those charged in mineral leases. The lease of the Coal Exchange in Mountstuart Square, granted for ninety-nine years in 1883, stipulated that for the first three years the rent should be one peppercorn, the following two years £100, the

[29] N.L.W., B., 101, 103 and 143.
[30] N.L.W., Jevons Papers, IV, 122.
[31] Ibid.; C.C.L., Cardiff supplementary rental, 1927–30.

next year £200, the following four years £700, and thereafter £1,000 a year for the duration of the lease.[32]

The ground-rents charged by the Bute estate in the valleys of the coalfield were markedly lower than those at Cardiff. Where the building-plot was in an isolated position, the rent was calculated in the first half of the nineteenth century, as a fraction of a charge of around £10 an acre. Thus, in 1827 the estate granted a building lease of ten perches at Aberdare at 15s. a year, and in the 1840s the usual rent for individual plots in the neighbourhood of Hirwaun and Llantrisant was 1d. a square yard for the house and ½d. for the garden.[33] Rents of around £10 an acre, the equivalent of ½d. a square yard or 1s. 3d. a perch, were also the payments generally made by the industrialists who, in the 1820s and 1830s, leased land upon which they erected workers' cottages.[34] Where the responsibility for laying out new streets was that of the Bute estate rather than of the lessee, charges were higher. Houses about sixteen feet wide were leased at Dumfries Street, Treorci, in the 1870s, at £1 10s., a payment which was general for terraced houses in the Rhondda in the late-nineteenth and early-twentieth centuries. Representing about 2s. a foot of frontage or 3d. a square yard, it was less than half the charge made for similar houses in Cardiff during the same period. The difference between the ground-rents of public buildings at Cardiff and those in the industrial valleys was even more marked: Gosen chapel, Treorci, bore a ground-rent of £4 7s. 6d. a year, while £20 was paid for a chapel at Pierhead in Cardiff.[35]

In the early-nineteenth century, the estate was not obliged to provide any services on the land leased for building, the only costs it incurred being the wages of estate officials for the time they spent marking out the plots.[36] Where such building was part of a planned urban development, however, the cost

[32] Ibid.; N.L.W., B., 103.
[33] Lease, 1827 (N.L.W., B., 31); Richards to Thomas, 27 May 1841 (C.C.L., B., IX, 27, 21); Corbett to Bute, 20 January and 30 May 1844, 15 September 1845 (N.L.W., B., 70, L. 1841–45).
[34] Note on Hirwaun common, 1825–26 (N.L.W., B., 47); indenture, 4 July 1837 (ibid., 106).
[35] Ibid., 101; C.C.L., Cardiff supplementary rental, 1927–30; N.L.W., Sale catalogues, 55, 213, 214.
[36] Richards to Stewart, 18 September 1824, to Bute, 22 November 1828 (C.C.L., MS. 4.713); Bute to Richards, 7 September 1824 (G.R.O. D/DA 11); C.C.L., B., XI, 35.

of road construction was a charge upon the estate and, as the century advanced, more elaborate services were required of the lessors. Initially, expenditure was low, sums of up to £100 a year being spent on the formation of Bute Street in the 1830s. With the expansion of Butetown in the 1840s, costs rose; most of the outgoings listed under the heading of 'Improvements' in Richards's 'Cardiff' accounts represented the costs of preparing building ground, and by the late-1840s such expenditure was running at between £1,000 and £3,000 a year. The Bute estate was responsible for the haulage of stones, the making of drains, the laying down of roads and the provision of sewerage for the whole of the new town which grew up around the dock.[37] Much of this work was severely criticised. In the 1880s, John Howell recalled the 'wretchedly inadequate Bute Street' of the 1840s while in 1849, Clark, the estate's mineral agent, noted that 'the exhalations from decomposed vegetable and animal matter lying about the streets and ditches are most offensive and dangerous'. The report on Cardiff's sanitary condition, published in 1850, revealed that the estate's sewerage system had been constructed without reference to the levels of the sewers installed by the town's Commissioners for Streets and argued that open or crudely-filled drains at Butetown were a direct cause of cholera.[38] The report stirred the Bute trustees to action. They appointed a clerk of works, and expenditure on roads and drainage soared. Between August 1851 and July 1859, £16,300 was spent on improvements at Cardiff, an expenditure equivalent to more than half the gross income from ground-rents in the town received by the estate in that period.[39] Under pressure from the newly established local Board of Health, ditches were covered in, sewers repaired, cesspools eliminated and streets drained. The 1850s were also a period of much activity in the valleys of the coalfield, where the report on the sanitary condition of Merthyr Tydfil had caused widespread shock and concern. In the Cynon valley in particular, the

[37] N.L.W., B., 60, 72 and 73; T. W. Rammell, op. cit., pp. 17–18; N.L.W., MS. 7454A, 17 February 1847.
[38] J. Howells, 'Reminiscences of Cardiff', *Red Dragon*, V (1884), 220; Clark to Bruce, 6 June 1849 (Scot. P.R.O., H.B. MSS., 197); T. W. Rammell, op. cit., *passim*.
[39] Letters, 1849–56, in G.R.O., D/DA 33–37; N.L.W., B., 60, 65, 72 and 73.

trustees initiated and financed work similar to that carried out at Cardiff.[40] Thereafter, the standard of the services provided for Bute lessees was high, even critics of the estate acknowledging in the early-twentieth century that insanitary constructions were very rare within its boundaries.[41]

As the marquesses of Bute were the owners of most of the land within the ancient borough of Cardiff, they had the opportunity to plan the rapidly growing town as a coherent whole. In the centre of Cardiff, which in the mid-nineteenth century was 'a most unlovely place, with narrow tortuous streets, the principal ones blocked by dilapidated buildings', their opportunities were admittedly limited.[42] The alignment of High Street and St. Mary's Street had long been established and most of the land between those streets and the dock feeder belonged to other landlords; even had this not been so, any ordered development there would have been hampered by the presence of the dock feeder and the Glamorganshire Canal. The suburb of Crockherbtown, the present Queen Street, also belonged to a number of landowners, and in consequence its development was piecemeal and its alignment crooked. Nevertheless, even though the site of central Cardiff was not part of his inheritance, a man of the second marquess's industry and influence could have commandeered the middle of the town and replanned it. A precedent for such an act would have been very familiar to him, for his close friend and adviser, John Clayton, undertook at Newcastle-upon-Tyne in the 1830s the complex task of cutting through a tangled web of legal rights, succeeding with his associates in obtaining full control over the land in the centre of Newcastle, and in making it the only major town then in England with a planned city centre.[43] This was not a task the second marquess felt called upon to

---

[40] Ibid.; T. W. Rammell, *Report . . . on the . . . sanitary condition of the town of Merthyr Tydfil* (1850); *Cambrian Journal*, 1 (1854), 312–13.

[41] See below, p. 203.

[42] *S.W.D.N.*, 2 April 1910.

[43] L. Wilkes and C. Dodd, *Tyneside classical, the Newcastle of Grainger, Dobson and Clayton* (1964); N. Pevsner, *The buildings of England, Northumberland* (1957), pp. 222–23.

undertake at Cardiff, and the chief glory of central Cardiff today is the result of negative rather than positive action by the Bute estate. By refusing to lease Cathays Park, Coopers Fields and much of the farms of Maendy, Mynachdy, Pontcanna, Plasturton and Blackweir for building purposes, the marquesses preserved a vast tract of open land in the heart of Cardiff long enough to ensure that its value would be recognised and that it would be preserved in perpetuity.

Where the Bute estate did enjoy unfettered control, there was a degree of enlightened town-planning. It was the second marquess's hope that the new town which grew up around his dock, and which he so 'highly approved of . . . being called Butetown', would be a dignified commercial and residential centre.[44] The straight Bute Street, over a mile long, was to be the processional way to the sea and adjoining it on the west the streets were laid out according to a grid-iron plan, centred upon Mountstuart Square, which was named after the marquess's ancestral home, and upon Loudoun Square, named after the ancestral home of his wife. 'The cornices [at Loudoun Square]', Richards was informed in 1853, 'are to be made with Roman cement as used in Belgravia.'[45] The second marquess's hopes of a fine residential district were dashed by the unsavoury reputation which Butetown very rapidly acquired. Before Loudoun Square had been finished, the *Merthyr Guardian* was describing the Bute Street area as 'increasingly vile and abominable . . . keepers of public houses and brothels are gradually obtaining possession of the whole street . . . Cardiff is gaining a world-wide reputation as one of the most immoral of seaports'.[46] Nevertheless, even today, with much of Butetown demolished, enough remains of the original concept to provide a striking example of Victorian architecture and town-planning in what has been described as 'perhaps the most tranquil and evocative commercial centre in Europe'.[47]

[44] Collingdon to Bruce, 23 March 1850 (Scot. P.R.O., H.B. MSS., 196).
[45] Rees to Richards, 1 June 1853 (C.C.L., B., IX, 27, 21). See also J. Summerson, op. cit., p. 179, and J. B. Hilling, *Cardiff and the valleys* (1973), pp. 88–89.
[46] *M.G.*, 8 January 1853.
[47] *Guardian*, 26 January 1968; J. B. Hilling, 'The buildings of Cardiff, an historical survey', *Glamorgan Historian*, VI (1969), 66–69.

Other areas of Cardiff also bear the imprint of the second marquess's ideas. It was he who was responsible for the diversion of the Taff, for it was at his prompting that Brunel, as engineer to the South Wales Railway Company, undertook the work. The diversion, completed by 1853, straightened the course of the river south of Canton Bridge, removed the danger of flooding in the town centre and led to the enlargement of the Great Park, the eventual site of Westgate Street and Cardiff Arms Park. Again, it was the second marquess who insisted that the South Wales Railway should be carried through Cardiff on an embankment rather than that all roads leading from the town to the dock should be intersected by level crossings.[48]

It is, however, in the residential districts of Cardiff developed in the second half of the nineteenth century that the hand of the Bute estate may be most clearly seen. The alignment of most of the streets of the Cathays, Adamsdown, Riverside and South wards of modern Cardiff, and the layout of substantial areas of the suburbs, are the work of Bute officials. The policy which they followed owed much to the experience of the second marquess. In the 1820s, he and his employees, while laying down the alignment of the streets and stipulating their width and the size of the plots, did not insist upon any specific style of building. 'The lots of ground at Crockherbtown', wrote Stewart in 1824, 'should certainly not be less than twenty-five foot and it would be desirable if the lessees should build upon a uniform plan—I doubt, however, the propriety of compelling them to do so.'[49] By the mid-1830s, indiscriminate building on the land of some of the smaller landowners was causing Richards, in particular, to argue for a more rigid control of building. One such landowner, Charles Vachell, allowed a number of squalid closes to be built on his land, Richards commenting that Vachell's 'system of building is most ruinous to the town . . . he lets his land to anyone without reference to any plan of building or of streets and he is

---

[48] Harris to Richards, 21 March 1846, Richards to Owen, 1 and 21 April 1846, Plews to Bute, 7 May 1846, Bute to Richards, 28 December 1846 (G.R.O., D/DA 30); Richards to Bute, 23 March 1846 (N.L.W., B., 70, L. 1845–46); Brunel to Collingdon, 18 September 1847 (C.C.L. MS. 329.51).
[49] Stewart to Richards, 8 September 1824 (G.R.O., D/DA 11); cf. Richards to Stewart, 3 September 1824 (C.C.L. MS. 4.713).

encouraged by some of the town attorneys who profit by preparing his leases'.[50]

The marquess responded by demanding that the layouts and elevations of prospective buildings should be sent to him for approval, and in 1837 he returned plans of the proposed Windsor Place with the comment: 'The roadway is too narrow and the fronts of the houses are too narrow for three windows'. At his insistence, the Place, which was to contain 'houses of a class much wanted [at Cardiff]', was provided with a road forty feet wide and a pavement fifteen feet wide on each side. 'The windows', wrote Richards, 'will not be too many for the first floor which will be 25 foot in some and 27 or 28 foot in width in others.'[51] In 1839, when discussing the rebuilding of Castle Street, he urged his employer 'to have a plan made of the New Buildings . . . and to compel the tenants to build accordingly'.[52] Demands that builders should adhere to a uniform plan became more insistent in the 1840s when, in some of the better residential districts of Butetown, such as Crichton Street, well-designed terraces with attractive pedimented doorways were built.

This trend towards greater direction by the lessors was continued by the trustees. In the 1850s, plans of prospective buildings were sent to them and concern was expressed that vigilance should be exercised in order to ensure 'that the terms and conditions of the Leases . . . are complied with'.[53] Yet, although elaborate hopes had been entertained over Butetown, much of the working-class housing built there in the mid-nineteenth century was inexpressibly dreary, George Santayana considering Cardiff's dockland, with its 'rows of mean little brick houses all alike', to be a place where 'ugliness and desolation could not be more constitutional'.[54] The decline of Butetown as a residential area may well have contributed to the determination of the Bute officials in the late-nineteenth century to be more stringent in controlling the activities of

[50] Richards to Bute, 14 February 1835 (ibid.); Bute to Richards, 11 February 1835 (N.L.W., B., 70, L. 6).
[51] Bute to Richards, 1 December 1837 (ibid.); Richards to Bute, 29 November and 2 December 1837 (C.C.L., MS. 4.860).
[52] Richards to Bute, 12 December 1839 (ibid.).
[53] Clinton to Lady Bute, 7 October 1850 (Scot. P.R.O., H.B. MSS., 196).
[54] G. Santayana, *Persons and places, the background of my life* (1944), pp. 137–38.

those who leased estate land for building. Professor Jevons's description of Bute leasing policy in the early-twentieth century shows that by then such control was complete. The builders 'take out leases for so many plots at a time and build according to the plans supplied by the estate architect . . . The building regulations of the estate are fairly but not unduly strict and are well-enforced, so that weak or insanitary construction is hardly to be found'.[55] By the late-nineteenth century, the spaciousness of planning and the quality of building on the estate were such that the boundary between Bute-owned land and that of other estates is immediately apparent.[56] Indeed, Jevons and other commentators on Bute policy accused the estate officials of doing their work too well, their expansive layouts and their demand for high-quality materials and workmanship causing, it was argued, most of the houses built under Bute leases to be beyond the means of working-class tenants.[57]

Evidence of Bute policy with regard to urban development in the valleys of the coalfield is far less plentiful than it is for Cardiff. The Bute estate owned virtually no building land at Merthyr and was therefore not the ground-landlord of any of the congested housing which sprang up around the ironworks there in the late-eighteenth century. Some iron companies did aim at a more ambitious level of working-class housing; the Union Iron Company, for example, built in the first decade of the nineteenth century three remarkable terraces of what was intended to be a new town, Y Drenewydd, near Rhymney. The initiative in their construction appears to have been entirely that of Johnson, the works manager. Although the houses came to be known as Butetown, the name recalls the Bute Ironworks rather than the family and there is no evidence that the first marquess and his agents had any part in the plan or its fulfilment.[58]

[55] N.L.W., Jevons Papers, IV, 122.
[56] M. J. Daunton, op. cit., p. 79, plates 3–5.
[57] N.L.W., Jevons Papers, IV, 122; E. L. Chappell, *Cardiff's housing problem* (1913), pp. 5, 12.
[58] J. B. Hilling, *Cardiff and the valleys*, p. 103.

From the 1820s onwards, dwellings to house employees of the iron companies were built on the Bute estate at Hirwaun and Aberdare, and sketches of such developments in Stewart's atlas suggest that their layout was more spacious and more carefully planned than was that of earlier clusters of iron-workers' cottages at Dowlais, Cyfarthfa and Penydarren.[59] It was in the second half of the nineteenth century, however, that the urbanization of Bute land within the coalfield gained momentum, in particular at Aberdare, where urban growth was especially rapid in the late-1850s and the early-1870s, and in the Rhondda, where 28,000 houses were built between the 1860s and the First World War.[60] Most of the houses built upon Bute-owned land within the coalfield were erected after the creation of the various local Boards of Health in the 1850s. As the nineteenth century advanced, building in the industrial valleys became subject to increasingly rigid by-laws enacted by the sanitary authorities, with the result that housing reformers in the early-twentieth century considered the mining population of south Wales to be better housed than were the populations of other British coalfields.[61]

There are no references to estate policy on the urban development of the industrial valleys of Glamorgan in the Bute correspondence. The diary of W. S. Clark, mineral agent to the estate from 1845 to 1864, contains occasional remarks about the supervision of the laying-out of building land in the upper Rhondda, and it may be assumed that the alignment of streets on Bute property at Treorci, Treherbert, Aberdare and else-where was the work of subordinate officials working under the supervision of Clark and later, of his successor, W. T. Lewis.[62] The by-laws to which urban development was subject were intended by their framers as minimum standards; many landowners and developers in industrial south Wales, however, viewed them as the maximum standard, and evidence on the ground suggests that housebuilders only rarely exceeded what they considered to be the norm laid down in the regulations.

[59] G.R.O., D/DB E 2.
[60] J. H. Richards and J. Parry Lewis, op. cit., pp. 297–99; E. D. Lewis, op. cit., p. 202.
[61] J. B. Hilling, *Cardiff and the valleys*, pp. 107–8; H. S. Jevons, *The British coal trade* (1915), pp. 128–29, 643.
[62] N.L.W., MSS. 7454A–7462A.

Houses on the Bute estate tended to be of a rather higher standard. In the Rhondda, for example, the Sanitary Authority laid down in 1879 that there should be a minimum of 150 square feet behind each house; plots leased by the Bute estate a decade earlier had allowed for backyards more than twice that size.[63]

Nowhere did the estate include a complete valley; thus, the opportunity for large-scale coherent planning was limited. In the upper Rhondda, however, Bute-owned land was sufficiently extensive to allow the planning of a major part of the town of Treorci, most of which was built on the land of the Bute farms of Abergorci and Ystradfechan. The width and straightness of Bute Street, the main thoroughfare, give Treorci a distinction among the urban settlements of the coalfield, a distinction which must be attributed to the work of Bute officials, for the layout of the town deteriorates rapidly at the boundary between the Bute and the Crawshay Bailey estates. The spaciousness and dignity of parts of the town of Aberdare can also be ascribed to Bute policy, as can other rare examples of attractive features in the urban landscape of the east Glamorgan coalfield, including the peaceful and archaic centre of Llantrisant and the splendidly uncluttered environs of Caerphilly Castle. It must be admitted, however, that the quality of urban development in the south Wales coalfield in the nineteenth century was such that even the most tentative evidence of a coherent plan elevates a township far above its neighbours.

Differences between the operation of the leasehold system at Cardiff and in the industrial valleys, which were apparent in the levels of ground-rent and in the availability of evidence of active participation by the Bute estate in urban planning, are equally apparent when the holders of Bute ground-leases are examined. At Cardiff, the payers of ground-rent listed in the rentals were overwhelmingly individuals who had leased houses which they let to tenants. In the coalfield, individual

[63] J. B. Hilling, *Cardiff and the valleys*, p. 107; personal observation.

landlord leaseholders were far less numerous, their place being taken either by owner-occupiers or by companies holding leases and renting houses to their employees. Both these categories were rare at Cardiff; only 9·7 per cent of the houses within the town were owned by their occupiers in 1884 and the proportion had fallen to 7·2 per cent by 1914. The most significant example of a company providing houses for its employees was the Dowlais Iron Company, whose 222 houses, built in the 1890s, represented 0·8 per cent of the tenanted houses of the town. House-ownership by companies other than employers was also unusual at Cardiff; the Cardiff Workmen's Cottage Company, founded in 1869, and the Glamorgan Workmen's Cottage Company, founded in 1881, owned between them in 1914 a total of 584 houses, compared with over 26,000 houses owned by individual landlords. Building societies played little part in financing house purchase in the town: the Starr-Bowkett clubs gained minimal support and the Principality Building Society, founded in 1869 'to provide working men . . . with a house at trifling cost', rapidly became the preserve of the middle class. [64]

The number of houses owned by an individual landlord and the number of dwellings let by holders of Bute leases at Cardiff varied from one to several hundred. One of the earliest holders of a Bute lease of a house intended for letting was John Bird, who in 1822 built himself a house at Crockherbtown, leasing two plots from the second marquess because, 'of building, I might as well build two'. In the 1840s David Storms, the dock contractor, became the landlord of a large number of houses leased from the estate at Butetown, as did William Vachell, the brother of Charles Vachell, the landowner, who in 1841 leased all the houses in John Street near the Gas Works. [65] The leasing of a whole street by an individual was a practice which continued into the late-nineteenth century, Edwin Trotman leasing in the 1880s the whole of May Street, Cathays. By then, however, it was more usual for a landlord to lease groups of houses in a number of streets, the rentals recording that between 1882 and 1886 David Thomas leased ten houses in Hirwaun Street, ten in Darran Street, fourteen

[64] M. J. Daunton, op. cit., pp. 108, 111, 115, 120; *C.T.*, 31 December 1859.
[65] Bird to Stewart, 23 April 1822 (N.L.W., B., 70, L. A); rentals (ibid., 65).

in Talbot Street, four in Pitman Street, eleven in Hamilton Street and fourteen in Ryder Street, and that in the same period John Evan Davies leased parts of half a dozen streets.[66] Generally, however, the landlords of dwelling-houses who held leases from the Bute and other estates at Cardiff were investors on a smaller scale. Only six individuals held more than fifty houses each in the town in 1884 and within the various quarters of Cardiff, owners of five houses or less constituted between 71 and 91 per cent of all tenanted dwellings. Investment in housing, often by people of modest means, could be profitable; a recent study suggests that the net returns at Cardiff varied between 4 and 12 per cent.[67]

In the valleys of the coalfield the earliest payers of ground-rent to the Bute estate were the encroachers on the commons of the Bute manors who were converted into leaseholders. Such a group emerged in the upper Cynon valley in the 1780s and the continuance of the practice into the mid-nineteenth century is indicated by a petition from squatters at Hirwaun in 1851 who, describing themselves as 'in low circumstances and entirely ignorant of the law', appealed to the marquess 'that some means will be taken by you to secure to them a title to the Erections in question by the payment from your Memorialists of a moderate ground rent'.[68] A less haphazard form of leasing began in the 1820s with the renting of building land by the acre to industrialists, the lessees being granted full powers to lay out streets and to build houses for their employees. The estate granted a number of such leases in the valleys of the Cynon and the Rhymney, and by 1845 the Rhymney Iron Company had built 333 houses on Bute land.[69] Clauses in the mineral leases of the 1870s specifying the rent to be paid for land leased for housing suggest that the practice continued into the late-nineteenth century,[70] but by then it was more usual for industrialists who became tenants of Bute building land to lease a number of houses in streets which the estate itself had laid out. Houses rented by colliery owners were more

[66] Ibid., 103; C.C.L., Cardiff supplementary rental, 1927–30.
[67] M. J. Daunton, op. cit., pp. 116–18, 121–23.
[68] Petition, 6 June 1851 (Scot. P.R.O., H.B. MSS., 196); see above, p. 40.
[69] C.C.L., B., VI, 33, 18; Crawshay to Tyndall, 11 April 1826 (N.L.W., B., 47).
[70] E.g., the lease to David Davies and others, 1867 (N.L.W., B., 106).

numerous in the south Wales coalfield than in any other coal-field of Britain apart from the Scottish.[71] Among such houses were those rented by Burnyeat Brown and Company, owners of the Abergorki colliery who in the 1870s leased Nos. 1–52 Glynrhondda Street and 166–88 Bute Street in Treorci from the Bute estate. Later in the century the estate granted similar leases to the Ocean Coal Company in the Rhondda and to the Powell Duffryn Steam Coal Company in the Cynon and Rhymney valleys.[72]

The provision of houses by coalowners caused the role of individual speculative landlords to be less important in the housing market of the industrial valleys than it was at Cardiff. Their role was lessened further by the high degree of owner-occupation which characterised the Glamorgan coalfield. Professor Jevons believed that the proportion of occupying owners varied in 1913 'from about 15 up to 60 per cent in the mining valleys', the highest proportions being in the Rhondda valleys; in 1919 the chairman of the South Wales Coalowners Association stated that 60 per cent of the houses of Tredegar were owner-occupied and that farther west the proportion was as high as 70 per cent.[73] Bute rentals, while listing all lease-holders, do not distinguish between those who occupied and those who let the houses for which they paid ground-rent. Oral evidence suggests that owner-occupiers such as Henry Davies, who leased No. 125 Dumfries Street, Treorci, in 1874, and his brother Evan Davies, who leased No. 126 in the same year, were typical of large numbers of holders of Bute leases in the Rhondda Valley and elsewhere. The widespread interest in the sales of leaseholds conducted by the estate in 1919 is a further indication of the degree to which Bute urban leases in the industrial valleys were held, not by a small group of landlords but by the actual occupiers of the houses.[74]

Owner-occupation was largely financed through building clubs, which were numerous in the coalfield long before the Starr-Bowkett type of club proliferated in the 1880s. 'Mr. Davies of Hirwaun', wrote Corbett in 1843, 'wants . . .

[71] *P.P.*, XII (1919), 1079–81; the Royal Commission on the coal industry (1925), *Appendix and Index* (1926), pp. 247–48.
[72] N.L.W., B., 101; N.L.W., Sale catalogues, 213.
[73] N.L.W., Jevons Papers, IV, 122; *P.P.*, XII (1919), 702, 1079.
[74] N.L.W., B., 103.

to build houses at Aberdare with the money of some club.'[75] The later decades of the nineteenth century saw the rapid growth of owner-occupation in the industrial valleys. By 1891 there were eighty-six building societies in Glamorgan, their membership totalling 12,760 and their annual receipts £351,795. In the first decade of the twentieth century, however, the massive influx of population into the coalfield and the sharp rise in building costs reversed the trend and the colliery companies were obliged to re-enter the housing market.[76]

As the Bute estate's income from ground-rents increased and as the power possessed by the estate over the development of land in east Glamorgan was more fully appreciated, Bute urban policy came increasingly under attack. In the coalfield, where a large proportion of the population was buying its own houses, the payment of ground-rent as well as mortgage redemption seemed an objectionable imposition. At Cardiff, where owner-occupation was rare, the leasehold system was held to be a major cause of the high rents characteristic of the town and was considered particularly burdensome to the working classes as ground-rent constituted a higher proportion of the rent of modest houses than it did of more substantial dwellings.[77]

The early-1870s saw the publication of a number of books and pamphlets attacking the position of the urban landlord and at the same time there was the tentative beginning of such agitation at Cardiff.[78] By the 1880s, the campaign was widely supported, the *Cardiff Times*, in particular, being diligent in searching for examples of Bute oppression not only in Glamorgan but also in Scotland. In 1884 a branch of Henry George's Land Reform League was founded at Cardiff, its

---

[75] Corbett to Bute, 19 April 1843 (N.L.W., B., 70, L. Corbett, 1841–45).
[76] *Return relating to building societies*, 1892, pp. 161–66; *P.P.*, XII (1919), 1079–81; P. N. Jones, *Colliery settlement in the south Wales coalfield, 1850 to 1926* (1969), pp. 12–14, 41–48; H. S. Jevons, op. cit., pp. 648–50.
[77] E. L. Chappell, op. cit., p. 13.
[78] E.g., J. Macdonell, *The land question* (1873), pp. 83–108, and *C.T.*, 31 January, 1874. Cf. D. A. Reeder, 'The politics of urban leaseholds in late-Victorian England', *International Review of Social History*, VI (1961).

aims including the compulsory sale of leaseholds. During the election of 1885, Sir Edward Reed, Cardiff's Liberal candidate, talked of leases being granted 'on terms which are . . . disgraceful to the trading and commercial character of this great town'.[79] Liberals in south Wales came to consider the policies and impositions of the urban landowner to be the determining factors in the housing problem which in Cardiff in the late-nineteenth century consisted not so much of slum dwellings as of an insufficiency of housing stock at rents which working-class families could afford. By the early-twentieth century, it was estimated that only a quarter of the dwellings of the town was let 'at rentals which may be regarded as reasonable from the standpoint of the average worker', the resultant 'cottage famine' being considered the consequence of the policies of the larger estates which had, it was claimed, given priority to the building of large and expensive villa-type houses.[80] In the coalfield, the rapid growth of population, allied to the problems of obtaining building land, moved Professor Jevons to state in 1915 that 'building enterprise has hopelessly failed and a serious house famine has resulted'.[81] It was gratifying for the Liberals to be able to place the blame for the housing problem upon the ground landlords, almost all of whom were political opponents. By the twentieth century, however, the more progressive of Cardiff's reformers were realising that the problem was more complex than had hitherto been believed, and in the 1920s E. L. Chappell in particular was to become, through his work with the Welsh Housing and Development Association, an ardent advocate of municipal and subsidised housing.[82]

In the campaign against ground-landlordism, the Bute estate was especially vulnerable. It had developed its land with a greater emphasis upon houses for the well-to-do than had the other major estates of Cardiff, and its refusal to sell building land was more rigid than theirs.[83] As some of the house leases granted in the 1820s and 1830s were for periods

[79] C.T., 25 February 1882, 14 November 1885; S.W.D.N., 18 February 1884.
[80] E. L. Chappell, op. cit., pp. 2, 5; cf. M. J. Daunton, op. cit., ch. 6.
[81] H. S. Jevons, op. cit., p. 637.
[82] The Welsh housing and development yearbook, 1911–34; E. L. Chappell, op. cit.; idem, Gwalia's homes (1911); cf. M. J. Daunton, op. cit., pp. 103–5.
[83] N.L.W., Jevons Papers, IV, 122.

shorter than ninety-nine years, by the 1880s the rights of the tenant at the expiration of the lease were under discussion. Demand arose for legislation which would 'prevent Lord Bute or any other man from taking . . . homes without compensation', and in 1897 the Cardiff and South Wales Leasehold Enfranchisement Association was founded.[84] In the years immediately before the First World War, Professor Jevons gathered a large body of evidence to support his contention that 'it was a generally well-known fact that applications for renewal [of leases] would not be entertained' by the Bute estate, and in 1909 the Cardiff City Council passed a motion demanding to know what Bute intentions were with regard to the 'renewal and extension on fair and equitable terms of Bute ground leases which are drawing to a close'.[85] Jevons alleged that estate policy on this matter was considerably relaxed when Lord Ninian Crichton-Stuart was adopted as Unionist candidate for Cardiff in 1910 and it may not be without significance that, following Lord Ninian's victory, the estate offered six acres of land for cottage building at Splott.[86]

Jevons and others also claimed that Bute policy on leasing sites for works and factories gravely hampered Cardiff's development as an industrial centre. The almost total absence of freehold sites in the neighbourhood of the docks, where the Bute estate had a virtual monopoly of land, the estate's policy of granting industrial leases for a maximum of sixty years and, in most cases, only for between twenty-one and thirty years and the high rents charged were factors, it was claimed, which had severely retarded Cardiff's growth. Cammell Laird, Jevons alleged, had investigated sites for a steel-works at Cardiff which would have employed 6,000 men, but the company had withdrawn from the area after failing to obtain satisfactory terms for leasing the necessary land. 'If the sale of freehold land or if long leases had been granted by the Bute estate', asserted Jevons, 'Cardiff would now [1913] be a town of 500,000 rather than 200,000.' It has recently been persuasively argued that the growth of Cardiff on such a scale was hindered

[84] *S.W.D.N.*, 24 October 1889 and 11 June 1897; *Merthyr Express*, 11 February 1888; *C.*, 16 March 1888.
[85] *S.W.D.N.*, 7 April 1909; N.L.W., Jevons Papers, IV, 122.
[86] Ibid.

by more complex factors than the single issue of the availability of land, but that such opinions were held and promulgated by a man of the integrity and standing of Jevons undoubtedly added to the antagonism felt by Cardiffians in the early-twentieth century towards the Bute estate and its policies.[87]

Other factors contributed to this antagonism. There was a feeling that the location of Cardiff's public buildings was subservient to the convenience of the Bute estate and that the religious denominations were at the mercy of the Roman Catholic predilections of the third and fourth marquesses. Among leaseholders, the estate's demand for a fee on the reassignment of a lease was resented as was the imposition of a fine of up to £50 if a house were turned into a shop. The situation was exacerbated, Jevons claimed, by the over-centralisation of the estate's administration under Lord Merthyr: 'every renewal of a lease . . . must receive Lord Merthyr's personal consideration, even sometimes to minutest details . . . so that . . . all kinds of negotiations for leases . . . are unduly protracted'. Above all, it was the far-reaching and interlocking nature of Bute interests which most disturbed radical critics of estate policy. 'It is almost certain', wrote Jevons, 'that there is no builder in Cardiff who would dare bring an action against the Bute; he never knows when he may want some concession down the Docks, from the Cardiff Railway, or from colliery or industrial enterprises out of the many [with] which Lord Bute or the trustees of the Bute estate or Lord Merthyr or the surveyors, architects or solicitors of the Bute estate are connected.'[88]

Not all local commentators viewed the Bute leasehold system in as negative a light as did Jevons. Questioned by the Select Committee on Town Holdings in 1887, a firm of Cardiff solicitors stated: 'We believe that if the tenure was altered, it would put an end to a great proportion of speculative building . . . we think the present system most satisfactory'.[89] In Cardiff, where most of the house building was undertaken by small speculative builders of little capital, the fact that the leasehold

[87] Ibid.; M. J. Daunton, op. cit., pp. 37–54.
[88] N.L.W., Jevons Papers, IV, 122; *W.M.*, 12 November 1885.
[89] *P.P.*, XIII (1887), 796–97.

system did not oblige the builder to raise the purchase price of the plot could be of material assistance to him, and in the industrial valleys, where home buyers were numerous, the fact that the price of the plot was not a component part of the price of the house may have enabled many to buy houses which they could not otherwise have afforded. Such considerations, however, may have carried less weight with late-nineteenth century Welsh Liberals than did the view of T. J. Wheldon, minister at Blaenau Ffestiniog, who told the Select Committee on Town Holdings: 'By paying a rent to his landlord [a tenant] satisfies his conscience . . . but in paying a lump sum down for the freehold, he feels himself a nobler man . . . The one would be an act of justice, the other would be an act of joy to him.'[90]

By the early-twentieth century attacks upon urban leases were creating apprehension among the ground landlords themselves and, believing that 'leasehold enfranchisement is bound to come', some estates, the Bute estate among them, began granting 999-year leases for which they could obtain a slightly higher ground-rent.[91] Agitation against the building-lease system developed hand in hand with the agitation against mineral royalties and had close links with the anti-landlordism of the countryside. For the agricultural tenant, his difficulties were alleviated by the various agricultural holdings acts of the late-nineteenth century and by the vast transfer of farms from landlord to cultivator which occurred in the twentieth century.[92] The position of the coalowner was improved by legislation and the whole private royalty system was abolished with the nationalisation of mineral reserves in 1938.[93] The holders of building leases had longer to wait. The antagonism felt towards the marquesses of Bute as owners of urban land was felt more intensely towards the anonymous Western Ground Rents Company. Despite the Leasehold Enfranchisement Act of 1967, legislation which was enacted largely as a response to vigorous campaigning in industrial south Wales, the issue has not yet been fully resolved.

[90] *P.P.*, XXII (1887), p. 222.
[91] N.L.W., Jevons Papers, IV, 122.
[92] J. Davies, 'The end of the great estates and the rise of freehold farming in Wales', *Welsh History Review*, VII, no. 2 (1974), pp. 186–212.
[93] See below, p. 243.

VI

THE MINERAL ESTATE*

'When I first went to investigate the very extensive mineral property of your lordship in South Wales [in 1823]', wrote Robert Bald to the second marquess of Bute in 1845, 'your lordship . . . had not the vestige of any mineral plans, records or sections of strata; . . . nevertheless, by perseverance . . . I was able to give a clear view of your lordship's mineral property [and] . . . was much complimented, not only by your lordship but also by your men of business and agents who . . . had not the least conception of the great value of these minerals.'[1] British landowners, unlike those of most of continental Europe, were the owners of the non-precious minerals beneath the surface land of their estates and thus mining developments could represent for them significant accretions of income.[2] Mining had taken place for centuries beneath the lands which constituted the Bute estate but eighteenth century leases, such as that of Dowlais, indicate that those who granted them had little notion of the wealth which their ownership of minerals could represent.[3] Despite the riches which the Welsh iron-masters had amassed by the early-nineteenth century, the extent and value of the south Wales coalfield were only slowly realised. The first to undertake a scientific study of the matter was Edward Martin, who in 1799 fired Bird's imagination with talk of iron ore enough to keep furnaces going for a hundred years and of coal sufficient to supply the whole kingdom. In 1806 Martin's notes were published by the Royal Society and his work was the basis of subsequent study of the south Wales mineral basin.[4]

---

* All references to mineral leases, unless otherwise stated, are drawn from material in N.L.W., Bute collection, Box 106.

[1] Bald to Bute, 4 December 1845 (C.C.L., B., XIV, 70, 14).

[2] R. A. S. Redmayne and G. Stone, *The ownership and valuation of mineral property in the United Kingdom* (1920), *passim*.

[3] J. Davies, 'The Dowlais lease, 1748–1900', *Morgannwg*, XII (1968), 37–66.

[4] E. Martin, 'Description of the mineral basin in the counties of Glamorgan, Monmouth, Brecknock, Carmarthen and Pembroke', *Philosophical Transactions of the Royal Society of London* (1806), pp. 342–47; C.C.L., MS. 2.716, 24 October 1799.

The second marquess of Bute, as lord of most of the manors of east Glamorgan, owned the minerals not only beneath his freeholds but also beneath the commons within the basin of the river Taff, commons which stretched almost precisely to the northern limits of the coalfield.[5] It was during the survey of the estate which Stewart commenced in 1817 that Bute began to appreciate the wealth that could accrue to him through the exploitation of the coalfield. 'The time must come', wrote Stewart, 'when either the present Marquess or one of his successors will reap the benefit of the present investigation and when the enormous wealth which now lies useless will be put into full activity.'[6] His optimism was confirmed by Bald's survey mentioned above, conducted during the winter of 1823–24. By the 1830s, when the second marquess embarked on the dock building project which was aimed at bringing that 'enormous wealth' into 'full activity', the riches of the coalfield were widely appreciated. Smyth, his dockmaster, who considered that Providence had ordained the universal deluge expressly to create the south Wales coalfield, estimated that it represented £375 million in royalties to its owners, figures which were confirmed by de la Beche's geological survey.[7]

Having been awakened to a realisation of the value of his inheritance, the second marquess, under Stewart's guidance, hastened to secure his rights over what he already owned and to enlarge his holdings within the coalfield through purchase. At Dowlais, Stewart discovered large-scale workings of minerals not leased to the company, instigated litigation for compensation and established the boundaries of those freeholds within the common which had not been included in the original lease. Counsel's opinion was obtained on Bute's right to the minerals beneath the wastes of his manors and Stewart urged the marquess to grant leases of small pits on the commons as acts of ownership. Substantial purchases of mineral land were made, some aiming at the command of

[5] The estate included minerals beneath 36,000 acres of the south Wales coal basin, although Bute freehold land within the basin was below 10,000 acres. Coal House, Llanishen, Cardiff, Claim Files, R.O./8/25, 41, 55, 56, 58, 62, 66, 67, 70, 72, 73, 74, 77, 82, 84, 85, 87, 89, 95, 97, 101, 103, 104, 106, 107, 113, 115, 116, 136, 154, 182, 281; C.C.L., B., VII, 13, 4.

[6] Ibid., IX, 19; ibid., MS. 4.850.

[7] W. H. Smyth, *Nautical observations on the port and maritime vicinity of Cardiff* (1840), p. vii.

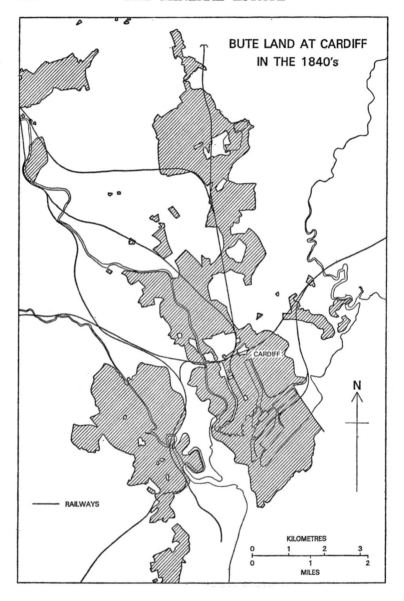

BUTE LAND AT CARDIFF
IN THE 1840's

CARDIFF

N

RAILWAYS

KILOMETRES
0   1   2   3
0   1   2
MILES

openings to the commons in places where surreptitious enclosure had created a barrier between Bute freeholds and the waste, and others representing significant extensions of the marquess's property within the coalfield. The Rhondda estate of Sir John Wood, purchased in 1824, included the land upon which the township of Treherbert was later built, and the Wyndham Lewis property in the Cynon valley, acquired in 1826, comprised much of the site of the town of Aberdare.[8] These purchases initiated a policy which was to continue throughout the nineteenth century and which made the Bute family the owners of by far the largest estate in the valleys of the Taff, the Rhondda, the Cynon and the Rhymney, the richest part of the coalfield. In 1919 the fourth marquess stated that the family had spent £220,000 on purchasing mineral land in the south Wales coalfield between 1814 and 1919, purchases which were among the most profitable investments made by any landed family.[9]

In seeking to profit from his mineral holdings, the second marquess was faced with two alternatives: either to exploit his minerals himself or to lease them in exchange for royalties, dead rents and wayleaves. By the early-nineteenth century, active participation by landowners in the exploitation of minerals had ceased to be common in the south Wales coalfield; it became increasingly rare in the course of the century and by 1919 less than 2 per cent of Welsh coal output was mined from freeholds.[10] Bute, however, ran collieries in county Durham and it might well have been expected that such an active landowner would have exploited his coal in Glamorgan, as did the Dudleys in Worcestershire and the Lowthers in Cumberland.[11] The marquess was indeed urged to become a large-scale coalowner and freighter but he was reluctant to do

[8] C.C.L., MS. 4.850; ibid., B., VII, 13, 4, IX, 17; Bute to Smyth, 19 August 1839 and 13 August 1840 (N.L.W., B., 70, L. 7); Steel to Smyth, 23 August 1841 (ibid., 141, 5); J. Davies, op. cit., pp. 41–47.

[9] P.P., XII (1919), 654; Coal House, Llanishen: Claim Files, see note 5.

[10] P.P., XXXVI (1890), 188; J. H. Morris and L. J. Williams, The south Wales coal industry, 1841–75 (1958), p. 116; A. H. John, The industrial development of south Wales, 1750–1850 (1950), pp. 8–10; G. E. Mingay, English landed society in the eighteenth century (1963), p. 65.

[11] F. M. L. Thompson, English landed society in the nineteenth century (1963), p. 264; 'English great estates, 1790–1914', Contributions to the first international conference of economic history (1960); D. Spring, 'Landed estate in the age of coal and iron', Journal of Economic History, XI (1951).

so in view of the circumstances which prevailed at Cardiff. 'I carry on collieries myself on the river Tyne', he wrote in 1841, 'but those are long established and well known . . . and moreover there is one ingredient in that concern which I look upon as a *sine qua non*—that is to say, a shipping merchant on a *del credere* commission—which is—the owners pay a higher rate of commission and have no risk of bad debts. I have never been able to find a merchant who would fit my coal in Glamorgan upon a *del credere* commission and until then I will have nothing to do with any coal trade.'[12]

Nevertheless, Bute had by 1841 already entered the coal trade on a small scale and his son's trustees were to become substantial coalowners. However, in every case where the Bute Glamorgan minerals were worked by their owner, direct profit from the undertakings was not the primary object. The second marquess's first such attempt in Glamorgan was motivated by social rather than economic reasons. In 1832 his mineral agent noted that 'his lordship is thinking of opening a colliery for sending a supply of stone coal to Neath and Swansea markets with a view to the employment of workmen'.[13] The site of the proposed colliery was at Rhigos on the great Hirwaun moor, where the Bute tenants were among the most poverty-stricken in Glamorgan. The difficulties facing the Rhigos colliery were considerable and the venture was hardly a success. Coal from the mine did not reach the market until 1836 and after building a tramroad, buying canal barges and leasing a wharf at Neath, the marquess failed to find anyone there capable of handling his coal on the terms he obtained at Newcastle.[14] By 1840 he was tired of the venture. 'Of all my concerns', he wrote, 'this Rhigos colliery is the only one which makes my patience give way. It takes my attention and my money in an annoying way from matters of larger importance.'[15] Between 1839 and 1841 he made three attempts to wind up the concern but each time he drew back, fearing for

[12] Bute to Smyth, 9 January 1841 (N.L.W., B., 70, L. 7).
[13] Memorandum, 1832 (ibid., 141, 5); Bute to Richards, 2 January 1833 (G.R.O., D/DA 18).
[14] Memorandum, 1833 (ibid.); C.C.L., B., XI, 55, XVI, 4 and 5; Richards to Bute, 23 February 1833 (ibid., MS. 4.713).
[15] Bute to Smyth, 25 and 31 July 1840 (N.L.W., B., 70, L. 7).

the sufferings of the dependent community. In 1841 David Davis of Hirwaun made an offer for the colliery and it was leased to him in the following year.[16]

The trouble and expense of the Rhigos work were powerful arguments against further such experiments and strengthened Bute in his resolve to lease profitably as much of his mineral land as possible. By the 1840s, the decade which saw the making of the reputation of the steam coal of Aberdare, most of his mineral land in the Cynon valley had been leased and Aberdare was becoming a major source of Bute income. The marquess therefore became anxious to promote the exploitation of the steam coal of the Rhondda valley where he owned 8,000 acres. An essential preliminary to such exploitation was the completion of the Rhondda branch of the Taff Vale Railway. 'Any scheme', wrote Bruce in 1845, 'which proposes to open the Rhondda valley and to bring its rich products to Cardiff is one essentially beneficial to his lordship's property.'[17] In that year an opportunity arose for Bute to add to his property there when William Davies, one of the last of the yeomen of the parish of Ystradyfodwg, offered his 600-acre farm of Cwmsaerbren for sale. Corbett was excited by Cwmsaerbren's possibilities. 'It extends across the valley', he wrote, 'so that no railway may be taken up without crossing it.' Agreement to purchase the property for £11,000 was signed in 1845, but difficulties over boundaries and title delayed the completion of the sale until 1848.[18]

Having purchased Cwmsaerbren, Bute failed to attract a coalowner prepared to mine steam coal at unknown depths on an inaccessible site. He also failed to persuade the Taff Vale Railway Company to construct its line up the valley. In April 1848 the second marquess died and by 1850 his trustees had decided to open a colliery at Cwmsaerbren themselves. The motives for so doing were strong. As the Bute mineral agent, W. S. Clark, pointed out when reporting on the proposed purchase of Blaenllechau in the Rhondda Fach in 1845:

---

[16] Collingdon to Smyth, 20 August 1840, Bute to Smyth, 12 August 1841 (ibid., L. 7); notes, 1840, lease to Davis (ibid., 141, 5).

[17] Bruce to Roy, 15 October 1845 (ibid., 70, L. 1845–46).

[18] Corbett to Bute, 8 and 27 March 1845 (ibid., L. Corbett, 1845–46); C.C.L., B., VII, 27, 2.

'Nothing has been done to prove the minerals in this property. This greatly lessens their value'.[19]

By proving that the steam coal of the Rhondda lay at exploitable depths, the trustees could demand royalties and rents there comparable with those charged at Aberdare, while successful borings would motivate the Taff Vale Railway Company to construct its Rhondda branch railway. In January 1850, Clark met the Rhondda landowner, Griffith Llewelyn, and representatives of the Taff Vale Railway Company, and it was agreed that the Bute trustees should sink a pit to prove the coal. The work was under way by September 1850, spurred on by the company's grant of £500 towards the cost. The experiment proved troublesome and expensive; the site was remote, all equipment having to be hauled from the Taff Vale's terminus at Dinas, and in 1854 and 1855 expenditure rose to the alarming average of £500 a month. In December 1855, the Cwmsaerbren pit, soon to be known as the Bute Merthyr colliery, produced the first wagon of steam coal to leave the Rhondda and the Taff Vale Railway Company extended its line to the pit in August 1856. The Bute role in initiating the working of steam coal in the most famous of coal valleys was commemorated when the township which grew near the new works was named Treherbert, the family name of the earls of Pembroke, whose estates the Butes had inherited.[20]

Having proved the case for charging substantial royalties for Rhondda coal, the Bute trustees sought to relieve themselves of the burden of running their colliery by leasing it to a company. After two years of operation the company failed and the colliery was virtually abandoned until it was re-started by the trustees in 1861. During the 1860s the Bute Merthyr pit was the responsibility of the estate's assistant mineral agent, the young W. T. Lewis; under him sinkings were extended to the three seams below the four-foot seam struck in 1853 and output increased from 34,000 tons in 1864 to 60,000 tons in 1869. Profits from the colliery rose from £3,500 a year in 1867–68 to over £10,000 during the boom years of the

---

[19] Ibid., 7 and 46, 1; J. H. Morris and L. J. Williams, op. cit., pp. 112–13.
[20] Ibid., pp. 114–15; C.C.L., B., VII, 46, 1; N.L.W., 7454A–7462A; E. D. Lewis, *The Rhondda valleys* (1959), pp. 69–70, 118.

early-1870s, but from the mid-1870s onwards, partly because of expenditure on the neighbouring Lady Margaret pit, the undertakings showed a deficit which rose to £11,360 in 1880.[21]

By the 1890s collieries managed directly by the Bute estate were producing over 160,000 tons of coal a year. In addition to the Treherbert enterprises, they included pits which the third marquess had taken over on the bankruptcy of lessees, among them the concerns which Richard Fothergill had leased in the Cynon valley and the Tylacoch colliery in the Rhondda.[22] Under the fourth marquess, the estate gave up colliery ownership. Fothergill's collieries at Aberdare were sold to the Powell Duffryn Company in 1915 and those at Hirwaun to D. R. Llewelyn in 1919. The Treherbert pits, together with the defunct Tylacoch colliery, were sold to the United National Collieries in 1915, a concern later absorbed by the giant Ocean Coal Company.[23]

Apart from becoming a colliery owner himself, there were other courses open to a landowner to accelerate the pace of industrial development and to shape its pattern to his own advantage. Cwmsaerbren was not an isolated example of proving the existence of exploitable minerals on the Bute estate. In the 1790s Bute agents had employed workmen to try for coal at Hirwaun as a preliminary to the letting of small levels to local farmers, and similar operations were undertaken at Rhigos in the 1820s. In 1827 the second marquess ordered borings for iron ore to be made at Castell Coch and, when low grade ore was found, considered establishing his own ironworks at Tongwynlais. On the commons of Caerphilly, Llantrisant and Eglwysilan, he and, later, his son's trustees made sinkings in search of exploitable seams, and successful trials were followed by profitable leases.[24]

As the greatest landowner within the Taff basin, the second marquess was expected by industrialists and by fellow landowners to be prepared to use his estate as a clearing house for mineral land. In 1825 Crawshay urged him to buy the Gwynn

[21] C.C.L., B., X, 2 and MS. 4.937.
[22] Ibid., B., XVI, 13; deeds relating to Tyla coch, 1891 (N.L.W., B., 28).
[23] Colliery Guardian, 19 February 1915 and 18 July 1919.
[24] Vouchers (G.R.O., D/DA 56–117); Lloyd to Dalrymple, 20 September 1825 (N.L.W., B., 70, L. 1825–36); C.C.L., B., VII, 26, XIV, 40; N.L.W., MSS., 7454A–7462A.

Holford properties near Hirwaun in order to augment the Hirwaun Iron Company's leaseholds. In the same year the marquess made a bid for the Rhymney ironworks with a view to leasing it to his tenants, the Bute Iron Company.[25] In 1843 Thomas of the Court, Merthyr, owner of the Werfa estate at Aberdare, offered to lease his minerals to Bute, promising to 'fall in with any agreement of his lordship, a nobleman from whom I have always experienced the most flattering kindness'.[26] Many of the smaller landowners of the coalfield, men such as Leigh of Pontlotyn, Davies of Cwmsaerbren and Thomas of the Court, discovering that their ancestral lands had become the object of intense interest and uncertain of how best to benefit from their good fortune, preferred to lease or sell their lands to a great mineral landowner rather than to treat directly with coalowners and ironmasters. Thus, from Leigh Bute leased the Pontlotyn estate, sub-leasing it to the Rhymney Iron Company; from Davies he leased Pwll yr hwyaid, sub-leasing it to the Penydarren Company and from Thomas he leased Werfa, sub-leasing it to Nixon.[27] Although these transactions were initially expensive, dead rents having to be paid whether or not the minerals had been sub-leased, the Bute estate ultimately benefited. By leasing adjacent or interlocking land, the marquess was able to offer industrialists more convenient mineral takings and could also prevent his tenants from working the coal of others to the exclusion of his own.

To ensure the success of his lessees, Bute was prepared to assist them financially. Loans by local landowners to ironmasters had not been uncommon in the eighteenth century and the practice was one which the marquess continued. When Beaumont, his mineral agent, set up as a coalowner in 1839, Bute lent him £1,200 to pay the first two years of his dead rent, and when disputes among the partners caused the Aberdare Iron Company to be sold in 1846, one of the partners turned for assistance to the marquess, his landlord, 'asking me

[25] Crawshay to Stewart, 18 February 1825, to Tyndall, 4 March 1825 (N.L.W., Cyfarthfa Papers III); Farrer to Richards, 31 July 1824 (G.R.O., D/DA 11); notes, 1825 (N.L.W., B., 47).
[26] Richards to Bute, 22 August 1843 (ibid., 70, L. 7).
[27] Roy to Bute, 23 March 1842 (ibid., L. Roy, 1840–43); C.C.L., B., IX, 18; J. E. Vincent, *John Nixon, pioneer of the coal trade* (1900), p. 155.

to advance the enormous sum of £150,000'.[28] To the Bute-Rhymney Iron Company, which was partly sponsored by Bute as a counter-weight to Dowlais, the financial assistance of the marquess was of crucial importance. In 1824, Stewart persuaded Forman, the principal partner at the Penydarren works, to lease the Carno lands recovered from Dowlais and the Pontlotyn lands leased from Leigh and to erect upon them a new ironworks to be known as the Bute works, which, the surveyor hoped, 'may become the first works in Wales and consequently in the world'. In 1825 Forman bought the Rhymney Ironworks, whose mineral taking lay on the Monmouthshire side of the river Rhymney opposite that of the Bute Company. The entire purchase price, £147,400, was raised through a loan from Messrs. Coutts, Bute's London bankers, the marquess negotiating the loan and guaranteeing it.[29] Bute found his financial commitment to the company an embarrassment which caused him protracted difficulties after Forman's death in 1831. Nevertheless, the transaction proved profitable: the eastern expansion of Dowlais was contained and, despite severe fluctuations of fortune, the royalties paid by the company loomed large in Bute mineral income.[30]

Although the Bute estate sank pits, proved minerals and made loans to industrialists, the usual relationship between the estate and the industrialist was that of landlord and tenant, and it was largely through its negotiations over mineral leases and royalties that the estate influenced the pattern of industrialisation in Glamorgan. Each coalfield in the United Kingdom developed its own distinct pattern of mineral leases. In the south Wales coalfield no estate was so dominant as to be able to dictate a regional pattern of leases and royalties as

[28] Bute to Geddes, 15 May 1846 (N.L.W., B., L. 1845–46); C.C.L., B., VII, 44, 5; A. H. John, op. cit., p. 46.
[29] C.C.L., B., IX, 13 and 19 and MS. 4.850; letterbook of Messrs. Coutts, etc., *passim* (N.L.W., B., 70); bond relating to Rhymney (ibid., 140).
[30] Bute to Roy, 19 December 1831 (ibid., L. Coutts, etc.); accounts (ibid., 36); C.C.L., B., XIV, 70, 3; J. P. Addis, 'The heavy iron and steel industry in south Wales, 1870–1950' (unpublished University of Wales Ph.D. dissertation, 1957), Appendix E; *P.P.*, XXXVI (1890), 2–10; *P.P.*, XII (1919), 596–603.

did the Ecclesiastical Commission in county Durham.[31] In Glamorgan the regional pattern developed in a more haphazard fashion and was the product of the hard-won experience of landowners and the accumulated knowledge of solicitors' offices. On the Bute estate, experience, particularly of the losses suffered through the Dowlais lease of 1748, which tied down much of the minerals of the estate for ninety-nine years for a trifling rent, went far to determine the second marquess's attitude to lease negotiations. 'It is curious', he wrote in 1840, 'to compare the leases of 1748, 1763, 1803, 1823 and 1840 and to observe how much landlords have been taught by experience.'[32] The drawing up of the mineral lease was the responsibility of the estate solicitor. In 1832, Jones and Powell, the Brecon solicitors at whose office E. P. Richards had served his apprenticeship, stated that 'over the last fifty years this office has been engaged in some way or other in nearly all the mineral leases that have been granted . . . in this county and the adjoining county of Glamorgan'.[33] His experience there and that which he later gained as solicitor to the Bute estate and to his nephew, joint landlord of the Cyfarthfa ironworks, caused Richards to be recognised as one of the leading experts on mineral leases in the south Wales coalfield. Roy, Blunt, Duncan and Co., the second marquess's London solicitors, were agents for much industrial litigation and they supervised the drawing up of Bute leases, drawing upon knowledge of practices in many parts of the United Kingdom.

Equally significant was the experience the second marquess gained as both lessor and lessee of minerals in county Durham.[34] Apart from Stewart, Geddes and Bald, all of Edinburgh, the mineral advisers of the marquess, Beaumont, Nixon, Gray, Steel, Fenwick, Clark and Clayton, were men from the Newcastle area. Bute's introduction of mineral experts from Newcastle to Glamorgan constituted one of the chief channels of communication between the well-established

[31] G. F. A. Best, *Temporal pillars* (1963).
[32] Bute to Smyth, 25 January 1840 (N.L.W., B., 70, L. 6).
[33] Jones and Powell to Richards, 20 February 1832 (G.R.O., D/DA 18).
[34] As descendant of the Clavering family, Bute was part-owner of the collieries of Tanfield Lea and Garesfield. The Claverings were founder-members of the committee for the regulation of the vend. E. Hughes, *North Country life in the eighteenth century: the north-east, 1700–1750* (1952), p. 167.

coalfield of north-eastern England and its youthful rival in south Wales. Reports by such men did much to improve the Dowlais Company's wasteful coal-mining methods, while Clayton's intervention in the Dowlais lease negotiations was of crucial importance.[35] In drawing up leases, Bute insisted that the most improved Newcastle systems should be followed and his advisers there scrutinised each lease, adding their own suggestions.

The willingness of the Bute authorities to grant leases, and the stipulations contained in them, strongly influenced the development of the south Wales coalfield, for the pace and pattern of exploitation depended to a large degree upon the readiness of major landowners to agree to the working of their minerals and the conditions upon which they did so. Looking upon the estate minerals as 'frozen capital', the second marquess was anxious to lease as much of them as possible without delay. In considering requests for leases, the over-riding factors were the credit worthiness of the applicants and their willingness to pay the charges demanded, although on occasion Bute's involvement in Glamorgan politics made him less than impartial in judging the claims of industrialists. 'I will not', he wrote in 1840, 'let Cwmbach to the Aberdare Company. I have not forgotten the election of 1837.'[36] His intransigence towards the Dowlais Company had undoubted political overtones and his generosity towards the Pentyrch Company reflected the fact that its owner, T. W. Booker, was his closest ally among the Glamorgan Conservatives. Nevertheless, as a largely absentee landlord, Bute was prepared to encourage a more rapid exploitation of his minerals than were smaller resident owners, who feared for the safety of the foundations of their mansions and who regretted the disruption of their rural pursuits and the despoliation of their estates.[37]

Until the 1820s, the mineral leases of the Bute estate were simple documents, based upon the example of agricultural practice rather than upon the concept of royalty. Those sanctioned by the Windsors in the eighteenth century differed

[35] J. Davies, op. cit., pp. 58–59.
[36] Bute to Richards, 25 January 1840 (G.R.O., D/DA 24).
[37] E.g., the restrictions in the Bedlinog and Werfa leases granted by small landowners (N.L.W., B., 106).

little from the sixteenth-century leases of the Pembrokes, containing as they did a grant of land and minerals for a period varying from five to ninety-nine years or from one to three lives and stipulating the payment of mere simple rent. It was in the 1820s during the dispute over the Dowlais encroachments that Bute came to understand the intricacies of mineral leases and the immense potential of royalty payments.[38] Beginning with Bute Iron Company lease of 1825, the mineral leases of the estate became vast indentures specifying in detail the rights and obligations of landlord and tenant.

Of central importance in these new-style leases was the level of royalty. This was determined by a variety of factors, the most basic being the relationship between supply and demand. 'The royalty rent [of Gadlys Iron Company]', wrote Bute in 1834, 'should be regulated according to their want of coal as well as by its quantity and their facility for getting it.'[39] A consideration which weighed heavily upon him was a reluctance to do anything which might weaken him in future renewal negotiations with the Dowlais Company. Thus, from the Bute Iron Company his object was to obtain a royalty of 1s. a ton on coal, partly for the sake of the immediate revenue but more particularly to strengthen his position when dealing with Dowlais, and when Thomas of the Court demanded the same royalty for Werfa coal, the marquess was delighted 'because it points out what I may ask from other people'.[40]

The state of the works at the time of the lease was also taken into account when assessing the level of royalty; the Dowlais Company, Bute considered, should on the renewal of its lease pay a higher coal royalty than the 1s. a ton paid by the Bute Company, for the latter had been burdened with the payments while also bearing the expense of the construction of its furnaces, pits and tramroads, while the former had made those investments when paying no royalty at all.[41] In addition,

[38] 'Royalty' was the usual term in Glamorgan, but 'galeage' and 'lordship' were sometimes used. The theory of royalty is discussed in *P.P.*, XLI (1890–91), 116–76.
[39] Bute to Richards, 20 January 1834 (N.L.W., B., 70, L. 6); J. H. Morris and L. J. Williams, op. cit., pp. 118–19.
[40] Bute to Roy, 5, 7 and 14 February 1832 (N.L.W., B., 70, L. Coutts, etc.); to Smyth, 23 and 25 July 1840 (ibid., L. 7).
[41] Bute to Geddes, 4 July 1846 (ibid., L. 1845–46).

consideration was given to the quality and accessibility of the mineral leased, for a uniform royalty would give a well-placed enterprise a marked advantage over those with inconveniently-placed or indifferent minerals. The Bute Company's payment of 1s. a ton was for 'some of the best and most easily worked [coal] in the whole South Wales coalfield'. In the Cynon valley, the Aberdare Company, whose leased minerals Bute had purchased from Wyndham Lewis in 1824, paid 6d. a ton in coal royalty but the Gadlys Company in its Tir Fryd lease of 1834 was obliged to pay 8d. in order 'to bring them on an equal with the Aberdare Company in the expense of obtaining their coal', for the Tir Fryd coal, although of similar quality, was better situated. At Hirwaun, Crawshay refused to pay the same royalties as those levied upon the Aberdare Company because 'the very inferior coal and five miles more distant carriage to market . . . [would make] a competition with that work untenable'.[42] Transportation costs were thus important in fixing the level of royalty. 'I know by my experience in the Newcastle coal trade', wrote Bute, 'how much the freights affect prices.'[43] When the Bute dock was opened in 1839, the second marquess expected higher royalties because the facilities there meant a reduction in the freight charges paid by coalowners.

In most south Wales leases coal consumed at the colliery, and that supplied free to workmen, was not subject to royalty. The second marquess, who disliked the practice, sought in the Bute Company lease of 1825 to establish the principle of half royalty for the coal of workmen other than colliers and by the late-nineteenth century it became customary on the estate to restrict the amount of royalty-free coal to 5 per cent of total output. Restriction on the amount of royalty-free coal was accompanied by a growing demand for royalties in kind. The Bargoed Coal Company's lease of 1864 obliged it to supply the Bute trustees with a maximum of one ton of free coal a week, a stipulation often found in the leases of the later-nineteenth century. The free coal was used to heat the mineral office at

[42] Bute to Roy, 14 February 1832 (ibid., L. Coutts, etc.); Crawshay to Stewart, 5 November 1823 (ibid., 141, 6); Beaumont to Richards, 4 February 1834 (G.R.O., D/DA 19).
[43] Bute to Smyth, 17 February 1840 (N.L.W., B., 70, L. 6).

Aberdare and the offices and the castle at Cardiff, the rest being consumed by engines at the Bute docks.

As the nineteenth century advanced, provisions relating to royalty on coal became more detailed and complex. Instead of a uniform rate being levied on all coal leased, it became common to specify different royalties for different seams. The lease of the Rhigos mine in 1842 charged 10*d*. per ton for coal from the upper four-foot seam and 6*d*. for coal from other seams and by the 1860s such terms had become almost universal.[44] A lease of minerals at Treorci in 1865 stipulated that 9*d*. should be paid for coal from the upper four-foot seam, 8*d*. for coal from seams below it, 7*d*. for coal from the two-foot-nine seam and 6*d*. for coal from the Abergorci seam and above. In the 1890s such complexities were largely superseded by a percentage royalty. The second marquess had been anxious to benefit from his tenants' periods of prosperity through a sliding-scale and a percentage system of royalty. 'It is dishonest of Messrs. Thompson and Co.', he wrote in 1832, 'to expect a reduction in royalty in bad times if they are not willing for an increase when prices are good.'[45] The complications of making such provisions alarmed his adviser John Geddes. 'Who will undertake', the latter wrote in 1846, 'to frame a lease providing for all the peculiarities that may come up in the selling prices for a lease of forty years?'[46] Despite the complications, a simplified sliding-scale was included in the Dowlais lease of 1854; by the late-nineteenth century sliding-scales and percentage royalties had become the standard practice of the Bute estate which, the Royal Commission on Mining Royalties was informed in 1891, was the pioneer in their introduction into the south Wales coalfield.[47] Typical of such agreements was that with Cope and Thomas of 1894, which stipulated that royalty on coal was to be one-twelfth of the selling price, with a minimum royalty of 6*d*. a ton. In some leases tonnage and percentage royalties were combined as in a lease of 1908, in which the royalty demanded was to be 9*d*. if the selling price of coal were under 8*s*. a ton,

[44] C.C.L., B., VII, 45.
[45] Bute to Roy, 14 and 18 February 1832 (N.L.W., B., 70, L. Coutts, etc.).
[46] Geddes to de Grave, 5 March 1846 (ibid., 141, 5).
[47] *P.P.*, XXXVI (1890), 189.

but if it were over 8s., then a royalty of one-tenth was to be paid. Such sliding-scales were unpopular with coal owners for, although they always stipulated a minimum royalty, they rarely stipulated a maximum one.[48] The system was clearly advantageous to landowners, especially in boom years. In 1919, when 14·69 per cent of the coal mined on the Bute estate was subject to percentage agreements, the average royalty per ton on coal so leased was nearly 1s. 6d., while the average on coal mined under fixed royalty agreements was only 6·42d.[49]

Another form of coal royalty which changed in the course of the nineteenth century was that on small coal which, in the early part of the century, was considered worthless by both freighters and ironmasters. In the late-nineteenth century, however, new uses were found for it and the Dowlais Company in particular reaped great benefits from the fact that its lease charged no royalty upon it.[50] Bute leases of the 1870s stated that large coal should be considered to be nine-tenths of all the coal raised and at the same time the royalty on small coal was increased from one-half to two-thirds that of large. By the turn of the century, the practice of differentiating between large and small coal had been abandoned, the last example in the Bute papers of such differentiation being a lease of coal at Abernant in 1899.

Royalties on minerals other than coal, although of little importance to the mineral income of the estate, were defined with care and precision. Royalty on iron ore, the most significant in terms of income, followed a pattern similar to that on coal. The Bute Iron Company lease of 1825, the Gadlys lease of 1845 and the Werfa lease of 1847 specified a royalty of 1s. per ton, but leases of the 1860s demanded rates of between 4d. and 8d., the level settling to a steady 6d. a ton in the 1890s. A few leases, such as that to the Bute Haematite Company in 1866, differentiated between various types of ore; haematite ironstone cost 1s. a ton while argillaceous ironstone cost 8d. if sold and 4d. if used on the premises. Blackband, which had so excited the iron-making world in the 1830s, was separately provided for: in some leases it was reserved to the landlord; in

[48] P.P., XLI (1890–91), 60.
[49] P.P., XII (1919), 653.
[50] J. Davies, op, cit., pp. 63–64.

others 1s. or 1s. 6d. was charged if the band were over six
inches and 8d. to 1s. if it were not. Despite intensive searches,
blackband was not found on the Bute estate and clauses
relating to it were omitted from the leases after about 1875.
Lead ore, which existed in small quantities at Llantrisant, was
not subject to a tonnage royalty; typical of the few Bute leases
of lead mines is one of 1826 which specified payments of
one-tenth of the selling price for the first eight years, rising to
one-ninth thereafter.[51]

Fireclay, surface clay, sand, limestone and building stone
were other materials for which the Bute leases designated
royalties. Parts of the estate, particularly Hirwaun and Llantrisant, were rich in these resources and they provided a useful
income during the lifetime of the second marquess. Royalties
on fireclay, surface clay and sand varied between 2d. and 4d.
a ton, but tonnage rates were occasionally abandoned in favour
of a charge on the finished materials, the Rhymney lease of
1837, for example, charging 1s. per thousand bricks or tiles.
Limestone was charged at 2d. or 3d. if used on the premises
and up to 9d. if sold. Building-stone royalties were usually 1d.
if used by the lessee and 3d. if sold, but Bute allowed stone for
turnpike roads to be quarried on his estate free of charge.[52]

Royalties were not the only source of Bute mineral income.
Leases almost invariably required wayleave payments, a charge
made for transporting across the lessor's land, above or below
ground, minerals mined under leases held from others. Wayleaves were not a heavy charge in south Wales, largely because
of the superabundance of public railways within the coalfield;
in 1890 wayleaves in county Durham produced £97,600
compared with £30,000 in south Wales.[53] On the Bute estate
they were usually 1d. a ton per mile, although underground
charges could be a $\frac{1}{2}d.$ more than those on the surface. David
Davies's lease of 1867 charged a lump sum of £250 a year
instead of a tonnage wayleave, but this was an isolated
example.

[51] Lease to Taylor, 1826 (N.L.W., B., 141, 6).
[52] C.C.L., B., VII, 34, 75.
[53] P.P., XLI (1893–94), 83–85. Shaft rents, a heavy burden in county Durham,
were unknown in south Wales.

Apart from royalties and wayleaves, each mineral lease specified the payment of a dead or sleeping rent. 'It is generally the practice here', wrote Richards in 1834, 'to reserve a fixed or dead rent . . . compelling the lessee to use the minerals under the demised premises.' 'The minimum rent', it was stated in 1925, 'is an inducement to the lessees to keep working steadily and so to spread the working and payment of the coal more evenly over the term of the lease.'[54] The Royal Commission on Mining Royalties was informed in 1891 that in south Wales the dead rent was calculated at a rate varying from £1 to £5 per acre.[55] On the Bute estate, however, the rent charged was a proportion, varying between a third and a half, of the anticipated return in royalty when the enterprise would be working at full capacity.[56] Dead rent in relation to acreage rose sharply in the course of the nineteenth century. In the 1840s it was under £1 an acre, £150, for example, being charged for 448 acres at Gadlys in 1845, but by the 1860s it was over £5 an acre, £1,000 being charged for 214 acres of the Senghennydd Common in 1861. It became common to graduate the dead rent in order to reduce the demands made upon a coalowner's capital during the initial boring operations. In 1863 a lease of Rhondda minerals stipulated a dead rent of £300 for the first two years, rising thereafter to £800 a year, and in the same year the lease of the Hirwaun ironworks allowed for a dead rent carefully graduated over five years. On occasion, the charge was linked to the lessee's success in reaching various seams of coal; £300 was required of David Davies in 1867 with the proviso that the dead rent would rise to £500 if the upper four-foot seam were reached. The dead rent invariably merged into the royalty payment; equally invariably Bute leases allowed for the spreading of the charge over a term of years. 'If in the first two half years of the term granted', stated a lease of 1867, 'the lessee shall not work a quantity of minerals sufficient to produce a royalty at least equal to the dead rent and shall in either of the succeeding ten half years obtain more than the dead rent, then, and as

[54] Richards to Roy, 9 August 1834 (G.R.O., D/DA 19); The Royal Commission on the coal industry (1925), *Minutes of evidence*, II, 738.
[55] *P.P.*, XXXVI (1890), 188.
[56] C.C.L., B., VII, 4; Steel to Smyth, 23 August 1841 (N.L.W., B., 141, 5).

often as this happens, they shall retain out of such excess the sum paid in deficiency in the first two half years.'[57]

The duration of the mineral leases granted by the Bute estate varied considerably. The second marquess, plagued by the losses sustained by his family under the ninety-nine year Dowlais lease, objected to long leases and quoted the example of the Durham coalfield, where the usual length was forty-two years.[58] The only ninety-nine year lease granted by the estate after 1814 was that to Sir Henry Bridges of twenty perches in 1858, clearly a small addition to a larger lease held by Sir Henry of another landlord.[59] The Bute Estate Act of 1848 empowered the trustees to grant mineral leases not exceeding sixty years, a duration which the second marquess had granted to most of his major lessees[60]. There were some shorter leases, even for extensive areas of minerals. In 1860 the Pentyrch works leased 266 acres of the Garth mountain for fifty years, and in 1874 Burnyeat, Brown and Co. leased the minerals of a number of Rhondda farms for forty-nine years. Later in the century, leases tended to become shorter and small portions of the estate were leased for twenty-one years or less. Among the Bute leases are some in which no specific duration was stipulated. In 1823 coal was leased at Penywaun 'during the marquess's pleasure' and in 1825 a lease at Llantrisant obliged the tenant to 'surrender his occupation . . . if the coalfield is required for a greater extension of trade than he is capable of', while in 1904 the Crawshay Brothers leased thirteen acres of coal near Aberdare from year to year.[61] With a usual duration of sixty years, however, the Bute estate's leases conformed to the pattern prevalent in south Wales, where the term was considerably longer than that granted in any other coalfield of the United Kingdom.[62]

In the first half of the nineteenth century it was usual for the estate to include in its lease all the minerals beneath a

[57] There is a mass of material on the way the system operated in the Claim Files; see note 5 above.
[58] Bute to Richards, 26 October 1846 (N.L.W., B., 70, L. 7); to Clark, 30 November 1846 (ibid., L. 1845–46).
[59] Lease to Bridges, 1858 (ibid., 143).
[60] 11–12 Victoria, cap. 20.
[61] Lease to Williams, 1823 (C.C.L., B., VII, 26); Bute to Richards, 11 November 1825 (G.R.O., D/DA 12).
[62] P.P., XXXVI (1890), 188.

tract of land, although the right to lease part of the building stone or limestone to other lessees was retained. By the 1840s blackband, if found, was reserved and this practice was extended later in the century to a reservation of everything except the coal and the minerals found in conjunction with it. By the 1870s leases of individual seams of coal became a regular practice; in 1874, for example, the trustees leased the Brithdir seam under the farm of Tir rhwng y ddaugae, and in 1904 the fourth marquess leased the Gerllwyn seam under sixteen acres of the upper Rhondda valley.

Unless the area of minerals was very small or was intended to be worked from an adjoining taking, Bute mineral leases made provision for the leasing of surface land which was needed as a site for the colliery and its sidings as well as for the deposit of waste, the erection of colliers' houses and to enable the lessee to control the water system of his works. The iron companies of south Wales had traditionally held large tracts of surface land, freehold and leasehold, but the demands of the colliery companies, which were the main applicants for Bute leases from the 1840s onwards, were more modest. Initially the same rent was charged for surface land regardless of the use to be made of it but by the second half of the nineteenth century differing rates were usually charged. Thus Insole's Treorci lease of 1864 specified £2 per acre for land for surface works, £2 10s. per acre for land for sidings and £20 for land for housing. Covenants relating to the use of land were often detailed; the Bute Iron Company's lease of 1837 contained elaborate provisions concerning care of trees, the Penydarren lease of 1857 stipulated the area, the situation and the sequence in which land was to be leased for tipping, and the Abernant lease of 1899 insisted that the angle of tips should not exceed forty-five degrees and that they should be planted with larch as soon as possible.

To the second marquess, one of the most important covenants in his leases was that which bound lessees to ship at his dock part or the whole of the minerals they exported. He saw his minerals and his dock as an integrated entity. In 1839 he declared: 'I intend to insist that all lessees come to my dock'.[63]

[63] Bute to Smyth, 17 November 1839 (N.L.W., B., 70, L. 6).

The usual provision was that all coal intended for export within fifty miles of the port of Cardiff had to be shipped at the Bute Docks, although this demand was usually halved in the late-nineteenth century. If the stipulation were ignored, the lessee was obliged to pay dock dues not exceeding 2d. a ton on the coal shipped elsewhere. Thus Nixon, a leading protagonist of the Penarth Dock, and Davies, the strongest advocate of the Barry Dock, were obliged, even while conducting parliamentary battles against the Bute estate, to ship at least part of their coal at the Bute Docks.

Each Bute mineral lease contained covenants relating to the termination or forfeiture of the lease and to the right of re-entry by the landlord. Bute leases, like those of the south Wales coalfield as a whole, were stricter over termination than were those of other British coalfields. In the first half of the nineteenth century, it was virtually impossible to abandon a mineral lease in south Wales. The second marquess, with his experience of the Durham coalfield, was surprised that the tenant of Llethrddu continued to pay him dead rent after the minerals had been exhausted and was annoyed that he had to go to law to abandon the lease, which he had taken on behalf of the Penydarren Company, of the depleted minerals at Pwllyrhwyaid.[64] By the 1830s leases contained provisions allowing breaks every seven years and surrender after exhaustion of the minerals, the Bute Iron Company lease of 1837 including such clauses and also specifying that the takings could be abandoned at twelve months' notice if two impartial judges agreed that the state of the iron trade was such that no reasonable profit could be made. Clauses of this kind became normal in the leases of the second half of the nineteenth century, although the right to surrender was usually strictly controlled during the first five or ten years. If termination by the lessee were difficult, forfeiture was almost impossible. The Royal Commission on Mining Royalties recognised that forfeiture was very rare in south Wales and that it only occurred following consistent breaches of covenant after notice. Despite the manifold misdeeds of the Dowlais Company, all efforts to cancel its lease failed; indeed, the only example of

[64] Bute to Clark, 30 November 1846 (ibid., L. 1845–46); letter-book of Messrs. Roy, 1844–46, *passim* (ibid.).

a forfeited lease among the Bute papers is that of the tenant of
a small colliery at Llantrisant whose agreement was cancelled
and whose coal was distrained upon after consistent non-
payment of rent.[65]

Detailed covenants specifying how the minerals were to be
worked were rare in the Bute leases of the first half of the
nineteenth century. Eighteenth century leases had contained
no such covenants and, in consequence, at Dowlais in particular, Bute minerals had been wastefully exploited and surface
land ruined. The first of the second marquess's leases, that to
the Bute Iron Company in 1825, broke new ground; it obliged
the company to build six furnaces by 1846 and when it seemed
reluctant to do so, Bute threatened to withdraw part of its
taking from it.[66] A large number of furnaces meant higher
royalties, as did rapid sinking to the steam coal seams. Davies's
lease of 1867, one of the foundation leases of the great Ocean
Coal Company, obliged the lessee to reach the nine-foot seam
by 25 March 1869 and a lease of 1894 stipulated that the
two-foot-nine seam was to be worked by 29 September of that
year, the upper four-foot seam by 29 June 1895 and the
six-foot seam by 29 September 1896. By the late-nineteenth
century the estate also demanded that all buildings should be
insured to their full value and should be kept in good repair,
some leases going so far as to stipulate how often buildings
were to be painted and with which companies they were to
be insured.

In the early years of the second marquess's period of ownership there was no specific administration of the Bute mineral
estate. Until 1825 Stewart the surveyor undertook responsibility for negotiating leases and inspecting the operations of
lessees. In 1823 Bald, of the Edinburgh firm of Geddes and
Bald, was employed to survey the mineral estate and thereafter
the second marquess leant heavily upon the firm's advice. By
the mid-1820s Bute came to feel the need of a full-time mineral

[65] Walker to Richards, 12 January 1820 (G.R.O., D/DA 8); *P.P.*, XXXVI
(1890), 213.
[66] Bute to Roy, 1 February 1834 (N.L.W., B., 70, L. Coutts, etc.).

agent in Glamorgan and Bald recommended to him Robert Beaumont, a mineral surveyor from Newcastle, who had previously been in the employ of the earl of Elgin. Beaumont moved to Cardiff in 1827 and, with his appointment, mineral matters were separated from other aspects of estate administration. Bute wanted his estate to be a nursery of mineral surveyors for the south Wales coalfield and instructed his new agent to take on local apprentices and teach them the techniques of the older coalfields.[67] Beaumont was a man of wide experience with a firm grasp of mineral geology and of the economics of coal-mining, but his lethargy and carelessness drove his employer to distraction. 'He is so inanimate', wrote Bute, '[that he cannot arrange a lease] if his life depended upon it.'[68] In the early-1830s he became a coalowner, running the Tophill colliery, Caerphilly, in partnership with Powell of Newport. He was dismissed from Bute service in 1833 but continued to be employed on special assignments until the late-1840s.

After Beaumont's dismissal, the administration of the mineral estate became one of Richards's many activities, assisted on the technical side by Fenwick, Bute's mineral agent in county Durham. During the 1830s Fenwick and his colleague Gray made regular visits to Glamorgan to advise the marquess on his mineral concerns, as did Geddes and Bald of Edinburgh. In the late-1830s Bute again felt the need for a permanent mineral agent in Glamorgan and offered the post in succession to two of Gray's pupils, John Nixon, later the successful coalowner, who declined it, and Edward Steel, who was appointed to the office in 1839.[69] In 1840 the mineral estate and the Bute dock were integrated into one concern under Captain Smyth and, as Smyth's assistant, Steel proved satisfactory. He died in 1842, however, and Bute reverted to the practice of employing advisers and temporary assistance. The Dowlais question, which loomed large in estate affairs in the early-1840s, was entrusted to Geddes and Robert Stephenson

[67] Bute to Mylne, 1 November 1843 (ibid., L. 1840–44).
[68] Bute to Richards, 2 January 1833 (G.R.O., D/DA 18).
[69] J. E. Vincent, op. cit., pp. 57, 69; Bute to Smyth, 27 July 1839, to Mrs. Smyth, 12 December 1839 (N.L.W., B., 70, L. 6).

and most of the mineral reports were prepared by Beaumont and William Struvé.

The continuous history of the Bute mineral agency begins in January 1845 with the appointment of W. S. Clark, a protégé of Clayton, town clerk of Newcastle. Clark, whose diary is an invaluable source of information on estate matters, was a man of great ability and integrity.[70] By appointing him at a salary of £600 a year (rising to £720 in 1854 and to £1,000 in 1860) the marquess was recognising the increasing importance of his mineral estate.[71] Until Clark's appointment there had been no specific centre for the transaction of Bute mineral business other than Richards's office and leases were stored at Cardiff castle, in London or at Luton, much to the confusion of the agents. In 1854 work began on the construction of a mineral office at Aberdare, together with a residence for the agent; the house and office, known as the Mardy, remained the centre of Bute mineral affairs until the nationalisation of mineral reserves in 1938.[72]

As Beaumont had done before him, Clark built up a group of apprentices, a policy triumphantly vindicated by the emergence of William Thomas Lewis, the Glamorgan estate's first native mineral agent, and the main architect of the fortunes of the estate in the late-nineteenth century. 'Wm. Lewis', noted Clark in his diary on 9 January 1855, 'came today as clerk.' Lewis was then seventeen years of age and had been apprenticed since he was thirteen to his father, T. W. Lewis, an engineer at the Plymouth Ironworks. W. T. Lewis represented the sixth generation of his family to be engaged in heavy industry in south Wales and this tradition was strengthened when, in 1864, he married Anne Rees, grand-daughter of Robert and Lucy Thomas, the pioneers of the south Wales coal trade. When Clark died in 1864, Lewis, who had proved himself to be the ablest of the Bute apprentices, was appointed Bute mineral agent, an office which he held until his retirement in 1913. In 1867 Lewis began acquiring collieries on his own account and by the end of the century was among the greatest of the south Wales capitalists and the leading figure in the

[70] N.L.W., MSS., 7454A–7462A.
[71] C.C.L., B., X, 2.
[72] N.L.W., MSS., 7458B, 7460B.

Monmouthshire and South Wales Coalowners Association. In 1880 he became chief agent of the Bute estate in Glamorgan and manager of the Bute Docks. On his retirement from the mineral agency he was succeeded by his nephew and pupil, R. T. Rees, while another of his nephews, W. L. Harris, was employed as legal adviser on mineral matters.[73]

As the nineteenth century advanced, the work of the mineral agent became more complex. The lease became an increasingly refined tool, adding to the work needed to ascertain that a lessee was fulfilling its covenants. Lewis's reports on Fothergill's Aberdare collieries are a far cry from Beaumont's scattered notes.[74] In 1919, even after the Bute collieries had been sold, the fourth marquess was employing 'a mining engineer, a staff of four or five and a lawyer'; by then most other landowners in south Wales had given up the task of administering their mineral estates and had farmed out the work to specialist firms.[75]

In the early-nineteenth century, the mineral receipts of the Bute estate were minimal. The earliest detailed information available refers to the second half of 1826, when mineral receipts amounted to £872 and included £570 from the Bute Iron Company, £150 from the Aberdare Iron Company and £87 from Crawshay's ironworks at Hirwaun.[76] This was small indeed compared with the £3,000 a year which the Grosvenor family received from their lead-mines alone in the mid-eighteenth century, or the £4,000 a year the Middleton family obtained in royalties in 1800.[77] In the second half of 1831, largely as a result of Bute's purchase of Wyndham Lewis's estate leased to the Aberdare Iron Company, gross mineral receipts had risen to £1,551. The mineral rent-book ends in 1832 with the departure of Beaumont and, thereafter, full details of mineral income are not available until 1848–49, when the series of trustees' accounts begins. Between 1833 and

---

[73] Files and press cuttings in the possession of Lord Merthyr.
[74] Compare C.C.L., B., VI, 30, with ibid., VII, 13, 2.
[75] *P.P.*, XII (1919), 579, 657, 698, 701.
[76] Rentals, 1826 (N.L.W., B., 60).
[77] G. E. Mingay, op. cit., p. 57.

1838, mineral income appears to be included in the section of the general account labelled 'miscellaneous receipts'. These show that between August 1836 and July 1837 Bute received £4,277 in mineral rents and royalties, including £2,140 from the Bute Iron Company and £1,632 from the Aberdare Iron Company.[78] This steady rise in the estate's mineral income was the one factor in the accounts which gave the second marquess some confidence during the years of heavy expenditure at the dock, and it was particularly gratifying that the rise was occurring before the estate came to share in 'the riches of the Dowlais mountain'.[79] Royalty arrears caused Bute severe annoyance. 'We must not', he wrote, 'let the Ironmasters divide profits while I am manifestly suffering from the delay of any payments to my account. These great ironmasters are ready to make any excuse for being irregular.'[80]

By the mid-nineteenth century the estate was coming to depend increasingly upon mineral royalties. 'The account' wrote Bruce in 1849, 'will be a little crippled until the Royalties are paid.'[81] In 1848–49, the year following the second marquess's death, the net mineral income of the Bute estate was £10,756, some £1,500 less than the net profit of the Bute docks. In the following year, the first full year of the new Dowlais lease, mineral income rose to £24,619, and thenceforward until 1875 the estate's net mineral income always exceeded the net profit of the dock. The growth in the net mineral income received by the third and fourth marquesses of Bute from Glamorgan is shown in the following table:[82]

1848–49	£10,756	1861–62	£34,240	1874–75	£81,000
1849–50	£24,619	1862–63	£20,792	1875–76	£52,086
1850–51	£21,435	1863–64	£35,913	1876–77	£81,707
1851–52	£26,993	1864–65	£36,277	1877–78	£51,898
1852–53	£36,528	1865–66	£48,997	1878–79	£41,236

[78] Rental of the mineral estate, 1831; accounts, 1836–37 (N.L.W., B., 60).
[79] Bute to Roy, 17 July 1834 (ibid., L. Coutts, etc.).
[80] Ibid., 10 July 1832, 13 December 1833 (ibid.); Bute to Smyth, 9 November 1840 (ibid., L. 7).
[81] Bruce to Richards, 6 November 1849 (G.R.O., D/DA 33).
[82] The figures for 1848–58 are in C.C.L., B., X, 2; those for 1858–66 in C.C.L., MS. 4.937; those for 1867–81 in C.C.L., B., X, 6, 2–6; those for 1913–18 in P.P., XII (1919), 653; that for 1918 in Royal Commission on the coal industry (1925), Minutes of evidence, II, 792; that for 1919 in P.P., XIII (1919), 230. The total for 1934–38 has been calculated from the Claim Files (see note 5 above).

1853–54	£28,699	1866–67	n.a.	1879–80	£56,184
1854–55	£26,918	1867–68	£44,699	1880–81	£48,900
1855–56	£26,002	1868–69	£39,358	1913–18	£115,742
1856–57	£41,884	1869–70	£47,276		(average)
1857–58	£39,634	1870–71	£47,991	1918	£115,000
1858–59	£41,021	1871–72	£40,204	1919	£117,477
1859–60	£33,842	1872–73	£55,207	1934–38	£94,966
1860–61	£35,881	1873–74	£51,340		(average)

In the 1850s the bulk of Bute mineral income came from four great ironworks; in 1851–52, the estate's gross mineral receipts included £12,000 from the Dowlais, £8,000 from the Penydarren, £6,237 from the Bute-Rhymney and £2,648 from the Aberdare Iron Companies, the payments being largely royalties on coal but including significant sums for ironstone. By the early-1870s royalty on ironstone had virtually come to an end and fuel economies allowed the companies to divert much of the coal they mined to the export market, such coal generally carrying a higher royalty than that consumed at the works.[83] By the year 1870–71, while the iron companies were still the chief source of Bute mineral income, contributing £34,960 of the gross receipts of £51,398, the income from coal companies was rising rapidly. In 1870–71, for example, Insoles paid £4,422, the Dunraven Coal Company £1,971 and the Bargoed Coal Company £1,264. In 1875 the landowners of south Wales received £360,000 in mineral income; in that year, when only half its mineral land had been let, the Bute estate's receipts amounted to £52,000, representing 14 per cent of the total.[84] The estate ranked among the richest of the mineral properties of the United Kingdom and in 1861 its royalties even exceeded those received by that wealthy mineral-owning body, the Ecclesiastical Commission. The Commission pulled ahead decisively in the 1870s and 1880s, but the Bute estate won and retained a leading position among secular owners. In 1919, when almost the entire mineral estate had been leased, Bute mineral income stood at £117,477, the highest in the kingdom apart from that of the Ecclesiastical

[83] The mining of iron ore in Wales fell from 970,000 tons in 1871 to 42,000 tons in 1889. S. Griffiths, *Guide to the iron trade of Great Britain* (1873), p. 181; *P.P.*, XLI (1893–94), 85.

[84] J. H. Morris and L. J. Williams, op. cit., p. 123.

Commission.[85] Even during the depressed years of the mid-1930s, the estate's receipts, averaging £94,966, held up well. By then, as a consequence of the amalgamation of coal concerns, 58 per cent of the receipts were paid by a single company, that of Powell Duffryn.

The level of royalty was of central importance to an ironmaster or a coal-owner, and it is no coincidence that the search for more economic methods of iron-making intensified following the expiration of royalty-free leases. In Pembrokeshire collieries in the eighteenth century, payments to the landlord took one-third of the profits of coalowners and at Beaumont's Tophill colliery in 1839 rents and royalties represented 28 per cent of the cost of coal at the pithead and 16 per cent of its cost at Cardiff. At Fothergill's collieries in the Cynon valley, royalties in 1882 represented 9 per cent of the working costs, a smaller proportion than usual but sufficient to rob the company of any profit.[86] During periods of difficulty, however, the estate was prepared to grant concessions to industrialists. The Aberdare leases of Thompson and Fothergill were modified in favour of the lessees in 1832, Booker received concessions to his Garth lease in 1844 because of his fruitless expenditure on iron-ore prospecting, and Nixon's royalty at Werfa was reduced by 2d. a ton in 1846 when he struck a swamp during mining operations.[87] When the Aberdare and Plymouth works stopped in 1875, the third marquess's willingness to waive a debt of £30,000 enabled them to be reopened, and when the enterprise finally collapsed in 1882, the Bute estate did not press its claim. In 1919 the fourth marquess claimed that the estate had given away £150,000 in concessions to mining companies since 1859.[88]

In the late-nineteenth century the cost of cutting coal rose rapidly, while the level of royalty remained fairly stable. Between 1887 and 1890, in a representative group of south Wales collieries, royalties as a proportion of total production

[85] G. F. A. Best, op. cit., p. 557.
[86] A. H. John, op. cit., p. 183; Beaumont to Bute, 5 March 1841 (C.C.L., B., VII, 44, 7); report on Aberdare collieries, 1882 (ibid., XVI, 13).
[87] Ibid., VII, 26; Bute to Roy, 7 January 1832 (N.L.W., B., 70, L. Coutts, etc.), to Clark, 2 September 1845 (ibid., L. 1845–46).
[88] W.M., 1 October 1908; P.P., XII (1919), 656.

costs fell from 13 per cent to 8 per cent.[89] Yet although a declining charge in the 1880s, it was in that decade that agitation against royalties first assumed serious proportions. Thomas Halliday, the Labour candidate at Merthyr in the general election of 1874, while demanding changes in land law, had made no specific reference to mineral leases. In the election of 1880, however, royalties came under severe attack. At the end of the decade even J. T. D. Llewelyn, the Unionist candidate at Swansea, and himself a major mineral landowner, felt obliged to support a revision of the system. In 1888 the miners of Merthyr and Aberdare demanded the abolition of all mineral royalties, while William Abraham, Lib-Lab member for the Rhondda, declared: 'No colliery can be opened without the consent of the landlord and the consent must be given in his own terms . . . even if the capital of the speculator had all been expended uselessly, the landlord must have his pound of flesh'.[90] The whole matter was ventilated by the Royal Commission on Mining Royalties of which both Abraham and W. T. Lewis were members; its report considered that the system had worked equitably and recommended only minor changes.

Although the third marquess of Bute was more generous in his patronage of miners' charities than were his fellow mineral landowners, he was particularly vulnerable to attacks upon mineral estates. The levels of Bute royalties were known to be higher than the south Wales mean, itself higher than that of any other British coalfield. In 1919 the average Bute coal royalty was 8·14*d*. per ton compared with 6·29*d*. in a representative group of other south Wales estates.[91] *The South Wales Daily News* was especially vocal in its attacks and sought to prove that Edward VI's grants of land to the Herbert family expressly reserved minerals to the crown. The paper's denunciations extended over a quarter of a century and more; in 1912, for example, it declared that 'the industrial classes had been giving millions to a family who had obtained their land by fraud'.[92]

[89] *W.M.*, 29 January 1874; *C.T.*, 11 September 1880; *C.*, 28 March 1888.
[90] Ibid.; *Merthyr Express*, 11 and 25 February, 3 March 1888; *P.P.*, XLI (1893–94), 92–93.
[91] *P.P.*, XII (1919), 579, 653; *S.W.D.N.*, 3 April 1889.
[92] Ibid., 11 May 1895, 1 June 1912.

The attack upon mineral landlords culminated in the Royal Commission of 1919 under Sir John Sankey, which unanimously recommended the nationalisation of mineral royalties. By then, agitation had won some victories, for mineral rights duties, excess mineral rights duties and other taxes reduced the gross £117,477 received by the fourth marquess in mineral income in 1919 to less than £25,000 net.[93] In 1923 the rights of a landlord over his coal were severely restricted by the Mines (Mineral Facilities) Act, which gave the Department of Mines wide powers over mineral reserves. During the bitter disputes which characterised the British coal industry in the inter-war years, the nationalisation of royalties was the only issue upon which both coalowners and miners agreed, and the delay in its implementation was seen as a handicap to the revival of the industry in south Wales. Mineral reserves were taken into state ownership in 1938, compensation being fixed at £76·5 million. Of this sum, £19,187,437 were allotted to the south Wales coalfield and included £1,222,425 paid to the Bute family company of Mountjoy Ltd. for coal and other minerals under a total of 36,456 acres within the south Wales coalfield.[94]

In the exploitation of the mineral wealth of Glamorgan, the landowners of the county could and did play a crucial role. The second marquess of Bute and, after him, his son's trustees did all in their power to accelerate mineral exploitation while at the same time, through the provisions in their leases, seeking to some degree to civilize the industrial process. Only in the case of Dowlais, where the second marquess, blinded by his dislike of Sir John Guest and anxious to recoup some of the losses suffered as a consequence of the folly of his ancestors, allowed a great ironworks to drift towards closure, did the estate in any way hinder the pace of industrial development. The incentive to encourage it was, of course, financial, and the British royalty system, allowing as it did the owners of surface land to share in the profits of extractive industries, may

[93] *P.P.*, XII (1919), 655.
[94] Calculated from the Claim Files listed in note 5 above; Central Valuation Board, *Valuation regions* (*P.P.* (1938), Cmd. 5904); *Times*, 17 December 1938.

have been a factor in enabling Britain to be the pioneer of the iron and coal industries, for elsewhere in Europe, where minerals were vested in the state, there was no financial gain to the landowner who promoted the despoliation of his estate by mines and collieries. It is also likely that in upland Wales, where agricultural rent was low, landowners were more desirous of encouraging industrial growth than were those in the richer agricultural areas of England.

During the nineteenth century the Bute property in Glamorgan was transformed from a large, but impoverished, agricultural estate into a great industrial concern. In consequence, the role of the landlord and that of the industrialist became blurred. A similar process was occurring elsewhere in the county. Leading landowners such as Talbot of Margam were prominent as railway company directors, and landowning families like the Llewelyns of Baglan and the Bruces of Duffryn became industrialists in their own right. On the other hand, industrial families like the Dillwyns and the Guests became major landowners. W. T. Lewis, the central figure of the Bute estate in the late-nineteenth century and perhaps the greatest of Welsh industrialists, himself became a landowner; his descendants' links with industry were weak and his son, the second Lord Merthyr, became famous for his herd of shorthorn cattle. Nowhere was this blurring of distinctions more evident than on the Bute estate. Before the death of the second marquess, industry had overtaken agriculture as the mainstay of the estate, a fact that the marquess tacitly recognised when he addressed the House of Lords on the subject of the Corn Laws. By the late-nineteenth century, the agricultural department was a small and unprofitable part of the estate, its improvements and deficits being financed out of the income from mineral royalties. Although the profits from the docks received greater publicity, the income from minerals was the real wealth and strength of the Bute estate. The debts which the second marquess incurred in dock building were cleared through the rise in mineral royalties in the 1850s and the dock expansion under the trustees was directly financed from mineral profits. Without royalties there would have been no incentive to construct the docks, for they were built primarily to accelerate the exploitation of Bute minerals; without

royalties, ownership of the docks would have driven the estate
to bankruptcy.

VII
DOCKS, RAILWAYS AND THE BUTE ESTATE

THE WEST BUTE DOCK, 1822–48

'There is probably no similar estate in the country', noted the *Daily Chronicle* in its obituary of the third marquess of Bute, 'where an immense commercial centre has been fostered on one man's property, and the rights of the landlord preserved . . . intact.'[1] The newspaper was referring in particular to the Bute Docks, the greatest enterprise of the Bute family in Glamorgan. The construction of the West Bute Dock by the second marquess and of other docks by the trustees gave Cardiff a dock system unrivalled among the ports of south Wales. The enterprise of the family, coupled with the favourable position of the port in relation to the coalfield and to the world sea routes, allowed Cardiff to become the greatest coal port in the world and the largest town in Wales.[2] From the opening of the West Bute Dock in 1839 until amalgamation with the Great Western Railway Company in 1922, Cardiff docks were a family concern, owned, financed and administered by the marquesses of Bute and their employees. They are of significance, therefore, not only in the history of the south Wales coalfield but also in the history of the participation by landed aristocrats in the economic development of the United Kingdom, since of the nineteenth century British towns in whose development a single landowning family played a crucial role Cardiff was undoubtedly the largest.[3] The impor-

---

[1] *Daily Chronicle*, 13 October 1900.

[2] M. Crubellier, 'Le developpement de Cardiff au cour du XIXᵉ siècle et jusqu'à la crise actuelle', *Annales de Géographie*, 45 (1936), 471; T. M. Hodges, 'A history of the port of Cardiff in relation to its hinterland' (unpublished University of London M.Sc. Econ. dissertation, 1948); M. J. Daunton, *Coal metropolis, Cardiff 1870–1914* (1977).

[3] On other such towns, see J. D. Marshall, *Furness and the industrial revolution* (1958); S. Pollard, 'Barrow-in-Furness and the seventh duke of Devonshire', *Economic History Review*, VII (1955), 213–21; A. S. Turberville, *Welbeck abbey and its owners* (1938–39), II, 369, 418–20; R. Mitchison, *Agricultural Sir John* (1962); E. G. Heape, *Buxton under the dukes of Devonshire* (1948); J. F. Rees, *The story of Milford Haven* (1954); D. Spring, 'English land-owners and nineteenth-century industrialisation', in J. T. Ward and R. G. Wilson (eds.), *Land and industry, the landed estate and the industrial revolution* (1971), pp. 39–40, 42–43.

tance of the Bute initiative was widely recognised by contemporaries. The second marquess was hailed as 'the creator of modern Cardiff' and as 'the most spirited nobleman in Great Britain'. When the West Bute Dock was opened, there was general admiration for 'an immense public work completed for the benefit of mankind by one individual'.[4]

The idea of constructing a dock at Cardiff came to the marquess in 1822, largely at the prompting of David Stewart, who pointed out that as most of the land around the estuary of the Taff, together with a vast acreage within the coalfield, belonged to the Bute estate, 'neither the port of Cardiff nor the mineral country can be opened properly without the consent of Lord Bute'. 'If the port of Cardiff', wrote Stewart, 'is not made the best port in the Bristol Channel it must be because Lord Bute does not choose to exert his power.'[5] The 1820s were not propitious times for the owner of the Bute estate; property and political influence had been neglected for generations; protracted lawsuits were in progress and administration was in confusion. The marquess had no son to whom to bequeath his estates and the ill-health of his wife made the birth of an heir unlikely, while his relations with his brother and heir presumptive were not altogether cordial. Nevertheless, he decided to equip Cardiff at his own expense with a system of docks which, he hoped, would rival those of Liverpool.[6]

From his enterprise, Bute could expect financial returns from three sources: the earnings of the docks themselves, the urban rents at Cardiff which would increase as a consequence of dock development, and the royalties from his mineral properties, the exploitation of which would be hastened by the provision of dock facilities. It was clear to him that the third consideration was the most important one. 'It is admitted', he wrote in 1832, 'that if I lay out a large sum to improve the port, the principal return to me must be the income which I may, directly or indirectly, derive from coals.'[7] Such a

[4] Press cutting, October 1837 (C.C.L., B., XI, 38); Finlay to Bute, 19 October 1839 (ibid., 55, 13).
[5] C.C.L., MS. 4.850; ibid., B., IX, 8; Bute to Crawshay, 18 September 1847 (N.L.W., B., 70, L. 1847–48).
[6] Lord Bessborough, *Lady Charlotte Guest; extracts from her journal, 1833–52* (1950), p. 206; C., 24 March 1848; *South Wales Echo*, 18 May 1892.
[7] Bute to Roy, 14 February 1832 (N.L.W., B., 70, L. Coutts, etc.).

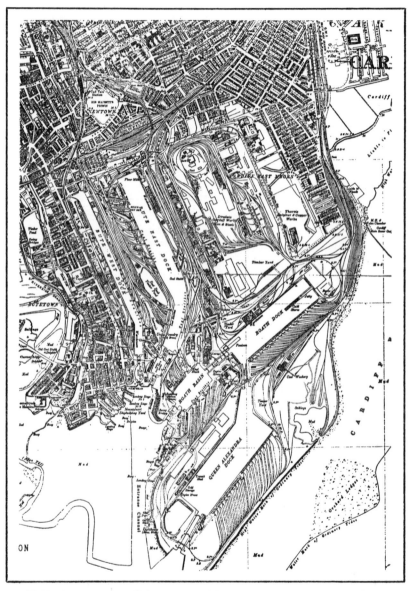

THE BUTE DOCKS IN THE EARLY TWENTIETH CENTURY

consideration did not make it necessary for the marquess to construct the dock himself. Indeed, in the early-1820s he seemed anxious that the task should be undertaken by others, expressing in 1821 a desire 'to show such a disposition on [my] part as would induce the great industrialists interested in the port of Cardiff to come forward and undertake the completion of the port'.[8] In the following year, however, when the Glamorganshire Canal Company sought to purchase Bute land in order to improve its facilities, the marquess refused because the company's scheme 'may defeat a very important plan that has been suggested to [me] to improve [my own] property at Cardiff', and in the mid-1820s, although not yet committed to building a dock himself, Bute was successful in thwarting every attempt by the canal company to modernise its facilities.[9] Such prevarication angered the ironmasters of Merthyr, whose trade was hampered by the inadequacies of the canal's outlet to the sea. In particular, it was resented by the Crawshays of Cyfarthfa, the main shareholders in the company, a Cyfarthfa employee complaining of the 'slippery attitude of Lord Bute'.[10] The marquess's plans for a dock were thus conceived in an atmosphere of suspicion towards him amongst the industrialists for whose trade the dock was built. Although there were to be periods of co-operation between dock-owner and dock-users, suspicion persisted throughout the nineteenth century.

In 1828 Bute's plans crystallized when James Green, the eminent canal engineer, submitted a report on the scheme. The main defect of the Glamorganshire canal was the location of its sea lock, $2\frac{1}{4}$ miles from low water, and Green urged that the first object of a new dock should be the avoidance of the long and intricate navigation of the Taff estuary. Furthermore, the lock was adequate only for ships of under two hundred tons, while the pond adjoining it was handling in the late-1820s ten times the trade of some ten thousand tons which had been loaded there in the late-1790s. Green was much impressed by the natural advantages of Cardiff as a port, noting that, despite

[8] C.C.L., B., I, 13, IX, 16.
[9] Case concerning the Glamorganshire Canal (N.L.W., B., 31); C. Hadfield, *The canals of south Wales and the border* (1960), pp. 100–1.
[10] Routh to Crawshay, 17 and 21 May 1824 (N.L.W., Cyfarthfa Papers, I); Stuart to Richards, 22 May 1824 (G.R.O., D/DA 11); W. H. Smyth, *Nautical observations on the port and maritime vicinity of Cardiff* (1840), p. 9.

its inadequate facilities, it shipped coal more cheaply than did the more important coal port of Newport. He estimated that a new ship canal, constructed upon the Bute-owned moors south of Cardiff, would cost £66,600; wharf and dock dues on current trade would produce £4,762 annually, representing a return of 7 per cent.[11]

In 1829 Green's plans were revised by Thomas Telford and a bill was prepared for presentation to parliament. The bill, which received royal assent in July 1830, was opposed by the Glamorganshire Canal Company, the Monmouthshire Canal Company and the Melingriffith Works, but with the skilled assistance of John Guest, then member for Honiton, it went through parliament virtually unchanged. It authorised the construction of a basin, a waterway a mile and a half long and a sea lock within less than a mile of low water.[12] Although armed with full parliamentary powers, Bute hesitated before implementing them. His advisers expressed their doubts over 'the magnitude of the undertaking for the capital of one individual where there is no positive interest on the part of others to co-operate so as effectively to promote the success of the scheme'.[13] In the early-1830s, the project was the subject of numerous conferences and by 1833 the marquess's vacillations were causing impatience among the freighters of the port. 'Indeed, my lord', wrote Crawshay, 'something should be done for the port of Cardiff. The power is in your hands alone now and we all earnestly hope that you will use it or delegate it to those who will.'[14] By 1833 Bute had come to the conclusion that Green's plans were unsuitable and, under the guidance of William Cubbitt, he applied to parliament for a new act believing that 'these repeated discussions and revisions of the plan [will be] of great advantage to me in the increased security which they promise for the safe and satisfactory

[11] C.C.L., B., XI, 3, 4; C. Hadfield, 'James Green as a canal engineer', *Journal of Transport History*, I (1953), 44–45; A. H. John, *The industrial development of south Wales, 1750–1850* (1950), pp. 116–17.
[12] I William IV, *cap.* CXXXIII; letters, 1829 in C.C.L., MS. 4.713; W. H. Smyth, op. cit., pp. 8–10; C.C.L., B., X, 34; Bute to Richards, 24 February 1829, Green to Richards, 14 March 1829 (G.R.O., D/DA 15).
[13] Anderson to Richards, n.d. (ibid., 17).
[14] Crawshay to Bute, 19 December 1833 (N.L.W., Cyfarthfa Papers, III); C.C.L., MS. D 305.51; letters, 1832–33, in C.C.L., MS. 4.713, N.L.W., B., 70, L. Coutts, etc., and G.R.O., D/DA 17 and 18.

expenditure of my money'.[15] The new scheme substituted an
entrance channel for the wide canal planned by Green, the
channel to be regularly scoured by a flood of water from a
reservoir. Legislation sanctioning these changes received the
royal assent in May 1834.[16]

Despite warnings from his brother and heir not 'to venture
[your] Fortune beyond a certain given amount', the marquess
proceeded in 1834 to implement his parliamentary powers.[17]
Work on the feeder from the Taff was under way by December
and, under the supervision of the resident engineer, George
Turnbull, Telford's former principal assistant, construction
proceeded satisfactorily; in June 1835 the excavation of the
entrance channel was begun, the rapid progress causing Cubbitt
to be in high spirits over the success of the work. The first stone
of the dock itself was laid in March 1837 and the completed
dock was opened on 8 October 1839. Much to Bute's delight,
the event was marked by great festivities at Cardiff, the
citizens realising that it inaugurated a new era in the history
of their town.[18]

The actual construction of the dock passed without serious
incident, but the first few years of its operation were for Bute
a period of acute anxiety. In the early-1840s he was plagued
by the financial difficulties encountered by Daniel Storms, the
chief contractor of the dock, whose blatant dishonesty and
eventual bankruptcy involved the marquess in several years
of arduous negotiations. Furthermore, faulty workmanship
caused the closure of the dock for repairs in the spring of 1840.
Parts of it were not re-opened until January 1841 and it was
not until 1843 that the undertaking was considered by Robert
Stephenson to be fully satisfactory. Thereafter, for the
remainder of the 1840s, annual expenditure on repairs rarely
exceeded £250.[19]

[15] Bute to Richards, 12 March 1833 (ibid., 18).
[16] 4 William IV, *cap.* XIX.
[17] Stuart to Richards, 23 November 1833 (letter in the possession of Mr. A.
Andrews, 19 Waungron Road, Llandâf, Cardiff).
[18] *M.G.*, 25 October 1834, 3 January and 27 June 1835, 10 October 1839;
Bute to Richards, 13 August 1834 (G.R.O., D/DA 19); Richards to Bute,
15 November 1834 (C.C.L., MS. 4.713); Lord Bessborough, op. cit., pp. 96–97.
[19] Indentures (N.L.W., B., 141, 6); letters, 1839–43, in ibid., 70, L. 6, L.Roy,
1840–43, L. Coutts, etc., G.R.O., D/DA 24–27 and C.C.L., MS. 4.860; *Times*,
17 and 21 October 1840; W. H. Smyth, op. cit., pp. 30–34.

Equally difficult were the complications which Bute encountered in seeking to create an effective system of dock administration. Anxiety over the success of his venture caused him great volatility of temper and although he had employed the most eminent men of the day to assist him, making his letters on dock matters read like a roll-call of the most distinguished engineers of the early railway age, he became dissatisfied in turn with the work of every one of his employees.[20] The early years of the dock coincided with a marked deterioration in the health of the marchioness: Bute's perturbation of mind was intensified by the feeling that he had sacrificed his wife to his preoccupation with the dock.[21] Dock officials, headed by the eminent Captain Smyth, were appointed in January 1839, when Bute also confirmed arrangements to place all his property south of the Cowbridge–Newport road under a Harbour Trust, created to ensure that all the proceeds of the dock should go 'towards the redemption of my great expenditure'.[22] He had by then already parted in anger with Green, Turnbull and Cubbitt. In 1841 he dismissed Abbott, his dockmaster, for wilful incapacity, Davies, his collector, for alleged embezzlement, and Captain Smyth for dishonesty, inefficiency and dilatoriness.[23] In 1842 de Grave, Bute's physician, anxious for the marquess to 'secure as far as it is in him Health, Comfort and Fortune, all those now scarcely as safe as they ought to be', urged him 'to get that immense and complicated [concern] out of his hands' by letting the docks, and a year later Lord James Stuart wrote of his brother as being 'so irritable and so apt to give way to such excitement'.[24] Plans to dispose of the dock failed and stability in administration did not come until the mid-1840s when Lieutenant Dornford, previously of the Glamorganshire Canal Company,

[20] In addition to Green, Telford and Cubbitt, advisers included Captain Beaufort, 'the most scientific navigator in the world', Sir John Hall and Captain Maugham of the London Docks, Smeaton, Rennie and Robert Stephenson.
[21] Bute to Smyth, 18 March 1841 (N.L.W., B., 70, L. 7).
[22] Bute to Richards, 11 March and 23 April 1839 (ibid., L. 6).
[23] Bute to Smyth, 18 March, 12 August, 3 and 8 September 1841 (ibid., L. 7); Smyth to Roy, 27 July 1841 (G.R.O., D/DA 25). Correspondence in N.L.W. and G.R.O. also contains bitter attacks on Smeaton, Swinburne, Richards, Roy and Stephenson.
[24] De Grave to Bruce, 22 December 1842; Stuart to Bruce, 17 March 1843 (Scot. P.R.O., H.B. MSS., 196).

was appointed dockmaster. Bute's ever-present fear of extravagance caused both the administrative and maintenance departments of the dock to be gravely understaffed. In 1845, when receipts exceeded £12,000, the enterprise employed a dockmaster, a collector and a clerk whose combined salaries amounted to £550, and an unspecified number of wharfingers, lock-keepers and labourers whose combined annual wages amounted to £1,030.[25] Apart from these full-time employees, Bute's secretary, Collingdon, acted as part-time accountant, his agent, Richards, as part-time legal adviser, and his mineral agent, Clark, as part-time engineer. Overall control remained vested in the marquess himself, who scrutinised every aspect of dock affairs up to the very day of his death.

DOCK EXPANSION, 1848–1922

'I am confounded', wrote Bruce to Richards in 1853, 'by the increasing demands forced upon the Trust by the growing trade of Cardiff; another thousand foot insisted upon in the new dock and a confident assurance that in two years, even that will be insufficient for the trade. The residue of my days, I feel, will be passed in a perpetual worry at an increasing expenditure and undiminished debt.'[26] Bruce's worries were to be shared by all those who were concerned with the Bute Docks in the second half of the nineteenth century. Their trade rose from 8,000 tons in 1839 to 827,000 in 1849 and to 1·3 million in 1854. C. F. Cliffe, visiting Cardiff in 1847, counted 160 vessels in the dock and recorded that Cardiff opinion already considered the facilities to be insufficient. W. J. Trounce, reminiscing in 1918, remembered seeing in the early-1850s American clippers, Dutch East Indian and French Long Couriers diverted to other ports because of the congestion at Cardiff. 'I have known', he wrote, 'vessels detained for a week and sometimes longer on the Penarth Roads, awaiting their turn to come into dock.'[27]

[25] C.C.L., B., XII, 20; Bute to Collingdon, 31 December 1845 (N.L.W., 70, L. 1845–46); accounts, 1847 (G.R.O., D/DA 56–117).
[26] Bruce to Richards, 22 January 1853 (ibid., 35).
[27] C.C.L., B., XI, 56; C. F. Cliffe, *The book of south Wales, the Bristol Channel, Monmouthshire and the Wye* (1847), p. 104; W. J. Trounce, *Cardiff in the fifties* (1918), pp. 24, 29.

Although Bute's Trust Deed of 1845 had granted the trustees the power to expand dock facilities, they were reluctant to commit the estate to large-scale expenditure and, despite the pleas of Lady Bute, nothing was done during the three years which followed the death of the second marquess. In 1851 a decision was forced by the freighters of Cardiff, who petitioned the trustees to construct a new dock, hinting that otherwise they would take their custom elsewhere. A report on the dock, prepared by Rennie and Plews in 1851, noted that its shallow, narrow sea gate and its small entrance basin prevented larger ships from using it and that the main basin of 200 feet by 4,000 feet could not provide sufficient frontage for the growing trade. The report estimated that a new dock could be constructed east of the existing one at a cost of £193,284.[28]

This report was accepted and in May 1852 the trustees committed themselves to the construction of a sea lock, an outer basin, an inner lock, a dock of forty-six acres and a communication canal at a cost of £155,000. The East Bute Dock, built under the supervision of Rennie and Plews, was completed in three stages, the first being opened in June 1855.[29] Meanwhile, pressure for more accommodation had caused the trustees to build a tidal harbour east of the new dock before the entire project was finished. This was opened in 1856 and proved useful for the small craft of the Irish trade. The second section of the dock was opened in January 1858 and the whole undertaking, which added 9,360 feet of quays to the 8,800 feet of the older dock, was completed in September 1859.[30] With the opening of the east dock, the earnings of the west dock fell rapidly and by the early-1860s its upper reaches had been given over to races and pleasure boats. Despite the increasing redundancy of the original dock, the Bute Docks, with sixty-seven acres of enclosed water, a tidal harbour, two miles of quays, ballast cranes, graving docks and forty-nine coal

[28] M. Elsas, *Iron in the making* (n.d.), p. 165; *C.*, 24 March 1848; C.C.L. IX, 15, XI, 29.
[29] Ibid., XI, 57; J. Rennie, *Autobiography* (1875), p. 367; Plews to Bute. 12 June 1869 (G.R.O., D/DA 46).
[30] N.L.W., MSS. 7458B–7459B; W. J. Trounce, op. cit., pp. 48, 51, 58; *Illustrated London News*, 1 October 1859; W. Turner, *The port of Cardiff* (1882), pp. 32–35; Bute to Richards, 1 May, 11 and 18 July 1835 (G.R.O., D/DA 20).

staithes, could in 1859 handle over two million tons of goods a year.[31]

Even with the additional accommodation, the docks soon reached maximum capacity. In 1859 they handled 1·8 million tons of goods; by 1864 this had risen to 2·6 million tons and the trustees were again under pressure to build. In 1864 they applied to parliament for permission to construct a new dock at an estimated cost of £1·2 million. During the discussions on the bill the disadvantages of family control of a large transport undertaking became apparent, for parliament refused to sanction the expenditure of so large a sum upon the estate of a minor. The trustees made another application to parliament in 1865 but that was also rejected. In 1866, the building of a new basin was sanctioned but permission to construct a new dock was refused on the grounds that as the third marquess was approaching his majority, he should be consulted before large expenditure was undertaken. The Roath Basin, twelve acres in extent, was commenced in 1868 and opened for trade in July 1874.[32]

While the basin was under construction, demands upon accommodation at Cardiff rose rapidly, the 2·6 million of 1864 becoming 3·6 million in 1874. Between 1874 and 1886, while the accommodation available remained virtually unchanged, trade rose from 3·6 million to 8 million tons, and by the early-1880s the tonnage of goods handled per acre at Cardiff was the highest of any port in the United Kingdom. Under the guidance of McConnochie, the able dock engineer, every method available was used to expand capacity but only a temporary respite was thereby gained. The early-1870s were a period of rapid expansion of the south Wales coal trade, the coal famine of 1873 bringing such high prices that the freighters became frantic over delays in shipment. In 1874 a deputation called upon the trustees to extend the docks, a demand to which the trustees responded by obtaining powers to build a new dock adjoining the Roath Basin. The year 1874 was

---

[31] C.C.L., B., XI, 56, XII, 23; S. W. Allen, *Reminiscences, being a few rambling recollections of some people and things I have met with* (1918), p. 53.

[32] 29–30 Victoria, *cap.* CCXCVI; *W.M.*, 24 July 1874; C. J. Howells, *Transport facilities in the mining and industrial districts of south Wales and Monmouthshire* (1911), p. 21.

a propitious time for dock expansion: dock profits were high, mineral royalties at £80,000 had reached a record level and trade was booming.[33] In the later-1870s, however, depression in the coal trade caused the marquess to doubt the wisdom of further heavy investment. 'The trustees and I', he informed the Cardiff Chamber of Commerce in 1876, 'have discussed and considered the subject at great length . . . and I do not see that it would be advantageous to me to begin at present the active construction of the proposed docks.'[34]

In 1881 Boyle resigned as chief trustee and dock matters came under the control of W. T. Lewis who, far more aware of the needs of the coal trade, succeeded in convincing the marquess of the need for dock expansion. By the early-1880s, with the coal trade rapidly reviving, congestion at the docks had become acute; by 1883, it was possible to walk across the docks upon the decks of the vessels moored within them.[35] The powers obtained in 1874 having lapsed, new legislation was obtained in 1882, and the act, although containing clauses strongly opposed by the freighters, gave 'the liveliest satisfaction' to the corporation of Cardiff. The new Roath Dock, designed by McConnochie, was ready for service by August 1887. One of its features was the efficiency of its mechanical appliances, particularly the Lewis-Hunter cranes, which had been invented by Lewis the dock manager and Hunter, a dock engineer.[36]

Despite very considerable expansion following the opening of the Roath Dock, the accommodation available remained insufficient. By 1888 the trade of the docks had risen to 9·2 million, and the directors of the newly-incorporated Bute Docks Company were informed by Pomeroy, their dockmaster, that shipping-power was unequal to demand.[37] In the following year, the Barry Docks were opened, causing the

[33] 37–38 Victoria, *cap.* CXVIII; C.C.L., B., XI, 56, XII, 31; W. Turner, op. cit., pp. 30–31; I. B. Thomas, *Top sawyer, a biography of David Davies, Llandinam* (1938), pp. 270–71; J. H. Morris and L. J. Williams, *The south Wales coal industry, 1841–75* (1958), p. 76.

[34] *S.W.D.N.*, 16 November 1876.

[35] C.C.L., B., XI, 56; D. S. Barrie, *The Taff Vale Railway* (1939), p. 24.

[36] 45–46 Victoria, *cap.* CCXLII; *W.M.*, 25 August 1887; C. J. Howells, op. cit., p. 28; J. H. Matthews, *Cardiff records, materials for a history of the county borough* (1898–1911), V, 60.

[37] C.C.L., B., XI, 56; minutes of the meeting of the directors of the Bute Docks Company, 28 September 1888 (B.T.H.R.O., B.D.C. 1).

export of coal from Cardiff to fall slightly. The challenge of Barry made Lewis more anxious to improve facilities at Cardiff.[38] The rapid expansion of the coal trade in the early-1890s caused rival companies to rush to parliament to seek permission for new docks and railways, and the Bute Company felt unable to stand aloof. The need for a new dock at Cardiff in the 1890s arose not because the existing docks provided a insufficient number of shipping places, but because those docks were unsuitable for the changed conditions of trade since they were unable to accommodate ships of larger size and were ill-adapted for that diversification of business which, the Bute directors believed, would be the company's salvation in the face of Barry's strong challenge to its coal exports.[39]

A bill for the construction of a new dock costing £800,000 was deposited in January 1893, but the uncertain state of the coal trade and fears of a renewed dock war with Barry led to its withdrawal.[40] Trade revived in 1893–94, causing pressure for extended and more suitable accommodation at Cardiff to become more intense. In December 1893, the company decided to seek parliamentary sanction for a new dock, with a lock gate which would take the largest vessels afloat, to be constructed on 320 acres of land reclaimed from the foreshore. The Act received the royal assent in 1894 despite the strenuous opposition of rival companies.[41] The marquess and his advisers were not enthusiastic over the new undertaking. 'Its formation has been forced upon the company', noted Jamieson the auditor, 'by the exigencies of trade; it is a measure of defence and precaution intended to preserve rather than extend the company's business. The rapid expansion of trade', he continued, 'the altered circumstances under which that trade is conducted, the rivalry of competitors [and] the unreasonable urgency of a jealous community . . . have imposed upon the owners of this property the necessity of continuous outlays which have often been necessary, not so much to enhance as to maintain the value of the property.'[42]

[38] Ibid., 28 January 1889; C.C.L., MS. 4.1033.
[39] *S.W.D.N.*, 18 June 1891; C.C.L., B., XI, 20, 23; minutes, B.D.C., 28 August and 21 October 1881 (B.T.H.R.O., B.D.C. 1).
[40] Ibid., 11 November and 24 March 1892; C.C.L., B., XI, 23.
[41] 57–58 Victoria, *cap*. CLIV.
[42] Minutes, B.D.C., 1 November 1894 (B.T.H.R.O., B.D.C. 1).

The construction of the new dock proved lengthy and troublesome; although begun in 1897, it was not ready for service until June 1907. Named the Queen Alexandra Dock by Edward VII, when opened it was the largest masonry dock in the world.[43] With its completion, the history of the expansion of the Bute docks came to an end. Their total trade in 1908, the first full operational year of the new dock, was slightly smaller than in 1907. During the intermittent depressions and labour troubles of the immediate pre-war years, the trade of the docks rose erratically from the 11·9 million tons of 1907 to the all-time record of 13·7 million tons of 1913. During the war the trade of Cardiff declined sharply; despite a remarkable post-war shipping boom it soon became obvious that the decline was not to be reversed and that Cardiff, through the efforts of the Bute family, had been endowed with a dock capacity in excess of its needs.[44]

THE PATTERN OF TRADE, 1839–48

The justification for the building of the West Bute Dock was the remarkable increase in the industrial output of the south Wales coalfield in the 1820s and 1830s and the belief that the export trade of the coalfield would gravitate to a modern dock if one were provided. The total tonnage of shipping using the port of Cardiff rose from 90,000 in 1826 to 125,000 in 1830 and to 213,000 in 1835. By the 1820s Cardiff was the leading iron port of the United Kingdom, shipping a total of 87,000 tons in 1829. Iron remained the most important item of export in terms of value until the 1850s but, in terms of weight, it was overtaken by coal in the early-1830s. Although Cardiff's coal trade was then small compared with that of the other south Wales ports and minute compared with that of the Tyne, it increased significantly during the construction period of the West Bute Dock. In the 1830s, the coal shipped from Cardiff

[43] *S.W.D.N.*, *W.M.*, 14 and 15 July 1907; *South Wales Coal Annual*, 1906; C.C.L., B., IV, 11.

[44] Ibid., XI, 56; the total trade of the Bute Docks fell from 13,054,419 tons in 1914 to 6,863,563 tons in 1938, coal exports falling from 10,278,963 tons to 4,980,479 tons (Annual Reports of the Cardiff Chamber of Commerce, cited in M. J. Daunton, 'Aspects of the social and economic structure of Cardiff, 1870–1914' (unpublished University of Kent Ph.D. dissertation, 1974), II, 508).

was largely house coal but that decade saw the beginnings of the trade in Welsh steam coal, a trade which was to transform Cardiff and Glamorgan. The rapidity of the growth of Cardiff's export trade, from 144,000 tons in 1827 to 344,000 tons in 1839, gave rise to widespread optimism and some dared to hope that the town, given a modern dock system, might escape from its thraldom to Bristol, the great emporium of the west.[45]

There were those at Cardiff, however, who considered Bute's investment in dock-building to be a 'wild speculation'. Early figures of the dock's trade give substance to this view, for the bigger ships, accommodation for which was the dock's main advantage over the Glamorganshire canal, did not immediately avail themselves of the new facilities. An eye-witness of the dock's opening recalled that it 'did not take to any extent when first opened . . . On opening day the entire channel had been swept with a view to inducing a few big ships to enter to add to the prestige of the occasion. Only one old wooden ship, one tug boat and the Bristol steamer was the whole flotilla.'[46] Between 1839 and 1841, the apparent ill-success of his venture caused Bute the most acute anxiety. 'I hope that some vessels have entered during this month', he wrote to Smyth in November 1839, ' . . . send me a weekly return for the present. You will not be surprised at my anxiety.'[47] In the first three months of the dock's operation, the total trade amounted to a meagre 8,000 tons, the marquess attributing the low figure to a 'combination of ironmasters and coalowners' intent on ruining him.[48] That there was tacit hostility among the freighters there can be little doubt although the dock was, to a high degree, a speculation in advance of trade. The two leading ironmasters, Crawshay and Guest, had sufficient reason to dislike the marquess and to be suspicious of his enterprises. Crawshay, as chief shareholder in the

[45] C.C.L., B., XI, 17, 3; W. H. Smyth, op. cit., p. 10; C. Hadfield, op. cit., p. 105; M.G., 10 August 1833, 11 January 1834; A. H. John, op. cit., p. 103. In 1833, 171,978 tons of coal and 112,315 tons of iron were carried to Cardiff via the canal.
[46] C. F. Cliffe, op. cit., p. 104; J. Howells, 'Reminiscences of Cardiff', Red Dragon, V (1884), 232.
[47] Bute to Smyth, 13 and 14 November 1839, 29 July 1840 (N.L.W., B., 70, L. 7); Roy to Bute, 9 October 1841 (ibid., L. Coutts, etc.).
[48] Bute to Smyth, 11 March 1841 (ibid., L. 7).

Glamorganshire Canal Company, was unlikely to bring
Cyfarthfa's trade to the canal's competitor, and Guest, while
suffering from Bute's intransigence over the Dowlais lease, was
also in dispute with him over the Taff Vale Railway. The other
ironmasters and coalowners, believing that delay would bring
them better terms, were not anxious to commit themselves.
'The mischief at Cardiff', wrote the marquess, 'is that until we
get a proper infusion of strangers, the present inhabitants
grumble at giving Lord Bute two per cent upon any capital he
expends although they are ready to give twenty per cent to
anyone else.'[49]

Bute, however, was in a position to coerce the freighters to
use his dock. Although the canal, with its combination of
shipping facilities and until 1841 a monopoly of communications with the hinterland, was well-placed to retain its trade,
it was, to a large extent, at the mercy of the marquess. He had
succeeded in thwarting all attempts by the company to improve
its facilities and his determination to persevere in this policy
increased in the 1840s. 'What extent of convenience', he asked
in 1841, 'can the Glamorganshire canal really be brought to
supply without the aid of my land adjoining and in the teeth
of every opposition from my property?'[50] In the early-1840s,
dock and canal officials were engaged in daily boundary warfare, which, to judge by the description of one encounter, did
much to enliven Cardiff life.[51] Bute's antagonism towards the
canal continued into the late-1840s, causing Crawshay to write
in 1847: 'The question between us is not whether we are
entitled to any specific quantity of land or not . . . [but] whether
you can so cripple us . . . at our shipping port at Cardiff that
you can obtain the whole trade of the port through your
superior and costly exit to the sea!! This, my lord, is the real
question and all the covering of the suits of ejectment and
equity . . . cannot hide the real question between us. My lord,
I venture further to tell you, not only as the Chairman of the
Canal Company but as an individual freighter of the port of

---

[49] Ibid., 12 November 1839 (ibid., L. 6).
[50] Bute to Roy, 9 December 1841 (ibid., L. Coutts, etc.); Bute to Smyth,
20 November 1844 (ibid., L. 13).
[51] Roy to Bute, 29 March 1842, 11 November 1845 (ibid., L. Roy 1840–43).
An encounter in August 1842 is described in Strawson to Richards, 19 August
1842 (G.R.O., D/DA 26).

Cardiff—that you cannot succeed in obtaining the whole trade of the port of Cardiff by force.'[52] While preventing the canal company from improving its facilities, thus causing it to be increasingly uncompetitive, Bute was also in a position to put pressure upon the shippers at the canal's sea-lock pond, twenty-four of whose thirty-five wharfs were situated on Bute land and were held on annual tenancies. 'Do not', urged Roy in 1840, 'hold out to the Glamorganshire canal tenants the possibility of remaining tenants at an increased rent, as it would have to be a very high rent indeed which could compensate your lordship for the loss of wharfage and dock dues and it would rather be in the nature of a penalty than a rent.'[53]

Other weapons were also ready to Bute's hand. As lord of the river Taff he insisted that Powell and Coffin, Cardiff's leading coal-shippers, should abandon the jetty adjoining the Taff and lease wharf ground at his dock.[54] As the owner of vast tracts of unleased mineral land, his favour was courted by industrialists seeking leases, while as an aristocrat with wide-ranging political connections, his support was canvassed by the keen politicians among the ironmasters, nine of whom entered parliament in 1841. Within Glamorgan itself, the marquess had formidable influence; the smaller ironmasters and emerging coalowners did not wish to antagonise the man who chose the magistrates and the deputy-lieutenants. Thus, Bute used every method available to increase the trade of his dock and the detailed information he received concerning those who used the canal sea-lock pond and the basin of the Taff Vale Railway left him in no doubt who were his friends and who his enemies.[55]

In the struggle to attract the whole of the trade of the port to the Bute Dock, the level of dock dues was of crucial importance. For ships of under two hundred tons, the canal was markedly cheaper, a 140-ton grain vessel discharging at the sea-lock pond in 1842 paying £3 0s. 9d. for services which would have cost £14 2s. 9d. at the dock. For larger ships,

[52] Crawshay to Bute, 15 September 1847 (C.C.L., MS. 329.51); Bute to Crawshay, 18 September 1847 (N.L.W., B., 70, L. 1847–48).
[53] Roy to Bute, 29 September 1840 (ibid., L. Roy 1840–43); Bute to Roy, 6 September 1841 (ibid., L. Coutts, etc.).
[54] Bute against Powell (ibid., 141, 6); Richards to Bute, 7 April 1832 (C.C.L., MS. 4.713).
[55] E.g., Bute to Smyth, 27 March and 7 August 1841 (N.L.W., B., 70, L. 7) and C.C.L., B., XI, 31–33.

however, the advantages of the dock were manifest; six hundred tons of corn could be loaded there for £45, an operation which would cost £90 if carried out in the roads.[56] 'If his lordship revises his rates', noted Booker in 1842, 'he will put his docks on such a footing as will command the trade of the Port and annihilate all competition which exists at present.' Bute refused to compete with the canal for the small ship trade. 'It is rather my interest', he wrote, 'to get the character of the Trade changed—to get the trade into vessels of larger class as soon as may be.'[57] His expenditure having been far greater than he had anticipated, he was anxious to increase rather than decrease his dock dues. 'The trade is kept at Cardiff', he argued, 'by the improved accommodation I have made for it—the trade can afford to pay for that accommodation and they must.'[58] Acting upon the advice of Sir John Hall of St. Catherine's Dock, the marquess decided upon a wharfage charge of 1s. a ton on iron and 3d. a ton on coal but reserved the right to negotiate different rates with individual freighters. Attacks upon his dock dues on coal, which were not exorbitant in comparison with other docks, caused him great annoyance. 'The coalowners of Glamorgan', he wrote, 'are getting much higher prices than anyone else and they therefore can well afford to pay higher dues . . . a penny per ton represents hundreds or rather thousands of pounds of income to me.'[59]

The marquess's coercion of the freighters and the desire of shipmasters to use his dock in preference to the canal pond caused the prospects of his venture to improve markedly in the early-1840s. In 1842, the Dowlais Company bound itself to ship all its iron at the dock under a three-year agreement and leased 535 feet of frontage at 10s. a foot. Dowlais was the first of the iron companies to sign such an agreement although the coal-shippers, Coffin and Powell, had taken a 360-feet frontage apiece in 1841.[60] In 1844, the trade of the dock, then standing at 490,000 tons, exceeded that of the Glamorganshire Canal

[56] Ibid., XII, 9.

[57] Ibid.; Bute to Richards, 29 June 1839 (N.L.W., B., 70, L. 6).

[58] Bute to Bruce, 21 November 1842 (Scot. P.R.O., H.B. MSS., 196).

[59] Bute to Smyth, 11 March 1841 (N.L.W., B., 70, L. 7); Bute to Roy, 9 December 1841 (ibid., L. Coutts, etc.).

[60] Ibid., 23 October 1841, 1 November 1842 (ibid.).

for the first time and by then all the freighters interested in the port of Cardiff, with the exception of the Cyfarthfa company, were shipping at least a proportion of their trade at the Bute Dock. Expansion was rapid in the late-1840s; by 1849, the year following the death of the second marquess, total trade had risen to 827,000 tons and, as the marquess himself had anticipated, facilities were becoming inadequate to meet demand.[61]

THE PATTERN OF TRADE, 1848–1922

The vast expansion of the trade of the Bute Docks under the third and fourth marquesses was the consequence of the world's insatiable demand for Welsh coal. As the second marquess had foreseen in 1832, the docks were from the beginning over-whelmingly concerned with coal. In the 1840s iron continued to be the most important commodity in value handled at the port of Cardiff, but the dock's share of that trade was slight; of the 737,000 tons of iron exported from Cardiff between 1840 and 1850 only 23 per cent passed through the West Bute Dock, whose iron trade did not exceed that of the Glamorganshire canal until 1851.[62] Throughout the period of Bute ownership, the tonnage of coal exported was never less than three-quarters of the total trade of the docks. Imports were of little account. In 1844 they constituted 3·1 per cent of the total tonnage handled and they rarely rose above 10 per cent in the first fifty years of the dock's existence. Of the export trade of 1844, coal and coke constituted 96·2 per cent of the total and the proportion stood at between 85 and 92 per cent during the three following decades. In addition to the export of coal and coke, there was a small but increasing trade in patent fuel. The Crown Preserve Patent Fuel works were established at Blackweir in 1857 and other works were later built on Cardiff's East Moors; exports began with 499 tons in 1858 and rose to 232,000 tons by 1890.[63]

[61] C.C.L., XI, 56.
[62] Ibid.; C. Hadfield, op. cit., p. 114; *Cambrian Journal*, I (1854), 316.
[63] C.C.L., XI, 56; leases to fuel works (N.L.W., B., 143); W. J. Trounce, op. cit., p. 71.

During the lifetime of the second marquess, the coal trade of Cardiff was almost exclusively with Ireland or with other British ports. In 1840 only 2·5 per cent of the coal shipped at the West Bute Dock went abroad. In the 1850s, however, foreign trade in coal outstripped local and coasting trade and in the first half of 1854 1,400 vessels sailed from Cardiff to foreign ports, representing by their flags a total of twenty-one different states. By 1860, 60 per cent of Cardiff's exports went abroad; 93 per cent of the total to the European continent, 53 per cent to France, the first country to appreciate the qualities of Welsh coal. These developments enabled Cardiff to avoid the fate of Middlesbrough whose docks, geared to the coastal trade, went into decline when it became cheaper to transport coal by rail rather than by sea.[64]

The 1860s saw steam tonnage overtaking sail tonnage in Britain. The demand for coal for steam-ships led to the establishment of coaling stations along the world's sea routes, a development of which Cardiff, with its matchless steam coal, its modern dock facilities and its advantageous geographical position, was well placed to take advantage. In the late-nineteenth century, the coal trade of the south Wales ports, under the leadership of Cardiff, outstripped that of the old-established coalfield of the Tyne. By 1890, when south Wales's share of British coal exports stood at 43 per cent, compared with the 31·7 per cent of north-eastern England, the third marquess had underlined the predominance of south Wales by disposing of the Bute collieries in county Durham which had once supplied Glamorgan with much of its mining expertise. Of the 15·7 million tons of coal exported from south Wales in 1890, the Bute Docks accounted for 7·4 million. By then Cardiff had earned universal recognition as the world's greatest coal port; there were twenty-four consuls and fourteen vice-consuls in the town and the very name 'Cardiff', when applied to coal, assured a higher price, for Rhondda coal

[64] Ibid., p. 35; D. A. Thomas, 'The growth and direction of our foreign trade in coal during the last half-century', *Statistical Journal*, LXVI (1903), 478; H. S. Jevons, *Foreign trade in coal* (1909), p. 18; A. Briggs, *Victorian cities* (1963), p. 252.

shipped there commanded at least 6*d*. a ton more than similar coal shipped from Swansea.[65]

Iron and iron products made up most of the rest of the exports of the Bute Docks. In the late-1840s these averaged 120,000 tons a year, representing about 10 per cent of the total exports. Railway-building booms in India and North America in the late-1860s and early-1870s led to an increase in the trade, the export of iron rails from Cardiff rising from 221,000 tons in 1866 to 314,000 tons in 1872. Thereafter there was a rapid decline; iron, as a proportion of the docks' total exports, fell from 12 per cent in 1872 to 3·8 per cent in 1880. Overseas demand for iron rails, Dowlais's great speciality, slumped; in 1890 only 74,000 tons of iron were exported and the south Wales ironworks adapted themselves to the domestic market.[66]

Imports, no less than exports, were geared to the coal and iron industries. Iron ore represented well over half the imports, rising from 39,000 tons in 1815 to 319,000 tons in 1873 and to 910,000 tons in 1903. The exhaustion of native supplies and the need for high-quality ores for new steel-making techniques caused the ironmasters to comb the world for raw materials and in 1873, the Dowlais Company, in cooperation with Krupp and the Consett Iron Company, formed the Orconera Company to co-ordinate trade in Basque ore. The import of ore from Spain, a major importer of Welsh coal, helped to reduce the number of ships arriving in ballast, as did the import of pitwood from the west coast of France, for more of Cardiff's coal ships went to Nantes and Bordeaux than to any other ports. During the first forty years of the Bute Docks' existence, iron ore, pig iron, timber and pitwood made up well over 80 per cent of their imports and the importance of pitwood increased as mines aged and more irregular seams were exploited. In 1845, Cardiff imported 2,700 tons of pitwood; this rose to 28,000 tons in 1860, to 208,000 tons in 1890 and to 700,000

[65] *Cardiff tide tables and almanack* (1893), pp. 155, 208; *The Mariner*, 15 September 1908; W. Turner, op. cit., p. 11; C. J. Howells, op. cit., p. 16; C.C.L., B., XI, 56.
[66] Ibid.; J. P. Addis, 'The heavy iron and steel industry in south Wales, 1850-1950' (unpublished University of Wales Ph.D. dissertation, 1958), p. 36; T. M. Hodges, op. cit., p. 315.

tons in 1913, making Cardiff second only to London as a timber-importing port.[67]

'Few seaports of the magnitude of Cardiff' noted E. L. Chappell in 1939, 'have . . . developed in so lopsided a fashion.' Indeed the inordinate reliance upon the coal and iron trades was a matter of anxiety to those concerned with the fortunes of the docks.[68] The second marquess had desired from the beginning to diversify the trade of the port and to encourage the import of general merchandise, but during his lifetime such trade was almost negligible. His son's trustees, hoping that Cardiff would become the import centre for the English midlands, built a bonded warehouse at the docks in 1861 and in 1868 co-operated with the town's newly-established Chamber of Commerce in advertising Cardiff's attractions as an import centre.[69] Their efforts had some measure of success; during the 1870s, while exports doubled, imports quadrupled and although iron ore and pitwood remained dominant, general merchandise increased in importance. The need to diversify the trade of Cardiff became more acute in 1889 with the opening of Barry Docks. W. T. Lewis, the dock manager, believed that because of the south Wales coal trade's apparently limitless capacity to expand, competition from Barry would not of necessity result in a decline in Cardiff's coal exports. Nevertheless, an expansion in such exports sufficient to provide a return on a vast investment in new docks was, he argued, unlikely and thus extra earnings would have to be sought from the more lucrative trade in general merchandise. His reasoning proved to be correct. The coal trade of the Bute Docks, which had risen by 42 per cent in the 1860s, by 104 per cent in the 1870s and by 44 per cent in the 1880s, rose by a mere 9·5 per cent in the 1890s and by only 5·5 per cent in the 1900s. The overall trade of the docks, however, rose by 15 per cent in the 1890s, imports rising by 33·3 per cent and by 12 per cent in the first decade of the twentieth century, imports rising by 28 per cent. Following the opening of the Barry Docks, it was the importa-

---

[67] C.C.L., B., XI, 56, XII, 31; W. Turner, op, cit., p. 4; Lady Rhondda (ed.), *D. A. Thomas, viscount Rhondda* (1921), pp. 129–30.
[68] E. L. Chappell, *History of the port of Cardiff* (1939), p. 120.
[69] Bute to Richards, 30 May 1839 (N.L.W., B., 70, L. 6); W. J. Trounce, op. cit., p. 28; C.C.L., B., XI, 56.

tion of general merchandise which represented the growth sector of the trade of the Bute Docks.[70]

Of the imports of general merchandise, grain was the most important commodity. In 1852 Spiller and Browne of Bridgwater leased land at the docks to build a warehouse for grain, and the firm of Spillers won a prominent role in the trade which rose from 46,000 tons in 1876 to 320,000 tons in 1908. Bute officials cherished their grain imports, seeking to provide adequate storage space and saving the Cardiff Milling Company from bankruptcy with a grant of £60,000.[71] They were equally anxious to expand the trade in live cattle; the Bute Docks, with their extensive lairs at the Roath Dock, were the only ones in south Wales with a Board of Trade licence to land foreign cattle. Efforts were also made to establish Cardiff as a leading port for the importation of frozen meat, and in 1907 £50,000 was spent on refrigeration machinery. Although the grandiloquent ambitions of some of the port's apologists were not fulfilled, these efforts did achieve some success and in the first decade of the twentieth century Cardiff's imports of general merchandise stood at 700,000 tons a year.[72]

The Bute authorities also sought other methods of diversifying activity at their port. Whilst enlarging the docks' import trade and outbidding Newcastle in the coal trade, they also saw Cardiff as a rival to the ship-building industry of the Clyde and to the passenger trade of Liverpool. 'The government', wrote Thompson of the Greenock Bank in 1845, 'is going to build a great establishment to create an iron steam navy. Why not at Cardiff as the materials and docks are there? I should rejoice to see Cardiff the great arsenal for the steam navy of Great Britain.'[73] Boat-building had long been established at Cardiff, and in the mid-nineteenth century the yards of Batchelor and Tredwen were particularly active. In the 1870s and 1880s Cardiff won recognition as one of Britain's chief centres of ship-repairing, an activity to which a ship-building industry seemed an obvious concomitant. The notion

[70] Ibid.; minutes, B.D.C., 28 January 1889, 13 February 1890 (B.T.H.R.O., B.D.C. 1).
[71] Ibid., 3 May and 10 June 1897; lease to Spiller and Browne, 1852 (N.L.W., B., 143); W. Turner, op. cit., pp. 78–82.
[72] S.W.D.N., 15 July 1907; Journal of Commerce, 24 April 1913; C.C.L., B., XI, 56.
[73] Thompson to Bute, 25 January 1845 (C.C.L., B., XI, 55).

of Cardiff as a leading shipbuilding centre fired the imagination
of W. T. Lewis, and in the late-1870s he promoted the
re-opening of the Rhymney Ironworks in order to supply
Cardiff with ship steel. In 1882 the Bute Shipbuilding
Engineering and Dry Dock Company was established which
in 1886 launched the first steel steamship to be built in south
Wales. Spurred on by this success, Lewis conceived a plan
whereby steel-making and ship-building would be an integrated concern at the Bute Docks. One reason for attracting
the Dowlais Iron Company to the East Moors was to ensure
a supply of steel for a large shipbuilding industry at Cardiff.
Dowlais open hearth steel had been approved by Lloyds and
the manufacture of ship steel was to be a function of the new
works. Cardiff, however, proved unable to compete with the
traditional shipbuilding centres; between 1890 and 1914 only
eight sailing vessels and two small steam ships were built at
the port.[74]

Schemes to encourage passenger traffic were equally
ambitious. The second marquess spent several thousands of
pounds on the provision of landing stages, largely to improve
communications between Cardiff and Bristol. By the 1850s
four passenger ships a day linked the two towns and the Bute
trustees invested over £15,000 in steamship companies serving
the Severn ports. The 1850s saw the beginning of passenger
traffic from Cardiff to the United States; a group of Mormons
made the voyage in 1854 perched on a cargo of iron rails and
in 1857 attempts were made to provide a more comfortable
clipper service.[75] A low-water pier with a floating pontoon was
constructed in 1868 and Boyle visited America to seek support
for a regular service between Cardiff and the United States.
The trustees invested £25,000 in the South Wales Atlantic
Steamship Company established in 1870 and provided the
company with free coal and free dock facilities. The company's
first ship, the *Glamorgan*, left Cardiff in 1873 but the scheme
soon collapsed. Similar attempts made by Boyle in 1877 and by
Lewis in 1894 also ultimately failed. In the early-1890s large
sums were spent on improving passenger facilities at Cardiff

[74] Minutes, B.D.C., 28 September 1888 (B.T.H.R.O., B.D.C. 1); T. M. Hodges,
op. cit., p. 379; J. P. Addis, op. cit., pp. 20, 72–73; E. L. Chappell, op. cit., p. 56;
W. J. Trounce, op. cit., pp. 19, 29, 35, 66.
[75] Ibid., pp. 16, 19, 30, 64; C.C.L., B., X, 6, XII, 31.

to allow embarkation at all tides, and by 1894 400,000 people a year were sailing from the port. The vast majority of them, however, went no farther than other Severn ports and all schemes for services to more distant destinations were doomed to disappointment.[76]

Thus, despite the aspirations of the Bute authorities, the docks, under Bute ownership, failed to emancipate themselves from their heavy dependence upon the coal and iron trades. Indeed, following a promising growth in the imports of general merchandise in the late-nineteenth century, the docks became, in the early years of the twentieth century, more rather than less dependent upon coal exports; in 1910 they represented 78 per cent of the trade of the dock compared with 73·3 per cent in 1900. With 80 per cent of the ships visiting the dock entering in ballast, there seemed ample opportunity to expand the import trade and with abundant supplies of coal and steel at hand, Cardiff seemed eminently well placed for the development of varied manufacturing industries. The failure to exploit these possibilities has been the subject of perceptive discussion; the main cause for such failure was undoubtedly the fact that 'the local man has given his attention to the local staple and may not be seduced into a consideration of anything else . . . He came here intent on coal and coal only. For the matter of that, he is making a sufficiently good thing of it'.[77]

Furthermore, although the Bute authorities were anxious to diversify activity at the port, the docks themselves were ill-adapted to such diversification. In 1877 Boyle informed the Cardiff Chamber of Commerce that 'It only requires a firm determination, a sound experience and a moderate capital to commence enterprises by land and sea which will make our port independent of the vicissitudes of the trades in coal and iron and will place the fortunes of her population on a better and more enduring basis'.[78] In subsequent decades it became clear that such determination and experience were lacking and

[76] Ibid.; W. Turner, op, cit., pp. 25, 55, 60, 61; agreement, 1879, indenture 1890 (N.L.W., B., 141, 6); minutes, B.D.C., 28 October 1888, 27 February and 24 May 1890, 2 August 1894, 8 October and 5 November 1896 (B.T.H.R.O., B.D.C. 1).

[77] *Maritime Review*, 29 March 1907; M. J. Daunton, *Coal metropolis*, pp. 37–54; C.C.L., B., XI, 56.

[78] W. Turner, op. cit., p. 62; M. J. Daunton, *Coal metropolis*, pp. 44–45.

that the necessary capital was not forthcoming. The ware-houses provided by the Bute authorities were wholly inadequate and so heavy was congestion at Cardiff that the handling of general cargoes there took three to six times longer than at Liverpool or Bristol. Withdrawal of dock space from the coal trade was impractical and the construction of an import dock involved additional expenditure which the third marquess refused to contemplate. Thus, the fact that the docks were owned by a single individual was in part the cause of Cardiff's lopsided development. Nevertheless, despite its world fame as a coal port, Cardiff did not rely as heavily upon the export of coal as did its rivals, Barry and Penarth. By the early-twentieth century, imports constituted between 16 and 20 per cent of the trade of the Bute Docks and general merchandise accounted for up to 30 per cent of the import trade. At Barry in the same period, trade of any kind, apart from the export of coal, never rose above 5 per cent and at Penarth rarely above 2 per cent.[79]

THE FINANCES OF THE WEST BUTE DOCK

The West Bute Dock cost the second marquess a total of £350,000, £222,000 in cash and the rest in the value of timber, stone and other materials from the Glamorgan estate. The degree to which actual expenditure exceeded Green's estimate of £66,000 and that of £76,669 mentioned in the act of 1830 reflects the fact that accurate costing and quantity surveying were still in their infancy in the 1830s. Costs were not heavy during the early stages of dock-building but by the autumn of 1835 they had risen to £1,000 a month and in the summer of 1837 they leapt alarmingly to around £10,000 a month.[80] The marquess was appalled by the huge expenditure to which he had committed himself and as early as 1834 he was obliged to seek temporary loans. 'Mr. Cubbitt', he informed Roy in September 1834, 'will not require more than £5,000 within the next few months. I cannot bring any more money from Scotland, either from the Royal Bank or from my private bankers, nor shall I have any free money of my own before

[79] C.C.L., B., XI, 56.
[80] Letters, Richards to Bute, 1833–37 (C.C.L., MSS. 4.713 and 4.860); W. H. Smyth, op. cit., p. 21.

Christmas. I wish for your friendly assistance. I shall not require the £5,000 in one payment but at £500 or £1,000 a time.' 'My expenditure', he wrote in 1839, 'has been so enormous that I must not sink any more capital until something like income has begun to accumulate.'[81]

The bulk of the money spent on dock-building was raised by mortgaging the Glamorgan estate to the Equitable and Pelican Assurance Societies. A small proportion came from the estate itself; the 1836 December audit yielded £3,373, of which £3,300 was immediately transferred to the Ship Canal Account. While this was by far the largest direct transfer of cash, indirect channelling of money from the Glamorgan estate into dock construction undoubtedly occurred. Between 1830 and 1839, Richards paid the gross revenue of the estate amounting to nearly £78,000, into the central Bute account and in the same period the marquess paid £32,000 into the Glamorgan general account. Some of the balance of £46,000 must have found its way back to Glamorgan in the form of payments to the Ship Canal Account.[82] The Bute estates in Scotland and England also made their contribution, the marquess expressing the hope in 1839 that 'the Glamorgan estate [will] pay back to me a little of the money that I have advanced to Cardiff from other quarters'.[83]

In seeking a return on his investment, Bute was guided by the example of the Glamorganshire Canal Company. 'I should take some ratio of interest', he wrote in 1839, 'with which the neighbourhood is familiar, upon my outlay . . . the Glamorganshire Canal Company are restricted by their act to a profit of 8 per cent . . . I think that the county will go along with me if I adopt such a rule.'[84] In 1840 Roy estimated that a trade of 388,000 tons of coal, 130,000 tons of general merchandise and 30,000 tons of iron would produce £23,700 in wharfage and lockage payments, thus yielding more than an 8 per cent return on an outlay of £222,000.[85] His estimate proved

[81] Bute to Roy, 26 September 1834 (N.L.W., B., 70, L. Coutts, etc.); Bute to Smyth, 12 November 1839 (ibid., L. 6).

[82] Richards to Bute, 3 December 1836 (C.C.L., MS. 4.860); accounts, 1830–39 (N.L.W., B., 60).

[83] Bute to Richards, 5 December 1839 (ibid., 70, L. 6).

[84] Bute to Smyth, 19 April 1839 (ibid.).

[85] Roy to Bute, 13 February 1840 (ibid., L. Roy, 1840–45).

wildly optimistic. Between 1841 and 1848 the total gross
income of the dock amounted to £67,949. In 1844 the tonnage
handled was little more than half that estimated by Roy and
produced a net profit of only £2,104 on gross receipts of
£6,893. There was a sharp increase in 1845, partly because of
the abolition of export duty on coal carried in foreign ships;
in that year, gross receipts amounted to £12,385 and net
receipts to £8,341. Apart from these two years, details of the net
receipts of the dock are not available until 1848 when the series
of the accounts of the Bute trustees begins. The income predicted
by Roy was not received until 1854 and by then the trustees
had committed themselves to massive new expenditure.[86]
The disappointing return on investment which was to be such
a marked feature of the Bute Docks in the late-nineteenth and
early-twentieth centuries thus manifested itself in the very
first years of the dock's existence.

THE FINANCES OF THE BUTE DOCKS, 1848–1922

In 1851–52, the last full year before work began on the East
Bute Dock, total capital expenditure had reached £463,000;
net receipts amounted to £19,465, representing a return of
4·25 per cent. Net receipts rose rapidly in the 1850s, reaching
£35,888 in 1860–61. Expenditure, however, rose even more
rapidly. In 1852–53, £41,617 was spent on new works; this
rose to £105,000 in 1856 and thereafter, for the rest of the
decade, annual expenditure did not fall below £80,000. By
1860, with the East Bute Dock completed, a total of £690,000
had been spent on construction since 1852 and the return on
capital expenditure had fallen to 3·15 per cent.[87]
    Although heavy, the strain of raising large sums of money
for dock expansion was not as severe as that experienced by the
second marquess when constructing the first dock. As the
owner of the estate was a minor, sums paid for his maintenance
were small and during the minority a total of £1,276,000 of
the third marquess's income was spent on the docks. That
income, particularly from minerals, was rising rapidly, royalty
receipts increasing from £10,765 in 1848 to £44,699 in 1868.

[86] C.C.L., B., X, 2, XI, 56, XII, 20.
[87] Ibid., and XII, 22, 25 and 32; C.C.L., MS. 4.937.

The resources of the estate, however, were not in themselves sufficient to finance the construction of the East Bute Dock. In 1855, when the total net receipts of the Glamorgan estate were £61,659, expenditure on the new dock amounted to £105,000, while interest on the debt created by the construction of the old stood at £10,836. Such expenditure and interest exceeded income for the rest of the decade and, to finance the new works, the trustees were obliged to resort to loans. Between 1855 and 1859, a total of £128,000 was borrowed, including £60,000 from Clayton and £30,000 each from the Union and National Provincial Banks.[88]

With the completion of the East Bute Dock in 1859, capital expenditure declined and in the first half of the 1860s the cost of new works was below £20,000 a year. In 1865, when net income from the docks stood at £39,800, the return on the capital outlay of £1·22 million was 3·1 per cent. During the late-1860s and the early-1870s, net income rose rapidly but was again out-distanced by outgoings on construction. With the commencement of the Roath Basin in 1868, annual expenditure soared to around £150,000 and on its completion in 1874 the Bute investment in dock construction had reached £2,285,000. In that year, when £133,000 was spent on new works and a further £29,000 on loan interest, the Glamorgan estate produced a net income of £114,000. Further loans were therefore obtained, the rise in interest paid suggesting borrowings in the region of £475,000 between 1868 and 1874. In 1874, when net dock receipts stood at £62,618, the return on investment was 2·7 per cent, while rates of up to 4·5 per cent were being paid on the money raised to finance dock construction.[89]

The position improved in the late-1870s. Following the completion of the Roath Basin, no large-scale extensions were undertaken until the Roath Dock was commenced in 1883. By the early-1880s, with the facilities at the docks stretched to their utmost capacity, net earnings rose well above £100,000 a year; in 1882, when they stood at £140,651, the dock investment, without allowing for depreciation, was showing a

---

[88] Indenture, 1879 (N.L.W., B., 137, 4); 49–50 Victoria, *cap.* LXXXVI, citing judgement of 1884; C.C.L., MS. 4.937; ibid., B., X, 2.
[89] Ibid., X, 1–6, XII, 23, 31–32.

return of 5·7 per cent. This satisfactory situation was not destined to endure. In 1882, authority was obtained to build the Roath Dock at an estimated cost of £550,000. The strain of raising such a sum, together with the involved finances of the docks, was among the factors which led in 1886 to the establishment of the Bute Docks Company. The act of 1886 incorporating the docks was the culmination of attempts by the trustees to disentangle the personal finances of the third marquess from those of the dock. By then, a total of £2,006,397 of the marquess's own money had been spent on the docks since the death of his father. In satisfaction of the debt, he was granted shares in the company worth £2,050,000 and was also to be paid one half-penny for every ton shipped to or from the docks, 10 per cent of all wharfage dues, 50 per cent of the net rents of warehouses and £1,112 10s. a year for the weir and feeder. From the rest of the £3·5 million declared capital of the company, the trustees were issued with 9,000 preference shares at 4 per cent and debenture shares worth £550,000, in exchange for which they conveyed to the company 500 acres on the south side of the town of Cardiff, land which included 111 acres of docks. A further £800,000 worth of debenture shares was submitted to the public. The response was enthusiastic, offers amounting to £3,660,000 being received. Of those applications, £350,000 were allotted to London, £225,000 to Edinburgh and £225,000 to Cardiff.[90]

The establishment of the company coincided with the last phase of the expenditure on the Roath Dock. By 1887, when it was opened, £636,000 had been spent upon it; thereafter, into the 1890s, expenditure on new equipment and on the modernisation of the older docks stood at around £35,000 a year. Borrowing had again to be resorted to: Coutts Bank advanced £60,000 in 1887 and the National Provincial Bank a further £60,000 in 1889, while loans from the third marquess amounted by 1891 to £150,000. In 1888, £200,000 was raised through new shares and in 1891 a further 2,000 shares of £100 were issued, of which 1,500 were granted to the marquess in place of his loan. During the earliest years of the company

[90] Ibid.; 49–50 Victoria, *cap.* LXXXVI; agreement, 1887 (N.L.W., B., 141); minutes, B.D.C., 29 July, 3 August, 28 September, 12 October 1886 (B.T.H.R.O., B.D.C. 1). The annual royalties in the early years of the company amounted to between £20,000 and £30,000 a year (ibid., 1 December 1887, 15 February 1895).

dividends rose. Between 1887 and 1889 the half-yearly net revenue available for dividend increased from £70,000 to £90,000 and the interest paid on ordinary shares went up from 4 per cent to 6 per cent. The opening of Barry Docks in 1889, however, slowed the expansion of Cardiff's trade and obliged the Bute directors to give concessions to freighters, while the labour agitation of the early-1890s led to a rise in working costs. Gross receipts increased by 21 per cent between 1887 and 1893, but in the same period the amount available for dividend decreased and by 1893 interest on ordinary shares had fallen to 2·5 per cent.[91]

In these circumstances, the Bute directors' lack of enthusiasm for the dock authorised by the act of 1894 is understandable. Attempts to build the dock jointly with other concerns failed and the company was obliged to raise the entire capital itself. When the Queen Alexandra Dock was opened in 1907, £2,238,000 had been spent upon it; by 1912 a further £704,000 had been spent on the company's railway. To cover this vast outlay, the share capital of the company was increased from the £3,800,000 of 1894 to £6,300,000 by 1913. In the same period, the total trade of the docks rose by 40 per cent, but the amount of money available for dividend rose by a mere 18 per cent. The directors struggled to maintain a 3 per cent dividend on ordinary shares but, lacking a substantial reserve fund, they were vulnerable to a crisis in the coal industry. During the troubles of 1898 and again in 1912 no dividend at all was paid, while in the immediate pre-war years, when the trade of the docks reached unprecedented levels, the dividend was 1 per cent in 1913 and nil in 1914.[92] This was a poor record indeed in a period when the railway and colliery companies of south Wales were paying dividends of up to 12 per cent.[93] In order to pay even their meagre returns on ordinary shares, the directors were obliged to reduce the interest on debentures and on new issues of preference shares. What saved the company from bankruptcy was the willingness

---

[91] C.C.L., B., XII, 35–39; minutes, B.D.C., 1887–93 (B.T.H.R.O., B.D.C. 1).
[92] Ibid., 1886–97; minutes, C.R.C., 1897–1908, 12 February and 12 August 1913 (B.T.H.R.O., R.A.C. 1/55).
[93] P.P., XIII (1919), pp. 7–12; C.C.L., B., XII, 40.

of the chief shareholder, the marquess of Bute, to be exploited. The third marquess surrendered 5,000 ordinary shares in 1896 and a further 2,500 in 1898, transactions representing a nominal loss to him of £750,000. From 1902 to 1907, in order 'to maintain a dividend during costly dock operations' the fourth marquess paid the interest on loans raised to finance the Queen Alexandra Dock, a commitment which, by 1907, amounted to £70,000. From 1907 to 1912 he paid the interest on the debts incurred through the construction of the company's railway at an annual cost of £20,000, while in June 1912, when the ordinary shares produced no dividend, a return on the preferred ordinary shares was only possible because the marquess forewent the payment of his royalties. Loans raised to finance new works stood at £2,275,000 in 1907, while other borrowings amounted to a further million pounds. Despite strenuous efforts to reduce debts following the opening of the Queen Alexandra Dock and the issue of shares worth £990,000 in 1908, the company still had a debt of £982,866 at amalgamation in 1922.[94]

The construction of docks at Cardiff was, therefore, a disappointing investment for the Bute family. The later ventures proved particularly unprofitable, for the railway produced virtually no receipts and the £2,238,000 spent on the Queen Alexandra Dock only increased the annual average earnings by some £17,000. To construct a dock which yielded a return of only 0·75 per cent seems an act of folly yet, under the circumstances, it is difficult to see that the Bute authorities had any choice. Not to have invested in larger docks would soon have made the whole undertaking uncompetitive; by building new docks at huge expense, the older docks became increasingly redundant. The financial weakness of the docks arose not because of the incompetence of management, but because of the rapidly changing conditions of the trade. The charge for shipping coal, which remained unchanged at 2·25d. a ton throughout the late-nineteenth and early-twentieth centuries, was insufficient to cover the cost of the service but

[94] W. E. Simnett, *Railway amalgamation in the United Kingdom* (1923), pp. 230, 262; minutes B.D.C., 26 August 1895, 10 December 1896 (B.T.H.R.O., B.D.C. 1); minutes, C.R.C., 16 December 1898, 11 August 1902, 12 August 1907, 9 February 1911, 8 August 1912 (ibid., R.A.C. 1/55).

raising the charge would have driven shippers to Barry, whose docks were not burdened with obsolete investments.[95]

Cardiff's burden of obsolete investment was largely caused by the marked increase in the size of the ships using the port; the average rose from 180 tons in 1865 to 627 tons in 1912, the average tonnage of the twenty largest ships visiting Cardiff rising from 2,400 to 11,900 in the same period. In 1839 much was made of the large entrance lock and the great depth of water at the new Bute Dock; within two decades that much-vaunted dock was virtually redundant. When the East Bute Dock was opened it accommodated the largest vessels used in the coal trade, yet, thirty years later, over five hundred of the vessels visiting the port could not be accommodated within it. With the opening of the Roath Dock, the gross receipts of the East Bute Dock fell by 20 per cent and a similar contraction occurred in the trade of the Roath Dock when the Queen Alexandra Dock was opened. Furthermore, the larger ships became, the more cargo they could carry in relation to their registered tonnage. As dock dues were levied on registered tonnage, the use of larger ships caused payments per ton of cargo to fall by 30 per cent between 1873 and 1911, while at the same time the facilities needed for handling their cargo became progressively more expensive.[96] While railway companies, in order to handle increasing trade, needed only to add to the number of their trucks, dock companies were obliged to construct entirely new undertakings, each investment reducing the value of the preceding one. The provision of dock facilities in the nineteenth and twentieth centuries was, by its very nature, a non-profit-making public service. This public service the Bute family performed for Cardiff.

RAILWAY COMPANIES AND THE WEST BUTE DOCK

'I very much regret', wrote William Crawshay in 1839, 'that an arrangement for Union appears so difficult at present between Dockists, Canalists and Railroadists for the general

[95] Ibid., 1907–14; C.C.L., B., XI, 20. The progressive increases in the dimensions in feet of the four docks, West, East, Roath and Alexandra, were as follows: width of entrance lock, 45, 54, 80, 90; length of communication channel, 35, 49, 80, 90; normal depth of water, 13–19, 25, 32½, 37.
[96] C.C.L., B., XI, 20; M. J. Daunton, *Coal metropolis*, pp. 26–27.

welfare of this part of the country, but I do not doubt that the time will come when all parties will see their real interests.'[97] Union, however, did not come until 1922. While the Cardiff docks were owned by the Bute family, relations with other transport concerns serving the port and the coalfield were matters requiring complex and often contentious negotiations. In the 1840s such negotiations worked generally in favour of the Bute Dock, for not only did the marquess succeed in emasculating the Glamorganshire Canal, but he also impeded the hostile plan of the Taff Vale Railway Company, while at the same time obstructing all lines which could work to the advantage of rival ports.

To promote the exploitation of his mineral land and to ensure the success of his dock, the second marquess considered undertaking the construction of railways as well as docks. In 1828 Beaumont reported upon the possibility of building a railway to link the proposed dock with the coalfield, and a plan for the construction of a line from Cardiff to the Rhondda and the vale of Neath via Llantrisant was prepared by Green in 1829. The notion of a railway to the Llantrisant coalfield was revived in 1837 when Gray prepared a scheme to link Llantrisant with the Glamorganshire Canal, the line to be built jointly by Bute and the coalowner Thomas Powell. Expenditure at the dock, however, made the marquess reluctant to pursue the project and, although Powell sought to revive it in 1842, the plan was abandoned.[98]

Bute's decision not to become a railway promoter did not make him an enemy of railway development. 'I am prepared', he wrote in 1846, 'to assent to all railways in Glamorgan except where the course is particularly objectionable.'[99] 'Objectionable' meant any alignment which did not give to Cardiff clear advantages over all other ports in south Wales. To secure the maximum trade for his dock, Bute scrutinised every south Wales railway bill and during the 1840s, when such bills were being promoted in bewildering variety, this

---

[97] Crawshay to Bute, 24 December 1839 (C.C.L., B., XX, 146).

[98] Beaumont to Bute, 23 June 1829 (C.C.L., B., XIV, 70); report, 1829 (G.R.O., D/DA 15); report, 1838 (N.L.W., B., 31); Richards to Bute, 17 and 24 February, 21 September 1838 (C.C.L., MS. 4.860); Bute to Richards, 20 December 1837 (N.L.W., B., 70, L. 1833–40); Richards to Bute, 26 November and 3 December 1842 (ibid., L. 1842–46).

[99] Bute to Clark, 12 January 1846 (ibid., L. 1845–46).

meant constant vigilance. It is in his dealings with the Taff Vale Railway Company that the second marquess's insistence upon the paramount rights of Cardiff and its dock emerge most clearly. The dock-building project had been initiated long before the Merthyr ironmasters brought forward a plan to link Cardiff with the Welsh iron metropolis. It has since been widely assumed that the Bute Dock, opened in 1839, and the Taff Vale Railway, opened in 1841, were both part of an overall project to develop the south Wales coalfield. The Bute papers show that this was in fact far from being the case for, although a dock at Cardiff and a railway to Merthyr are clearly complementary undertakings, the industrialists who sponsored the Taff Vale Railway were deeply suspicious of Bute and he was equally suspicious of them.

The leading figure in the early history of the Taff Vale Railway was Sir John Guest, who had long been in dispute with the marquess, and it was no part of Guest's intention to ensure the success of the Bute Dock by making it the sole outlet of the new railway. The railway, as planned in 1835, was to have three termini, at the mouths of the Taff, the Ely and the Rhymney, with the Taff terminus alone being linked to the Bute Dock. Furthermore, the promoters, having no desire to use a dock which would not be under their own control, proposed that they should lease all the wharfs and take the entire Bute concern into their hands. Their attitude angered the marquess. 'I am afraid', he wrote, 'that the Taff Vale Railway Company is not much else than a combination of certain Merthyr ironmasters and tradespeople. We should find a company of strangers much more reasonable to deal with.'[100] When the railway bill was brought before parliament in 1836, it contained no mention of a terminus on the Ely or on the Rhymney, and Bute, therefore, made no effort to oppose it. The marquess invested in the company in the names of Richards, Bird and Lord James Stuart and attempted to create a Bute party among the Bristol shareholders. Although suspicious of any undertaking in which Guest was prominent, Bute was anxious to speed up the railway project for 'it cannot

---

[100] Bute to Roy, 19 December 1835, to Richards, 9 November and 5 December 1835 (ibid., L. 6); lists of shareholders in the Taff Vale Railway Company (N.L.W., B., 31, B.T.H.R.O., TV2/1A).

be denied that it is an advantage to me to get the railway finished as soon as may be after my dock is open'.[101]

While being well disposed to a line linking Merthyr to Cardiff, the marquess was ready to fight any plan designed to link that railway with any dock other than his own. By November 1836 it was widely rumoured that the Taff directors were planning to build a dock on the Ely and to link it with their proposed railway. Although Bute believed that they could not afford to undertake such a project, the possibility caused him grave concern.[102] When the company brought forward a bill in 1840 which referred to an Ely line, the marquess retaliated by persuading Stephenson to publish arguments proving the folly of the scheme, by pressurizing Hill, the Merthyr ironmaster, into threatening to resign from the board of directors, and by seeking to raise a petition at Cardiff opposing the bill. The offending clauses were eventually dropped from the Taff company's act of 1840 but the preamble which referred to the desirability of an Ely dock was passed by parliament. 'The Ely', argued Serjeant Wrangham, 'would be an open and free port while the new harbour was the private property of the marquess of Bute.' 'The advantages of a second outlet to the sea', stated the Taff directors, 'in the event of any obstruction at either place of shipment is too obvious to require comment.'[103] These arguments foreshadow those which were later to be used by the promoters of the Penarth and Barry docks. The Taff Vale Railway Company, destined to be the most prosperous railway company in Britain in the 1870s, was considered an unsound investment in the early-1840s and it was widely believed at Cardiff that its weakness was the result of Bute hostility. The marquess, always sensitive to local opinion, sent Roy to company meetings to put his point of view and he also briefed the Tory gentry of Glamorgan on his

[101] Bute to Richards, 30 March and 20 May 1836 (N.L.W., B., 70, L. 6); Bute to Smyth, 22 July 1840 (ibid., L. 7); 6–7 William IV, *cap.* LXXXII; Richards to Bute, 7 June 1837 (C.C.L., MS. 4.860).

[102] Richards to Bute, 11 November 1836 (ibid.); Bute to Smyth, 22 July 1840 (N.L.W., B., 70, L. 7).

[103] Correspondence in ibid., C.C.L., MS. 4.860, ibid., B., IX, 27, 21 and G.R.O., D/DA 24–28; W. H. Smyth, op. cit., p. 47; report to the ninth half-yearly meeting of the Taff Vale Railway Company (B.T.H.R.O., TV2/1A); 3–4 Victoria, *cap.* CX.

case.[104] In 1840, at Bute's instigation, Captain Smyth published his *Nautical Observations on the Port and Maritime Vicinity of Cardiff*, ostensibly a description of the Bute Docks but in fact an attempt to portray the Ely project as a cynical plot by a section of the Taff directors to force Bute to accommodate the railway at his dock on their own terms.

Bute's measures were successful, Stephenson considering by August 1840 that the Ely project was dead.[105] The question of the railway's access to the Bute Dock remained as a fruitful source of dispute and in 1842, with the issue still unresolved, the railway company made increasing use of a small dock which they had built adjoining the Taff. The marquess insisted that the small dock should be done away with before any final settlement was made and the company retaliated by reviving the Ely project.[106] Bute for once reacted in a conciliatory if ambiguous manner. 'Lord Bute', it was stated in September 1843, 'is disposed to look upon the Taff Vale Railway as a great work, admirably adapted to extend the development of the principle upon which he engaged in the construction of his dock, namely to provide a sufficient outlet for the vast mineral wealth of the district . . . He considers that the Interest of each party is to support and not to oppose the other and, if the company will pay that respect to his interests which they can justly claim for their own, an arrangement may easily be made for mutual benefit.'[107] This olive branch was immediately seized, and within a month discussions were afoot for the lease of the dock to the Taff Vale Railway Company. Under an agreement of November 1843, Bute was to be paid £12,000 a year together with half of all receipts beyond £12,000, while the company was to bear full responsibility for dock repairs and was to bind itself to ship all its traffic at the Bute Dock. To Crawshay, the chief proprietor of the canal company, the proposed union between Taff and Bute posed a grave threat and he suggested that the three concerns should

[104] Bute to Richards, 12 January 1841 (G.R.O., D/DA 25); Roy to Bute, 6 and 7 August 1840 (N.L.W., B., 70, L. Roy, 1840–43).
[105] Ibid., 22 August 1840 (ibid.).
[106] Ibid., 14 February 1842 (ibid.); Bute to Smyth, 28 February 1840 (ibid., L. 6); Bute to Richards, 14 and 19 August 1843 (ibid., L. 7).
[107] Memorandum in Bute to Richards, 8 September 1843 (G.R.O., D/DA 27); report to the fifteenth half-yearly meeting of the Taff Vale Railway Company (B.T.H.R.O., TV2/1A).

be merged, a course to which the marquess did not in principle object.[108] Crawshay's exaggerated demands jeopardized the scheme and in January 1844 the Taff shareholders repudiated the agreements made by their directors. This made the need for a working arrangement between Taff and Bute even more urgent. The marquess's objective was a settlement which would bring the entire Taff traffic to his dock and rule out the possibility of the construction of a dock on the Ely. Under the agreements of May and November 1844 and of May 1846 these objectives were realised and the Bute–Taff arrangements received parliamentary sanction in August 1846.[109]

The settlement of 1846 and the negotiations which led up to it provided precedents for the agreements later made with the South Wales Railway. When the Great Western Railway Company launched its plan to link south Wales with London in 1844, Bute was immediately sympathetic. Lord James Stuart presided over the initial discussions in London and the marquess himself took part in the meetings held to explain the project to the citizens of Cardiff. Negotiations with the South Wales Railway Company, which were less bedevilled by personal animosities than the Bute–Taff discussions, were satisfactorily concluded in 1851 when the company received parliamentary permission to build a railway to the proposed East Bute Dock.[110]

In dealing with railway companies, Bute was not merely concerned to ensure that those lines serving Cardiff should be linked with his dock on his terms. He was also vitally interested in opposing any company which sought to encroach upon the trade of the basin of the Taff and its tributaries and in seeking to extend Cardiff's catchment area beyond the limits of the port's natural hinterland. Green had predicted in 1829 that the district between the valleys of the Neath and the Taff

---

[108] Leaflet, 9 November 1843 (C.C.L., MS. D 305.51); letters, October–December 1843 (N.L.W., B., 70, L. 6 and L. Roy, 1840–43); Jones to Richards, 11 December 1843 (G.R.O., D/DA 27).
[109] Letters, 1844 (N.L.W., B., 70, L. 6, 7, and Roy 1844–46, C.C.L., B., V, and Scot. P.R.O., H.B. MSS., 196); reports of the eighteenth and twenty-first half-yearly meetings of the Taff Vale Railway Company (B.T.H.R.O., TV2/1A); C. J. Howells, op. cit., p. 13; M. J. Daunton, *Coal metropolis*, p. 20.
[110] Richards to Bute, 14 September 1844 (N.L.W., B., 70, L. 7); Roy to Bute, 7 May 1845 (ibid., L. Roy, 1844–46); 20–21 Victoria, *cap.* CXI; C.C.L., B., XII, 30; E. T. Macdermot, *A history of the Great Western Railway Company* (1927), I, 579.

would become an area of dispute between the ports of Neath and Cardiff. This threat became serious in 1845 with the sponsoring of a railway to link Neath and Swansea not only with the upper reaches of the vale of Neath but also with Merthyr Tydfil. The Vale of Neath railway, which reached Hirwaun in 1851, proved less of a danger than Bute had feared, for the steep gradients along its course and the lack of adequate dock facilities at Neath led to very little leakage of trade.[111] A graver danger was the possibility that the trade of the Aberdare valley would be diverted to Neath. The Aberdare railway was opened in 1846 and in that year the Vale of Neath Railway Company sought to lease or purchase it. 'The effect of a lease of it to the Neath people', wrote Roy, 'would be to enable them to take its traffic to Neath'. By the 1840s there were indications that the Aberdare coal trade would become as profitable as the Merthyr iron trade and its diversion to Neath would have gravely damaged the Bute Dock. Roy urged Bute 'to spur on the [Taff company] to outbid the Neath company for the Aberdare line' and to outbid it himself if the Taff company were reluctant to do so. The Neath company's interest did in fact stir the Taff directors to action and in January 1847 the Aberdare line was leased to the Taff Vale Railway Company in perpetuity.[112]

It was also feared that the Neath company would seek to tap the trade of the Rhondda. The Taff company built a branch into the lower Rhondda in 1841 and the landowners of the valley, Bute among them, urged the company to extend its line to the upper Rhondda Fawr, for as Richards noted, 'it will be most extraordinary if the valley should remain much longer unopened, considering the vast quantity of valuable mineral property there'.[113] The upper Rhondda Fawr is considerably nearer to Neath than it is to Cardiff and the Vale of Neath directors considered Neath to be the natural outlet for Rhondda traffic, a point of view which Bute vigorously opposed. 'An outlet to Neath or Swansea [from the

[111] Report, 1829 (G.R.O., D/DA 15); J. H. Morris and L. J. Williams, op. cit., pp. 94–95; Bute to Stuart, 22 May 1845, to Thomas, 15 December 1845, to Collingdon, 21 March 1846 (N.L.W., B., 70, L. 1845–46).
[112] Roy to Collingdon, 18 October 1846 (ibid., L. Roy, 1844–46); D. S. Barrie, op. cit., p. 14.
[113] Richards to Bute, 20 January 1844 (N.L.W., B., 70, L. 7); E. D. Lewis, op. cit., pp. 116–26.

Rhondda]', wrote Bruce, 'must be attended with an effect prejudicial to Cardiff.'[114] Pressure from landowners and coal-owners, together with threats that other interests would link Cardiff with the upper Rhondda, forced the Taff Vale Railway Company in 1846 to obtain an act authorising it to build a railway to the upper Rhondda. The line reached Dinas in 1849 and there it stopped until it could be proved that the steam coal of the upper Rhondda was commercially exploitable. Bute's purchase of Cwmsaerbren and the sinking of a pit to the steam coal measures at Treherbert were motivated in part by the need to induce the Taff Vale Railway Company to extend its line to the upper Rhondda, thereby forestalling rivals from Neath and Swansea and ensuring that Rhondda coal would be conveyed to Cardiff.[115]

While endeavouring to ensure that all the trade of the basin of the Taff and its tributaries would come to the port of Cardiff, the second marquess also sought to extend the influence of the port beyond the natural limits of Cardiff's hinterland. In 1846, he supported the proposed Ogmore and Garw and Port of Cardiff junction railway; nothing came of this scheme but later in the century the mid-Glamorgan valleys were linked to Cardiff by branches of the Great Western Railway and much of their coal came to be shipped at the Bute Docks.[116] It was in the Rhymney valley, however, that the marquess and, later, his son's trustees intervened most effectively to expand the trade of Cardiff at the expense of its rivals. 'The Rumney', wrote Thompson of the Rhymney Ironworks in 1825, 'was destined by nature for Newport.' Bute, however, thought otherwise. 'It is my clear rule', he declared, 'not to grant facilities for carrying any minerals to Newport which might be brought to the Bute Dock.'[117] The Rhymney Iron-works, of which the marquess was part-landlord, sent its iron by tramroad to Newport but Bute insisted that, once his dock were opened, he would not allow that arrangement to endure.

[114] Bruce to Roy, 15 October 1845 (N.L.W., B., 70, L. 1845–46).
[115] See above, pp. 219–20. On the Rhondda and Swansea Bay Railway completed in 1885, see C. J. Howells, op. cit., p. 116, and E. D. Lewis, op. cit., p. 120.
[116] Bute to Clark, 12 January 1846 (N.L.W., B., 70, L. 1845–46).
[117] Bute to Richards, 28 January 1843 (G.R.O., D/DA 27); Thompson to Crawshay, 27 January 1825 (N.L.W., Cyfarthfa Papers, I); Bute to Roy, 7 December 1831 (ibid., B., 70, L. Coutts, etc.).

Beaumont urged him to build a railway up the Rhymney valley, but Bute felt that as his expenditure on the dock had been so large, no other enterprise could be contemplated. Instead he urged the Taff Vale Railway Company to build a branch up the Rhymney valley; plans for such a line were drawn up in 1846 but were not proceeded with. The whole matter remained in abeyance until the early-1850s, when the third marquess's trustees sponsored the Rhymney Railway Company, an action which significantly enlarged Cardiff's catchment area and materially increased the trade of the Bute Docks.[118]

DOCKS AND RAILWAYS, 1848–1922

The tension between the Bute authorities and the freighters of Cardiff did not abate significantly following the death of the second marquess in 1848. The urgent need to expand dock accommodation and the antagonism aroused by the Cardiff parliamentary election of 1852 led to the revival of the scheme for a dock on the Ely. The Ely Tidal Harbour bill, sponsored by the Taff directors in 1855 and vigorously opposed by the Bute trustees, received the royal assent in July 1856. The promoters obtained further powers under the Penarth Harbour, Dock and Railway Act of 1857 which also authorised the Taff Vale Railway Company to take a perpetual lease on the proposed Penarth dock. When the dock was opened in 1865, the Taff company became the first concern in the Cardiff area to own both dock facilities and a railway to the coalfield; such an integrated transport undertaking was to become the goal of all those concerned with docks and railways in south Wales.[119]

Having provided themselves with their own dock, the Taff directors proceeded to divert to it a considerable proportion of their trade. Under their agreement with the second marquess they were obliged to ship all their goods at the Bute Docks or pay the equivalent in dock dues. The directors took the issue

[118] Bute to Roy, 26 September, 2 and 9 October 1846 (ibid., L. Roy, 1844–46), to Clark, 23 and 26 September 1846, to Roy, 5 October 1846 (ibid., L. 1845–46); J. Davies, 'The Rhymney Railway and the Bute estate', *Gelligaer*, VIII (1971), 7–10; see below, pp. 286–87.
[119] 19–20 Victoria, *cap.* CXXII; 20–21 Victoria, *cap.* LXIX; N.L.W., MS. 7458B, January to March 1854.

to the House of Lords, which freed the company from this obligation while at the same time prohibiting it from under-cutting the Bute Docks by charging lower rates at Penarth. Although the construction of the Penarth Dock did not lead to a price war between it and Cardiff, loss of trade to Penarth was considerable. By 1870, Penarth was exporting 1·18 million tons of coal a year; this represented 28 per cent of the total coal brought down by the Taff Vale Railway and until the opening of the Barry Docks in 1889 it was the most considerable diver-sion from the Bute Docks of the trade of the basin of the Taff. Despite the Taff Vale Railway Company's anxiety to have a dock under its own control, the venture brought it little profit. The return rarely rose above 4 per cent and in 1880, when Penarth made a loss, the company's chairman noted 'The undertaking has always been a sort of incubus upon the company'.[120]

While the Taff Vale Railway Company was anxious to have its own outlet to the sea, the Bute trustees were equally anxious to have a measure of control over a railway to the hinterland. Their opportunity came with the passage of the Rhymney Railway Act in 1854. The connection with the Bute estate was made explicit in the act and, as the work proceeded, the project became increasingly a Bute concern. Boyle, the most active of the Bute trustees, was appointed chairman of the company, Clark, the estate's mineral agent, supervised the construction of the railway and the estate assumed responsi-bility for raising the initial capital of £100,000. The trustees relieved the company of the expense of building a line linking the railway with the East Bute Dock, a costly project requiring several bridges and high embankments. In 1863, when £80,000 had been spent on the dock branch, the whole of the east side of the dock was leased to the company, the Bute authorities at their own expense providing all necessary shipping appliances. Preferential treatment for the Rhymney Railway Company exacerbated relations between the Bute trustees and the Taff Vale Railway Company, whose lease of a large portion of the increasingly redundant West Bute Dock was by the 1860s proving an embarrassment. The fact that the Taff company

---

[120] *Weekly Mail*, 22 January 1881; C.C.L., B., XI, 56; D. S. Barrie, op. cit., p. 20; W. Turner, op. cit., p. 24.

could only reach the East Bute Dock over the lines of the Rhymney company caused tension and the matter was not settled until 1866, when the Taff company was allowed its own access to the east dock in exchange for withdrawing its opposition to the Rhymney company's Cardiff and Caerphilly line which gave Rhymney access to Cardiff without being obliged to use Taff lines.[121]

In its early years the Rhymney Railway did not justify the optimism of its promoters. In 1871, however, with the opening of its tunnel under Caerphilly mountain, the company was freed from its dependence upon Taff lines and at the same time the Powell Duffryn Company extended its mining operations in the Rhymney valley. Thereafter the Rhymney Railway Company's success was assured and it became one of the most prosperous concerns in south Wales, its stock reaching 218 in 1882 and its shares paying over 10 per cent. By sponsoring a railway linking the Rhymney valley to Cardiff, the Bute trustees captured for their dock the entire traffic of the valley and, through a junction with the Great Western Railway, were also able to tap the riches of the western and eastern valleys of Monmouthshire, thus expanding Cardiff's hinterland at the expense of Newport. In 1880 Rhymney Railway carried over a million tons of coal to Cardiff, representing 20 per cent of the entire coal export trade of the dock. This traffic was almost wholly unaffected by the opening of the Barry Docks; indeed, between 1888 and 1895 Rhymney's traffic in coal to the Bute Docks increased from 1·7 million to 2·5 million tons, its share of the total trade rising from 22 per cent to 32 per cent.[122] The connection with Rhymney was a major factor in ensuring that the opening of the Barry Docks and Railway was not as severe a blow to the Bute Docks as it was to the Taff Vale Railway.

During the 1870s there was outward harmony between the various transport undertakings serving the port of Cardiff. The 1880s saw the renewal of strife and, before the end of the century, dock and railway warfare was to be waged on a grand

[121] 17–18 Victoria, *cap.* CXCIII; *C.T.*, 30 March 1907; N.L.W., MS. 7458B, June and September 1854, February 1855; C.C.L., MS. 4.937; ibid., B., XII, 28.
[122] D. S. Barrie, *The Rhymney Railway* (1952), pp. 47, 56–59; W. Turner, op. cit., p. 23; C.C.L., B., XI, 56.

scale. The Bute authorities, while participating in the battle, were becoming increasingly disillusioned with their position and were anxious to come to an arrangement which would allow them to divest themselves of their responsibilities. The third marquess had little aptitude for business and the constant demands of the docks distracted him from more congenial pursuits. In 1880 he resolved to let the docks, and approaches were made to the corporation of Cardiff. The negotiations were initially promising but they broke down over disputed clauses in the Bute Docks bill of 1882 and in October of that year the marquess extricated himself from all discussions with the corporation.[123]

In 1883 the threat that the freighters of the Taff basin would build a major system of docks away from the town of Cardiff hardened into reality. In the 1840s, when the great ironmasters had considered building their own dock, the coalowners, who then lacked the resources for such a venture, had been the earliest and most consistent users of the Bute Dock. In the intervening forty years the profits from the coal industry had grown sufficiently to provide the means for an investment in dock-building, while a strong motive for such an investment was provided by calculations that its cost would be less than the losses sustained by the coalowners as a result of delays at Cardiff's congested docks. The Barry Dock scheme was frankly aimed at the Bute monopoly at Cardiff, and David Davies of the Ocean Coal Company, its leading protagonist, prophesied that grass would grow in the streets of Cardiff as a result of the construction of docks elsewhere.[124] The Liberal newspapers of south Wales saw the scheme as a weapon with which to attack the Bute position at Cardiff. 'Thus the high handed policy of the Bute trustees would be avenged', wrote the *Weekly Mail*, 'and the craven-spirited town council which had meekly bowed its head before the iron hand of tyranny would

[123] Ibid., IX, 29, 6 November and 9 December 1880, 7, 17 and 18 March 1882; ibid., XI, 5; *C.T.*, 1 July and 28 October 1882; *S.W.D.N.*, 26 May, 6 June and 10 July 1882; J. H. Matthews, op. cit., V, 60, 69, 70–71.
[124] C. S. Howells, op. cit., p. 41; I. B. Thomas, op. cit., pp. 270–311; L. N. A. Davies, 'The history of the Barry Dock and Railway Company in relation to the development of the south Wales coalfield' (unpublished University of Wales M.A. dissertation, 1938).

learn that their miserable sycophancy was unprofitable as well
as unmanly.'[125]

To some of its supporters, the main purpose of bringing
forward the Barry project was to use it as a bargaining counter
with the Bute estate. The promoters' attacks upon the Bute
Docks were often without foundation and served to veil the
real point at issue, which was the freighters' desire to have a
major complex of docks under their own unfettered control.
Cardiff's dock dues, declared exorbitant by the Barry promoters, were among the lowest in the United Kingdom and
the third marquess's vast profits were a myth.[126] Congestion
and delay there were but, by the time the Barry Dock bill was
before parliament, work had already begun on the Roath
Dock. Among the Barry promoters were those who were
prepared to abandon their project if the marquess made over
his docks to a trust which would be under their control. It was
to a trust representative of all interests rather than to a speculative company of freighters, however, that the marquess
wished to sell his docks and the attempted negotiations of the
coalowners proved abortive.[127]

The Barry Dock and Railway Act received the royal assent
in August 1884, the *South Wales Daily News* exulting over the
destruction of the monopoly of 'venal peers and conscienceless
incapables'.[128] With the threat of massive competition now a
reality, an ally was found in the old rival, the Taff Vale
Railway Company, to whom the competition from the Barry
Dock and Railway was more menacing than it was to the
Bute Docks, with their secure trade from the Bute lessees, from
the Rhymney valley and from their increasing import business.
Bute and Taff co-operated closely in the lengthy battle against
the Barry bill. At the same time, they jointly sponsored the
Cardiff and Monmouthshire Railway bill, which sought to
compensate for the trade which would be lost to Barry by

[125] *Weekly Mail*, 18 February 1882; *S.W.D.N.*, 31 January 1883; *W.M.*,
21 April 1884.
[126] C.C.L., B., IV, 4, XII, 35. Between 1865 and 1913 the maximum rates at
Cardiff remained unchanged, although in that period the expenses of coal
shipment increased fourfold. Bute dock dues were 20–30 per cent lower than those
of other United Kingdom ports of similar rank (*Journal of Commerce*, 24 April 1913).
[127] C.C.L., B., IX, 29, 14 December 1883; 20 February 1884; ibid., XI, 5;
answer to the proposals of the Barry promoters (G.R.O., D/DA 52); *S.W.D.N.*,
7 March and 14 April 1884.
[128] *S.W.D.N.*, 16 August 1884.

improving Cardiff's links with the Monmouthshire coalfield.[129] During their joint resistance, Inskip, the Taff company chairman, suggested that his company should take over the Bute Docks; a bill authorising the sale of the docks to the Taff Vale Railway Company was placed before parliament in 1885 but was defeated because of the opposition of rival companies.[130]

Having failed to prevent the construction of rival docks or to dispose of their own, the Bute authorities decided that the docks should be incorporated. While wishing to free the marquess from day-to-day decision-making on dock matters, they were also anxious to quell agitation against the dock as a private concern owned by one man. Setting up a company with published accounts dispelled the air of secrecy which had surrounded dock investment and profit, while offering shares in the new company allowed those interested in the port of Cardiff to obtain a financial stake in the Bute Docks.[131] The board of directors appointed under the incorporation act of 1886, however, included no one from Cardiff. It consisted of the marquess of Bute, his kinsmen H. Dudley Ryder and Lord E. B. Talbot, his secretary G. E. Sneyd and his commissioner Frederick Pitman; the company secretary was an Edinburgh solicitor and the auditors were an Edinburgh firm. Later directors included the fourth marquess of Bute, the duke of Norfolk, A. R. C. Pitman and Sir John King. W. T. Lewis, appointed manager of the company at a salary of £2,500 in 1886, joined the board in 1898. His plea that the docks should be more closely identified with Cardiff bore fruit with the appointment to the board of John Gunn and Thomas Morel in 1898 and of W. J. Tatem in 1914.[132]

In 1889 the Barry Docks were opened. Although their coal trade was eventually to exceed that of Cardiff, their opening did not cause a catastrophic fall in the earnings of the Bute Docks. Gross receipts, which amounted to £352,000 in 1888, rose to £380,000 in 1889, falling back to £364,000 in 1890. It

[129] Minutes, B.D.C., 5 August 1886, 25 August 1887, 24 April 1888 (B.T.H.R.O., B.D.C. 1); C.C.L., B., IV, 19, 26; ibid., IX, 29, 26 August and 26 September 1884.

[130] Ibid., September and October 1884; C.T., 29 November 1884, 14 February 1885; W.M., 9 May 1885.

[131] 49–50 Victoria, cap. LXXXVI; minutes, B.D.C., 29 July 1886, 9 May 1889 (B.T.H.R.O., B.D.C. 1).

[132] Ibid., 1886–97; minutes, C.R.C., 1897–1914 (B.T.H.R.O., R.A.C. 1/55).

was with relief that the directors noted that 'the trade of the docks for the half year ending 31 December 1889 has been fairly well maintained notwithstanding the new competition created by the opening of the Barry Dock in July last'.[133] The Taff Vale Railway Company suffered more heavily. Its coal-carrying trade fell from 5·2 million tons in 1889 to 4·2 million in 1891 and its dividend, which had been 18 per cent in 1882, fell to 3 per cent. Penarth dock was even worse affected, its trade of 1890 being only a quarter of that of 1889. There was uproar among the Taff shareholders and the board was reconstituted under a new manager.[134] Recognising that Barry's strength would lie in its possession of both docks and railways, the Taff Vale Railway Company in 1887 made a further abortive attempt to buy the Bute Docks. In 1888 an agreement was made to work the two concerns together, with the profits to be divided in the ratio of 71 per cent for the Taff and 29 per cent for the Bute company. Parliament refused to sanction this arrangement and the two companies were obliged to seek a more informal association.[135]

Relations between the rival companies changed dramatically in 1890. The catalyst was labour agitation. The Dockers Union, established at Cardiff in 1889, brought its members out on strike in 1891 in support of the seamen's attempt to exclude non-union labour. Such activity found a stern opponent in Lewis. 'The crux of the matter to many of the men', he wrote, 'is that only Unionist men should be employed. This the board refuses to consider.'[136] In resisting the demands of the men, the Bute company joined with the Rhymney, Taff and Newport companies and even with Barry to co-ordinate strategy. From these meetings emerged a scheme for the amalgamation of all the concerns, a course strongly urged by Jamieson, the Bute company's auditor. 'Much benefit would result for all parties', he wrote, 'from a cessation of hostilities and much more from

---

[133] Minutes, B.D.C., 13 February 1890 (B.T.H.R.O., B.D.C. 1).
[134] C.C.L., B., XI, 56; W. Turner, op. cit., p. 22; D. S. Barrie, *Taff*, p. 26.
[135] C.C.L., B., IV, 17, 19, XI, 5; ibid., XI, 33, July 1889; E. D. Lewis, *The Rhondda valleys* (1959), p. 124; minutes, B.D.C., October 1888–June 1889 (B.T.H.R.O., B.D.C. 1).
[136] Ibid., 27 March 1890; Lewis to Ellis, 10 March 1890 (N.L.W., Ellis Papers, 1421).

a complete identification.'[137] The prospect of union between the companies without reference to any other organisations alarmed the corporation of Cardiff, which declared in October 1890 that it viewed 'with grave concern the amalgamation of docks and railways serving Cardiff and suggests that negotiations should begin to place these bodies under a public trust'. The Mersey Docks and Harbour Board, the Tyne Improvement Commission and the Swansea Harbour Trust were cited as models for Cardiff. 'The Corporation', wrote Councillor Carr, 'is the only official mouthpiece of the town and should have an effective voice in arranging the terms upon which a Harbour Trust would be formed. All property values depend upon the amount of shipping done in the docks and the corporation would be utterly insolvent if anything happened to them.'[138]

The Bute authorities viewed with sympathy the notion of a harbour trust under the corporation, particularly when hopes of a grand amalgamation foundered following turmoil within the Taff company and the excessive demands of the Rhymney company.[139] By 1894 valuations had been agreed upon and the corporation had committed itself to pledge the town rates as security for the money needed to acquire the dock. Jamieson warmly endorsed the plan. 'To hand over this undertaking', he wrote, 'created by the marquess's predecessors and himself to the community to the growth of which in wealth and importance it has so materially contributed, is a transaction of a different type from the merging of such an undertaking in the commercial enterprise of the minor competitors which have risen to rival it.' Financially, too, sale to the corporation had great merits. 'The revenue from corporation bonds', wrote Jamieson, 'is perpetual, whereas the property for which they are to be substituted is subject to many contingencies . . . grave responsibility and consequent liability.'[140] The corporation's Harbour Trust Committee sought to widen the proposed trust and initiated discussions with other concerns. The antagonistic

[137] Minutes, B.D.C., 23 October 1890 (B.T.H.R.O., B.D.C. 1); C.C.L., B., IX, 28.
[138] Ibid., IX, 5.
[139] Ibid., XI, 20; minutes, B.D.C., 9 December 1890 (B.T.H.R.O., B.D.C. 1).
[140] Ibid., 14 February 1893, 11 January, 1 and 15 November 1894; J. H. Matthews, op. cit., V, 174.

attitude of some of the members of the corporation and its refusal to proceed solely with the Bute Docks Company angered Lewis who, on his own initiative, broke off the negotiations and, before the end of 1894, the whole attempt had been abandoned.[141] The notion of a grand amalgamation of all companies was revived in 1895, but the attempt failed because of the opposition of the Taff company which was then seeking parliamentary permission to build its own dock. Fears that Taff as well as Barry would come to possess massive integrated dock and railway facilities brought the Bute and Rhymney companies together and several unsuccessful attempts were made to merge them between 1895 and 1897.[142]

Following failure to amalgamate with a company owning a railway to the hinterland, the Bute directors resolved to construct their own direct link between the docks and the coalfield, possession of which, it was believed, would give them parity with Barry. The company already possessed a link of sorts in the form of the Glamorganshire Canal which had been purchased in 1882.[143] Ambitious schemes for the improvement of the canal were prepared and between 1885 and 1906 £25,000 was spent upon its modernisation. These efforts were in vain; subsidence wrought havoc with the banks and the fifty-one locks of the canal made the use of steamboats impractical. 'Everything has been done . . . by Lord Bute', stated the canal manager in 1906, ' . . . to try and create and improve the traffic . . . but it has been found to be useless.'[144] A scheme to construct a railway along part of the canal bed was prepared in 1888 'with a view to give independent communication between the Bute Docks and the collieries, a necessity because the companies which bring coal to the Bute Docks also have an interest in taking it to other docks', but fears that its implementation would prejudice the proposed working agreement with the Taff Vale Railway Company led to its abandonment. When Parliament refused to sanction that agreement,

[141] *W.M.*, 9 and 14 November 1894; Bute to Lewis, 15 November 1894 (note in a volume of press cuttings labelled K.H.G., vol. II, in the possession of Lord Merthyr); minutes, B.D.C., 15 November 1894 (B.T.H.R.O., B.D.C. 1).

[142] Ibid., October 1895–February 1897.

[143] C. Hadfield, op. cit., pp. 113, 116; C.C.L., B., IX, 32, 23 November and 14 December 1883.

[144] *P.P.*, XXXII (1906), questions 10781–10854; minutes, B.D.C., 15 November 1894 (B.T.H.R.O., B.D.C. 1).

the Bute company was authorised in 1890 to take over the powers obtained by the Rhymney Railway Company in 1888 to build a railway to the heart of the Monmouthshire coalfield but because of financial weakness these powers were allowed to lapse in 1891.[145]

Plans to link the Bute Docks with the coalfield were revived in a more modest form in 1897 with the passage of an act authorising the company to construct a railway to Trefforest; the act also changed the company's name to the Cardiff Railway Company, a name more attractive to investors. In seeking such powers, the Bute authorities were motivated in part by the desire to have a weapon with which to 'bring the Taff and the Rhymney into line, with the object of forming a combination of interests to fight the Barry Company who are now fast coming to be regarded as the avowed enemies of Cardiff'. 'Barry', noted *Lloyd's List*, 'has a simple and common interest in the fight whereas at Cardiff there are many conflicting interests.'[146] The use of its new powers as a threat proved fruitless, for a full decade was to pass before the companies interested in the port of Cardiff again moved towards union. Thus, the Cardiff Railway Company felt that it had little choice but to turn its threat to build a railway to the coalfield into reality, an action the company recognised as 'our last resort'.[147]

The difficulties faced by the builders of the new railway were formidable. Construction involved five crossings of the Merthyr road, three of the Glamorgan Canal, one of the Taff, a diversion of the river, a viaduct, a 108-yard tunnel, eleven cuttings, twelve under-bridges and fifteen over-bridges in a total length of nine miles. The railway, completed in 1911, hardly fulfilled the hopes that it would emancipate the Bute Docks from dependence upon rival companies. Its coal traffic consisted of whatever the Taff Vale Railway Company cared to direct to it at Trefforest and that proved to be little. It was in fact an irrelevant encumbrance, its main traffic consisting

[145] Ibid., 31 May, 28 September, 22 November 1888, 13 February, 27 March, 8 August 1889, 27 February 1891; 51–52 Victoria, *cap.* CLXXVII; 53–54 Victoria, *cap.* CXXXIX.

[146] *Shipping Gazette and Lloyd's List*, 19 July 1897; C.C.L., B., IV, 16; 60–61 Victoria, *cap.* CCVII.

[147] M. J. Daunton, *Coal metropolis*, p. 35.

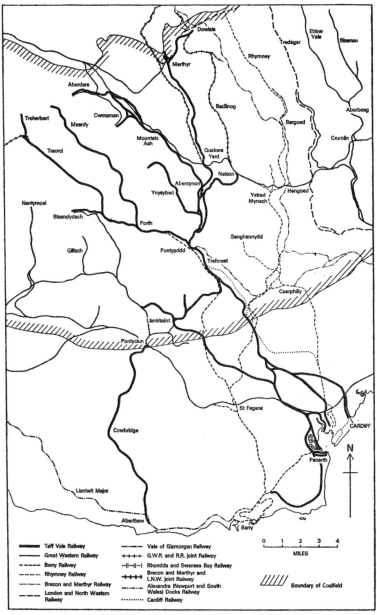

THE RAILWAYS SERVING CARDIFF, 1914

of a trickle of coal from the Nantgarw district and some passengers from the northern suburbs of Cardiff; following its opening there was no discernible rise in the total company receipts.[148]

The fourth marquess, who inherited his father's shares and position in the Cardiff Railway Company in 1900, was as anxious as his predecessor to divest himself of his responsibilities. In 1906 he sought to interest the corporation in the purchase of the docks but the project found little support among the councillors. D. A. Thomas commented: 'I look upon the Cardiff Docks and Railways today as a white elephant. I can quite understand the marquess of Bute being wishful to sell'.[149] In 1908 came yet another attempt to amalgamate the companies serving the port of Cardiff when the Taff Vale Railway Company sought to buy the Cardiff and Rhymney Railway Companies, thereby creating a 'gigantic corporation with a capital of £20 million'. For the Cardiff company, whose capitalisation by 1909 was £6,300,000, the Taff company offered Taff shares worth £4,445,300, a handsome offer, for the Bute investment gave a maximum return of 3 per cent while the Taff shares paid between 4 and 5 per cent. The scheme received the enthusiastic support of the Cardiff Shipowners Association and Chamber of Commerce, the *Western Mail* rejoicing that the docks would 'pass to the control of a native company'.[150] On submission to parliament, however, the plan was defeated and in 1910, when it was submitted again, it suffered the same fate.[151]

No further attempts were made at amalgamation. An anonymous report of a discussion in July 1914 notes that D. A. Thomas had approached the company concerning the purchase of the docks with a view to linking them with the Taff Vale Railway. Nothing came of the plan and within a few weeks of the conversation the docks, following the outbreak of war, had been taken over by the government.[152] During the war a degree of amalgamation did in fact take place; in 1917

---

[148] *Railway News*, 18 March 1911.
[149] *S.W.D.N.*, 27 and 29 September, 6 and 10 October 1906, 15 July 1907.
[150] C. S. Howells, op. cit., p. 44; C.C.L., B., XI, 56; *W.M.*, 13 November 1908; minutes, C.R.C., 10 February and 13 August 1909 (B.T.H.R.O., R.A.C. 1/55).
[151] Ibid., 9 February, 9 August 1910, 9 February 1911.
[152] C.C.L., MS. D 321.51.

E. A. Prosser, the general manager of the Rhymney Railway Company, also became general manager of the Cardiff and of the Taff Vale Railway Companies. This unified management continued after the war until all the south Wales railway and dock companies were amalgamated with the Great Western Railway Company. The amalgamation acts of the early-1920s, which reduced the number of railway companies in Britain to five, recognised only twenty-five constituent companies; among the twenty-five were the Cardiff Railway Company and its four rivals. On vesting day, 1 January 1922, the independent existence of the Bute Docks and the Cardiff Railway Company and that of all its old competitors came to an end.[153] After eighty-four years of antagonism and hesitant co-operation, that 'arrangement for Union . . . between Dockists, Canalists and Railroadists for the general welfare' which Crawshay had hoped for in 1839 had at last come to pass.[154]

CONCLUSION

Among landlord entrepreneurs the Bute family deserves an honoured place. Nevertheless, it was not always to Cardiff's advantage that its docks were the enterprise of a single family and that they were controlled by that family for almost a century. D. A. Thomas was convinced of the disadvantages of their private ownership. 'So far from the late Lord Bute being the creator of modern Cardiff', he wrote in 1906, 'the docks, in the hands of a private individual, have greatly retarded the progress of the port.'[155] There is much evidence to support this view. In the 1860s, expansion was held up because parliament would not sanction vast expenditure upon the estate of a minor, while in the 1870s the much-needed new dock was not constructed because the owner was reluctant to commit all his available assets to the dock. During the 1880s decisions on dock matters were delayed as a result of the marquess's fondness for spending long periods in Greece and Palestine. The fact that the most important outlet for the richest part of

[153] D. S. Barrie, *Taff*, p. 39; E. T. Macdermot, op. cit., II, 463–64; W. E. Simnett, op. cit., pp. 5, 50–51, 230, 262.
[154] Crawshay to Bute, 24 December 1839 (C.C.L., B., XX, 146).
[155] *S.W.D.N.*, 27 September 1906.

the coalfield was in the hands of one man made the freighters suspicious of the Cardiff docks, while the right-wing complexion of the Bute organisation exacerbated relations between it and the coalowners, many of whom were Liberals and radicals.

Nevertheless, there can be no doubt that the second marquess's initiative in the 1830s was of crucial importance in the development of Cardiff and of the south Wales coal trade. In the decade 1830–40, when intimations of the potential of the coal trade first became apparent, it was only at Cardiff that any decisive action was taken to provide that trade with docks adequate to its needs. Cardiff's chief rivals, Newport and Swansea, took no steps during that period. When the Bute Dock was opened in 1839, Newport's coal trade was three times that of Cardiff but by 1848 Cardiff, largely because of its superior dock facilities, had outstripped Newport and it never lost the lead it had won. Newport did build a dock in 1842 and the town was talked of as an 'infant Liverpool', but its dock was only four and a half acres compared with Cardiff's nineteen. Throughout the 1840s coal ships at Swansea lay in the mud at low tide, where they were loaded from small boats; at Cardiff, from 1839 onwards, they were loaded afloat in the security of the dock.[156]

As significant as that early initiative was the success of the Bute authorities, in the years between the 1840s and the 1880s, in retaining for their docks almost the entire trade of the basin of the Taff and in capturing for them the trade of the Rhymney valley. The advantage which Cardiff thereby won was the consequence not only of hard bargaining by the second marquess and his son's trustees, but also of the fact that the Bute family, as well as owning docks, was also the leading land and mineral royalty owner within the coalfield. This virtual monopoly of the trade of the basins of the Taff and the Rhymney was massively breached following the opening of the Barry Docks in 1889. By then, however, Cardiff had established itself securely as the leading regional capital of south Wales and as the acknowledged administrative centre of the coal trade, roles which were strengthened rather than weakened by the growth of Barry. Cardiff's rise to the headship

[156] J. H. Morris and L. J. Williams, op. cit., pp. 26, 100–1; W. H. Jones, *A history of the port of Swansea* (1922).

of the local urban hierarchy occurred between the 1840s and the 1880s, and was the direct result of its superior transport facilities. The decline in the importance of those facilities caused its administrative and commercial functions to become its primary role, a role enhanced by its recognition as the capital of Wales in 1956.[157]

Active participation in dock development by local land-owners was a feature of south Wales during the nineteenth century. Lord Tredegar was chairman of the Alexandra Dock Company of Newport, Lord Windsor was active in promoting the Penarth and Barry Docks, C. R. M. Talbot floated a company to build docks at Aberafan, Lord Jersey lent money to the Briton Ferry Dock Company and the duke of Beaufort gave assistance to dock-building at Swansea. None of these men, however, exerted himself to the extent of the Butes at Cardiff. When the Swansea Dock Bill of 1847 received the royal assent, the chairman of the dock company, in proposing a toast to the marquess of Bute as lord-lieutenant, declared that his company 'could not do better than emulate the zeal of this enterprising gentleman' and added with perhaps less conviction that 'he had no doubt that his grace the duke of Beaufort would be found as noble a supporter of the town of Swansea as the marquess of Bute had been for the town of Cardiff'.[158]

For the Bute family itself, the advantages of its investment in dock building are ambiguous. The second marquess's anxiety over the success of his investment undoubtedly hastened him to a premature death and his son's trustees found dock administration a severe burden. To the third and fourth marquesses the docks were an embarrassment of which they sought every opportunity to rid themselves. The return on capital was meagre, becoming more meagre as trade increased and on the eve of the First World War, when the trade of the docks had reached heights beyond the dreams of their founder, the undertaking was not paying its way. The great source of wealth on the Bute estate was the mineral royalties, much of which were swallowed up by the dock's insatiable demands.

[157] H. Carter, *The towns of Wales* (1965), pp. 110–17; M. J. Daunton, *Coal metropolis*, pp. 53–54.
[158] *C.*, 9 July 1847.

The return to the family was indirect, through the more rapid increase in mineral royalties because of good dock facilities and through the rise of land values at Cardiff. These profits, however, would have come to the Butes even if others had undertaken dock construction. It is difficult to resist the conclusion that, where Cardiff is concerned, D. A. Thomas's comment had a considerable element of truth in it, and where the Bute family itself is concerned, Crawshay's opinion, given in 1833, was even more apposite: 'Your lordship would do better to let others take the Port making, yourself keeping every ulterior and collateral advantage'.[159]

---

[159] Crawshay to Bute, 19 December 1833 (N.L.W., Cyfarthfa Papers, III).

BIBLIOGRAPHY

I. PRIMARY MATERIAL

A. UNPUBLISHED

1. Libraries, museums and record offices.

(a) *The British Transport Historical Record Office*
   1. B.D.C. 1 (1), (2) and (3): Minute Books of the meetings of the directors of the Bute Docks Company, 1886–98.
   2. R.A.C. 1/55: Minute Books of the meetings of the directors of the Cardiff Railway Company, 1898–1922.
   3. T.V. 2/1A: Registers of the shareholders of the Taff Vale Railway Company; Reports of the general meetings of the Taff Vale Railway Company.

(b) *Cardiff Central Library*
   1. The Bute Collection, Boxes I–XLI. This collection consists of a great mass of material, meticulously arranged, numbered and catalogued. Of particular value are Boxes VI and VII (reports on the mineral estate), Box IX (material relating to the activities of David Stewart and of the employees of the third marquess), Box X (accounts of the trustees), Boxes XI and XII (material relating to the Bute Docks) and Boxes XX and XXI (letters relating to the Chartists and the Glamorgan Police Force.)
   2. MS. 2.716: The diary of John Bird, 1790–91, 1792–1803, 1826.
   3. MSS. 4.713 and 4.860: The letterbooks of E. P. Richards, 1824–40.
   4. MS. 4.850: David Stewart, 'The extent of the mineral property of the marquess of Bute in Glamorgan', 1823.
   5. MSS. 4.459, 4.899 and 4.1130: collections of press cuttings.
   6. MS. 4.937: Payments and receipts of the trustees of the marquess of Bute, 1858–70 and miscellaneous material relating to the Bute estate.
   7. MS. 6.4: Scrapbook of T. J. Robinson.
   8. MS. D296.51: Material relating to Pwllypant.
   9. MS. D300.51: Miscellaneous Bute documents.
   10. MS. 305.51: Industrial documents, 1833–73.
   11. MS. 321.51: Miscellaneous Bute documents.
   12. MS. 329.51: Correspondence relating to the Bute estate, 1816–54.
   13. Box labelled 'Posters *etc.*': materials relating to early-nineteenth century elections and to the coming of age of the third marquess.
   14. Papers relating to the political affairs of Cardiff, 1815–19.
   15. Cardiff supplementary rental, 1927–30.

(c) *Coal House, Llanishen, Cardiff*
   1. Claim Files relating to the nationalisation of mineral reserves. Maps and valuations of Bute mineral property are contained in Files R.O. 8/25, 41, 55, 56, 58, 62, 66, 67, 70, 72, 73, 74, 77, 82, 84, 85, 87, 89, 95, 97, 101, 103, 104, 106, 107, 113, 115, 116, 136, 154, 182 and 281.

(d) *Companies House, Cardiff*
   1. Material relating to the Mountjoy Company Ltd.

(e) *The Glamorgan Record Office*
1. D/DA 1–55: Letters of the second marquess of Bute and others to agents in Glamorgan, 1787–1909.
2. D/DA 56–117: Vouchers relating to the Bute estate.
3. D/DB E, 1–2: Atlas and terrier of the Bute estate, 1824.
4. D/DC 514–600: Material relating to the Dowlais Iron Company.

(f) *The Office of the Department of the Environment, Cardiff*
Plans and photographs relating to the restoration of Castell Coch and Caerphilly castle.

(g) *The National Library of Scotland, Edinburgh*
1. MSS. 3419, 3444 and 3445: Letters written to and by the second marquess of Bute.
2. MSS. 2851, 3446 and 3447: Letters written by Lady Bute.
3. MS. 3654: Letters relating to the *Scottish Review*.

h) *The National Library of Wales, Aberystwyth*
1. The Bute Collection. This vast collection, consisting of sixty-seven tin boxes, was deposited at the National Library by the fifth marquess of Bute in 1948. The boxes are numbered up to 143 but there are no boxes 1–16, 18–19, 22, 29–30, 36–46, 51, 53–57, 62, 76–81, 94–98, 102, 105, 107–117, 119–123, 125, 127, 129–131, 133–135 and 138; there are two boxes numbered 70. See B. G. Charles, 'The Marquess of Bute Collection', *National Library of Wales Journal*, VII (1951–52), 246–58 The typescript schedule is haphazard in its arrangement and does not provide a complete guide to the contents of the boxes but a complete catalogue of the papers is in progress. A considerable proportion of the collection relates to the period when the Cardiff Castle estate was owned by the earls of Pembroke, but the nineteenth century material is rich and varied. Of particular value are Boxes 26, 27 and 35 (deeds and conveyances), Box 31 (law suits and reports), Box 33 (agreements for tenancies), Boxes 58, 64, 65, 75 and 100–103 (estate rentals), Boxes 60, 73 and 74 (estate accounts), Boxes 66–70 (private acts of parliament), Box 70 (twenty-two letterbooks), Boxes 71 and 82–99 (manorial material), Box 104 (surveys and valuations), Box 106 (mineral leases), Box 124 (papers relating to Pwllypant), Boxes 136–137 and 139–140 (wills and marriage settlements) and Boxes 141–143 (letters, indentures, reports and agreements). In addition, the map collection contains several hundred maps and plans of farms, commons, railways, docks and mineral holdings.
2. The Cyfarthfa Papers: Letters to the second marquess of Bute and his employees in Box 1, vols. I–VI.
3. MSS. 7454A–7462A: The diaries of W. S. Clark, 1845–58.
4. MS. 2340C: A letter in Welsh by the third marquess of Bute.
5. Ellis Papers, no. 1421.
6. Rendel Papers, Box 9, no. 94.
7. The collection of sale catalogues.
8. The commutation of tithe, Glamorgan, maps and apportionments.
9. The diary of L. W. Dillwyn, typescript calendar.
10. Jevons Papers, IV, 122: material relating to leaseholds at Cardiff.

(i) *The Public Record Office*
1. Ministry of Agriculture MSS: Loans under the Improvement of Land Act, 1862–1912.
2. H.O. 40/46, 52/21 and 52/25: Letters by the second marquess of Bute concerning unrest in Glamorgan.

(*j*) *The Scottish Public Record Office, Register House, Edinburgh*
    1. The Hamilton Bruce MSS., Boxes 196–98: letters written by the Bute family and its agents, largely to O. T. Bruce, 1825–53.

(*k*) *University of Nottingham Library*
    The Portland Papers.

2. Privately owned collections.

(*a*) The Harrowby Papers, by courtesy of the earl of Harrowby, especially vols. XX and XXI (letters relating to the Bute family, 1787–1813) and vols. XXXVII, XXXVIII and XXXIX (letters of Lady Bute and Lord James Stuart, 1848–55).

(*b*) The Hean Castle collection of newspaper cuttings, by courtesy of Lord Merthyr, especially the volumes relating to W. T. Lewis and to the death of the third marquess of Bute.

(*c*) Papers in the possession of Mr. A. Andrews, 19 Waungron Road, Llandaf, Cardiff: A letter written by Lord James Stuart to E. P. Richards.

B. PUBLISHED

(*a*) Official Papers.

  (i) General.
    Hansard's *Parliamentary Debates*, second and third series.
    Parliamentary Debates, fourth and fifth series.
    Censuses of Great Britain, 1801 *et seq.*

  (ii) Reports.
    1833, V, *Report and minutes of evidence of the Select Committee on Agriculture.*
    1835, XXIII–XXIV, *Report of the Royal Commission on Municipal Corporations in England and Wales.*
    1836, VIII, *Report of the Select Committee on the state of Agriculture.*
    1837, V, *Report and minutes of evidence of the Select Committee of the House of Lords on Agriculture.*
    1839, XIX, *First Report of the Royal Commission on the establishment of a constabulary force for the counties of England and Wales.*
    1847, XXVII, *Report and minutes of evidence of the commissioners of enquiry into the state of education in Wales.*
    1847–48, VII, *Report and minutes of evidence of the Select Committee on agricultural customs.*
    1871, XXXVI, *Report of the Commission on the truck system.*
    1874, LXXII, parts I and II, *Return of owners of land, England and Wales.*
    1874, LXXII, part III, *Return of owners of land, Scotland.*
    1880, XXXI, *Report and minutes of evidence of the Royal Commission on municipal corporations not subject to the Municipal Corporations Act.*
    1881, XV–XVII, 1882, XIV, *Report and minutes of evidence of the Royal Commission on the depressed condition of the agricultural interests.*
    1884–85, XXX, *Report and minutes of evidence of the Royal Commission on the housing of the working classes.*
    1886, XII, 1887, XIII, 1888, XXII, 1889, XV, *Report and minutes of evidence of the Select Committee on town holdings.*
    1890, XXXVI, 1890–91, XLI, 1893–94, XLI, *Report and minutes of evidence of the Royal Commission on mining royalties.*
    1892, *Return relating to building societies.*

1894, XVI, 1896, XVI–XVII, 1897, XV, *Report and minutes of evidence of the Royal Commission on agricultural depression.*

1894, XXXVI–XXXVII, 1895, XL–XLI, 1896, XXXIII–XXXV, *Report and minutes of evidence of the Royal Commission on land in Wales and Monmouthshire.*

1906, XXXII, 1907, XXXIII, 1909, XIII, 1910, XII, *Report and minutes of evidence of the Royal Commission on canals and waterways.*

1919, XI–XIII, *Royal Commission on the coal industry.*

1926, XIV, *Royal Commission on the coal industry, Report, Minutes of evidence.*

1938, Cmd. 5904, Central Valuation Board, *Valuation Regions.*

(iii) Acts of Parliament

14 George III c. 7	20/21 Victoria c CXI
42 George III c. 67	24/25 Victoria c. CCXXXVI
3/4 George IV c. 22	28/29 Victoria c. CCCXXV
7/8 George IV c. 25	29/30 Victoria c. CCXCVI
1 William IV c. CXXXIII	37/38 Victoria c. CXVIII
4 William IV c. XIX	45/46 Victoria c. CCXLII
5/6 William IV c. 76	49/50 Victoria c. LXXXVI
6/7 William IV c. LXXXII	49/50 Victoria c. CII
7 William IV c. XVIII	51/52 Victoria c. CXIV
1 Victoria c. 42	53/54 Victoria c. CXXXIX
11/12 Victoria c. 20	57/58 Victoria c. CLIV
16/17 Victoria c. 22	60/61 Victoria c. CCVII
19/20 Victoria c. CXXII	61/62 Victoria c. CCLXII
20/21 Victoria c. LXIX	62/63 Victoria c. LXI

(*b*) Newspapers and Periodicals.

1. Newspapers.

Aberdare Leader	*The Leader*
The Age	*Merthyr Express*
Brecon County Times	*Merthyr Guardian*
The Buteman	*Merthyr Telegraph*
Cambrian	*Silurian*
Cardiff Mercury	*South Wales Daily News*
Cardiff Recorder	*Star of Gwent*
Cardiff Reporter	*The Times*
Cardiff Times	*Weekly Mail*
Daily Chornicle	*Western Mail*
The Guardian	

2. Periodicals

Annual Register	*Journal of Commerce*
The Athenaeum	*The Mariner*
Barn	*The Maritime Review*
Cambrian Journal	*Railway News*
Cymru	*St. Peter's Magazine*
Y Diwygiwr	*The Scottish Review*
Estates Gazette	*Shipping Gazette and Lloyd's List*
Economist	*South Wales Coal Annual*
Gentleman's Magazine	*Truth*
Greal y Bedyddwyr	*The Welsh Housing and*
Illustrated London News	*Development Yearbook*
The Jewish Chronicle	

(c) Contemporary Works (Place of publication, Cardiff, unless otherwise stated).

ALEXANDER, B. (ed.), *Life at Fonthill, 1807–1822, from the correspondence of William Beckford* (London, 1957).

ALLEN, S. W., *Reminiscences, being a few rambling recollections of some people and things I have met with* (1918).

ANONYMOUS, *A sketch of the life of John, second marquess of Bute, reprinted principally from the Cardiff and Merthyr Guardian* (1848).

ASHLEY, W. J. (ed.), J. S. Mill, *Principles of Political Economy* (London, 1929).

ASPINALL, A. (ed.), *The later correspondence of George III*, 4 vols. (Cambridge, 1963–68).

The correspondence of George, Prince of Wales, 1770–1812, 3 vols. (London, 1963–65).

BAMFORD, F. and WELLINGTON, duke of, *The Journal of Mrs. Arbuthnot, 1820–32* (London, 1950).

BEDFORD, duke of, *A great agricultural estate* (London, 1897).

BELL, G. H. (ed.), *The Namwood Papers of the Ladies of Llangollen and Caroline Hamilton* (London, 1930).

BENTINCK, Lady Norah, *My wanderings and memories* (London, 1924).

BERRETT, C. (ed.), *The diary and letters of Madame d'Arblay* (London, 1905).

BESSBOROUGH, earl of (ed.), *Lady Charlotte Guest; extracts from her journal, 1833–52* (London, 1950).

Lady Charlotte Schreiber; extracts from her journal, 1853–1891 (London, 1952).

BIRD, J., *The directory of Cardiff* (1794).

BOWEN, I., *The great enclosures of common land in Wales* (London, 1914).

BRADY, F. and POTTLE, F. A. (eds.), *Boswell on the Grand Tour, Italy, Corsica and France* (London, 1955).

Boswell in search of a wife (London 1957).

BRAYE, Lord, *The fewness of my days* (London, 1927).

BUTE, marchioness of (ed.), *The private journals of the marquess of Hastings*, 2 vols. (London, 1858).

Calendar of Patent Rolls 1547–48 (Record Commission, London, 1924).

CARDIGAN, countess of, *My recollections* (London, 1909).

CARTWRIGHT, J. (ed.), *The journals of Lady Knightley of Fawsley* (London, 1915).

CLARKE, T. E., *Guide to Merthyr Tydfil* (Merthyr Tydfil, 1848).

CLIFFE, C. F., *The book of south Wales, the Bristol Channel, Monmouthshire and the Wye* (London, 1847).

CORBETT, J. A. (ed.), *Rice Merrick's Booke of Glamorganshires Antiquities* (London, 1887).

DAVIES, E. (ed.), *Coxe's Historical Tour through Monmouthshire* (London, 1934).

DAVIES, W., *A general view of the agriculture and domestic economy of south Wales*, 2 vols. (London, 1814).

DISRAELI, B., *Lothair* (The Bradenham edition of the novels of Disraeli, London, 1927, vol. XI).

DONOVAN, E., *Descriptive excursions through south Wales and Monmouthshire in 1804* (London, 1805).

DOWDEN, W. S. (ed.), *The letters of Thomas Moore* (Oxford, 1964).

DUFF, M. E. G., *Notes from a diary, 1851–72*, 2 vols. (London, 1897).

ELSAS, M., *Iron in the making* (n.d.).

EVANS, J., *Letters written during a tour through south Wales in the year 1803 and at other times* (London, 1804).

FITZROY, A., *Memoirs* (London, n.d.).

FOX, J., *General view of the agriculture of Glamorgan* (London, 1796).

GALBRAITH, G. (ed.), *The journal of the Reverend William Bagshaw Stevens* (Oxford, 1965).

GIBSON, J., *Agriculture in Wales* (London, 1879).

GILPIN, W., *Observations on the River Wye and several parts of south Wales etc. made in the summer of the year 1770* (5th edition, London, 1800).

GRANT, J., *Random recollections of the House of Lords, 1830–36* (London, 1836).

GRANVILLE, Castalia, Countess (ed.), *Lord Granville Leveson Gower, private correspondence, 1781–1821* (London, 1957).

GRIEG, J. (ed.), *The Farrington diary*, 8 vols. (London, 1923–28).

GRIFFITHS, S., *Guide to the iron trade of Great Britain* (London, 1873).

HARE, J. C. A., *The story of my life*, 6 vols. (London, 1896–1900).

HASTINGS, Lady Sophia (ed.), *The poems of Lady Flora Hastings* (London, 1841).

HILL, G. B. (ed.), and POWELL, L. F. (revised), *Boswell's Life of Johnson*, 6 vols. (Oxford, 1934).

HOME, J. A. (ed.), *The letters of Lady Louisa Stuart and Miss Louisa Clinton* (Edinburgh, 1901).

JAMES, C. H., *What I remember about myself and old Merthyr* (Merthyr Tydfil, 1892).

OH NES, A. J., *An essay on the causes which have produced dissent from the established church in the principality of Wales* (London, 1832).

JONES, E. P., *Oes gofion* (Bala, n.d.).

KNIGHT, W., *Some nineteenth century Scotsmen, being personal recollections by William Knight, Professor of Philosophy in the University of St. Andrews* (London, 1903).

LEWIS, E. A., *The Welsh port books, 1550–1603* (London, 1927).

LEWIS, H. (ed.), *Llanwynno* (1949).

LEWIS, W. S., *The Yale edition of the letters of Horace Walpole* (Yale, 1937 et seq.).

MACDONNELL, J., *The land question* (London, 1873).

MALKIN, B. H., *The scenery, antiquities and biography of south Wales from materials collected during two excursions in the year 1803*, 2 vols. (London, 1807).

MATTHEWS, J. H. (ed.), *Cardiff Records, materials for a history of the county borough*, 6 vols. (1898–1911).

MINGAY, G. E. (ed.), J. Caird, *The landlord interest and the supply of food* (London, 1967).

MOGG, E. (ed.), *Paterson's Roads* (18th ed., London, n.d.).

The National Farm Survey of England and Wales, *A summary report* (London, 1944).

NEVILLE, S., *The diary of Sylas Neville, 1767–1788* (Oxford, 1950).

NICHOLSON, C., *The Cambrian traveller's guide* (London, 1813).

PATERSON, D. R. (ed.), J. S. Corbett, *Glamorgan, papers and notes on the lordship and its members* (1926).

PEARSON, A., *Some account of a system of garden labour* (London, 1831).

PHILLIPS, S., *The history of the borough of Llantrisant* (Bristol, 1866).

RAMMELL, T. W., *Report on a preliminary inquiry into the . . . sanitary condition of the inhabitants of the town of Cardiff* (London, 1850).

Report on a preliminary inquiry into the . . . sanitary condition of the inhabitants of the town of Merthyr Tydfil (London, 1850).

REES, T., *Description of south Wales* (London, 1815).

RENNIE, Sir J., *Autobiography* (London, 1875).

Theory, formation and construction of British and foreign harbours, 2 vols. (London, 1851–54).

ROSCOE, T., *Wanderings and excursions in south Wales* (London, 1836).

RUSSELL, G. E. (ed.), *Malcolm Maccoll, memoirs and correspondence* (London, 1914.)

RYSKAMP, C. and POTTLE, F. A. (eds.), *Boswell, the ominous years,1774–76* (London, 1963).
SANFORD, J. L. and TOWNSEND, M., *The great governing families of England* (London, 1865).
SANTAYANA, G., *Persons and places, the background of my life* (London, 1944).
SHAW, M. T., *Memorials of two sisters, Susanna and Catherine Winkworth* (London, 1908).
SKRINE, H., *Two successive tours through the whole of Wales* (London, 1798).
SMYTH, W. H., *Nautical observations on the port and maritime vicinity of Cardiff* (London, 1840).
STEVENSON, W. H., and others, *Records of the borough of Nottingham*, 7 vols. (London, 1882).
STUART WORTLEY, Mrs., *A prime minister to his son* (London, 1925).
TEMPLE, A. G., *Guildhall memories* (London, 1918).
Transactions of the National Eisteddfod of Wales, Cardiff (1883).
Transactions of the National Eisteddfod of Wales, Rhyl (1892).
TROUNCE, W. J., *Cardiff in the fifties* (1918).
TURNER, W., *The port of Cardiff* (1882).
VAUGHAN, H. M., *The south Wales squires* (London, 1926).
VINCENT, J. E., *The land question in south Wales* (London, 1897).
WALPOLE, H., *Memoirs of the reign of George III*, 4 vols. (London, 1894).
WARNER, R., *A second walk through Wales in August and September, 1798* (London, 1799).
WINSTATT, K. and POTTLE, F. A. (eds.), *Boswell for the defence* (London, 1960).
WILLIAMS, T. (Brynfab), *Pan 'roedd Rhondda'n bur* (Pontypridd, 1912).
WILSON, J., *Tourists' guide to Rothesay and the Isle of Bute* (Rothesay, 1862).
YOUNG, A., *A six weeks' tour through the southern counties of England and Wales* (3rd ed., London, 1772).
YOUNG, G. M. and HANDCOCK, W. D. (eds.), *English historical documents, 1833–1874* (London, 1956).

II. SECONDARY WORKS

A. WORKS OF REFERENCE

BALLINGER, J. and JONES, J. I., *Catalogue of printed literature in the Welsh department at the Cardiff Free Library* (1898).
BATEMAN, J., *The great landowners of Great Britain and Ireland* (London, 1883).
The Black Book (London, 1820).
BLACK, G. F., *A list of works relating to Scotland in the New York Public Library* (New York, 1916).
BOASE, F., *Modern English biography* (London, 1965).
Burke's Landed Gentry.
Burke's Peerage, Baronetage and Knightage.
Cardiff tide tables and almanack (1893).
CARLISLE, N., *A topographical dictionary of the dominion of Wales* (London, 1811).
CHALMERS, G., *Caledonia, or a historical and topographical account of north Britain*, 6 vols. (Paisley, 1894).
COCKAYNE, G. E. (ed.), GIBBS, V. and others (revised), *The Complete Peerage*, 13 vols. (London, 1910–59).
COLVIN, H. M., *Biographical dictionary of English architects, 1666–1840* (London, 1954).

308 BIBLIOGRAPHY

DAVIES, E., *Rhestr o enwau lleoedd; a gazetteer of Welsh place-names* (1957).
Dictionary of Welsh Biography (London, 1959).
Dod's Parliamentary Companion.
FORD, P. and G., *Select list of British parliamentary papers, 1833–1899* (Oxford, 1953).
        Guide to parliamentary papers . . . (Oxford, 1955).
        A breviate of parliamentary papers, 3 vols. (Oxford, 1951–61).
FOSTER, J., *Alumni Oxoniensis*, 8 vols. (London, 1887–92).
GROSS, C., *A bibliography of British municipal history* (2nd ed., Leicester, 1966).
HANDCOCK, P. D., *A bibliography of works relating to Scotland, 1916–1960* (Edinburgh, 1960).
HUGHES, W. J., *Wales and the Welsh in English literature* (Wrexham, 1924).
JENKINS, R. T. and REES, W., *A bibiography of the history of Wales* (2nd ed., 1962).
JONES, T. I. J. (ed.), *Acts of Parliament concerning Wales, 1714–1901* (1959).
LEWIS, S., *A topographical dictionary of Wales*, 2 vols. (London, 1833).
A list of paintings at Cardiff Castle (1893).
Map of the steam and anthracite takings in the south Wales coalfield (n.d.).
NAMIER, L. and BROOKE, J., *The House of Commons, 1757–1790*, 3 vols. (London, 1964).
NICHOLAS, T., *Annals and antiquities of the counties and county families of Wales*, 2 vols. (London, 1872).
OLDFIELD, T. H. B., *The representative history of Great Britain and Ireland*, 6 vols. (London, 1816).
PAUL, J. B., *Scots Peerage*, 9 vols. (Edinburgh, 1904–14).
PORRIT, E. and A. G., *The unreformed House of Commons*, 2 vols. (Cambridge, 1903).
REES, W., *Map of south Wales and the border in the fourteenth century* (Southampton, 1933).
        A historical atlas of Wales (1951).
A register of persons entitled to vote at any election of a member or members to serve in Parliament for the county of Glamorgan (1844).
RICHARDS, M., *Welsh administrative and territorial units* (1969).
SEYMOUR, C. T., *Electoral reform in England and Wales, 1832–1885* (Newhaven, Connecticut, 1915).
Slater's Directory of Cardiff and its suburbs (Manchester, 1883).
STAMP, L. D., Land Utilisation Survey of Britain, *Map, Great Britain*, sheet 2 (London, 1944).
The Times tercentenary list of English and Welsh newspapers, magazines and reviews, 1620–1920 (London, 1920).
VENN, J. and J. A. *Alumni Cantabrigenses*, 10 vols. (Cambridge, 1922–54).
WALMSLEY, R. C. and others, *Rural estate management* (London, 1948).
The Western Mail Cardiff Directory, 1898 (1898).
Who's Who in Wales (eds. 1920, 1933 and 1937).
Who was Who.
WILLIAMS, W. R., *Parliamentary history of Wales, 1541–1895* (Brecknock, 1895).

B. OTHER BOOKS

ADDIS, J., *The Crawshay dynasty* (1957).
ALGER, J. G., *Napoleon's British visitors and captives* (London, 1904).
ASHBY, W. and EVANS, I. L., *The agricultural history of Wales and Monmouthshire* (1944).

ASPINALL, A. *Politics and the press* (London, 1949).
ATTWATER, D., *The Catholic church in modern Wales* (London, 1935).
BALLINGER, J. (ed.), *Cardiff: an illustrated handbook* (1896).
BARRIE, D. S., *The Taff Vale Railway* (Sidcup, 1939).
   The Rhymney Railway (South Goldstone, 1952).
BERESFORD, M., *New towns of the middle ages* (London, 1967).
BEST, G. F. A. *Temporal pillars* (Cambridge, 1963).
BLAIR, D. H., *John Patrick, third marquess of Bute, K.G., 1847–1900, a memoir* (London, 1921).
BLYTH, H., *The pocket Venus* (London, 1966).
BRIGGS, A., *Victorian cities* (London, 1963).
BRIGGS, A. (ed.), *Chartist studies* (London, 1959).
British Association for the advancement of science, *Handbook to Cardiff and the neighbourhood* (1920).
BYLES, C. E., *The life and letters of R. S. Hawker, vicar of Morwenston* (London, 1905).
CARLETON, W., *Valentine M'Clutchy, the Irish agent* (Dublin, 1847).
CARTER, H., *The towns of Wales* (1965).
CHAMBERS, J. D. and MINGAY, G. E., *The agricultural revolution, 1750–1860* (London, 1966).
CHAPPELL, E. L., *Gwalia's homes* (Ystalyfera, 1911).
   Cardiff's housing problem (1913).
   History of the port of Cardiff (1939).
   Historic Melingriffith: an account of Pentyrch ironworks and Melingriffith tinplate works (1940).
   Old Whitchurch: the story of a Glamorgan parish (1945).
CLAPHAM, J. H., *An economic history of modern Britain*, 3 vols. (Cambridge, 1950–52).
CLARK, G. T., *The land of Morgan, being a contribution towards the history of the lordship of Glamorgan* (London, 1883).
CLEVELAND, duchess of, *The life and letters of Lady Hester Stanhope* (London, 1914).
COBBE, H., *The history of Luton church* (London, 1899).
COLERIDGE, E. H., *The life of Thomas Coutts, banker*, 2 vols. (London, 1919).
CREWE, marquess of, *Lord Rosebery* (London, 1931).
CUST, N., *Wanderers—episodes from the travels of Lady Emmeline Stuart and her daughter Victoria* (London, 1928).
DAUNTON, M. J., *Coal metropolis, Cardiff 1870–1914* (Leicester, 1977).
DAVIES, E. T., *Religion in the industrial revolution in south Wales* (1965).
ERNLE, Lord, *English farming, past and present* (6th edition, London, 1961).
EVANS, E. W., *Mabon, a study in trade union leadership* (1959).
EVANS, T., *The background of modern Welsh politics, 1789–1846* (1936).
FLATRÈS, P., *Géographie rurale de quatres contrées celtiques, Irlande, Galles, Cornwall et Man* (Rennes, 1957).
FULFORD, R., *Samuel Whitbread, 1764–1815* (London, 1967).
GASH, N., *Politics in the age of Peel* (London, 1953).
GIROUARD, M., *The Victorian country house* (Oxford, 1971).
GOODWIN, A. (ed.), *The European nobility in the eighteenth century* (London, 1953).
GORDON, Lady, *The winds of time* (London, 1934).
GORMAN, W. J. B., *Converts to Rome* (London, 1910).
GRANT, J. P., *Cardiff Castle, its history and architecture* (1923).
GRANT, R., *The parliamentary history of Glamorgan, 1542–1976* (Swansea, 1978).
GRIFFITHS, R. A. (ed.), *Boroughs of medieval Wales* (1978).

HADFIELD, C., *The canals of south Wales and the border* (1960).
HALSBAND, P., *The life of Mary Wortley Montagu* (Oxford, 1956).
HAMEL, F., *Lady Hester Lucy Stanhope* (London, 1913).
HANHAM, H. J., *Elections and party management* (London, 1959).
HARE, J. C. A., *The story of two noble lives, being memorials of Charlotte, countess Canning and Louisa, marchioness of Waterford*, 3 vols. (London, 1893).
HEALEY, E., *Lady unknown, the life of Angela Burdett-Coutts* (London, 1978).
HEAPE, E. G., *Buxton under the dukes of Devonshire* (London, 1948).
HICKEY, J. V., *Urban catholics* (London, 1967).
HILLING, J. B., *Cardiff and the valleys* (London, 1973).
HITCHCOCK, H. R., *Architecture, eighteenth and nineteenth centuries* (London, 1958).
HOWELL, D. W., *Land and people in nineteenth century Wales* (London, 1978).
HOWELLS, C. J., *Transport facilities in the mining and industrial districts of south Wales and Monmouthshire* (1911).
HUGHES, E., *North Country life in the eighteenth century, the north-east, 1700–1750* (Oxford, 1952).
ILCHESTER, earl of, *Chronicles of Holland House, 1820–1900* (London, 1927).
ILCHESTER, countess of and SLAVERDALE, Lord, *The life and letters of Lady Sarah Lennox, 1745–1826*, 2 vols. (London, 1901).
JAMES, L. H., *Old Cowbridge* (1922).
JENKINS, J. A., *Glamorgan at the opening of the twentieth century* (Brighton, 1907).
JENKINS, R. T., *Hanes Cymru yn y ddeunawfed ganrif* (1928).
            Hanes Cymru yn y bedwaredd ganrif ar bymtheg, y gyfrol gyntaf, 1789–1843 (1933).
JENKINS, W. L., *A history of the town and castle of Cardiff* (1854).
JEVONS, H. S., *Foreign trade in coal* (1909).
            The British coal trade (London, 1915).
JOHN, A. H., *The industrial development of south Wales, 1750–1850* (1950).
JONES, D. W., *Hanes Morgannwg* (Aberdar, 1874).
JONES, G. A., WARD, J. W. and COE, H. A., *Father Jones of Cardiff* (London, 1907).
JONES, G. E., *The gentry and the Elizabethan state* (1977).
JONES, J., *River out of Eden* (London, 1951).
JONES, J. I., *A history of printing and printers in Wales to . . . 1923* (1925).
JONES, P. N., *Colliery settlement in the south Wales coalfield, 1850 to 1926* (Hull, 1969).
JONES, W. H., *History of the port of Swansea* (Carmarthen, 1922).
KEETON, G. N., *Lord Chancellor Jeffreys and the Stuart cause* (London, 1965).
LEVER, T., *The Herberts of Wilton* (London, 1967).
LEWIS, E. D., *The Rhondda valleys* (London, 1959).
LLOYD, J., *The early history of the old south Wales ironworks, 1760–1840* (London, 1906).
LOVAT-FRASER, J. A., *John Stuart, earl of Bute* (Cambridge, 1919).
MacCUNN, Florence, *Sir Walter Scott's friends* (London, 1909).
MacDERMOT, E. T., *History of the Great Western Railway*, 2 vols. (London, 1927–31).
McKELWAY, J. E., *George III and Lord Bute* (London, 1973).
MACPHERSON, N., *The appellate jurisdiction of the House of Lords in Scotch cases, illustrated by the litigation relating to the custody of the marquess of Bute* (Edinburgh, 1861).
McROBERTS, D. (ed.), *Modern Scottish Catholicism* (Glasgow, 1979).
MAGUIRE, W. A., *The Downshire estates in Ireland, 1801–1845* (Oxford, 1972).
MARSHALL, J. D., *Furness and the industrial revolution* (Barrow-in-Furness, 1958).
MINGAY, G. E., *English landed society in the eighteenth century* (London, 1963).

MITCHISON, R., *Agricultural Sir John* (London, 1962).
M'KERLIE, P. M., *History of the lands and their owners in Galloway*, 2 vols. (Paisley, 1906).
MONYPENNY, W. F. and BUCKLE, G. E., *The life of Disraeli*, 2 vols. (London, 1929).
MORGAN, K. O., *Wales in British politics, 1868-1922* (1963).
MORGAN, O. M., *The history of Pontypridd and Rhondda valleys* (Pontypridd, 1903).
MORRIS, J. H. and WILLIAMS, L. J., *The south Wales coal industry, 1841-1875* (1958).
NASH-WILLIAMS, V. E., *The Roman frontier in Wales* (1969).
OGBORN, M. E., *Equitable Assurance, 1762-1961* (London, 1962).
PATERSON, D. R., *Early Cardiff* (Exeter, 1926).
PEARCE, C. E., *The jolly duchess* (London, 1915).
PETTIGREW, A., *The public parks and recreation grounds of Cardiff* (1926).
PEVSNER, N., *The buildings of England, Northumberland* (Harmondsworth, 1957).
PHILLIPS, E., *A history of the pioneers of the Welsh coalfield* (1925).
PHILLIPS, J. R., *An attempt at a concise history of Glamorgan* (London, 1879).
POLLOCK, F., *The land laws* (London, 1896).
PRICE, C. J. L., *The English theatre in Wales in the eighteenth and nineteenth centuries* (1948).
REDFORD, A., *Labour migration in England, 1800-1850* (London, 1926).
REDMAYNE, R. A. S. and STONE, G., *The ownership and valuation of mineral property in the United Kingdom* (London, 1920).
REES, J. F., *The story of Milford* (1954).
REES, J. F. (ed.), *The Cardiff region, a survey* (1960).
REES, W., *Cardiff, a history of the city* (1962).
RHEE, H. A., *The rent of agricultural land in England and Wales, 1870-1943* (London, 1949).
RHONDDA, Viscountess (ed.), *Life of D. A. Thomas, Viscount Rhondda* (London, 1921).
RHYS, J. and JONES, D. B., *The Welsh people* (London, 1900).
RICHARDS, J., *The Cowbridge story* (Bridgend, 1956).
RICHARDSON, R., *Coutts and Co., bankers, Edinburgh and London* (London, 1901).
RIDDELL, Lord, *The story of the Western Mail* (1927).
ROBBINS, H. H., *Our first ambassador to China* (London, 1908).
ROBERTS, G., *The municipal development of the borough of Swansea to 1900* (1940).
ROLT, L. T. C., *George and Robert Stephenson* (London, 1960).
ROSKELL, Dame M. F., *Memories of Francis Kerril Amherst, D.D., lord bishop of Northampton* (London, 1903).
RUSSELL, G. W. E., *Portraits of the seventies* (London, 1916).
SCOTT-THOMSON, G., *The Russells in Bloomsbury, 1669-1771* (London, 1940).
SCRIVENOR, H., *History of the iron trade from the earliest records to the present period* (London, 1854).
SHERRINGTON, C. E. R., *The economics of rail transport in Great Britain* (London, 1928).
SIMNETT, W. E., *Railway amalgamation in Great Britain* (London, 1923).
SPRING, D., *English landed estate in the nineteenth century; its administration* (Baltimore, 1963).
STONE, L., *The crisis of the aristocracy, 1558-1641* (Oxford, 1965).
STUART WORTLEY, Mrs., *Highcliffe and the Stuarts* (London, 1927).
SUMMERSON, J., *Georgian London* (London, 1948.)
THOMAS, D., *Agriculture in Wales during the Napoleonic Wars* (1963).

THOMAS, I. B., *Top sawyer, a biography of David Davies of Llandinam* (London, 1938).

THOMPSON, F. M. L., *English landed society in the nineteenth century* (London, 1963).

THOMPSON, H. M., *Cardiff from the coming of the Normans to the dominance of Cromwell* (1930).

TURBERVILLE, A. S., *The House of Lords in the age of reform* (London, 1938).
  Welbeck Abbey and its owners, 2 vols. (London, 1938–39).

VAN THAL, H., *The prime ministers*, I (London, 1974).

Victoria history of the county of Cambridge and the Isle of Ely, 4 vols. (London, 1938–53).

Victoria history of the county of Bedford, 3 vols. (London, 1908–12).

VINCENT, J. E., *John Nixon, pioneer of the coal trade* (London, 1900).

WARD, J. T. and WILSON, R. G. (eds.), *Land and industry, the landed estate and the industrial revolution* (Newton Abbot, 1971).

WARD, W., *The life of Cardinal Newman* (London, 1912).

WEBB, S. and B., *The manor and the borough* (London, 1908).

WESTCOTT, A., *Life and letters of Brooke Foss Westcott, D.D., D.C.L., sometime bishop of Durham*, 2 vols. (London, 1903).

WILKES, L. and DODDS, G., *Tyneside classical, the Newcastle of Grainger, Dobson and Clayton* (London, 1964).

WILKINS, C., *The south Wales coal trade and its allied industries from the earliest days to the present time* (1888).
  The history of the iron, steel, tin-plate and other trades of Wales (Merthyr Tydfil, 1903).
  The history of Merthyr Tydfil (Merthyr Tydfil, 1867).
  Wales, past and present (Merthyr Tydfil, 1870).

WILLIAMS, C., *A Welsh family* (London, 1893).

WILLIAMS, D., *The history of Monmouthshire* (London, 1796).

WILLIAMS, D., *John Frost, a study in chartism* (1939).
  A history of modern Wales (London, 1950).
  The Rebecca Riots; a study in agrarian discontent (1955).

WILLIAMS, G. (ed.), *Merthyr politics: the making of a working-class tradition* (1966).
  Glamorgan County History, IV (1974).

WILLIAMS, G. A., *The Merthyr Rising of 1831* (London, 1978).

WILLIAMS, G. J., *Traddodiad llenyddol Morgannwg* (1948).
  Iolo Morganwg, I (1950).

WILLIAMS, P., *The Council in the Marches of Wales under Elizabeth I* (1958).

WILLIAMS, W. P., *A monograph of the Windsor family* (1879).

WILSON, J. A., *The life of Bishop Hedley* (London, 1930).

WOODWARD, E. L., *The age of reform* (Oxford, 1958).

WORTLEY, Baron and GROSVENOR, C., *The first Lady Wharncliffe and her family, 1779–1856*, 2 vols. (London, 1927).

YOUNG, W., *A noble life, incidents in the career of Lewis Davis of Ferndale* (London, 1899).

C. ARTICLES

ANONYMOUS, 'Recent manuscript accessions', *Bulletin of the John Rylands Library*, XXXIII (1950–51).
  'Deposits by the most honourable, the marquess of Bute', *National Library of Wales Annual Report*, 1950–51.
  'Cardiff before 1890', *Glamorgan Historian*, I (1963).

BAKER, E. R., 'The beginnings of the Glamorgan County Police', *Glamorgan Historian*, II (1965).

BALLINGER, J., 'Elections in Cardiff and Glamorgan, 1818–1832', *Cymru Fu*, I (1889).
CANNADINE, D. N., 'From "feudal" lords to figureheads', *Urban History Yearbook*, 1978.
CHARLES, B. G., 'The marquess of Bute collection', *National Library of Wales Journal*, VII (1951–52).
CLARK, G. K., 'The electorate and the repeal of the Corn Laws', *Transactions of the Royal Historical Society*, fifth series, I (1951).
　　'The repeal of the Corn Laws and the politics of the forties,' *Economic History Review*, second series, IV (1950–51).
CLARK, G. T., 'Castell Coch', *Archaeologia Cambrensis*, first series, IV (1850).
　　'The manorial particulars of the county of Glamorgan', *Archaeologia Cambrensis*, fourth series, VIII (1877–78).
CROOK, J. M., 'Patron extraordinary, John, third marquess of Bute, 1847–1900', *Victorian south Wales, the seventh conference report of the Victorian Society*, 1969.
CRUBELLIER, M., 'Le developpement de Cardiff au cour du XIXe siècle et jusqu'à la crise actuelle', *Annales de Géographie*, 45 (1936).
DAVIES, E., 'The small landowner, 1780–1832, in the light of the land tax assessments', *Economic History Review*, first series, I (1927).
DAVIES, J., 'The Dowlais lease, 1748–1900', *Morgannwg*, XII (1968).
　　'The end of the great estates and the rise of freehold farming in Wales', *Welsh History Review*, 7, no. 2 (1974).
　　'The Rhymney Railway and the Bute estate', *Gelligaer*, VIII (1971).
　　'The second marquess of Bute; a landowner and the community in the nineteenth century', *Glamorgan Historian*, VIII (n.d.).
DODD, A. H., 'Wales's parliamentary apprenticeship, 1536–1625', *Transactions of the Honourable Society of Cymmrodorion*, 1942.
　　'The pattern of politics in Stuart Wales', *Transactions of the Honourable Society of Cymmrodorion*, 1948.
ENGLAND, J., 'The Dowlais iron works, 1759–1763', *Morgannwg*, III (1959).
EVANS, L. V., 'The Royal Glamorgan Militia', *Glamorgan Historian*, VIII (n.d.).
FLETCHER, T., 'The great depression of English agriculture, 1873–1896', *Economic History Review*, second series, XIII (1961).
FUSSELL, G. E., 'Glamorgan farming; an outline of its modern history', *Morgannwg*, I (1957).
HABAKKUK, H. J., 'English landownership, 1680–1740', *Economic History Review*, first series, X (1940).
　　'Marriage settlements in the eighteenth century', *Transactions of the Royal Historical Society*, fourth series, XXXII (1950).
　　'The economic functions of English landowners in the seventeenth and eighteenth centuries', *Explorations in entrepreneurial history*, VI, no. 2 (1953–54).
HADFIELD, C., 'James Green as canal engineer', *Journal of Transport History*, I (1953).
HARGEST, L., 'Cardiff's "spasm of rebellion" in 1818', *Morgannwg*, XXI (1977).
HILLING, J. B., 'The buildings of Cardiff, an historical survey', *Glamorgan Historian*, VI (1969).
HODGES, T. M., 'The peopling of the hinterland and the port of Cardiff', *Economic History Review*, first series, XVII (1947).
　　'Early banking at Cardiff', *Economic History Review*, first series, XVIII (1947).
HOWELLS, J., 'Reminiscences of Cardiff', *Red Dragon*, V (1884).
HOWELLS, J. M., 'The Crosswood estate, 1547–1947', *Ceredigion*, III (1956).

HUGHES, E., 'The eighteenth century land agent', in H. A. Cronne, T. W. Moody and D. B. Quinn (eds.), *Essays in English and Irish history in honour of J. E. Todd* (London, 1949).

HUMPHRIES, I., 'Cardiff politics, 1850–74', *Glamorgan Historian* VIII (n.d.).

JOHN, A. H., 'Insurance investment and the London money market of the eighteenth century', *Economica*, new series, XX (1953).

      'Iron and coal on a Glamorgan estate, 1700–1740', *Economic History Review*, first series, XIII (1943).

JONES, I. G., 'Franchise reform and Glamorgan politics, 1832–67', *Morgannwg*, II (1958).

      'The election of 1868 in Merthyr Tydfil', *Journal of Modern History*, XXXIII (1961).

JONES, T., 'The place-names of Cardiff', *South Wales and Monmouthshire Record Society Publications*, II (1950).

LITTLE, W., 'The agriculture of Glamorgan', *Journal of the Royal Agricultural Society of England*, second series, XXI (1885).

MARTIN, E., 'Description of the mineral basin in the counties of Glamorgan, Monmouth, Brecknock, Carmarthen and Pembroke', *Philosophical Transactions of the Royal Society of London*, 1806.

MOORE, P., 'Cardiff slums in 1849', *Glamorgan Historian*, II (1965).

MORGAN, K. O., 'Democratic politics in Glamorgan, 1884–1914', *Morgannwg*, IV (1960).

MINGAY, G. E., 'The large estate in eighteenth century England', *Contributions to the first international conference of economic history* (Stockholm, 1960).

OWEN, L., 'The population of Wales in the sixteenth and seventeenth centuries', *Transactions of the Honourable Society of Cymmrodorion*, 1959.

PETTIGREW, A., 'The vineyard at Castell Coch', Cardiff Naturalists' Society, *Report and Transactions*, XVI (1884).

POLLARD, S., 'Barrow-in-Furness and the seventh duke of Devonshire', *Economic History Review*, VIII (1955).

READ, C. S., 'On the farming of south Wales', *Journal of the Royal Agricultural Society of England*, X (1849).

REEDER, D. A., 'The politics of urban leaseholds in late Victorian England', *International Review of Social History*, VI (1961).

REES, R. D., 'Glamorgan newspapers under the Stamp Acts', *Morgannwg*, III (1959).

      'South Wales newspapers under the Stamp Acts', *Welsh History Review*, I (1962).

REES, W., 'The lordship of Cardiff', Cardiff Naturalists' Society, *Reports and Transactions*, LXIII (1932).

RICHARDS, J. H. and LEWIS, J. P., 'Housebuilding in the south Wales coalfield', *Journal of the Manchester School of Economic and Social Studies*, XXIV (1956).

SPRING, D., 'The English landed estate in the age of coal and iron, 1830–1880', *Journal of Economic History*, XI (1951).

      'The earls of Durham and the great northern coalfield, 1830–1880', *Canadian Historical Review*, XXXIII (1952).

      'A great agricultural estate: Netherby under Sir James Graham 1820–45', *Agricultural History*, XXIX (1955).

      'The role of the aristocracy in the late nineteenth century', *Victorian Studies*, IV (1960).

THOMAS, B., 'The migration of labour into the Glamorganshire coalfield', *Economica*, X (1930).

THOMAS, D. A., 'The growth and direction of our foreign trade in coal during the last half century', *Statistical Journal*, LXVI (1903).

THOMPSON, F. M. L., 'The end of a great estate', *Economic History Review*, second series, VIII (1955).

'The land market in the nineteenth century', *Oxford Economic Papers*, new series, IX (1957).

'English landownership: the Ailesbury Trust, 1832–56', *Economic History Review*, second series, XI (1958).

'English great estates, 1790–1914', *Contributions to the first international conference of economic history* (Stockholm), 1960).

TROTT, A. L., 'The Society for the Diffusion of Useful Knowledge in Wales', *National Library of Wales Journal*, XI (1959–60).

WARD, J., 'Cardiff Castle: its Roman origin', *Archaeologia*, LVII (1901).

'Roman Cardiff', *Archaeologia Cambrensis*, sixth series, VIII (1908), XIII (1913), XIV (1914).

WILLIAMS, D., 'A note on the population of Wales, 1536–1801', *Bulletin of the Board of Celtic Studies*, VIII (1935–36).

'Rural Wales in the nineteenth century', *Journal of the Royal Agricultural Society of England*, second series, LXXVIII (1953).

WILLIAMS, G. A., 'The making of radical Merthyr, 1800–1836', *Welsh History Review*, I (1961).

'The Merthyr Riots; settling the account', *National Library of Wales Journal*, XI (1959).

WILLIAMS, J. E., 'Whitehaven in the eighteenth century', *Economic History Review*, second series, VIII (1955).

WINSTONE, J., 'Reminiscences of old Cardiff', *Cardiff Naturalists' Society, Report and Transactions*, XV (1883).

D. UNPUBLISHED DISSERTATIONS

ADDIS, J. P., 'The heavy iron and steel industry in south Wales, 1870–1950' (Ph.D., Wales, 1958).

BALL, E., 'Glamorgan, a study of the concerns of the county and the work of its members in the House of Commons from 1825 to 1835' (Ph.D., London, 1965).

DAUNTON, M. J., 'Aspects of the social and economic structure of Cardiff, 1870–1914' (Ph.D., Kent, 1974).

DAVID, I. W. R., 'Political and electioneering activity in south-east Wales, 1820–51' (M.A., Wales, 1959).

DAVIES, A. C., 'Aberdare, 1750–1850, a study in the growth of an industrial community' (M.A., Wales, 1963).

DAVIES, J., 'The historical geography of the Rhymney valley' (M.Sc., Wales, 1926).

DAVIES, J. M., 'A study of the effect of the Reform Act of 1884 and the Redistribution Act of 1885 upon the political structure of Glamorgan' (M.A., Wales, 1979).

DAVIES, L. N. A., 'The history of the Barry Dock and Railway Company in relation to the development of the south Wales coalfield' (M.A., Wales, 1938).

FRASER, D. B., 'The development of the road system in Glamorgan up to 1844, with special reference to turnpike roads' (M.A., Wales, 1940).

HICKEY, J. V., 'The origin and growth of the Irish community at Cardiff' (M.A., Wales, 1959).

HODGES, T. M., 'A history of the port of Cardiff in relation to its hinterland with special reference to the years 1830–1914' (M.Sc., Econ., London, 1948).

HUGHES, M., 'The economic activities of the landowners in north-eastern England in the first half of the nineteenth century' (Ph.D., Newcastle, 1963).

JOHN, L. B., 'The parliamentary representation of Glamorgan, 1536–1832' (M.A., Wales, 1934).

JONES, G. E., 'The Glamorgan gentry, 1540–1640' (M.A., Wales, 1963).

PAINTING, D., 'A critical examination of Disraeli's novels from Sybil to "Falconet" ' (Ph.D., Wales, 1963).

REES, R. D., 'The parliamentary representation of south Wales, 1790–1830' (Ph.D., Reading, 1962).

RICHARDS, J. H., 'Fluctuations in house-building in the south Wales coalfield, 1851–1954' (M.A., Wales, 1956).

WILLS, W. D., 'Ecclesiastical reorganisation and church extension in the diocese of Llandaf, 1830–50' (M.A., Wales, 1965).

INDEX

Aberafan, 86, 97, 105, 299
Abercorn, duke of, *see* Hamilton, James, first duke of Abercorn
Aberdare: building leases at, 197; church at, 98, 99, 100; collieries at, 238, 241; election of 1837 at, 126; farms at, 147, 149, 175; ground-rents at, 190; mineral leases at, 219, 232; mineral office at, 237; mineral royalties at, 220; parishioners of, 40; railways at, 283; school at, 97; urban land at, 78, 186, 187, 204, 205, 209; woodlands at, 183, 184. *See also* Cynon valley
Aberdare Iron Company, 49, 222, 238, 239, 240, 241
Abergorci, 41
Abernant, 229, 233
Abraham, William (Mabon), 242
Adam brothers, 6
Adare, Lord, *see* Wyndham-Quin, Edwin, third earl of Dunraven
Advowsons of the Cardiff Castle estate, 41, 95–6, 98–9, 100, 131
Age, The, 125
Agreements, agricultural, 169, 178, 179–80
Agricultural Holdings Act (1883), 163
Agriculture: Bute investment in, 170, 172–3; industry and, 146–50; land lost by, 147–8; markets for the products of, 148–9. *See also* Farms; Leases; Rents
Alexandra Dock Company, 299
All Saints, church of, Cardiff, 131
Allotments, 152–3
Anderson, Sir Rowand, 29
Anne, Queen, 5
Annual Register, 7, 13
Archaeologia Aeliana, 114
Auditors, 59
Audits, 37, 58–9, 164, 166
Ayr, boroughs of, *see* Constituencies, parliamentary
Ayrshire, 12, 48, 181. *See also* Constituencies, parliamentary

Bald, Robert, 214, 215, 224, 235, 236
Ballot Act, 142
Banks: 59–60; Barclays, 59; Coutts, 46, 59, 66n., 71, 223, 274; London and Westminster, 18n., 20, 46, 59, 66n., 67; National and Provincial, 51, 60, 274; Royal, 59, 270; Savery, Towgood and Company, 60; Sharples, 59; Sir William Forbes and Company, 59; Wood's, 59, 118
Bargoed Coal Company, 227, 240
Barry Docks, *see* Docks, Barry
Barry Dock and Railway Act, 289
Barry Railway, 295 (fig.)
Batchelor and Tredwen, boat builders, 267
Beauchamp, Lady, *see* Seymour, Alice Elizabeth Conway, Viscountess Beauchamp
Beauchamp, Lord, *see* Seymour, Francis Conway, second marquess of Hertford
Beauchamp, Richard, earl of Worcester (d. 1422), 80
Beauclerc, Harriet, duchess of St. Albans (née Mellon), 10 and n.
Beaufort, duke of, *see* Somerset, Henry, fifth duke of Beaufort
Beaufort, duke of, *see* Somerset, Henry Charles, sixth duke of Beaufort
Beaufort, duke of, *see* Somerset, Henry, seventh duke of Beaufort
Beaufort, dukes of, *see* Somerset family, dukes of Beaufort
Beaumont, Robert: appointment as mineral agent, 54; character of, 236; as coalowner, 222, 241; dismissal of, 55, 236; and railways, 285
Beche, de la, Henry, 215
Bedlinog, 225n.
Belgravia, 193
Bentinck, William Henry Cavendish, third duke of Portland, 9
Bird, John: as agent, 35–6, 58; and castle social life, 91; diary of 35,

INDEX

19, 238–43, 244, 299; on clay, 230; on coal, 226–9; as a proportion of colliery costs, 241–2; on iron ore, 229–30; in kind, 227; on lead, 230, 238; on limestone, 230; payers of, 240, 241; percentage, 228–9, 230; on sand, 230; *mentioned*, 217, 223, 225, 226 and n., 231, 235

Rudry, 97

Russell family, dukes of Bedford, 85, 173

Ruthin, lordship of, 57

Ryder, Dudley, first earl of Harrowby, 18

Ryder, Dudley, second earl of Harrowby, 42n.

Ryder, Henry Dudley, fourth earl of Harrowby, 73, 187, 290

St. Albans, duchess of, *see* Beauclerc, Harriet, duchess of St. Albans

St. Andrews, 25, 26, 29

St. Andrew's church, Cardiff, 131

St. German's church, Cardiff, 132

St. John's church, Aberdare, 100

St. John's, Cardiff: church of, 28, 84, 85, 91, 98, 187; parish of, 98, 189

St. John's Gospel, 139

St. John's Lodge, 26

St. Margaret's church, Roath, 10, 11, 84, 95

St. Mary's, Cardiff: church of, 98; parish of, 39, 42, 98, 189

Sandon Hall, 42n.

Sanitary reform, 136–7, 198

Sankey, Sir John, first Viscount Sankey, 145, 243

Sanquhar, 12, 29

Santayana, George, 140, 202

Savery, Towgood and Company, *see* Banks

Schools, 97–8, 112, 131–2, 139

Scotland: banks in, 59; Bute properties in, 46, 69, *see also* Dumfries estate, Mountstuart estate; second marquess of Bute's commitment to, 17, 94–5, 101; third marquess of Bute's commitment to, 27–8; fourth marquess of Bute's commitment to, 30; Catholicism in, 24, 25 and n.; Dumfries properties in, 12; education in, 24, 95, 97;

farming in, 169; history of, third marquess's interest in, 23, 27, 29, 45; home rule for, 27–8; mortgages in, 72; peers of, 5, 9, 12, 28; King Robert II of, 5; Union of, with England, 5; *mentioned*, 22, 29, 47, 54, 66, 85, 119, 138, 139, 186, 209

Scotland, Church of, 19, 20 and n., 95, 97

Scottish Review, 27

Senghennydd, lordship of, 38, 40, 57

Senghennydd Common, 38, 39, 153, 231

Settlements, marriage: of the second marquess of Bute, 15, 44–5, 64; of Lord Mountstuart (1767–94), 12–13; of the Windsor family, 34, 42

Seymour, Alice Elizabeth Conway, Viscountess Beauchamp (née Windsor), 4

Seymour, Francis Conway, first marquess of Hertford, 4

Seymour, Francis Conway, second marquess of Hertford (Lord Beauchamp), 4

Sheep, 166–7

Shirley, L. V., 26, 71, 74, 135, 141–2

Silurian, The, 125

Smeaton, Mr., 187, 252n.

Smyth, Captain W. H., 55, 215, 236, 252, 259, 281

Sneyd, G. E., 187, 290

Somerset, Charles, first earl of Worcester, 1

Somerset family, dukes of Beaufort, 1, 3

Somerset, Henry, fifth duke of Beaufort, 86, 88

Somerset, Henry, sixth duke of Beaufort, 119

Somerset, Henry, seventh duke of Beaufort, 299

Sophia Gardens, 131, 141

South Wales Atlantic Steamship Company, 268

South Wales Daily News, 144, 242, 289

Spiller and Brown Ltd., 267

Splott, 211

Squatters, 40, 41, 58

Staël, Germaine, Mme. de (née Necker), 14

Star of Gwent, 51

Starrbowkett clubs, 208